T0246614

THE

50 GREATEST PLAYERS

IN

SAN FRANCISCO 49ERS

HISTORY

ROBERT W. COHEN

LYONS
PRESS

ESSEX, CONNECTICUT

An imprint of The Globe Pequot Publishing Group, Inc.
64 South Main Street
Essex, CT 06426
www.globepequot.com

Distributed by NATIONAL BOOK NETWORK

British Library Cataloguing in Publication Information available

Library of Congress Cataloging-in-Publication Data

The hardback edition of this book was previously cataloged as follows:

Names: Cohen, Robert W., author.
Title: The 50 greatest players in San Francisco 49ers history / Robert W. Cohen.
Other titles: Fifty greatest players in San Francisco 49ers history
Description: Guilford, Connecticut : Lyons Press, 2021.
Identifiers: LCCN 2021004478 (print) | LCCN 2021004479 (ebook)
Subjects: LCSH: San Francisco 49ers (Football team)—History. | Football players—
    California—San Francisco—Biography.
Classification: LCC GV956.S3 C63 2021 (print) | LCC GV956.S3 (ebook) | DDC
    796.332/640979461—dc23
LC record available at https://lccn.loc.gov/2021004478
LC ebook record available at https://lccn.loc.gov/2021004479

ISBN 9781493086412 (paperback)
ISBN 9781493058198 (cloth)
ISBN 9781493062898 (epub)

CONTENTS

ACKNOWLEDGMENTS

I wish to thank Troy Kinunen of MEARSonlineauctions.com, Kate of RMYauctions.com, FootballCardGallery.com, Mike Traverse, George A. Kitrinos, Stu Jossey, Jeffrey Beall, Mike Morbeck, Keith Allison, and Aaron Sholl, each of whom generously contributed to the photographic content of this work.

INTRODUCTION

THE 49ER LEGACY

A charter member of the short-lived All-America Football Conference (AAFC) that lasted only four seasons, the San Francisco 49ers came into being in 1946, joining the Los Angeles Dons of the AAFC and the Los Angeles Rams of the rival National Football League as the first three major-league professional sports franchises to be based in the Western United States. Founded by San Francisco native Tony Morabito, the owner of a successful lumber hauling business who earlier tried unsuccessfully to establish an NFL expansion team in his hometown, the 49ers took their name from the prospectors who arrived in Northern California during the Gold Rush of 1848–1855.

Co-owned by Morabito, his younger brother Vic, and their partners in the Lumber Terminals of San Francisco, Allen E. Sorrell and Ernest J. Turre, the 49ers began play in the AAFC's inaugural season of 1946, taking up residence in the league's Western Division, which they shared with the Cleveland Browns, Los Angeles Dons, and Chicago Rockets. Coached by longtime college head coach Buck Shaw, the 49ers played their home games in Kezar Stadium, a 50,000-seat arena located in the southeastern corner of Golden Gate Park that originally opened in 1925. Although the 49ers fared extremely well from 1946 to 1949, compiling an overall record of 38-14-2, they finished second in the division to the Browns each year, with Cleveland losing a total of only four contests, en route to winning four straight AAFC championships.

Absorbed by the NFL, along with the Browns and the original Baltimore Colts, when the AAFC folded following the conclusion of the 1949 campaign, the 49ers joined the Colts, Los Angeles Rams, Chicago Bears, Green Bay Packers, Detroit Lions, and New York Yanks in the league's

Western Division, where they experienced a moderate amount of success under Shaw the next five seasons, earning two second-place finishes, while posting an overall mark of 33-25-2. But, with the Morabito brothers and 49ers general manager Louis Spadia unhappy over the team's inability to capture a division title, they replaced Shaw at the helm with 49ers assistant Red Strader at the end of 1954. Strader remained in charge for just one year, leading the 49ers to a record of 4-8, before Frankie Albert, who starred for the 49ers at quarterback during their formative years in the AAFC, assumed control of the team in 1956. Although the 49ers compiled a mediocre record of 19-16-1 under Albert the next three seasons, they nearly advanced to the NFL championship game in 1957, posting a regular-season mark of 8-4 that tied them with Detroit for the best record in the Western Division, before losing to the Lions by a score of 31–27 in a one-game playoff to determine the division champion.

Sadly, the 49ers suffered another major loss in 1957 when Tony Morabito died of a heart attack during an October 27 home game against the Chicago Bears. Learning of their beloved owner's passing at halftime, an emotional and extremely motivated 49ers team subsequently scored 14 unanswered points, to come away with a 21–17 victory.

Following Morabito's passing, his brother, Vic, and widow, Josephine, assumed full control of the team, retaining Albert for one more year, before relieving him of his duties after the 49ers finished just 6-6 in 1958. Red Hickey, an assistant under Albert, subsequently took over as head coach, guiding the 49ers to a record of 7-5 in 1959 that enabled them to finish the decade with an overall mark of 63-54-3. Yet, even though the 49ers failed to distinguish themselves as a team during the 1950s, they featured some of the greatest individual stars in the game, including future Hall of Famers Y. A. Tittle, Joe Perry, Hugh McElhenny, John Henry Johnson, Bob St. Clair, and Leo Nomellini, with the first four members of that troupe acquiring the nickname "The Million Dollar Backfield" for their ability to create excitement on offense.

Hickey continued to coach the 49ers for another three years, during which time he became the first NFL head coach to employ the shotgun formation on offense. However, with the 49ers hovering right around the .500-mark much of the time, Hickey received his walking papers during the early stages of the 1963 campaign, with Hall of Fame defensive back and 49ers assistant Jack Christiansen replacing him at the helm. Vic Morabito died shortly thereafter, with his passing at only 45 years of age on May 10, 1964, leaving primary ownership of the team to the Morabito widows.

Faring no better under the new regime, the 49ers continued to flounder until shortly after former Dallas Cowboys defensive coordinator Dick Nolan assumed head-coaching duties in 1968. After struggling their first two seasons under Nolan, the 49ers won three straight division titles and appeared in two NFC championship games from 1970 to 1972, although they ended up losing to Dallas both times, suffering a 17–10 defeat at the hands of the Cowboys in the 1970 title tilt, before losing to them again the following year, this time by a score of 14–3. Outstanding performers for the 49ers who helped facilitate their rise to prominence included quarterback John Brodie, running back Ken Willard, wide receiver Gene Washington, offensive linemen Forrest Blue and Len Rohde, defensive tackle Charlie Krueger, linebacker Dave Wilcox, cornerback Jimmy Johnson, and defensive ends Cedrick Hardman and Tommy Hart.

As the 49ers rose to elite status during the early 1970s, they found themselves sharing the NFC Western Division with the Los Angeles Rams, Atlanta Falcons, and New Orleans Saints following the NFL-AFL merger at the end of 1969 that resulted in a new two-conference setup that featured three divisions in each conference. And, after calling Kezar Stadium home for the previous 25 seasons, the 49ers moved into Candlestick Park in 1971, giving them a more modern facility that served as their home venue for the next 43 years.

Unfortunately, the success that the 49ers experienced from 1970 to 1972 proved to be short-lived, as they subsequently suffered through a horrendous eight-year stretch during which they posted just one winning record, as Dick Nolan (1968–1975), Monte Clark (1976), Ken Meyer (1977), Pete McCulley (1978), and Fred O'Connor (1978) all took turns coaching the team. However, things finally began to turn around after real estate developer Edward J. DeBartolo Jr. purchased the 49ers in 1977, fired general manager Joe Thomas two years later, and hired former Stanford University head coach Bill Walsh to run the team.

A disciple of legendary NFL head coach Paul Brown, under whom he served as offensive coordinator in Cincinnati from 1968 to 1975, Walsh proved to be extremely effective at stockpiling draft picks, making wise selections in the annual draft, and filling holes in his roster by acquiring key free agents. Walsh is also credited with popularizing the "West Coast Offense," which predicates much of its success on a short, precise, well-timed passing game and an effective running game that helps keep the opposing defense off balance.

It took some time for Walsh to find the right players to implement his system in San Francisco, resulting in a pair of losing seasons for the 49ers, who compiled an embarrassing record of 2-14 in 1979 that remains tied for the worst mark in franchise history. But, after drafting quarterback Joe Montana, inserting unproven Dwight Hicks at free safety, overhauling the rest of his secondary by drafting defensive backs Ronnie Lott, Eric Wright, and Carlton Williamson, and acquiring veteran linebacker Jack "Hacksaw" Reynolds and sack specialist Fred Dean over the course of the next two seasons, Walsh suddenly found himself in charge of a team ready to compete for the league championship.

Beginning an extended period of excellence in 1981, the 49ers won the NFC Western Division title by going 13-3 during the regular season, before defeating the Giants by a score of 38–24 in the divisional round of the postseason tournament. The Niners subsequently earned their first conference championship by recording a memorable 28–27 victory over the Cowboys in the NFC title game, scoring the winning points on a last-minute TD grab by wide receiver Dwight Clark that has since become known simply as "The Catch." The 49ers then emerged victorious in Super Bowl XVI, building an early 20–0 lead over Cincinnati, before holding on for a 26–21 win.

A players' strike in 1982 threw everything out of kilter, contributing to a disappointing 3-6 record by the 49ers. However, they subsequently began an exceptional 16-year run during which they advanced to the playoffs 15 times, captured 12 division titles, and won four more Super Bowls. After suffering a 24–21 defeat at the hands of the Washington Redskins in the 1983 NFC championship game, the 49ers rebounded in a big way the following year, outscoring their opponents by a combined margin of 475–227 during the regular season, en route to compiling a franchise-best 15-1 record. Continuing their dominant play in the postseason, the 49ers defeated the Giants by a score of 21–10 in the opening round of the playoffs, before shutting out the Bears 23–0 in the NFC championship game. The 49ers subsequently put the finishing touches on their banner year by recording a convincing 38–16 victory over Dan Marino and the Miami Dolphins in Super Bowl XIX, with Joe Montana earning game MVP honors for the first of three times. At season's end, Ronnie Lott, Eric Wright, Dwight Hicks, and Carlton Williamson all received invitations to the Pro Bowl, marking the first time ever that an entire defensive backfield earned that honor.

Although the 49ers made the playoffs in each of the next three seasons, they failed to advance beyond the opening round of the postseason tournament, losing twice to the Giants and once to the Vikings, with their unexpected 36–24 loss to Minnesota in the divisional round of the 1987 playoffs prompting Eddie DeBartolo Jr. to strip Bill Walsh of his team president title. After finishing first in the NFC West for the third straight time in 1988, the 49ers gained a measure of revenge against the Vikings in the divisional round of the playoffs, recording a resounding 34–9 victory over their overmatched opponents, before defeating the Bears by a score of 28–3 in the NFC championship game. The 49ers then earned a hard-fought 20–16 victory over the Cincinnati Bengals in Super Bowl XXIII, with Joe Montana delivering the game-winning 10-yard touchdown pass to John Taylor in the final minute of regulation. Bill Walsh subsequently announced his retirement, turning over control of the team to his defensive coordinator and handpicked successor, George Seifert. In his 10 seasons as 49ers head coach, Walsh led the team to seven playoff appearances, six division titles, three Super Bowl wins, and an overall record of 92-59-1 in regular-season play.

On a mission to prove they had the ability to win without Walsh, the 49ers performed magnificently in 1989, going 14-2 during the regular season, before outscoring the Vikings and Rams by a combined margin of 71–16 in the playoffs. The Niners then won their fourth NFL championship by routing the Denver Broncos by a score of 55–10 in Super Bowl XXIV, with Joe Montana's five touchdown passes earning him game MVP honors for the third and final time.

The driving force behind San Francisco's first four Super Bowl championships, Montana established himself as the finest quarterback of his era, displaying an ability to excel under pressure that few others have ever even approached. Yet, as great as Montana proved to be, he received a considerable amount of help from his teammates, with Ronnie Lott, Dwight Hicks, Eric Wright, Charles Haley, and Keena Turner all excelling on defense, and Roger Craig, Brent Jones, Dwight Clark, and Jerry Rice starring on the offensive side of the ball. Rice, in fact, contributed nearly as much to the success of the 49ers as did Montana, with his extraordinary skill set making him easily the league's most lethal wide receiver.

Hoping to "three-peat," the 49ers once again compiled a regular-season record of 14-2 in 1990. However, after disposing of the Washington Redskins in the divisional round of the playoffs, they suffered a heartbreaking 15–13 defeat at the hands of the Giants in the NFC championship game, losing the contest on a 42-yard field goal by Matt Bahr as time expired.

The 49ers' loss to the Giants ended up having a profound impact on the organization. With Joe Montana having sustained a serious injury during the latter stages of the contest, he had to sit out the entire 1991 campaign, allowing Steve Young to assert himself as the team's new signal-caller.

A quarterback controversy subsequently developed upon Montana's return to the team the following year, resulting in the four-time Super Bowl champion requesting a trade to another team. Prior to dealing Montana to the Kansas City Chiefs, though, the 49ers allowed Ronnie Lott and Roger Craig to leave via Plan B free agency, stripping away much of the heart and soul of the team.

Yet, even with all the changes, the 49ers remained perennial contenders in the NFC the next several years, advancing to the playoffs seven times between 1991 and 1998, while making four conference championship game appearances. After failing to make the playoffs for the first time in nine years in 1991 despite finishing the regular season with a record of 10-6, the 49ers won four straight division titles and advanced to the NFC championship game three consecutive times, losing to Dallas in both 1992 and 1993, before finally defeating the Cowboys by a score of 38–28 in 1994. The Niners then posted a convincing 49–26 victory over the San Diego Chargers in Super Bowl XXIX, with Steve Young's record-setting six TD passes earning him game MVP honors.

Certainly, the free-agent acquisitions of veterans Ken Norton Jr., Rickey Jackson, Bart Oates, Richard Dent, Charles Mann, and Deion Sanders, who earned NFL Defensive Player of the Year honors, contributed greatly to the success the 49ers experienced during their championship campaign of 1994. But the combination of Steve Young and Jerry Rice proved to be too much for opposing teams to handle, with Young's 3,969 passing yards and league-leading 35 touchdown passes prompting the Associated Press to accord him NFL MVP honors and Rice's 112 receptions and 1,499 receiving yards earning him his ninth consecutive trip to the Pro Bowl and eighth First-Team All-Pro nomination.

The 49ers advanced to the playoffs in each of the next two seasons as well, although they ended up losing to the Green Bay Packers in the divisional round of the postseason tournament both times. Choosing to announce his retirement following the conclusion of the 1996 campaign, George Seifert left behind a legacy as head coach that included six division titles, one Super Bowl win, and an overall record of 98-30. Seifert also helped oversee the development of outstanding young players such as Terrell Owens, Bryant Young, Dana Stubblefield, and Merton Hanks during his time in San Francisco.

Moving expeditiously to replace Seifert, the 49ers immediately hired former University of California head coach Steve Mariucci, who had only one year of previous head-coaching experience at any level. Proving to be an excellent choice, Mariucci led the 49ers to four playoff appearances and two division titles between 1997 and 2002, a period during which a series of lawsuits over control of the family's vast holdings forced Eddie DeBartolo Jr. to surrender controlling interest of the team to his sister, Denise, and her husband, Dr. John York, with Denise becoming chairwoman of the board and John assuming the role of CEO. Meanwhile, on the playing field, after finishing the 1997 regular season with a record of 13-3, the 49ers posted a convincing 38–22 win over Minnesota in the opening round of the post-season tournament, before losing to the Packers by a score of 23–10 in the NFC championship game. Returning to the playoffs the following year, the 49ers once again faced the Packers, this time in the wild card round. However, unlike the previous three playoff meetings between the two teams, the 49ers emerged victorious, winning the game in dramatic fashion by a score of 30–27 on a 25-yard touchdown pass from Steve Young to Terrell Owens in the closing moments. One week later, though, the 49ers suffered a 20–18 defeat at the hands of the Super Bowl–bound Atlanta Falcons.

The 49ers subsequently got off to a fast start in 1999, winning three of their first four games, before a concussion sustained by Steve Young during a 24–10 victory over the Arizona Cardinals convinced him to announce his retirement. Struggling without their leader the rest of the year, the 49ers won just one of their remaining 12 contests, giving them their first losing season since they finished 3-6 during the strike-shortened 1982 campaign. Former CFL star Jeff Garcia took over behind center full-time the following year and performed well. But a porous defense relegated the 49ers to a record of 6-10 and their second consecutive fourth-place finish in the NFC West.

With Garcia, Terrell Owens, and star running back Garrison Hearst leading the way, the 49ers made the playoffs in both 2001 and 2002, compiling an overall record of 22-10 over the course of those two seasons. But they failed to advance beyond the divisional round of the postseason tournament both years, losing in the wild card round to the Packers by a score of 25–15 in 2001, before suffering a 31–6 defeat at the hands of the Tampa Bay Buccaneers in the divisional round the following year, just one week after mounting a miraculous fourth-quarter comeback against the Giants that resulted in a 39–38 victory.

The first few years of the 21st century ushered in several changes in San Francisco, with the first of those being the addition of two new divisional foes following the NFL's realignment prior to the start of the 2002 season. The Seattle Seahawks and Arizona Cardinals joined the 49ers and Rams in the NFC West, while the Atlanta Falcons, New Orleans Saints, and Carolina Panthers moved to the newly formed NFC South. Meanwhile, the 49ers fired head coach Steve Mariucci on January 15, 2003, after he reportedly lost a power struggle with general manager Terry Donahue, contributing to a dismal eight-year stretch during which the Niners failed to post a winning record as Dennis Erickson (2003–2004), Mike Nolan (2005–2008), Mike Singletary (2008–2010), and Jim Tomsula (2010) took turns coaching the team.

The hiring of former Stanford University head coach Jim Harbaugh by new general manager Trent Baalke in 2011 brought a level of stability to the organization that it had been lacking for nearly a decade. And, with the consistently excellent running of Frank Gore and a swarming defense that featured end Justin Smith and standout linebackers Patrick Willis and NaVorro Bowman, the 49ers once again emerged as an elite team, appearing in three consecutive NFC championship games and one Super Bowl between 2011 and 2013. After losing to the Giants in overtime by a score of 20–17 in the 2011 NFC title tilt, the 49ers earned their sixth trip to the Super Bowl the following year by posting victories over the Packers (45–31) and Falcons (28–24) in the playoffs. However, they came up just a bit short against the Baltimore Ravens in Super Bowl XLVII, losing to their AFC counterparts by a score of 34–31. Returning to the championship game in 2013 after defeating the Packers (23–20) and Panthers (23–10) in the first two rounds of the playoffs, the 49ers lost to the eventual Super Bowl champion Seattle Seahawks by a score of 23–17, ending their three-year run as one of the NFL's foremost teams.

The 2013 campaign marked the end of another era in San Francisco, since the 49ers christened brand new Levi's Stadium the following year, ending in the process a 43-year stint during which they played their home games at Candlestick Park. Located some 40 miles south of San Francisco, in Santa Clara, Levi's Stadium is named for Levi Strauss & Co., which purchased its naming rights in 2013. Designed as an open stadium with a natural grass field, it has a seating capacity of 68,500.

Jim Harbaugh remained in San Francisco for one more year, before he and the 49ers agreed to part ways after the 49ers finished 8-8 in 2014. The 49ers subsequently suffered through two horrific campaigns, posting an overall record of just 7-25 under head coaches Jim Tomsula and Chip Kelly in 2015 and 2016, prompting team president Jed York, the oldest son of John York and Denise DeBartolo York, to clean house. After firing Kelly and general manager Trent Baalke, York replaced Kelly with former Atlanta Falcons offensive coordinator Kyle Shanahan and Baalke with former NFL standout John Lynch, who had spent the previous few seasons working as a color commentator for the *NFL on Fox*. Although the 49ers continued to struggle their first two seasons under the new management team, winning a total of just 10 games from 2017 to 2018, strong coaching by Shanahan and several wise moves made by Lynch, including the free agent signing of quarterback Jimmy Garoppolo and the drafting of talented players such as tight end George Kittle, defensive end Nick Bosa, and wide receiver Deebo Samuel, eventually restored the organization to prominence. After finishing first in the NFC West with a regular season record of 13-3 in 2019, the 49ers posted impressive wins over Minnesota and Green Bay in the playoffs, defeating the Vikings by a score of 27–10, before recording a resounding 37–20 victory over the Packers in the NFC championship game. The Niners then gave the Chiefs all they could handle in Super Bowl LIV, holding a 20–10 lead through three quarters, before Kansas City scored 21 unanswered points in the final period to come away with a 31–20 victory.

Decimated by injuries in 2020, the 49ers failed to earn a playoff berth, finishing the regular season with a record of just 6-10. But a return to full health by standout performers such as Kittle, Bosa, and Samuel in 2021 should enable the 49ers to mount a serious challenge for the division title, which would be their 21st. The 49ers have also won seven conference championships and five Super Bowls, which ties them with the Cowboys for third all-time, with only the Patriots (7) and Steelers (6) having won more. Meanwhile, the 49ers have made more NFC championship game appearances (16) than any other team. Featuring a plethora of exceptional performers through the years, the 49ers have inducted 22 players into their Hall of Fame, 12 of whom have had their numbers retired by the team. Meanwhile, 24 members of the Pro Football Hall of Fame spent at least one full season in San Francisco, with 14 of those men wearing a 49ers uniform during many of their peak seasons.

FACTORS USED TO DETERMINE RANKINGS

It should come as no surprise that selecting the 50 greatest players ever to perform for a team with the rich history of the San Francisco 49ers presented quite a challenge. Even after narrowing the field down to a mere 50 men, I still needed to devise a method of ranking the elite players that remained. Certainly, the names of Joe Montana, Jerry Rice, Steve Young, Ronnie Lott, Leo Nomellini, and Jimmy Johnson would appear at, or near, the top of virtually everyone's list, although the order might vary somewhat from one person to the next. Several other outstanding performers have gained general recognition through the years as being among the greatest players ever to wear a 49ers uniform, with Joe Perry, Bob St. Clair, John

Brodie, and Roger Craig heading the list of other 49ers icons. But how does one compare players who lined up on opposite sides of the ball with any degree of certainty? Furthermore, how does one differentiate between the pass-rushing and run-stopping skills of linemen such as Leo Nomellini and Bryant Young and the ball-hawking skills of defensive backs such as Jimmy Johnson and Ronnie Lott? And, on the offensive end, how can a direct correlation be made between the contributions of Hall of Fame lineman Bob St. Clair and skill position players such as Jerry Rice and Joe Perry? After initially deciding whom to include on my list, I then needed to determine what criteria I should use to formulate my final rankings.

The first thing I decided to examine was the level of dominance a player attained during his time with the 49ers. How often did he lead the league in a major statistical category? Did he ever capture league MVP honors? How many times did he earn a trip to the Pro Bowl or a spot on the All-Pro Team?

I also chose to assess the level of statistical compilation a player achieved while wearing a 49ers uniform. I reviewed where he ranks among the team's all-time leaders in those statistical categories most pertinent to his position. Of course, even the method of using statistics as a measuring stick has its inherent flaws. Although the level of success a team experiences rushing and passing the ball is impacted greatly by the performance of its offensive line, there really is no way to quantifiably measure the level of play reached by each individual offensive lineman. Conversely, the play of the offensive line affects tremendously the statistics compiled by a team's quarterback and running backs. Furthermore, the NFL did not keep an official record of defensive numbers such as tackles and quarterback sacks until the 1980s (although the 49ers kept their own records prior to that). In addition, when examining the statistics compiled by offensive players, the era during which a quarterback, running back, or wide receiver competed must be factored into the equation.

To illustrate my last point, rules changes instituted by the league office have opened up the game considerably over the course of the last two decades. Quarterbacks are accorded far more protection than ever before, and officials have also been instructed to limit the amount of contact defensive backs and linebackers are allowed to make with wide receivers and tight ends. As a result, the game has experienced an offensive explosion, with quarterbacks and receivers posting numbers players from prior generations rarely even approached. That being the case, one must place the numbers Jeff Garcia compiled during his career in their proper context when comparing him to earlier 49ers quarterbacks such as Y. A. Tittle and John Brodie. Similarly, the statistics posted by Terrell Owens, Vernon Davis, and George Kittle must be viewed in moderation when comparing them to previous 49ers pass-catchers Gene Washington, Dwight Clark, and Brent Jones.

Other important factors I needed to consider were the overall contributions a player made to the success of the team, the degree to which he improved the fortunes of the club during his time in San Francisco, and the manner in which he impacted the team, both on and off the field. While the number of championships and division titles the 49ers won during a player's years with the team certainly factored into the equation, I chose not to deny a top performer his rightful place on the list if his years in San Francisco happened to coincide with a lack of overall success by the club. As a result, the names of players such as Hugh McElhenny and Kermit Alexander will appear in these rankings.

One other thing I should mention is that I only considered a player's performance while playing for the 49ers when formulating my rankings. That being the case, the names of exceptional players such as Charles Haley and Ken Norton Jr., both of whom had many of their finest seasons for other teams, may appear lower on this list than one might expect. Meanwhile, the names of Hall of Famers Randy Moss and Chris Doleman are nowhere to be found.

Having established the guidelines to be used throughout this book, the time has come to reveal the 50 greatest players in 49ers history, starting with number 1 and working our way down to number 50.

1

JERRY RICE

Despite the greatness of Ronnie Lott and Steve Young, the choice for the number one position in these rankings ultimately came down to either Jerry Rice or Joe Montana. On virtually any other team, Montana would be a lock for the top spot. A two-time NFL MVP who served as the unquestioned leader of 49er teams that won nine division titles and four Super Bowls, Montana can boast an extremely impressive list of credentials that also includes seven Pro Bowl selections, five All-Pro nominations, three Super Bowl MVPs, and a number four ranking on the NFL Network's 2010 list of the 100 Greatest Players in NFL History. But Rice finished three spots ahead of his longtime teammate on that same list, earned 12 Pro Bowl selections and 10 All-Pro nominations, gained NFL Player of the Year recognition once and NFL Offensive Player of the Year recognition twice, and played for 49er teams that won 10 division titles and three Super Bowls. Furthermore, after Montana left San Francisco, Rice continued to star at wideout for the 49ers for another eight years, performing equally well while teaming up with Steve Young. And finally, while Montana's name invariably comes up in any conversation regarding the greatest quarterback in NFL history, Rice is the unquestioned king of wide receivers, with many of the finest players who ever manned that position ceding that title to him. As a result, "Joe Cool" must settle for a very close second-place finish behind Rice, who many people consider to be the greatest player in the history of the game.

The NFL's all-time leader in every major pass-receiving category, Jerry Rice spent 16 seasons excelling for the 49ers at wide receiver, surpassing 80 receptions 10 times and 1,000 receiving yards on 12 separate occasions. Establishing himself as the game's ultimate offensive weapon during his time in San Francisco, Rice scored more touchdowns, amassed more yards from scrimmage, and accumulated more all-purpose yards than any other player in league history, prompting Ronnie Lott to once say, "Without a doubt—hands down—Jerry Rice is the best receiver to play in the National

Jerry Rice is widely considered to be the greatest wide receiver in NFL history.
Courtesy of George A. Kitrinos

Football League." One of the few players to earn a spot on the NFL All-Decade Team for two distinct 10-year periods, Rice received the additional honors of being named to the NFL 100 All-Time Team in 2019, having his #80 retired by the 49ers, and gaining induction into the Pro Football Hall of Fame in his very first year of eligibility.

Born in Starkville, Mississippi, on October 13, 1962, Jerry Lee Rice grew up some 20 miles southeast, in the town of Crawford, where he spent the hot summer months assisting his father in his bricklaying business, saying years later, "It taught me the meaning of hard work." Developing into an outstanding all-around athlete at B.L. Moor High School in nearby Oktoc, Rice excelled in football, basketball, and track and field, beginning his career on the gridiron as a sophomore after being discovered by the school's principal sprinting away to avoid being reprimanded for truancy.

Offered an athletic scholarship to Mississippi Valley State University, a historically black college located in the Leflore County city of Itta Bena, Rice spent three years starring at wide receiver in head coach Archie Cooley's spread offense, setting 18 Division I-AA records. After making 66 receptions for 1,133 yards and seven touchdowns as a sophomore, Rice earned Division I-AA All-America honors his junior year by establishing new NCAA marks for most receptions (102) and receiving yards (1,450), with his 24 catches against Louisiana's Southern University also setting a single-game NCAA record. Rice followed that up by making 112 receptions and amassing 1,845 receiving yards in his senior year, with his 27 TD catches setting a new single-season NCAA record for all divisions. Named to every Division I-AA All-America team, Rice finished his college career with 301 receptions, 4,693 receiving yards, and 50 touchdowns, with his ability to catch anything near him earning him the nickname "World."

Yet, despite the extraordinary numbers that Rice compiled at Mississippi Valley State, some pro scouts remained uncertain about his ability to excel at the next level heading into the 1985 NFL Draft due to his small-college background. The 49ers, though, had no such doubts, trading their first two picks to the New England Patriots for the right to select him with the 16th overall pick after learning that the Dallas Cowboys also had him high on their board. Commenting on the selection of Rice, 49ers head coach Bill Walsh stated, "I thought Jerry would be picked in the first five selections in the draft. But, as we talked to our colleagues in the NFL, somehow, some way, he had run a 4.6 40 [yard dash] at the scouting combine. So, he had been downgraded. It was easy for scouts to dismiss Jerry because of his time. Because, otherwise, they would have had to project a player from Mississippi Valley State as a major NFL contributor, and that's a tough one to sell to management and coaches. This way, they could deflect the idea by saying, 'Well, it's a small college, and he has a slow time.'"

Coming from a tiny town with fewer than 1,000 people, Rice experienced a great deal of uneasiness upon his arrival in San Francisco, recalling, "I'm coming to this big city, and there's nobody that I know. I wanted to turn around and go back on the plane, go back home."

Adding to Rice's anxiety, he got off to an extremely slow start on the football field, acquiring the nickname "Butterfingers" before long due to his inability to hold onto the football. Looking back at his early struggles, Rice remembered, "Oh man, there were many games where I just went in and tried. I tried because I had always been able to catch a football and make a play, and now I was dropping footballs, and I just couldn't pinpoint what was going on."

The turning point of Rice's rookie campaign finally came on December 9, when he gathered in 10 passes for 241 yards and one touchdown during a 27–20 loss to the Los Angeles Rams, with Rice later saying, "When it was all over, I knew I could play professional football."

His confidence buoyed by his outstanding performance against the Rams, Rice ended up making 49 receptions for 927 yards and four touchdowns his first year in the league, earning in the process NFC Offensive Rookie of the Year honors. Rice followed that up by beginning an amazing 11-year run during which he posted the following numbers:

YEAR	RECS	REC YDS	TD RECS	TDS
1986	86	1,570*	15	16
1987	65	1,078	22	23
1988	64	1,306	9	10
1989	82	1,483	17	17
1990	100	1,502	13	13
1991	80	1,206	14	14
1992	84	1,201	10	11
1993	98	1,503	15	16
1994	112	1,499	13	15
1995	122	1,848	15	16
1996	108	1,254	8	9

* Please note that any numbers printed in bold throughout this book indicate that the player led the NFL in that statistical category that year.

Establishing himself as the most prolific wide receiver in the game, Rice consistently ranked among the NFL leaders in all four categories, finishing either first or second in the league in receptions six times, receiving yards eight times, TD catches seven times, and touchdowns six times. Named NFL Player of the Year in 1987, Rice set a new league record (since broken) by scoring 23 touchdowns, doing so in only 12 games due to the players' strike. Rice also surpassed 100 receptions and 1,500 receiving yards four times each, with his 122 catches and 1,848 receiving yards in 1995 both setting single-season franchise records that still stand. Named NFL Offensive Player of the Year for the second time in 1993, Rice also earned Pro Bowl honors each season and 10 First-Team All-Pro selections, with his magnificent play helping the 49ers win nine division titles and three Super Bowls.

Although the 6'2", 200-pound Rice had good size and speed, he was neither the strongest nor the fastest wide receiver in the league. Nevertheless, he proved to be extremely difficult to bring down in the open field, with Joe Montana saying, "Jerry has the ability to turn a short pass into a long gain very easily. He has great 'going from zero to full speed' speed. You don't see him being caught from behind by guys who are faster than him."

Addressing his ability to run with the football after the catch, Rice said, "So many receivers, once they catch the football they just fall down. But, with me, once I catch the football, I feel that the excitement is just starting. So, somehow, I'm gonna try to keep my balance and try to get into the end zone."

Steve Young discussed his former teammate's ability to break away from opposing defenders, stating, "Jerry got faster in uniform. He carried the equipment better than anyone who has ever played. On the street he might not be the fastest, but on the field, he was faster than everybody."

Blessed with a unique ability to create separation between himself and his defender, Rice also excelled as a route-runner, with former NFL head coach Dennis Green calling him "the best route-runner I've ever seen."

Steve Young agreed with Green's assessment, saying, "Jerry was a supreme route-runner. The way he moved was somehow predictable, and he really made it easy for me to throw the football. He was just so consistent in his motion and movement that I always knew where he was going to be. . . . And he was a star. He rose to every occasion. The bigger the moment, the better he played."

Jon Gruden, who served as Rice's head coach in Oakland for three years, expressed similar sentiments when he said, "His best football was played in the two-minute drill. Late in the game, most of the guys get a little tired. Not this guy. . . . When the games got bigger and the situations got tighter, Jerry Rice played his best football."

Gruden further praised Rice by stating, "He is the most dominant player at his position that I've ever seen. You could not cover him. He could beat double coverage. You could put man-to-man with help over the top. However you want to try to defend him, he can beat any coverage. He can take a short pass to the house. Probably the greatest receiver after the catch. I don't know how many yards this guy made throughout his career after the catch, but it was a lot because I charted it for three years."

Joe Montana discussed the challenge that covering Rice presented to opposing defenders when he said, "I watch the league all the time, and there's no one who compares to his consistency, and the first thing is catching the football. He was just so good, and then John Taylor came along and made it hard for teams to double Jerry. And I can tell you, it's impossible to cover Jerry Rice one-on-one. Jerry got to the post more than anyone in history. . . . Somehow, he always got behind the safety. I don't know how he did it, but I was happy he did."

Revealing that he dreaded going up against Rice, Hall of Fame cornerback Deion Sanders claimed, "I couldn't sleep at all the night before playing him."

An outstanding blocker as well, Rice excelled at every aspect of wide receiver play. Yet, Rice's most special qualities may well have been his tremendous desire, determination, and dedication to his profession, with his grueling workout regimen that included running up a long and steep hill in Edgewood County Park and Natural Preserve nearly every day becoming the stuff of legend.

In discussing Rice's incorporation of "The Hill" into his daily exercise routine, Jon Gruden recalled, "We sent some guys with him to work out a couple of times and they'd come back saying, 'That man's crazy! He's running up and down hills.' You cannot imagine this guy's stamina."

Steve Mariucci also expressed amazement over Rice's incredible endurance, saying, "He would come out 45 minutes early. Sometimes he would work on covering kicks, returning punts, doing this, stretching, working on stance and starts, and catching. Then, after practice, he would be out there running gassers. . . . I once asked him why he worked so hard and he said, 'I want to be stronger at the end of the game than the guy I'm playing against.'"

Commenting on Rice's desire to perform at the highest level possible, Eddie DeBartolo stated, "I've never seen a player more driven or willing to work harder to become the greatest of all time. His perfectionism was evident in everything he did, in the way he carried himself both on and off the field."

Ronnie Lott claimed, "He always had that fire inside of him. If you doubted it, he wanted to destroy you. He wanted to show you that he was better than anybody that ever played. . . . Jerry was so explosive off the line and had the ability to always finish plays like no one else before or after. One thing he had was an insatiable appetite to get an edge and be the best."

In describing his mindset, Rice said, "Fear of failure pushed me. If I had a year where I had over 1,000 yards and 90 catches, I felt like I had to have a better year the next season. . . . I had that hunger, that desire, to be successful, and I wasn't going to let anything stand in my way."

Rice's determination and tremendous conditioning enabled him to appear in 189 consecutive non-strike games from 1985 to 1996, before he suffered a torn anterior cruciate and medial collateral ligament in his left knee in the opening game of the 1997 regular season that forced him to miss the next 13 contests. Returning to action much sooner than expected, Rice scored a touchdown during a 34–17 victory over the Denver Broncos in Week 16. But, when he came down with the catch, he cracked the patella in his left kneecap, sidelining him for the remainder of the year.

Healthy again by the start of the 1998 campaign, Rice earned his 12th trip to the Pro Bowl by making 82 receptions for 1,157 yards and nine touchdowns. Continuing to perform well over the course of the next two seasons, Rice totaled 142 receptions, 1,635 receiving yards, and 12 touchdowns, before the emergence of Terrell Owens and a desire to rebuild following consecutive losing seasons prompted the 49ers to allow him to enter free agency at the end of 2000. Signing with the Oakland Raiders, Rice left San Francisco with career totals of 1,281 receptions, 19,247 receiving yards, 19,872 yards from scrimmage, 176 TD catches, and 187 touchdowns, all of which represent franchise records. Rice also appeared in more games (238) and scored more points (1,130) than anyone else in team annals.

Rice ended up spending three full seasons in Oakland, surpassing 1,000 receiving yards twice and earning the last of his 13 Pro Bowl nominations in 2002, before splitting the 2004 campaign between the Raiders and Seattle Seahawks. Announcing his retirement at the end of the year, Rice left the game with a long list of NFL records that includes most receptions (1,549), receiving yards (22,895), TD catches (197), touchdowns (208), yards from scrimmage (23,540), and all-purpose yards (23,546). Rice later signed a one-day contract with the 49ers on August 24, 2006, that enabled him to officially call it quits as a member of the team. The 49ers later retired his jersey #80 during halftime of a game against the New Orleans Saints on

September 20, 2010. Since retiring as an active player, Rice has spent much of his time playing golf. He has also appeared on several TV commercials.

Widely considered to be the most dominant player ever to man his position, Rice has drawn praise from many of the game's most accomplished wideouts, with both Michael Irvin and Terrell Owens calling him "the greatest receiver of all time." George Seifert took it one step further, saying of Rice, "He may have been the *greatest football player* of all time."

Former 49ers teammate Steve Wallace expressed similar sentiments when he stated, "Having played with great quarterbacks in Joe Montana and Steve Young, this guy is on planet Pluto. He's beyond the Pro Bowl and Hall of Fame. He's the only guy that dominated a position so far beyond anyone else."

Jon Gruden agreed, saying, "He did it for two decades. If you look at his statistics, where he is, and where the number 2, 3, and 4 guys are, it's amazing what he accomplished. He's a work of art."

49ERS CAREER HIGHLIGHTS

Best Season

There are so many great seasons from which to choose, with the 1987 and 1995 campaigns heading the list. In addition to catching 65 passes and amassing 1,078 receiving yards in 1987, Rice set a new single-season NFL record by making 22 touchdown receptions, with his fabulous performance earning him NFL Player of the Year honors. However, Rice posted better overall numbers in 1995, when he scored 16 touchdowns and established single-season franchise records with 122 receptions and 1,848 receiving yards.

Memorable Moments/Greatest Performances

Rice scored his first touchdown as a pro when he caught a 25-yard pass from Joe Montana during a 38–17 win over Atlanta on October 6, 1985.

Rice had his breakout game on December 9, 1985, earning NFC Offensive Player of the Week honors for the first of 12 times by making 10 receptions for 241 yards and one TD during a 27–20 Monday night loss to the Rams, with his TD coming on a 66-yard connection with Montana.

Rice helped lead the 49ers to a 35–14 win over the Indianapolis Colts on October 5, 1986, by making six receptions for 172 yards and three touchdowns, which came on hookups of 45, 16, and 58 yards with Jeff Kemp.

Rice contributed to a 43–17 victory over the St. Louis Cardinals on November 9, 1986, by making four receptions for 156 yards and three touchdowns, collaborating with Joe Montana on scoring plays that covered 45, 40, and 44 yards.

Although the 49ers lost to the Washington Redskins 14–6 on November 17, 1986, Rice earned NFC Offensive Player of the Week honors by making 12 receptions for 204 yards.

Rice gave the 49ers a dramatic 27–26 victory over the Cincinnati Bengals on September 20, 1987, by gathering in a 25-yard touchdown pass from Joe Montana on the game's final play.

Rice proved to be the difference in a 24–10 win over Tampa Bay on November 22, 1987, scoring all three 49ers touchdowns on passes from Joe Montana, with his seven catches, 103 receiving yards, and three TDs gaining him recognition once again as NFC Offensive Player of the Week.

Rice followed that up by making seven receptions for 126 yards and three touchdowns during a 38–24 win over Cleveland on November 29, 1987, with one of his TD catches covering 30 yards.

Rice gave the 49ers a 20–17 win over the Giants on September 11, 1988, by collaborating with Joe Montana on a 78-yard scoring play in the fourth quarter. He finished the game with four catches for 109 yards and that one TD.

Rice helped lead the 49ers to a lopsided 38–7 victory over Seattle on September 25, 1988, by making six receptions for 163 yards and three TDs, two of which went for more than 60 yards.

Rice earned NFC Offensive Player of the Week honors by making six receptions for 171 yards and two touchdowns during a 48–10 win over the San Diego Chargers on November 27, 1988, with one of his TDs coming on a career-long 96-yard connection with Joe Montana.

Rice helped the 49ers begin the 1989 campaign on a positive note by making six receptions for 163 yards and one touchdown during a 30–24 win over the Colts in the regular-season opener, with his 58-yard fourth-quarter TD connection with Montana providing the margin of victory.

Rice's eight receptions for 171 yards and one TD during a 19–13 win over Atlanta on September 23, 1990, gained him recognition as NFC Offensive Player of the Week for the fifth time.

Rice torched the Atlanta defensive secondary once again on October 14, 1990, making 13 receptions for 225 yards and five touchdowns during a 45–35 49ers win, with his five TDs and 30 points scored both setting single-game franchise records.

Rice helped lead the 49ers to a 24–20 victory over the Packers on November 4, 1990, by making six receptions for 187 yards and one touchdown, which came on a 64-yard pass from Joe Montana in the fourth quarter that provided the winning margin.

Rice starred during a 34–14 win over the Chargers on September 8, 1991, making nine receptions for 150 yards and two TDs, which came on hookups of 32 and 70 yards with Steve Young.

Rice earned NFC Offensive Player of the Week honors by catching seven passes, amassing 103 receiving yards, and scoring three touchdowns during a 56–17 rout of Atlanta on October 18, 1992, with one of his TDs coming on a 25-yard run and the other two on connections with Steve Young that covered 80 and 40 yards.

Rice earned that distinction again by making eight receptions for 172 yards and four touchdowns during a 45–21 win over Tampa Bay on November 14, 1993, with the longest of his TDs coming on a 51-yard pass from Young.

Rice led the 49ers to a convincing 44–14 victory over the Raiders in the opening game of the 1994 regular season by making seven receptions for 169 yards and scoring three touchdowns, one of which came on a 23-yard run, and the other two on receptions of 69 and 38 yards.

Rice gained recognition as NFC Offensive Player of the Week by making a career-high 16 receptions for 165 yards and three touchdowns during a 31–27 win over the Rams on November 20, 1994, with his 18-yard TD grab with just over two minutes remaining in the final period providing the margin of victory.

Rice contributed to a 41–10 win over Atlanta on September 10, 1995, by catching 11 passes for 167 yards and two touchdowns, the longest of which covered 29 yards.

Rice earned NFC Offensive Player of the Week honors for the 12th and final time by making 14 receptions for 289 yards and three TDs during a 37–30 win over Minnesota on December 18, 1995, with his 289 receiving yards setting a single-game franchise record that still stands.

An outstanding postseason performer throughout his career, Rice first exhibited his ability to excel under pressure in the divisional round of the 1988 playoffs, when he made three touchdown receptions during a 34–9 win over the Vikings.

Rising to the occasion once again in the 1988 NFC championship game, Rice made five receptions for 133 yards and two touchdowns during a 28–3 victory over the Bears, with his TDs coming on passes of 61 and 27 yards from Joe Montana.

Rice subsequently earned game MVP honors in Super Bowl XXIII by making 11 receptions for 215 yards and one touchdown during a 20–16 win over Cincinnati, with his TD coming on a 14-yard connection with Montana that tied the score at 13–13 early in the fourth quarter.

Rice also starred in Super Bowls XXIV and XXIX, leading the 49ers to a 55–10 rout of Denver in the first of those contests by making seven receptions for 148 yards and three touchdowns, before contributing to a 49–26 victory over San Diego five years later by making 10 receptions for 149 yards and three TDs, the longest of which covered 44 yards.

Notable Achievements

- Surpassed 100 receptions four times, catching at least 80 passes on six other occasions.
- Surpassed 1,000 receiving yards 12 times, topping 1,500 yards on four occasions.
- Scored at least 10 touchdowns 10 times.
- Scored more than 100 points three times.
- Averaged more than 20 yards per reception once.
- Led NFL in receptions twice, receiving yards six times, touchdown receptions six times, touchdowns twice, and points scored once.
- Finished second in NFL in receptions four times, receiving yards twice, touchdown receptions once, and touchdowns four times.
- Led 49ers in receptions 11 times and receiving yards 13 times.
- Holds 49ers single-game records for most receiving yards (289), touchdowns scored (5), and points scored (30).
- Holds 49ers single-season records for most receptions (122 in 1995), receiving yards (1,848 in 1995), touchdown receptions (22 in 1987), and touchdowns scored (23 in 1987).
- Holds 49ers career records for most games played (238), receptions (1,281), receiving yards (19,247), touchdown receptions (176), touchdowns (187), points scored (1,130), yards from scrimmage (19,872), and all-purpose yards (19,878).
- Tied for second in franchise history in seasons played (16).
- Holds NFL career records for most receptions (1,549), receiving yards (22,895), touchdown receptions (197), touchdowns (208), yards from scrimmage (23,540), and all-purpose yards (23,546).

- 10-time division champion (1986, 1987, 1988, 1989, 1990, 1992, 1993, 1994, 1995, and 1997).
- Three-time NFC champion (1988, 1989, and 1994).
- Three-time Super Bowl champion (XXIII, XXIV, and XXIX).
- 12-time NFC Offensive Player of the Week.
- November 1986 NFC Offensive Player of the Month.
- Member of 1985 NFL All-Rookie Team.
- 1985 NFC Offensive Rookie of the Year.
- Super Bowl XXIII MVP.
- 1987 Newspaper Enterprise Association (NEA) NFL MVP.
- 1987 Dan Bell Award winner as NFL Player of the Year.
- Two-time NFL Offensive Player of the Year (1987 and 1993).
- 12-time Pro Bowl selection (1986, 1987, 1988, 1989, 1990, 1991, 1992, 1993, 1994, 1995, 1996, and 1998).
- 10-time First-Team All-Pro selection (1986, 1987, 1988, 1989, 1990, 1992, 1993, 1994, 1995, and 1996).
- 11-time First-Team All-NFC selection (1986, 1987, 1988, 1989, 1990, 1991, 1992, 1993, 1994, 1995, and 1996).
- Pro Football Reference All-1990s First Team.
- NFL 1980s All-Decade First Team.
- NFL 1990s All-Decade First Team.
- Named to NFL's 75th Anniversary All-Time Team in 1994.
- Named to NFL 100 All-Time Team in 2019.
- Number two on the *Sporting News*' 1999 list of the 100 Greatest Players in NFL History.
- Number one on the NFL Network's 2010 list of the NFL's 100 Greatest Players.
- #80 retired by 49ers.
- Inducted into 49ers Hall of Fame in 2010.
- Elected to Pro Football Hall of Fame in 2010.

2
JOE MONTANA

Having fallen just short of earning the top spot on this list, Joe Montana lays claim to the number two position, finishing just ahead of Ronnie Lott and Steve Young. The holder of virtually every 49ers' career passing record, Montana is generally considered to be one of the two or three greatest quarterbacks ever to play the game. The NFL's all-time leader in passer rating and pass-completion percentage at the time of his retirement, Montana led the league in each of those categories on multiple occasions, while also topping the circuit in touchdown passes twice. One of only two quarterbacks in NFL history to win as many as four Super Bowls and not lose any, Montana led the 49ers to nine division titles and four league championships, earning in the process numerous individual accolades that included seven Pro Bowl selections, five All-Pro nominations, and two NFL MVP awards. Further honored following the conclusion of his playing career, Montana later received the additional distinctions of being named to the NFL 100 All-Time Team in 2019, being accorded a top-five ranking on both the *Sporting News'* and the NFL Network's respective lists of the 100 Greatest Players in NFL History, having his #16 retired by the 49ers, and gaining induction into the Pro Football Hall of Fame.

Born in the Washington County borough of New Eagle, Pennsylvania, on June 11, 1956, Joseph Clifford Montana Jr. grew up in nearby Monongahela, a coal mining town some 25 miles south of Pittsburgh. Displaying an affinity for sports at an early age, Montana began playing youth football at the age of eight, while also successfully competing in baseball and basketball. Continuing his athletic development at Ringgold High School, Montana starred in all three sports, proving to be especially proficient on the hardwood, where he earned All-State honors his senior year by leading Ringgold to the 1973 WPIAL Class AAA boys' basketball championship. A standout in football as well, Montana spent his final two seasons starting for the Rams at quarterback, gaining All-America recognition from *Parade* magazine as a senior. After seriously considering attending North Carolina

Joe Montana led the 49ers to four Super Bowl victories.
Courtesy of George A. Kitrinos

State University on a basketball scholarship, Montana ultimately chose to enroll at the University of Notre Dame, where he hoped to follow in the footsteps of his boyhood hero, quarterback Terry Hanratty.

Montana subsequently spent most of his first two seasons at Notre Dame sitting on the bench, before missing his entire junior year with a separated shoulder. Returning to action in 1978, Montana began starting behind center during the early stages of the campaign, after which he went on to lead the Fighting Irish to an 11-1 record and the National Championship, with his extraordinary effort against Houston in the 1979 Cotton Bowl making him a legendary figure in school history. Playing on a frozen field in Dallas with winds gusting up to 30 miles an hour, a cut and bleeding Montana returned to the fray late in the third quarter after having spent all of halftime and most of the third period being treated for hypothermia that left him with a body temperature of 96 degrees. Displaying tremendous resolve, Montana led the Fighting Irish on three fourth-quarter scoring drives that gave them a 35-34 victory in a game they trailed by 22 points heading into the final period, completing his final TD pass as time expired.

Yet, despite his heroics at Notre Dame, Montana received mixed reviews heading into the 1979 NFL Draft, with many pro scouts questioning his arm strength. Bill Walsh, though, expressed no such reservations after the 49ers selected him in the third round, with the 82nd overall pick, saying at the time, "I can't find any negatives about Joe Montana's arm. Maybe the so-called experts can. People who say it's only an average arm are mistaken. And they always will be. Because his delivery is not a flick of the wrist like Terry Bradshaw's, they think it's not strong. He throws on the run while avoiding a pass rush, and he does not have to be totally set."

Following his arrival in San Francisco, Montana spent his rookie season serving as a backup to Steve DeBerg, starting just one game and completing only 13 of 23 pass attempts for a 49ers team that finished just 2-14. However, after assuming a similar role during the early stages of the ensuing campaign, Montana replaced DeBerg behind center, starting seven contests and finishing the year with 1,795 yards passing, 15 touchdown passes, 9 interceptions, and a league-leading 64.5 completion percentage. Assuming the mantle of leadership full-time in 1981, Montana began an exceptional five-year run during which he posted the following numbers:

YEAR	YDS PASSING	TD PASSES	INTS	COMP %	QBR
1981	3,565	19	12	**63.7**	88.4
1982	2,613	**17**	11	61.6	88.0
1983	3,910	26	12	64.5	94.6
1984	3,630	28	10	64.6	102.9
1985	3,653	27	13	**61.3**	91.3

Establishing himself as the finest all-around quarterback in the game during that time, Montana finished either first or second in the NFL in pass-completion percentage in four of those five seasons, while also consistently ranking among the league leaders in passing yards, touchdown passes, and passer rating, with his outstanding play earning him four trips to the Pro Bowl, two All-Pro nominations, and three All-NFC selections. More importantly, Montana led the 49ers to four playoff appearances, three division titles, and two NFL championships, earning game MVP honors in Super Bowls XVI and XIX.

A perfect fit for Bill Walsh's West Coast Offense, the 6'2", 200-pound Montana excelled at getting the ball out quickly to his receivers and using the short passing game very much like the running game. Although Montana lacked a powerful throwing arm, he possessed perfect timing, the ability to read defenses quickly, excellent mobility, outstanding pocket presence, and tremendous accuracy on his passes, making him extremely effective at delivering the ball to his receivers on routes of the short and intermediate variety.

In discussing his former teammate, Charles Haley said, "I always thought he had the weakest arm in the world because every pass was so soft. He never threw hard. Everything was timed. He read things so fast; he was so smart. He controlled everything on offense. He got it done; he was a doer."

Assessing his own strengths at one point during his career, Montana stated, "What I have is recognition. The ability to see everything on the field. Position the other team to death. Keep the ball alive and keep it moving forward. Then, at the right moment, knock them on their ass; Own the field."

Describing the approach that he took to his craft years later, Montana said, "I wanted to play the game as more of a chess game. One move's going to lead to another, and you're not always going to get the king immediately. . . . Four yards here, five yards there, 10 yards there. It's more wearing on a defense than one 70-yard touchdown. That was more my style than anything."

Jerry Rice also shared his thoughts on what he considered to be some of his former teammate's greatest assets when he said, "He could feel pressure, and he would get rid of that football. If he didn't have the primary, it was the second or third receiver. . . . He knew exactly where everybody was going to be on that football field, and I think that's really what made him the best quarterback. Plus, he was 'Joe Cool.'"

Rice added, "Those little skinny legs that he had; they were so skinny—he didn't have a calf. I'm like, 'How can this guy move around like that?' But, you know, the thing about him, he was elusive. You couldn't catch him."

Impressed with Montana's ability to navigate the ball downfield, former 49ers quarterback Frankie Albert said in 1985, "I wasn't bad as a scrambler or ball-handler, but, after watching Montana play, I don't think I could carry that guy's helmet. I've seen some great quarterbacks—Otto Graham, Bob Waterfield, Norm Van Brocklin—and I'd say Montana ranks with the top two or three to ever play the game. When things break down and people start to scatter, he's at his best. He can get out of trouble and do things no other quarterback can do. He makes plays out of nothing. That's a gift."

Still, Montana's greatest gift may well have been his ability to perform well under pressure. Blessed with tremendous poise, Montana never seemed flustered, inspiring confidence in his teammates with the calmness he displayed in the most stressful of situations. In discussing his teammate's ability to block out external distractions, longtime 49ers offensive lineman Randy Cross stated, "He's not so far into the game that he loses perspective. He's rather detached. It's like he's able to do it in the third person."

The master of late-game heroics, Montana led his team to 31 fourth-quarter come-from-behind victories over the course of his career, prompting Ronnie Lott to once say, "He's like Indiana Jones. He can go up against odds, and he just believes in himself. He believes nothing can stop him . . . Joe finds a way to come out on top."

Revealing the confidence that he had in his teammate, Jerry Rice stated, "You knew that when everything was on the line, if you had a minute left in the ballgame, Joe wouldn't let us down. . . . Super Bowl XXIII, on the final drive, we were at ease because we had the best quarterback, and that was Joe Montana."

Claiming that Montana also proved to be an outstanding teammate who never let the success he experienced go to his head, Rice recalled how the 49ers quarterback treated him when he first arrived in San Francisco, saying, "I had watched him on television. I had seen him make so many incredible plays and pull out so many last-minute victories. I was a little bit in awe. . . . I thought a guy of his status would be conceited, not give me the time of day. But it was the opposite. He was very relaxed and willing to talk to you and help you out in any way possible."

After gaining Pro Bowl recognition for the third straight time in 1985, Montana missed the first half of the ensuing campaign with an injured back. Appearing somewhat frail upon his return to the team at midseason, Montana nevertheless led the 49ers to the division title and their fourth straight playoff appearance by compiling a 6-2 record in his eight starts, earning in the process NFL Comeback Player of the Year honors. However, the 49ers subsequently suffered a humiliating 49–3 defeat at the hands of the eventual Super Bowl champion New York Giants in the opening round of the postseason tournament, with Montana exiting the game shortly before halftime after being knocked unconscious by New York nose tackle Jim Burt.

Fully healthy by the start of the 1987 campaign, Montana ended up having one of his finest seasons, earning Pro Bowl honors and the first of his three First-Team All-Pro nominations by throwing for 3,054 yards and leading the NFL with 31 touchdown passes, a pass-completion percentage of 66.8, and a passer rating of 102.1. However, despite posting a league-best 13-2 record during the regular season, the 49ers once again exited the playoffs quickly, losing to the Minnesota Vikings by a score of 36–24 in their divisional round matchup.

Although neither the 49ers nor Montana performed as well during the 1988 regular season, with the team finishing 10-6 and Montana throwing for only 2,981 yards and 18 touchdowns, they both rose to the occasion in the playoffs, with the 49ers posting a 20–16 victory over Cincinnati in Super Bowl XXIII when Montana hit John Taylor with a 10-yard touchdown pass in the game's closing moments. Repeating as NFL champions the following year, the 49ers concluded the regular season with a record of 14-2, before outscoring their three playoff opponents by a combined margin of 126–26. Meanwhile, despite missing three games due to injury, Montana passed for 3,521 yards, threw 26 touchdown passes, completed a league-leading 70.2 percent of his passes, and topped the circuit with a passer rating of 112.4, with his fabulous performance earning him Pro Bowl, First-Team All-Pro, and NFL MVP honors. Montana then capped off his brilliant year by throwing five touchdown passes during a 55–10 manhandling of Denver in Super Bowl XXIV, earning in the process game MVP honors for the third time.

Seeking to capture their third consecutive NFL championship in 1990, the 49ers once again finished 14-2 during the regular season, with Montana earning Pro Bowl, First-Team All-Pro, and NFL MVP honors for the second straight time by ranking among the league leaders with 3,944 yards passing, 26 touchdown passes, and a 61.7 pass-completion percentage. But after handily defeating the Washington Redskins in the divisional round of the postseason tournament, the 49ers saw their dreams of a three-peat come to an end when they lost to the Giants by a score of 15–13 in the NFC championship game. Making matters worse, Montana had to leave the contest with 9:42 remaining in the fourth quarter after Giants defensive lineman Leonard Marshall delivered a vicious blindside hit to his back that left him with a bruised sternum, bruised stomach, cracked ribs, and a broken hand.

Forced to undergo offseason surgery on his throwing arm, Montana subsequently missed the entire 1991 campaign, and much of 1992 as well, during which time Steve Young performed exceptionally well in his absence. Unhappy with his role as Young's backup after he returned to the team midway through the 1992 season, Montana requested a trade to another team at the end of the year, prompting the 49ers to deal him to the Kansas City Chiefs. Montana left San Francisco with career totals of 35,124 yards passing, 244 touchdown passes, 123 interceptions, 1,595 yards rushing, and 20 rushing touchdowns. He also completed 63.7 percent of his passes and posted a passer rating of 93.5 while playing for the 49ers.

Montana ended up spending two seasons in Kansas City, leading the Chiefs to one division title and two playoff appearances, before announcing his retirement following the conclusion of the 1994 campaign. Ending his career with 40,551 yards passing, 273 touchdown passes, a pass-completion percentage of 63.2, and a passer rating of 92.3, Montana ranked among the NFL's all-time leaders in all four categories at the time of his retirement.

Pursuing a career in business following his playing days, Montana spent several years serving as a managing partner of HRJ Capital, which he co-founded with former teammates Harris Barton and Ronnie Lott. Montana later found success in the tech sector, investing in top firms such as Pinterest and DropBox, before launching in 2015 Liquid 2 Ventures, an investment fund at which he currently serves as a general partner.

Although the rules governing football the past two decades have enabled several quarterbacks to surpass the figures that Montana compiled during his playing career, there are those who still consider "Joe Cool" to be the greatest signal-caller in the history of the game. Among Montana's most ardent supporters is Jerry Rice, who said, "I think the greatest quarterback that ever put on football cleats is two words—Joe Montana."

49ERS CAREER HIGHLIGHTS

Best Season

Although Montana performed brilliantly for the 49ers throughout most of his 13-year stay in San Francisco, three seasons stand out above all others as the greatest of his career. Despite being relegated to Second-Team All-Pro honors by Dan Marino in 1984, Montana had one of his finest statistical seasons, ranking among the league leaders with 3,630 yards passing, 28 touchdown passes, a passer rating of 102.9, and a pass-completion percentage of 64.6. En route to earning First-Team All-Pro honors for the first time in 1987, Montana threw for 3,054 yards and led all NFL quarterbacks with 31 touchdown passes, a passer rating of 102.1, and a pass-completion percentage of 66.8. But Montana reached the apex of his career in 1989, when he earned NFL MVP and NFL Player of the Year honors by passing for 3,521 yards, throwing 26 TD passes and only eight interceptions, and leading the league with a passer rating of 112.4 and a pass-completion percentage of 70.2.

Memorable Moments/Greatest Performances

Montana threw his first touchdown pass as a pro in a mop-up role, delivering a 16-yard scoring strike to Bob Bruer during a 38–28 loss to the Denver Broncos on November 18, 1979.

Montana first displayed his ability to excel in the NFL when he ran for one score and passed for 285 yards and two touchdowns during a 38–35 overtime win over the New Orleans Saints on December 7, 1980, with the longest of his TD passes being a 71-yard hookup with Dwight Clark.

Montana led the 49ers to a 28–17 victory over the Bears on September 13, 1981, by throwing for 287 yards and three touchdowns, the longest of which went 46 yards to Freddie Solomon.

Montana starred during a 31–20 win over the St. Louis Cardinals on November 21, 1982, passing for 408 yards and three touchdowns, with his longest TD pass going 33 yards to Dwight Clark.

Montana guided the 49ers to a 30–24 victory over the Rams on December 2, 1982, by completing 26 of 37 pass attempts for 305 yards and two touchdowns, both of which went to Jeff Moore.

Montana threw four touchdown passes in one game for the first time as a pro during a 48–17 rout of Minnesota on September 8, 1983, with his longest TD toss going 21 yards to Dwight Clark.

Montana followed that up with a strong outing against the St. Louis Cardinals 10 days later, passing for 341 yards and three touchdowns during a 42–27 49ers win on September 18, 1983.

Continuing his outstanding play in the month of October, Montana threw for 358 yards and three touchdowns during a 45–35 victory over the Rams on October 23, 1983.

Montana led the 49ers to a 37–31 win over the Washington Redskins on September 10, 1984, by running for one score and passing for 381 yards and two touchdowns.

Montana earned NFC Offensive Player of the Week honors for the first of eight times by throwing for 353 yards and three TDs during a 34–21 win over the Houston Oilers on October 21, 1984, with his longest completion of the day being an 80-yard TD pass to Dwight Clark.

Montana followed that up by passing for 365 yards and three touchdowns during a convincing 33–0 victory over the Rams on October 28, 1984, hooking up with Dwight Clark and Roger Craig on scoring plays that covered 44 and 64 yards, respectively.

Montana gained recognition as the NFC Offensive Player of the Week by passing for 429 yards and five touchdowns during a 38–17 win over the Atlanta Falcons on October 6, 1985.

Montana led the 49ers to a 28–14 win over the Rams on October 27, 1985, by completing 22 of 30 pass attempts for 306 yards and three touchdowns.

Montana had another huge game later in the year, throwing for 354 yards and three touchdowns during a 31–19 win over New Orleans on December 15, 1985, with the longest of his TD passes going 52 yards to Mike Wilson.

Showing no signs of rust after missing the previous eight games due to injury, Montana earned NFC Offensive Player of the Week honors by passing for 270 yards and three touchdowns during a 43–17 win over the St. Louis Cardinals on November 9, 1986.

Montana gave the 49ers a dramatic 27–26 victory over the Cincinnati Bengals on September 20, 1987, when he hit Jerry Rice with a 25-yard scoring strike on the final play of the game. He finished the contest with 250 yards passing and three TD passes.

Montana earned NFC Offensive Player of the Week honors by throwing for 342 yards and four touchdowns during a 38–24 win over the Cleveland Browns on November 29, 1987, with three of his TD passes going to Jerry Rice and the other to Dwight Clark.

Montana earned that distinction again by passing for 302 yards and four touchdowns during a 38–7 win over the Seattle Seahawks on September 25, 1988.

Almost exactly one year later, on September 24, 1989, Montana led the 49ers to a 38–28 come-from-behind win over Philadelphia by throwing four fourth-quarter TD passes, the longest of which came on a 70-yard connection with John Taylor. Finishing the game with 428 yards passing and five TD passes, Montana again earned NFC Offensive Player of the Week honors.

Montana had a hand in all four touchdowns the 49ers scored during a 31–13 win over the Saints on November 6, 1989, running for one TD and passing for three others, the longest of which went 46 yards to John Taylor.

Montana threw for 458 yards and three touchdowns during a 30–27 win over the Rams on December 11, 1989, with his two TD passes to John Taylor each covering more than 90 yards.

Montana earned NFC Offensive Player of the Week honors by passing for 390 yards and two touchdowns during a 26–13 win over Washington on September 16, 1990.

Montana followed that up by throwing for 398 yards and two TDs during a 19–13 win over Atlanta on September 23, 1990, with the longest of his TD passes going 67 yards to Brent Jones.

Montana led the 49ers to a 45–35 win over Atlanta on October 14, 1990, by passing for a career-high and franchise-record 476 yards and six touchdowns, five going to Jerry Rice.

Montana had another huge game against Green Bay on November 4, 1990, throwing for 411 yards and three touchdowns during a 24–20 win over the Packers.

Yet, as well as Montana performed during the regular season, he became known for his ability to excel under playoff pressure, first exhibiting that quality in the divisional round of the 1981 postseason tournament when he threw for 304 yards and two touchdowns during a 38–24 win over the Giants.

Montana followed that up by leading the 49ers to a 28–27 win over the Dallas Cowboys in the NFC championship game, with his touchdown pass to Dwight Clark in the closing moments providing the margin of victory. Displaying tremendous poise throughout the 49ers' game-winning TD drive that began on their own 11 yard line, Montana calmly drove his team downfield, before finding himself in a third-down-and goal situation on the Dallas 6 yard line. Flushed out of the pocket by three Cowboy defenders, Montana lured Dallas defensive lineman Ed "Too Tall" Jones into leaving his feet by faking a pass. With Jones no longer in his line of vision, Montana tossed the ball toward the back of the end zone in the direction of Clark, who leaped high in the air to make the grab that subsequently became known simply as "The Catch."

Two weeks later, Montana led the 49ers to a 26–21 victory over Cincinnati in Super Bowl XVI by running for one score and throwing for another, with his outstanding play earning him game MVP honors for the first of three times.

Although the 49ers ended up losing the 1983 NFC championship game to Washington by a score of 24–21 on a late Mark Moseley field goal, Montana brought them back from a 21–0 deficit by throwing three fourth-quarter touchdown passes, the longest of which went 76 yards to Freddie Solomon. Montana finished the game with 347 yards passing and those three TD passes.

Outplaying Dan Marino in Super Bowl XIX, Montana passed for 331 yards, ran for one score, and threw for three others, in leading the 49ers to a 38–16 victory over Miami, earning in the process Super Bowl MVP honors for the second time.

Montana again performed brilliantly in Super Bowl XXIII, leading the 49ers to a 20–16 win over Cincinnati by passing for 357 yards and two touchdowns, with his 10-yard TD pass to John Taylor with just 34 seconds remaining in regulation providing the margin of victory.

After throwing four touchdown passes during a 41–13 rout of Minnesota in the divisional round of the 1989 playoffs, Montana led the 49ers to a 30–3 win over the Rams in the NFC championship game by completing 26 of 30 passes for 262 yards and two TDs. Montana then earned Super Bowl MVP honors for the third time by passing for 297 yards and five touchdowns during a 55–10 blowout of Denver in Super Bowl XXIV.

Notable Achievements

- Passed for more than 3,500 yards six times.
- Threw more than 25 touchdown passes six times, topping 30 TD passes once (31 in 1987).
- Completed more than 60 percent of passes 10 times, topping 70 percent once.
- Posted touchdown-to-interception ratio of better than 2–1 five times.
- Posted passer rating above 90.0 five times, finishing with mark above 100.0 on three occasions.
- Led NFL in touchdown passes twice, pass completion percentage five times, and passer rating twice.
- Finished second in NFL in pass completions three times, passing yards once, touchdown passes once, pass completion percentage three times, and passer rating once.

- Finished third in NFL in pass completions twice, passing yards once, touchdown passes twice, pass completion percentage twice, and passer rating once.
- Holds 49ers career records for most pass attempts (4,600), pass completions (2,929), passing yards (35,124), and touchdown passes (244).
- Nine-time division champion (1981, 1983, 1984, 1986, 1987, 1988, 1989, 1990, and 1992).
- Four-time NFC champion (1981, 1984, 1988, and 1989).
- Four-time Super Bowl champion (XVI, XIX, XXIII, and XXIV).
- Eight-time NFC Offensive Player of the Week.
- November 1989 NFC Offensive Player of the Month.
- 1986 NFL Comeback Player of the Year.
- Three-time Super Bowl MVP (XVI, XIX, and XXIV).
- Two-time NFL MVP (1989 and 1990).
- 1989 Bert Bell Award winner as NFL Player of the Year.
- 1989 NFL Offensive Player of the Year.
- 1990 *Sports Illustrated* Sportsman of the Year.
- Seven-time Pro Bowl selection (1981, 1983, 1984, 1985, 1987, 1989, and 1990).
- Three-time First-Team All-Pro selection (1987, 1989, and 1990).
- Two-time Second-Team All-Pro selection (1981 and 1984).
- Six-time First-Team All-NFC selection (1981, 1984, 1985, 1987, 1989, and 1990).
- 1990 Second-Team All-NFC selection.
- Pro Football Reference All-1980s First Team.
- NFL 1980s All-Decade First Team.
- Named to NFL's 75th Anniversary All-Time Team in 1994.
- Named to NFL 100 All-Time Team in 2019.
- Number three on the *Sporting News'* 1999 list of the 100 Greatest Players in NFL History.
- Number four on the NFL Network's 2010 list of the NFL's 100 Greatest Players.
- #16 retired by 49ers.
- Inducted into 49ers Hall of Fame in 2009.
- Elected to Pro Football Hall of Fame in 2000.

3

RONNIE LOTT

One of the greatest defensive players in NFL history, Ronnie Lott excelled at all four defensive back positions at different points in his career, which he spent primarily in San Francisco. A member of the 49ers from 1981 to 1990, Lott recorded more interceptions and amassed more interception-return yards than any other player in team annals, while also instilling fear in opposing wide receivers and running backs with his aggressive style of play that prompted longtime 49ers owner Eddie DeBartolo to describe him as a "mad man." Ranking among the franchise's all-time leaders in tackles, forced fumbles, and fumble recoveries as well, Lott earned nine Pro Bowl selections and six All-Pro nominations during his time in San Francisco, with his brilliant all-around play helping the 49ers win eight division titles and four Super Bowls. And, following the conclusion of his playing career, Lott received the additional honors of being named to the NFL 100 All-Time Team, being included on the *Sporting News'* and the NFL Network's respective lists of the 100 Greatest Players in NFL History, having his #42 retired by the 49ers, and gaining induction into the Pro Football Hall of Fame.

Born in Albuquerque, New Mexico, on May 8, 1959, Ronald Mandel Lott grew up in a military family, with his father spending much of his life serving in the US Air Force. Moving with his family from New Mexico to Washington, DC, before finally settling in Rialto, California, Lott starred on the gridiron at Eisenhower High School, excelling at quarterback, wide receiver, and safety. First exhibiting his commitment to winning in high school, Lott typically prepared himself mentally for each game by listening to the opening speech delivered by George C. Scott in the film *Patton*, during which Patton/Scott states emphatically, "Americans love a winner and will not tolerate a loser . . . the very thought of losing is hateful to Americans. . . ."

Recruited by several major colleges, Lott ultimately chose to play for head coach John Robinson at USC, where he ended up starting at safety

Ronnie Lott holds franchise records for most interceptions and most
interception-return yards.
Courtesy of Mearsonlineauctions.com

for three seasons. A key contributor to Trojan teams that won two Rose
Bowls and one National Championship, Lott gained consensus All-America
recognition in both his junior and senior years, performing especially well
in his final season, when, as team captain, he led the Pac-10 with eight
interceptions.

Subsequently selected by the 49ers with the eighth overall pick of the 1981 NFL Draft, Lott made an immediate impact upon his arrival in San Francisco, helping the 49ers win their first NFL championship by making 89 tackles, picking off seven passes, and scoring three touchdowns after laying claim to the starting left cornerback job during the preseason. In addition to being accorded Pro Bowl and First-Team All-Pro honors for his outstanding play, Lott finished runner-up to New York Giants linebacker Lawrence Taylor in the voting for NFL Defensive Rookie of the Year. Continuing to excel at cornerback for the next three seasons, Lott earned three more trips to the Pro Bowl and helped the 49ers win another NFL title by recording 10 interceptions, amassing more than 100 tackles once, and scoring another TD on defense.

However, after Lott struggled somewhat during the 1985 campaign, surrendering several big plays to opposing wide receivers, the 49ers decided to move him back to his original position of free safety, where he ended up spending his five remaining seasons in San Francisco. Performing magnificently at that spot, Lott gained Pro Bowl and First-Team All-Pro recognition in 1986 by leading the NFL with 10 interceptions, which he returned for a total of 134 yards and one touchdown. Lott followed that up by intercepting another 18 passes over the course of the next four seasons, earning in the process Pro Bowl and All-Pro honors each year.

Although Lott lacked great running speed, his superior instincts and uncanny feel for the game enabled him to diagnose plays almost immediately and break quickly on the football, with former USC and Oakland Raiders teammate Marcus Allen saying, "You look at all the interceptions that he's gotten—he always saw the ball." Meanwhile, Lott's tremendous intensity and powerful 6-foot, 203-pound frame, which he used as a weapon to launch himself into opponents, helped him develop a reputation as one of the league's hardest hitters and surest tacklers, with Allen also saying, "He was a destroyer. I think he realized that to really play this game at the level, and to be recognized as one of the best ever, you have to have a little bit of craze inside you. . . . He wanted to hurt you. He wanted to hurt your family that was listening. He wanted the entire family to be upset and worried. I mean, that's just the way he played."

In discussing the attitude that he brought with him to the playing field, Lott said, "When you go play the game of football, it's a violent game. Can you be psychotic and yet under control? Can you be neurotic and yet under control?"

Revealing that he greatly admired boxer Mike Tyson for his ability to deliver resounding hits to his opponent, Lott stated, "You could feel all his energy go through somebody. That's how I felt. I wanted it to come from my toes, all the way up through my soul. I wanted everything to go into the hit."

Lott added, "The way I play is important to me because I know I'm not gifted with great athletic ability or speed. But God always gives you the ability to do one thing, and that's to try hard. That's my attitude. If that means going out and running into somebody who's bigger or faster or tougher than you, you just do it."

Commenting on Lott's ability to impact the outcome of games from the 49ers' defensive backfield, Dallas Cowboys head coach Tom Landry said, "He's like a middle linebacker playing safety. He's devastating. He may dominate the secondary better than anyone I've seen.

John Madden expressed similar sentiments when he stated, "Ronnie Lott is probably the best guy who's ever played safety in this league."

Displaying his total dedication to his profession and some of that "craze" of which Marcus Allen spoke, Lott famously elected to have his broken left pinky finger amputated in April 1986 to avoid the long recovery time that would have followed reconstructive surgery. Lott's fearless attitude, sense of self-sacrifice, and unwillingness to accept mediocrity earned him the respect and admiration of everyone within the organization, with Charles Haley, who experienced problems with many of his teammates through the years, once saying, "We never got tense about the game because everyone was cracking jokes. Ronnie, on the other hand, I don't know if he ever smiled during a game. If he did, it was at the end, if we won. He was intense. He had every tendency down. He would remind you about everything. It was guts and glory with him. He was the glue to the thing on defense. He didn't accept mediocrity. He didn't accept low standards—everyone had to perform to their max and above that."

Claiming that Lott's high expectations extended to the coaching staff as well, Bill Walsh stated, "He's the only player I've ever had that just challenged me and took me on right in front of the rest of the team. We had a player strike and then, when the players rejoined the team, Ronnie proceeded to tell me what I had done wrong, why I had failed a lot of the team, and I proceeded to explain to him exactly why. And then he challenged me that much more. And then I explained even further. When it broke up, we were great friends again. But you can count on one thing—he speaks his mind."

Unfortunately, Lott's time in San Francisco came to an end following the conclusion of the 1990 campaign when the 49ers allowed him to become a Plan B free agent, giving him the opportunity to sign with another team providing they did not match whatever offer he received.

With Lott having missed five games in each of the previous two seasons, the 49ers chose not to pay him what the Oakland Raiders offered him, ending his 10-year stint in the City by the Bay. After essentially being released, Lott expressed his dissatisfaction with the 49ers' decision by saying, "I guess loyalty has an age limit."

Continuing to vent his frustration after officially becoming a member of the Raiders, Lott told the media, "The thing with the 'Niners was that everyone talked about family. But, when it all came down, well. . . . People asked me, 'Why did you leave?' I say, 'Why did they put me on Plan B?' You talked about family and loyalty. I told them I'd take a salary cut and all those things. What more can you ask?"

Years later, though, Lott took a somewhat softer stance, even questioning his decision to sign with the Raiders when he said:

To me, I've always had this mantra in life of exhaust every moment, exhaust life, and give it your all. For me, I always thought that was the idea of exhausting everything. Play as long as you can. No matter what team you play for, just exhaust it. Now, looking and reflecting back, there are things that I think about.

When I think about the 49ers and I think about what we were trying to accomplish and what we were doing, I've seen the Warriors break up. When you start to have people leave and things go in a different direction, it's really challenging. Sometimes I sit there and say, "Maybe winning is more important than exhausting life." I've debated about that in my head. . . .We might have won another championship. Those things, you think about. At the same time, exhausting life and giving our all and knowing you don't have any regrets is really interesting to me. When I look back at football, I know I left everything on the field. I gave everything I could. And yet, I could have possibly thought about that moment of saying, "If I stayed, what would that have been like?"

During his 10 seasons in San Francisco, Lott recorded 51 interceptions, amassed 643 interception-return yards, scored five touchdowns, made 721 tackles, forced eight fumbles, recovered 12 others, and registered 5½ sacks. After leaving the 49ers, Lott spent two seasons in Oakland playing strong safety, earning Pro Bowl and All-Pro honors for the final time in his career in 1991 by recording 93 tackles and leading the league with eight interceptions, before registering a team-high 103 tackles the following year. Lott then moved back to free safety after he signed with the Jets as a free agent at the end of 1992, manning that post for two seasons, before announcing his retirement prior to the start of the 1995 campaign. Ending his career with 63 interceptions, Lott currently ranks eighth in NFL history in that category. Lott also amassed 730 interception-return yards, scored five touchdowns on defense, recorded 1,146 tackles, forced 16 fumbles, recovered 17 others, and registered 8½ sacks.

Following his playing days, Lott began a brief career in broadcasting, serving as an analyst on *Fox NFL Sunday* for three years, before co-founding HRJ Capital, a private equity investment company that now boasts $2.4 billion in total assets. Lott also owns Toyota and Mercedes-Benz car dealerships, provides guidance to professional athletes who are transitioning to careers in the business world, and gives back to the community through All-Stars Helping Kids, a nonprofit organization he founded in 1989 to help promote a safe and healthy learning environment for disadvantaged children in low-income communities.

Praised by *USA Today* as "one of the most successful athletes at making the transition to business," Lott, who currently lives in Cupertino, California, with his wife, Karen, continues to be held in extremely high esteem by all those he played with and against, with Marcus Allen saying, "He is a legend of the game—not just a guy who played. He's what the game is all about. Ronnie Lott is the heart and soul of the National Football League. People should remember his name 150 years from now."

49ERS CAREER HIGHLIGHTS

Best Season

Lott performed brilliantly as a rookie in 1981, earning First-Team All-Pro honors and a runner-up finish to Lawrence Taylor in the NFL Defensive Rookie of the Year voting by recording 89 tackles and seven interceptions, three of which he returned for touchdowns. But Lott had his finest all-around season after he moved to free safety in 1986, leading the league with 10 interceptions, amassing 134 interception-return yards, scoring one touchdown, and registering 77 tackles, two sacks, and three forced fumbles, with his 10 picks setting a single-season franchise record that still stands.

Memorable Moments/Greatest Performances

Lott returned the first interception of his career 26 yards for a touchdown during a 21–14 win over New Orleans on September 27, 1981.

Lott contributed to a 45–14 victory over the Dallas Cowboys on October 11, 1981, by recording a pair of interceptions, one of which he returned 41 yards for a touchdown.

Lott lit the scoreboard again during a 33–31 win over the Los Angeles Rams on November 22, 1981, when he returned his interception of a Dan Pastorini pass 25 yards for a touchdown.

Lott punctuated his exceptional rookie campaign by recording two interceptions during the 49ers' 38–24 victory over the Giants in the divisional round of the 1981 playoffs, returning one of his picks 20 yards for a touchdown.

Lott clinched a 26–13 win over the Kansas City Chiefs on December 26, 1982, when he returned his interception of a Bill Kenney pass 83 yards for a touchdown late in the fourth quarter.

Lott helped lead the 49ers to a 23–10 victory over the Buffalo Bills on December 11, 1983, by intercepting Joe Ferguson twice.

Lott picked off another two passes during a 31–7 win over Tampa Bay in the opening game of the 1986 regular season.

Lott earned NFC Defensive Player of the Week honors by intercepting Dan Marino twice during a 31–16 win over the Miami Dolphins on September 28, 1986.

Lott earned that distinction once again by returning one of his two interceptions 55 yards for a touchdown during a 31–17 win over the Packers on October 26, 1986.

Lott contributed to the 49ers' 34–9 victory over Minnesota in the divisional round of the 1988 playoffs by intercepting Wade Wilson twice.

Lott continued to be a thorn in the side of the Vikings when the two teams met again in the divisional round of the 1989 playoffs, recovering a fumble and returning his interception of a Wilson pass 58 yards for a touchdown during a 41–13 49ers win.

Notable Achievements

- Scored five defensive touchdowns.
- Recorded at least five interceptions six times.
- Amassed more than 100 interception-return yards twice.
- Recorded more than 100 tackles twice.
- Led NFL with three touchdown interceptions in 1981.
- Led NFL with 10 interceptions in 1986.
- Led 49ers in interceptions five times.
- Holds 49ers single season record for most interceptions (10 in 1986).

- Holds 49ers career records for most interceptions (51), interception-return yards (643), and touchdown interceptions (5).
- Ranks among 49ers career leaders with 721 tackles (2nd), eight forced fumbles (11th), and 12 fumble recoveries (tied for 6th).
- Ranks among NFL career leaders with 63 interceptions (8th).
- Eight-time division champion (1981, 1983, 1984, 1986, 1987, 1988, 1989, and 1990).
- Four-time NFC champion (1981, 1984, 1988, and 1989).
- Four-time Super Bowl champion (XVI, XIX, XXIII, and XXIV).
- Two-time NFC Defensive Player of the Week.
- Finished second in 1981 NFL Defensive Rookie of the Year voting.
- Nine-time Pro Bowl selection (1981, 1982, 1983, 1984, 1986, 1987, 1988, 1989, and 1990).
- Five-time First-Team All-Pro selection (1981, 1986, 1987, 1989, and 1990).
- 1988 Second-Team All-Pro selection.
- Seven-time First-Team All-NFC selection (1981, 1983, 1986, 1987, 1988, 1989, and 1990).
- 1984 Second-Team All-NFC selection.
- Pro Football Reference All-1980s First Team.
- NFL 1980s All-Decade First Team.
- Named to NFL's 75th Anniversary All-Time Team in 1994.
- Named to NFL 100 All-Time Team in 2019.
- Number 23 on the *Sporting News'* 1999 list of the 100 Greatest Players in NFL History.
- Number 11 on the NFL Network's 2010 list of the NFL's 100 Greatest Players.
- #42 retired by 49ers.
- Inducted into 49ers Hall of Fame in 2009.
- Elected to Pro Football Hall of Fame in 2000.

4

STEVE YOUNG

Relegated to backup duty by Joe Montana his first four years in San Francisco, Steve Young did not assume full control of the 49er offense until shortly before he celebrated his 30th birthday. However, after replacing Montana behind center in 1991, Young went on to establish himself as one of the most accurate passers and finest all-around quarterbacks in NFL history over the course of the next eight seasons, leading the league in touchdown passes four times, pass-completion percentage five times, and passer rating six times, while also gaining more than 400 yards on the ground on four separate occasions. Winning close to 75 percent of the games he started, Young led the 49ers to five division titles and one NFL championship, serving as a member of 49er teams that won nine division titles and three Super Bowls in all. Along the way, Young earned seven Pro Bowl selections, six All-Pro nominations, and two league MVP trophies, before being further honored following the conclusion of his playing career by being included on the *Sporting News'* and the NFL Network's respective lists of the 100 Greatest Players in NFL History, having his #8 retired by the 49ers, and being inducted into the Pro Football Hall of Fame.

Born in Salt Lake City, Utah, on October 11, 1961, Jon Steven Young spent the early part of his childhood living in his home state, before moving with his family to Greenwich, Connecticut, at the age of eight. A member of a prominent family that founded Brigham Young University, Young displayed a fondness for football as a young boy, first playing quarterback in the midget leagues, while spending his formative years rooting for the Dallas Cowboys and his favorite player, Roger Staubach.

Establishing himself as an outstanding all-around athlete at Greenwich High School, Young starred in multiple sports, serving as co-captain of the school's baseball, basketball, and football teams his senior year, when he averaged 15 points a game on the hardwood, batted .384 and compiled a record of 5-1 while splitting his time between center field and pitcher on the diamond, and earned All-FCIAC West Division First-Team honors

Steve Young won two NFL MVP awards as a member of the 49ers.
Courtesy of George A. Kitrinos

and a spot on the CIAC All-State team by rushing for 13 touchdowns as a quarterback on the gridiron.

Heavily recruited by the University of North Carolina for his prowess on the football field, Young instead chose to enroll at BYU, where he spent his first two seasons sitting behind Jim McMahon, before joining the starting unit as a junior. After initially struggling somewhat with his passing, Young improved himself greatly in that area, performing brilliantly his senior year, when he led the Cougars to an 11-1 record by throwing for 3,902 yards and 33 touchdowns, gaining another 544 yards on the ground, and setting a then single-season NCAA record by completing 71.3 percent of his passes. In addition to gaining First-Team All-America recognition from several news organizations, Young finished second to Nebraska running back Mike Rozier in the voting for the Heisman Trophy and received the Davey O'Brien Award, which is presented annually to the best collegiate quarterback in the nation.

Choosing to bypass the 1984 NFL Draft and play immediately for the Los Angeles Express, who selected him with the 11th overall pick of that year's USFL Draft, Young signed a record-setting 10-year, $40 million contract with the Express in March 1985, agreeing to take his payment in the form of an annuity spread out over a 40-year period. Nevertheless, the Tampa Bay Buccaneers acquired Young's NFL rights when they made him the first overall pick of the 1984 NFL supplemental draft.

Young performed well his first year in Los Angeles, with the highlight of his rookie season coming when he became the first pro player ever to surpass 300 yards passing and 100 yards rushing in the same game. But, after the USFL ceased operations following the conclusion of the 1985 campaign, Young bought himself out of his big contract and joined the Buccaneers, who had posted a total of just eight victories over the course of the previous two seasons.

Faring no better with Young starting for them behind center in 1985 and 1986, the Buccaneers won only two games each year, with the former BYU All-American compiling an overall record of 3-16 as a starter. And, with Young completing just 53 percent of his passes, while also throwing only 11 touchdown passes and 21 interceptions, the Buccaneers became convinced that he did not represent the solution to their problems, prompting them to trade him to the 49ers on April 24, 1987, for second- and fourth-round draft picks.

Expressing his glee over acquiring Young, who he believed was merely a victim of circumstance in Tampa Bay, 49ers head coach Bill Walsh said after completing the deal, "We think that Steve's style of play will fit into our system and he will be able to display his vast talents. This move is not a reflection on Joe Montana. We fully expect Joe to continue as the leader and mainstay of our team."

Meanwhile, upon learning of the trade, Young stated, "I'm pretty excited. There are a lot of plusses for me. First, playing in the city itself. The town's 49er-crazy. And playing for Coach Walsh. He's obviously a genius in coaching quarterbacks. Being around a legend like Joe Montana will help me."

Young ended up seeing very little action his first four years in San Francisco, starting a total of only 10 games while serving as Montana's backup. Nevertheless, Young played well in his limited opportunities, winning seven of his starts, completing 60 percent of his passes, throwing 23 touchdown passes and just six interceptions, and running for 659 yards and four touchdowns.

Finally given a chance to start when Montana underwent offseason surgery on his throwing arm that forced him to sit out the entire 1991 campaign, Young made the most of his opportunity, passing for 2,517 yards, throwing 17 TD passes and eight interceptions, completing 64.5 percent of his passes, and leading all NFL quarterbacks with a passer rating of 101.8 and 415 yards rushing despite missing five games with a knee injury. Taking his game up a notch the following year, Young earned Pro Bowl, First-Team All-Pro, AP Offensive Player of the Year, and NFL MVP honors by throwing for 3,465 yards and leading the league with 25 touchdown passes, a pass-completion percentage of 66.7, and a passer rating of 107.0, with his superb play leading the 49ers to a regular-season record of 14-2 and the first of four straight division titles.

With Young's magnificent performance making it impossible to return him to the bench when Montana rejoined the 49ers midway through the 1992 season, friction soon developed between the two men, causing Montana to eventually request a trade to another team. Given sole responsibility for running the 49ers offense, Young embarked on an exceptional six-year run during which he posted the following numbers:

YEAR	YDS PASSING	TD PASSES	INTS	COMP %	QBR
1993	4,023	29	16	68.0	101.5
1994	3,969	35	10	70.3	112.8
1995	3,200	20	11	66.9	92.3
1996	2,410	14	6	67.7	97.2
1997	3,029	19	6	67.7	104.7
1998	4,170	36	12	62.3	101.1

Establishing himself as the NFL's most accurate passer, Young led the league in pass-completion percentage and passer rating four times each, while also topping the circuit in touchdown passes on three separate occasions. Young also finished second in the league in passing yards twice and rushed for a total of 25 touchdowns during that time, with his brilliant all-around play earning him Pro Bowl honors each year, five All-Pro selections, and his second NFL MVP award in 1994. More importantly, the 49ers made the playoffs each season, winning four division titles and their fifth NFL championship in the process, with Young being named MVP of Super Bowl XXIX.

Blessed with a considerable amount of natural ability, Young possessed size, speed, strength, and a good arm, making him equally effective as a runner and passer. Standing 6'2" and weighing 215 pounds, Young not only moved well in the pocket but also often used his legs to pick up huge chunks of yardage, recording five runs of more than 30 yards during his career. In fact, Young had to make a conscious effort not to stray from the pocket, as teammate Roger Craig suggested when he said, "Steve had to really work. I felt bad for him when he first took over because he was searching, trying to find himself. Steve was a running back caught in a quarterback's body. But he knew that, if he was going to be great, he had to stop running. He had to learn how to be a pocket thrower, and he proved that he could be a pocket thrower. And he shocked the NFL when he had the highest rating in the league for like four years in a row."

Agreeing with Craig's assessment, Mike Holmgren, who coached Young at BYU and in San Francisco, stated, "To be great as Steve became—Hall of Fame and all that stuff—he had to discipline himself as a thrower. 'I can't rely on using my legs to get out of this all the time.' And, with Steve, you coach him, but he kind of figured these things out for himself."

Praising Young for his intelligence, Holmgren continued, "There's a real side of him, like a lot of really bright guys, that he really thinks he knows how to do it better than his coach does. But he's smart enough to know 'this is the way I have to do it to be successful.'"

Holmgren then added, "What was most striking about Steve to me was he is very, very bright, I mean, very bright. He went to law school. I don't think he's ever practiced law. He can do whatever he wants. I always thought he'd be the governor of Utah."

Although Young had already spent 12 years in the league and won two MVP awards by the time Steve Mariucci assumed head-coaching duties in San Francisco in 1997, he remained one of the team's finest all-around athletes and best-conditioned players, with Mariucci recalling, "When we came into training camp, most teams will test their athletes to see if they're in shape, and high schools and colleges will do the same thing. . . . Steve Young would really be the best guy as far as our test was concerned. He was right up there and would pass most of the time all the receivers, running backs, and corners. . . . This guy was a great athlete. Forget about being 36, 37, and 38 years old, he was really a top-shelf, well-trained athlete."

Unfortunately, Young sustained a series of concussions through the years, with the most serious of those coming just three games into the 1999 campaign. After sitting out the rest of the season, Young announced his retirement, ending his NFL career with 33,124 yards passing, 232 touchdown passes, 107 interceptions, a pass completion percentage of 64.3, and a passer rating of 96.8 that ranked as the best in league history at the time. Young also rushed for 4,239 yards and 43 touchdowns, with both figures placing him among the NFL's all-time leaders among quarterbacks. During his time in San Francisco, Young passed for 29,907 yards, threw 221 touchdown passes and 86 interceptions, completed 65.8 percent of his passes, compiled a passer rating of 101.4, and ran for 3,581 yards and 37 touchdowns.

Lamenting the fact that he did not have more time to work with Young, Steve Mariucci said, "It's a shame. I really do believe I had him in his prime. Had he not gotten a couple of concussions, I think he could have played into his 40s, just like we saw Brett Favre, Tom Brady, and Drew Brees do. Steve Young was still throwing the ball very, very well late in his 30s."

Since retiring as an active player, Young, who received a JD from BYU's J. Reuben Clark Law School in 1994, one year after he founded the Forever Young Foundation, which provides financial, academic, and therapeutic assistance to children facing significant physical and emotional challenges, has continued his philanthropic work in that area. Young also serves as a national advisor to ASCEND: A Humanitarian Alliance, a nonprofit organization that provides life skills mentoring to residents of impoverished African and South American countries. A successful businessman as well, Young serves as a managing director at Huntsman Gay Global Capital, a private equity firm he co-founded in 2007 with billionaire industrialist Jon M. Huntsman and former Bain Capital executive Robert C. Gay. When not involved in those ventures, Young works as an NFL analyst for ESPN.

49ERS CAREER HIGHLIGHTS

Best Season

Young had a tremendous year for the 49ers in 1992, earning NFL MVP and NFL Player of the Year honors by finishing second in the league with 3,465 passing yards, running for 537 yards and four touchdowns, throwing only seven interceptions, and leading all NFL quarterbacks with 25 TD passes, a QBR of 107.0, and a pass-completion percentage of 66.7. He also performed brilliantly in 1998, setting a single-season franchise record by throwing 36 touchdown passes, completing 62.3 percent of his passes, and passing for a career-high 4,170 yards. However, Young had his finest all-around season in 1994, gaining NFL MVP and NFL Player of the Year recognition for the second time by passing for 3,969 yards and leading the league with 35 touchdown passes, a QBR of 112.8, and pass-completion percentage of 70.3, with each of the last two figures representing a single-season franchise record.

Memorable Moments/Greatest Performances

Young threw his first touchdown pass as a member of the 49ers when he connected with Jerry Rice on a 46-yard scoring play during a 26–24 loss to the New Orleans Saints on November 15, 1987.

Young earned NFC Offensive Player of the Week honors for his performance during a 24–21 win over the Vikings on October 30, 1988, when, in addition to passing for 232 yards and one touchdown, he scored the game-winning TD in the fourth quarter on a memorable 49-yard run during which he broke six tackles before finally collapsing in the Minnesota end zone. Mike Holmgren, his quarterback coach at the time, later called Young's miraculous run "the greatest play I ever saw him make, and one of the greatest offensive plays that I've ever seen in my life." Young's 49-yard jaunt later received a number 27 ranking on the list of the "100 Greatest Plays in NFL History."

Although the 49ers lost to the Saints by a score of 13–10 on December 23, 1990, Young rushed for a career-high 102 yards, with his longest run of the day covering 31 yards.

Young followed that up by leading the 49ers to a 20–17 win over the Vikings in the final game of the 1990 regular season, earning NFC Offensive Player of the Week honors by rushing for 59 yards and throwing for 205 yards and two touchdowns, with his 34-yard TD pass to John Taylor in the closing moments providing the margin of victory.

Young led the 49ers to a 34–14 win over San Diego on September 8, 1991, by throwing for 348 yards and three touchdowns, the longest of which came on a 70-yard connection with Jerry Rice.

Young earned NFC Offensive Player of the Week honors by completing 18 of 20 pass attempts for 237 yards and two TDs during a convincing 35–3 win over the Lions on October 20, 1991.

Young led the 49ers to a 52–14 rout of the Bears in the final game of the 1991 regular season by passing for 338 yards and three TDs, one of which came on a 69-yard hookup with Jerry Rice.

Young starred in defeat on September 13, 1992, throwing for 449 yards and three TDs during a 34–31 loss to the Bills, with his longest TD pass of the day going 54 yards to John Taylor.

Young guided the 49ers to a lopsided 56–17 victory over Atlanta on October 18, 1992, by passing for 399 yards and three TDs, the longest of which came on an 80-yard pass to Jerry Rice.

Young helped the 49ers turn a 20–7 deficit into a 21–20 win over the Saints on November 15, 1992, by completing a pair of fourth-quarter touchdown passes to Brent Jones.

Young earned NFC Offensive Player of the Week honors by throwing for 462 yards and four touchdowns during a 35–10 win over the Los Angeles Rams on November 28, 1993, with the longest of his TD passes going 76 yards to John Taylor.

Young earned that distinction again by passing for 354 yards and four touchdowns during a 55–17 pasting of the Detroit Lions on December 19, 1993, connecting with John Taylor from 68 yards out, while also collaborating with Jerry Rice on an 80-yard scoring play.

Young proved to be too much for the Rams to handle on September 18, 1994, running for two scores and completing 31 of 39 passes for 355 yards and two TDs during a 34–19 49ers win.

Young continued his success against the Rams in the second meeting between the two teams on November 20, 1994, throwing for 325 yards and four touchdowns during a 31–27 49ers victory, with his 18-yard TD pass to Jerry Rice with just over two minutes remaining in the final period providing the winning margin.

Young punctuated his banner year of 1994 with an exceptional performance against San Diego in Super Bowl XXIX, earning game MVP honors by passing for 325 yards and six touchdowns during a 49–26 win over the Chargers, with his six TD tosses setting a Super Bowl record.

Young led the 49ers to a 37–30 victory over Minnesota on December 18, 1995, by throwing for 425 yards and three touchdowns, all of which went to Jerry Rice.

Young used his legs as well as his arm to lead the 49ers to a 31–20 win over Atlanta on September 27, 1988, running for 50 yards and passing for 387 yards and three touchdowns, the longest of which came on a 66-yard hookup with Jerry Rice.

Young helped the 49ers overcome an early 21–0 deficit to the Indianap-olis Colts on October 18, 1998, by passing for 331 yards and two touch-downs, and running for 60 yards and another two TDs, with his stellar play earning him NFC Offensive Player of the Week honors.

Young earned that distinction for the 12th and final time by running for one score and passing for 288 yards and two TDs during a 38–19 win over the Rams in the 1998 regular-season finale.

Young subsequently made arguably the biggest play of his career in the closing moments of the 1998 NFC wild card game when he gave the 49ers a 30–27 win over the Green Bay Packers by hitting Terrell Owens with a 25-yard touchdown pass with just eight seconds left on the clock.

Notable Achievements

- Passed for more than 3,000 yards six times, topping 4,000 yards twice.
- Threw more than 25 touchdown passes four times, topping 30 TD passes twice.
- Completed more than 65 percent of passes seven times, topping 70 percent once.
- Posted touchdown-to-interception ratio of better than 2–1 nine times.
- Posted passer rating above 90.0 11 times, finishing with mark above 100.0 on seven occasions.
- Ran for more than 500 yards once.
- Led NFL in touchdown passes four times, pass completion percentage five times, and passer rating six times.
- Finished second in NFL in passing yards three times and pass comple-tion percentage once.
- Finished third in NFL in pass completions once, pass completion per-centage twice, and passer rating once.
- Holds 49ers single-season records for most touchdown passes (36 in 1998), highest completion percentage (70.3 in 1994), and highest passer rating (112.8 in 1994).
- Holds 49ers career record for highest passer rating (101.4).
- Ranks among 49ers career leaders with 3,648 pass attempts (3rd), 2,400 pass completions (3rd), 29,907 passing yards (3rd), 221 touch-down passes (2nd), 3,581 yards rushing (9th), and 37 rushing touch-downs (tied for 5th).
- Nine-time division champion (1987, 1988, 1989, 1990, 1992, 1993, 1994, 1995, and 1997).
- Three-time NFC champion (1988, 1989, and 1994).

- Three-time Super Bowl champion (XXIII, XXIV, and XXIX).
- 12-time NFC Offensive Player of the Week.
- Six-time NFC Offensive Player of the Month.
- Super Bowl XXIX MVP.
- 1992 NFL Offensive Player of the Year.
- Two-time NFL MVP (1992 and 1994).
- Two-time Bert Bell Award winner as NFL Player of the Year (1992 and 1994).
- Seven-time Pro Bowl selection (1992, 1993, 1994, 1995, 1996, 1997, and 1998).
- Three-time First-Team All-Pro selection (1992, 1993, and 1994).
- Three-time Second-Team All-Pro selection (1995, 1997, and 1998).
- Four-time First-Team All-NFC selection (1992, 1993, 1994, and 1998).
- 1996 Second-Team All-NFC selection.
- Pro Football Reference All-1990s First Team.
- Number 63 on the *Sporting News*' 1999 list of the 100 Greatest Players in NFL History.
- Number 81 on the NFL Network's 2010 list of the NFL's 100 Greatest Players.
- #8 retired by 49ers.
- Inducted into 49ers Hall of Fame in 2009.
- Elected to Pro Football Hall of Fame in 2005.

5

LEO NOMELLINI

T he first player ever selected by the 49ers in the NFL Draft, Leo Nomellini established himself as the dominant defensive tackle of his era during his time in San Francisco, earning 10 Pro Bowl selections and six First-Team All-Pro nominations over the course of his 14-year professional career. Known for his speed, strength, stamina, and ferocious style of play, Nomellini spent his first few seasons with the 49ers starring on both sides of the ball, before playing almost exclusively on defense his last several years in the league. One of the few players ever to gain All-NFL recognition both on offense and defense, Nomellini, who never missed a game his entire career, earned many other individual accolades with his fabulous play, including being named to the NFL's 50th Anniversary All-Time Team in 1969, having his #73 retired by the 49ers, and being inducted into the Pro Football Hall of Fame.

Born in Lucca, Tuscany, Italy, on June 19, 1924, Leo Joseph Nomellini immigrated to the United States with his family as an infant, spending most of his youth living on Chicago's West Side, where he attended Crane High School. Growing up in poverty, Nomellini had to work while in high school to help support his family, preventing him from competing in organized sports until he became a member of the Cherry Point Leathernecks football team after he enlisted in the US Marine Corps shortly after the attack on Pearl Harbor.

Offered an athletic scholarship to the University of Minnesota after serving his country in the Pacific during World War II, Nomellini went on to star for the Golden Gophers as a two-way lineman, gaining All-America recognition twice, while also becoming Big Ten heavyweight wrestling champion, competing in the shotput, and serving as anchor man on the school's 440-yard relay team. Referred to as "Leo the Lion" throughout his career, Nomellini acquired his famous nickname while in college, with former Gophers teammate and Hall of Fame Minnesota Vikings head coach Bud Grant recalling, "We would pull him, we were running the single

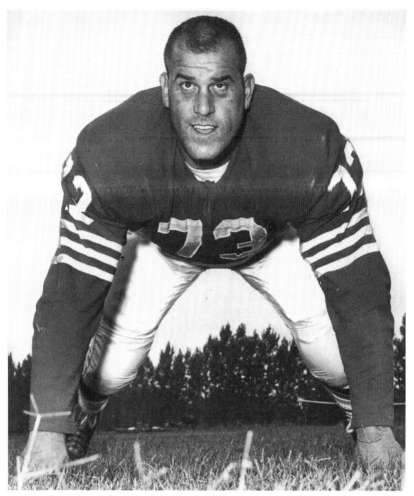

Leo Nomellini earned a spot on the NFL's 50th Anniversary Team with his magnificent play at defensive tackle.
Courtesy of Mearsonlineauctions.com

wing then, and, when he'd come around the corner, he would just roar. His blocking technique wasn't so great, but he'd just run you over like a truck."

Impressed with Nomellini's exceptional play at the collegiate level, the 49ers selected him in the first round of the 1950 NFL Draft, with the 11th overall pick, making him their first-ever NFL draft choice (they spent the previous four years competing in the AAFC). Making an immediate impact upon his arrival in San Francisco, Nomellini started for the 49ers on both sides of the ball as a rookie, earning Pro Bowl honors for the first of four straight times with his outstanding two-way play. Nomellini followed that up by gaining First-Team All-Pro recognition in each of the next four seasons, being named to the squad as an offensive tackle the first two years, before being similarly honored for his superb play at left defensive tackle in 1953 and 1954.

Commenting on Nomellini's brilliant performance in 1951, one newspaper account claimed, "The most outstanding 49er for the season is All-Pro right offensive tackle Leo Nomellini. Powerful as a drive blocker, and more than adequate in pass protection, he also is a destructive force at left defensive tackle. Amazingly quick for a man his size, he is an outstanding pass rusher and virtually unblockable as a run defender."

Standing 6'3" and weighing close to 265 pounds, Nomellini possessed good size for a defensive tackle of his era. But his strength and quickness are the things that truly set him apart from the other players who manned his position, with tales of his legendary power abounding.

Former 49ers general manager Lou Spadia related one such story when he recounted a time in 1955 that the 49ers enlisted the services of Dr. Jay Bender of Southern Illinois University to test the strength of their players. With Dr. Bender having invented a muscle-measuring machine consisting of two-by-fours, pulleys, and wires, he asked Nomellini to test its functionality by lying on his stomach and pulling on a strap wrapped around one of his legs designed to measure the size of a muscle above the ankle. Recalling the events that subsequently transpired, Spadia said, "The two-by-fours started flying, the wires broke, the scales fell off, and the doctor's eyes popped out. I remember having to duck pieces of flying wood. Leo just exploded the machine, blew it apart. Bender had to start it all over again, with six-by-sixes instead of two-by-fours, and thicker wires. He made a big mistake in telling Leo to pull as hard as he could."

49ers Hall of Fame running back Joe Perry also discussed his former teammate's great strength, saying, "He was as strong as three bulls. He'd slap you on the back and knock you 20 feet."

Nomellini's strength, speed, tenacity, and tremendous conditioning helped make him arguably the league's top pass-rusher, with Bud Grant stating, "In his day, he was as good as there was."

Equally adept at stuffing enemy runners, Nomellini enjoyed every aspect of the game, once saying, "I really like to play football. It's tough, and it's hard, and no pro football owner can pay a player enough for the punishment he takes. You just have to like it—and I do."

Nomellini's fondness for the physicality of the game prompted him to spend his offseasons wrestling professionally around the Bay Area as

"Leo the Lion"—a practice he continued throughout his playing career. A 10-time tag team champion, Nomellini once defeated National Wrestling Alliance (NWA) heavyweight champion Lou Thesz in a two-out-of-three falls match, although he failed to take the title from Thesz because he won the first fall on a disqualification. Choosing to employ the same tactics of intimidation he used in the wrestling ring on the football field, Nomellini could often be found snorting, growling, and contorting his face into an ugly mask prior to the snap of the football.

After failing to gain Pro Bowl recognition for just the second time in his career in 1955—a season in which injuries to San Francisco's offensive line forced him to play virtually 60 minutes every game—Nomellini appeared in each of the next six Pro Bowls, while also earning three more All-Pro nominations. And, during that time, Nomellini continued his string of 174 consecutive games played that lasted until he announced his retirement at the end of 1963. The Pro Football Hall of Fame subsequently wasted little time in opening its doors to Nomellini, who gained induction the first time his name appeared on the ballot in 1969, the same year the NFL named him to its 50th Anniversary All-Time Team. Two years later, Nomellini received the additional honor of having his #73 retired by the 49ers.

Following his playing days, Nomellini spent many years working for a title insurance company in the San Francisco Bay Area, before retiring to private life. Nomellini lived until October 17, 2000, when he passed away at 76 years of age from complications of a stroke that he suffered three weeks earlier.

Upon learning of his longtime teammate's passing, Bob St. Clair, who had visited him in the hospital several days earlier, said, "It's just a shock. We all thought he was coming back."

Former Gophers and 49ers teammate Gordy Soltau stated, "He was a great teammate and one of the best linemen we ever had. He loved to play, and he loved people."

Hall of Fame quarterback Y. A. Tittle, who spent 10 years playing with Nomellini in San Francisco, added, "Let's just put it this way: Leo was one of the kindest, gentlest, biggest tough men you'd ever want to meet. He was big and strong, a weightlifter. . . . More than that, though, he was just a great human being. He never had any bad things to say about anyone. He wasn't a gossiper. . . . He was a guy you could poke fun at, and he'd poke fun at you. He's a friend I hate to see go. . . . He was a loyal 49er. Every home game, he was at the 49er alumni barbecue. I just can't say enough good things about him."

CAREER HIGHLIGHTS

Best Season

Nomellini gained First-Team All-Pro recognition six times, earning his initial selection in 1951, when, in addition to recovering two fumbles, he scored the only touchdown of his career. Since the 49ers fielded one of the NFL's most imposing defenses in 1951, surrendering a total of only 205 points to the opposition, we'll identify that as the finest season of Nomellini's career.

Memorable Moments/Greatest Performances

Nomellini scored his only career touchdown when he ran 20 yards to paydirt after recovering a blocked punt during a 44–17 win over the Los Angeles Rams on October 28, 1951.

Nomellini contributed to a 20–10 victory over the Lions on December 2, 1951, by recovering a fumble and ending a Detroit scoring threat by sacking quarterback Bobby Layne.

Nomellini anchored a 49ers defense that recorded five sacks and allowed just 40 yards rushing and 65 yards of total offense during a 28–0 shutout of the Lions on October 12, 1952.

Nomellini helped the 49ers dominate Baltimore at the line of scrimmage in the final game of the 1953 regular season, with the Colts gaining just 57 yards on the ground and amassing only 136 yards of total offense during a 45–14 Niners win.

Nomellini and his line-mates once again dominated the opposition at the point of attack in the 1954 regular-season opener, with the 49ers recording eight sacks and allowing just 184 yards of total offense during a 41–7 manhandling of the Washington Redskins.

Nomellini led the defensive charge when the 49ers registered eight sacks during a 10–7 win over the Colts in the final game of the 1954 regular season.

Nomellini scored the first points of a 23–20 victory over the Rams on October 6, 1957, when he tackled running back Tommy Wilson in the end zone for a safety early in the second quarter.

Although the 49ers ended up losing the 1960 regular-season opener to the Giants by a score of 21–19, Nomellini brought them to within two points in the fourth quarter when he sacked quarterback Charlie Conerly in the end zone for a safety.

Nomellini helped lead the 49ers to a lopsided 35–3 victory over Washington in the opening game of the 1961 regular season by anchoring a defense that surrendered just 37 yards rushing and 135 yards of total offense.

Notable Achievements

- Scored one touchdown on special teams.
- Never missed a game his entire career, appearing in 174 consecutive contests.
- Ranks among 49ers career leaders with 14 seasons played (tied for 6th) and 13 fumble recoveries (5th).
- 10-time Pro Bowl selection (1950, 1951, 1952, 1953, 1956, 1957, 1958, 1959, 1960, and 1961).
- Six-time First-Team All-Pro selection (1951, 1952, 1953, 1954, 1957, and 1959).
- 1960 Second-Team All-Pro selection.
- Pro Football Reference All-1950s First Team.
- NFL 1950s All-Decade Team.
- Named to NFL's 50th Anniversary All-Time Team in 1969.
- #73 retired by 49ers.
- Inducted into 49ers Hall of Fame in 2009.
- Elected to Pro Football Hall of Fame in 1969.

6

JIMMY JOHNSON

Called "the best defensive back I have ever seen" by former 49ers head coach Dick Nolan, Jimmy Johnson gained general recognition as the premier man-to-man defender of his time during his 16 seasons in San Francisco. A true "shutdown" corner before the term became popular, Johnson did such an exceptional job of blanketing opposing wide receivers that quarterbacks rarely threw the ball in his vicinity, directing almost all their passes to the opposite side of the field. Nevertheless, Johnson managed to record the second-most interceptions and amass the second-most interception-return yards in franchise history, earning in the process five Pro Bowl selections and six All-Pro nominations. Following the conclusion of his playing career, Johnson received the additional distinctions of having his #37 retired by the 49ers and being inducted into both the 49ers and the Pro Football Hall of Fame.

Born in Dallas, Texas, on March 31, 1938, James Earl Johnson moved with his family at an early age to Kingsburg, California, where he starred in multiple sports while attending Kingsburg High School, serving as captain of the school's football, basketball, and baseball teams. The younger brother of 1960 Olympic decathlon champion Rafer Johnson, Jimmy found himself being constantly compared to his older sibling as a teenager, stating years later, "I've got another brother who dropped out of sports because he got tired of having people tell him to follow in Rafer's footsteps. They gave me the same jazz. I didn't like it either, but instead of letting it bug me, I decided to accept it as a challenge to see if I could make it on my own in sports."

Continuing to display his outstanding all-around athletic ability after accepting a scholarship to UCLA, Johnson not only excelled as a wingback and defensive back on the gridiron, but, also, as a member of the school's track and field team, earning All-America honors his senior year by winning the NCAA 110-meter hurdles championship with a time of 13.9 seconds, while also leaping 25 feet in the broad jump. In fact, Johnson, who initially did not expect to play football professionally, at one point considered giving

Jimmy Johnson proved to be the premier shutdown corner of his time.
Courtesy of Mike Traverse

up the sport to focus exclusively on track. But, after establishing himself as a dual threat on offense and being named UCLA's best blocker and tackler as a senior, Johnson began to seriously consider pursuing a career in football for the first time.

Selected by the 49ers with the sixth overall pick of the 1961 NFL Draft and by the San Diego Chargers in the fourth round of that year's AFL Draft, with the 32nd overall pick, Johnson chose to sign with the 49ers, who initially intended to use him at wide receiver. But after Johnson dislocated his wrist while practicing for the College All-Star Game, forcing him to wear a cast for the next few months, his inability to catch the football prompted the 49ers to play him at right cornerback his first year in the league. Performing exceptionally well as a rookie, Johnson recorded five interceptions and amassed 116 interception-return yards, prompting Hall of Fame defensive back Jack Christiansen—then an assistant coach with the 49ers—to say of his protégé, "He's a real good one. Mark my words. He'll be around for a while. He has the three requirements. Tremendous speed, great reflexes, and the willingness to tackle with authority."

Despite his outstanding play at corner, Johnson moved to the offensive side of the ball in 1962, finishing the season with 34 receptions, 627 receiving yards, and four TD catches, before being shifted back to defense the following year, when he picked off another two passes while playing safety. Finally finding a permanent home in 1964, Johnson laid claim to the starting left cornerback job, which he retained for the next 13 seasons.

After recording three interceptions in his first year at his new post, Johnson earned Second-Team All-Pro honors in each of the next two seasons by picking off a total of 10 passes, one of which he returned for a touchdown. Johnson then recorded a total of three interceptions over the course of the next two seasons, before gaining Pro Bowl and First-Team All-Pro recognition four straight times from 1969 to 1972.

Gradually establishing himself as arguably the finest cover corner in the league, the 6'2", 187-pound Johnson possessed all the qualities needed by a cornerback to excel in the NFL, including great speed, outstanding ball skills, superior tackling ability, and a sharp mind. Describing his temperament as a "little non-aggressive," Johnson preferred to avoid critical errors by blanketing his man in coverage, rather than constantly seeking interceptions, once telling the *Sporting News*, "I'm a defensive-minded back first. My job is to keep the receiver from catching the ball. I don't start thinking about interceptions until I'm sure the receiver can't get the ball. Some cornerbacks are always thinking about interceptions, and that can get you in trouble when you play the ball instead of the man."

Johnson added, "I don't look at someone and think that he can't beat me. If you play long enough, you're going to get beat. The question and the key to your effectiveness is how often."

Claiming that Johnson's ability to stay with wide receivers often prompted opposing quarterbacks to completely ignore his side of the field, 49ers QB John Brodie stated, "Jim doesn't receive much publicity because the opposition avoids him as much as possible. Talk to veteran quarterbacks like John Unitas and Bart Starr and they'll tell you they call few patterns in Jimmy's area. The only reason Johnson doesn't lead the league in interceptions is he doesn't get the chance."

Oakland Raiders Hall of Fame receiver Fred Biletnikoff expressed his admiration for Johnson when he said, "I feel Jim is one of the best corners in pro football. I just hope he makes a mistake of some sort so I can get an advantage. He covers all the pass patterns so well."

Kermit Alexander, who spent seven seasons playing alongside Johnson in the 49ers' defensive backfield, said of his longtime teammate, "He's one of the most phenomenal athletes I've ever seen. There are so many things he can do. He's an extremely controlled person and very, very talented. In the whole time we played together, I never saw him lose his cool, on or off the field. The reason his honors were so late in coming was that he never beat the drums for himself."

Meanwhile, Dick Nolan paid Johnson the ultimate compliment when he stated, "I coached three defensive backs I felt were great—Mel Renfro and Cornell Green with the Dallas Cowboys, and Johnson. Jimmy is the best I've ever seen."

Nolan also spoke of Johnson's leadership ability when he said, "He is the kind of individual who can get along with anybody, a leader in many ways. His leadership was very evident in the 1974 player strike. He kept things from getting out of hand. He's a guy of few words. He doesn't say much, but when he does, everybody listens."

Nolan added, "Whenever the team wanted something, they'd send Jim to see me. If it was foolish, he wouldn't bother with it. But if he came to me, I knew it was doggone important."

Extremely durable, Johnson started every game for the 49ers in nine of his 16 seasons, missing just three contests his last nine years in the league. Displaying his ability to play with pain in 1971, Johnson spent most of the year wearing a cast on his wrist after breaking it during a Week 2 victory over the New Orleans Saints. Making many one-handed tackles and recording three interceptions despite his injury, Johnson ended up winning the Pro Football Writers' George Halas Award as the league's most courageous player, while also being named the winner of the Len Eshmont award, presented annually to the 49ers player who best exemplifies the "inspirational and courageous play" of Eshmont, the former 49er who died of infectious hepatitis in 1957.

After helping the 49ers capture the division title three straight times from 1970 to 1972, Johnson continued to excel for them at left cornerback when they fell on hard times the next three years, earning the last of his five Pro Bowl nominations in 1974. Agreeing to play one final season after his high school teammate and good friend Monte Clark became head coach of the 49ers prior to the start of the 1976 campaign, Johnson later received words of praise from Clark, who said, "One of my first moves was to change our coverage to mostly zone. It was amazing to see Jim accept the challenge after being a man-to-man defender most of his career. He enjoyed it — like a rookie. And it was great having him around the young players—he helped them on the field, and I just hope they learned something about his approach to the game—his concentration."

Questioned at one point during the season about how he managed to play such a demanding position at the age of 38, Johnson responded, "Obviously, there is luck involved. I never had a serious knee injury, and I was able to maintain my speed and agility. Also, I am active in the off-season, playing racquetball, handball, tennis, or pickup basketball games. I'm never completely out of shape."

Johnson added, "People overplay the point of my age. Age doesn't play a major part in what a person can do. I think I can still cover any receiver in the league. When I get a group of receivers who can prove to me that I don't have the speed, agility or quickness to cover them, then I'll have to stop."

Choosing to announce his retirement following the conclusion of the 1976 campaign, Johnson ended his playing career with 47 interceptions and 615 interception-return yards, both of which remained franchise records until Ronnie Lott eventually established new marks. Johnson also recovered seven fumbles, scored two touchdowns on defense, and made 40 receptions for 690 yards and four touchdowns on offense.

Johnson, who continues to grace us with his presence at 83 years of age, had his #37 retired by the 49ers one year after he played his last game as a member of the team. Elected to the Pro Football Hall of Fame in 1994, Johnson later received the additional honor of being inducted into the 49ers Hall of Fame in 2009.

CAREER HIGHLIGHTS

Best Season

Johnson performed exceptionally well for the 49ers in 1965 and 1966, recording a career-high six interceptions in the first of those campaigns, before picking off four passes, recovering two fumbles, and scoring one touchdown in the second. However, he played the best ball of his career from 1969 to 1972, gaining First-Team All-Pro recognition four straight times. Although any of those four seasons would make a good choice, we'll go with 1969 since Johnson finished third in the NFL with six interceptions while serving as a member of a 49ers defense that applied only a moderate amount of pressure to opposing quarterbacks, with their 30 sacks representing easily their lowest total during that four-year period (they recorded 38 sacks in 1971 and 46 sacks in 1972).

Memorable Moments/Greatest Performances

Johnson contributed to a 49–0 blowout of the Detroit Lions on October 1, 1961, by recording the first interception of his career, which he subsequently returned 31 yards.

Johnson helped the 49ers forge a 20–20 tie with the Lions on November 5, 1961, by picking off two passes in one game for the first time as a pro.

Johnson made a key play during a 22–21 victory over the Packers on December 10, 1961, when he helped set up a San Francisco score by returning his interception of a Bart Starr pass 63 yards, deep into Green Bay territory.

Johnson made the first of his four career touchdown receptions on offense when he collaborated with John Brodie on an 80-yard scoring play that provided the margin of victory in a 34–27 win over the Chicago Bears on October 14, 1962.

Although the 49ers lost to the Lions by a score of 38–24 on November 11, 1962, Johnson had a big day at wide receiver, making 11 receptions for 181 yards.

Johnson scored his first touchdown on defense when he ran 35 yards to paydirt after picking off a pass during a 44–7 rout of the Atlanta Falcons on October 16, 1966.

Johnson helped the 49ers record a 14–13 victory over the Philadelphia Eagles in the final game of the 1969 regular season by intercepting two George Mira passes.

Johnson contributed to a 26–17 win over the Washington Redskins in the 1970 regular-season opener by tackling running back Larry Brown in the end zone for a safety.

Johnson lit the scoreboard again in the 1970 regular-season finale when he returned his interception of a Daryle Lamonica pass 36 yards for a touchdown during a lopsided 38–7 victory over the Raiders.

Johnson picked off Archie Manning twice during a 37–2 win over the Saints on October 1, 1972.

Johnson recorded another two interceptions during a 36–34 win over the Denver Broncos on September 23, 1973, returning his two picks a total of 45 yards.

Johnson recorded the final interception of his illustrious career during a 37–21 win over the Seattle Seahawks on September 26, 1976.

Notable Achievements

- Scored two defensive touchdowns.
- Recorded at least five interceptions three times.
- Amassed 116 interception-return yards in 1961.
- Finished third in NFL with six interceptions in 1965.
- Led 49ers in interceptions four times.
- Ranks among 49ers career leaders with 16 seasons played (tied for 2nd), 213 games played (2nd), 47 interceptions (2nd), and 615 interception-return yards (2nd).
- Three-time division champion (1970, 1971, and 1972).
- Five-time Pro Bowl selection (1969, 1970, 1971, 1972, and 1974).
- Four-time First-Team All-Pro selection (1969, 1970, 1971, and 1972).
- Two-time Second-Team All-Pro selection (1965 and 1966).
- Three-time First-Team All-NFC selection (1970, 1971, and 1972).
- 1974 Second-Team All-NFC selection.
- NFL 1970s All-Decade First Team.
- #37 retired by 49ers.
- Inducted into 49ers Hall of Fame in 2009.
- Elected to Pro Football Hall of Fame in 1994.

7
PATRICK WILLIS

Patrick Willis's decision to retire at only 30 years of age due to concerns over his long-term health will likely prevent him from going down as one of the greatest inside linebackers in NFL history. But, for the better part of his abbreviated eight-year career, Willis proved to be the league's premier player at his position, earning seven Pro Bowl nominations and six All-Pro selections. Serving as the anchor of San Francisco's defense, Willis recorded more than 100 tackles six times, retiring with more stops than anyone else in franchise history. A consummate team player who possessed extraordinary leadership ability, Willis played a key role in restoring the 49ers to prominence during the second decade of the 21st century, leading them to two division titles and their first Super Bowl appearance in 18 years. Accorded NFL Alumni Linebacker of the Year honors on three separate occasions, Willis later received the additional distinction of being named to the NFL 2010s All-Decade Team.

Born in Bruceton, Tennessee, on January 25, 1985, Patrick L. Willis grew up in abject poverty, barely knowing his mother, who deserted him at an early age. Forced to care for his three younger siblings due to the irresponsible nature of his alcoholic and abusive father, young Patrick went to work in the cotton fields at the age of 10, before finally taking his sister and two brothers and moving in with his high school basketball coach when his father became increasingly violent.

Despite his difficult childhood, Willis went on to star in multiple sports at Hollow Rock-Bruceton Central High School, lettering in baseball, basketball, and football. Particularly outstanding on the gridiron, Willis earned All-State honors twice and gained Regional Most Valuable Player and West Tennessee Player of the Year recognition as a senior. Even more impressive, Willis became the first player in state history to be nominated for the Mr. Football Award at two different positions (linebacker and running back) in the same season.

Patrick Willis recorded more tackles than anyone else in franchise history.
Courtesy of Stu Jossey

After fielding scholarship offers from several colleges, Willis ultimately chose to enroll at the University of Mississippi, where he spent three years starting at middle linebacker for the Rebels, recording a total of 335 tackles, en route to earning SEC Defensive Player of the Year honors twice and a pair of First-Team All-America nominations. Also named the winner of both the Jack Lambert Award and the Dick Butkus Award as the most outstanding linebacker in college football his final season, Willis drew high praise from Ole Miss head coach Ed Orgeron, who said, "Patrick leads by example. He is not a big talker. He just gets in there and does his job every day and makes everybody around him better."

Feeling that he had nothing left to prove at the collegiate level, Willis declared himself eligible for the 2007 NFL Draft following his junior year, after which the 49ers wasted little time in selecting him in the first round, with the 11th overall pick. Willis subsequently spent his first season in San Francisco being tutored by Hall of Fame middle linebacker Mike Singletary, then an assistant on the 49ers' coaching staff. Learning his lessons well, Willis recorded a league-leading 174 tackles, earning in the process Pro Bowl, First-Team All-Pro, and NFL Defensive Rookie of the Year honors. Willis followed that up with another outstanding season, finishing second in the NFL with 141 combined tackles and 109 solo stops, with his exceptional play enabling him to continue his string of seven straight Pro Bowl selections and six consecutive All-Pro nominations. Performing magnificently again in 2009, Willis led the league with 152 combined tackles and 114 solo stops, prompting Singletary to compare him to Hall of Fame linebacker Ray Lewis, who he earlier coached in Baltimore, with Singletary telling the NFL Network, "Patrick is very coachable, just like Ray. They're a gift, and they want to learn as much as they can handle. Patrick comes to me every day and says, 'Coach, I just need more.'"

Singletary added, "I've coached two of the greatest linebackers—one that has already proven to be one of the greatest [Lewis], and one who will prove to be [Willis]."

Lewis saw similarities between himself and Willis, saying, "I love the way he plays the game. He plays with fire. He reminds me of myself—a lot, a lot, a lot!"

In addition to his considerable physical talent, which included outstanding strength and excellent speed that made him equally effective in pass coverage and run defense, the 6'1", 242-pound Willis possessed several intangible qualities that enabled him to establish himself as one of the premier defenders in the game. Extremely intelligent, Willis did a superb job of reading opposing offenses and adjusting the 49ers' defense accordingly. Willis also displayed marvelous instincts, tremendous desire, and a selfless attitude that helped make him an exceptional team leader. Often delivering inspirational pep talks to his teammates before games, Willis proved to be a true leader in the locker room and on the playing field, spending most of his time in San Francisco serving as defensive captain. A solid citizen as well, Willis frequently visited area hospitals to bring cheer to those in need and gave much of his time to several charitable causes, including the Childhood Cancer Society.

Willis continued to perform at an elite level in 2010, recording 128 tackles and a career-high six sacks, despite suffering an assortment of injuries that included a broken hand that forced him to undergo season-ending surgery prior to the regular-season finale. Subsequently voted the NFL's best linebacker in a poll taken by ESPN prior to the start of the 2011 season, Willis received the following rave review from Matt Williamson of Scouts Inc.: "Nobody in the NFL plays their position better than Patrick Willis, and that is saying a lot. He is as good a linebacker as Peyton Manning is a quarterback, as Andre Johnson is a receiver, as Adrian Peterson is a running back. He has no weaknesses."

Unfortunately, the injuries continued to mount in subsequent seasons, with Willis missing the final three games of the 2011 campaign with a hamstring injury, undergoing surgery on August 5, 2013, to repair a fractured hand he suffered during training camp, and sustaining a groin injury later that year that forced him to sit out two games. Nevertheless, Willis remained a huge contributor to 49er teams that made three straight playoff appearances, won two division titles, and captured one NFC championship. Earning three more trips to the Pro Bowl and two more All-Pro nominations from 2011 to 2013, Willis finished second on the 49ers in tackles all three years, with only NaVorro Bowman recording more stops.

However, Willis finally reached a point of no return in 2014, when, after undergoing season-ending surgery on November 11 to repair his ailing left big toe that had been troubling him for years, he felt compelled to announce his retirement during the subsequent offseason. Citing his aching feet and worries about his future health as his primary reasons for making his decision, Willis told those in attendance at his March 10, 2015, press conference, "Honestly, I pay attention to guys when they're finished playing, walking around like they've got no hips, and they can't play with their kids. They can barely walk. People see that and they feel sorry, but they don't realize it's because they played a few extra years."

Willis continued, "You've seen me break my hand on Sunday, have surgery on Monday, and play on Thursday with a cast on. But there's something about these feet. And those are what made me who I am. They had you all saying, 'Wow, where'd he come from?' I know I no longer have it in these feet to go out there and give you guys that kind of 'Wow.'"

Willis then added, "As much as I'd love to win a Super Bowl and to bring number six back here, I have to be honest. I have to tell y'all that, if I don't have what I know I need to give to my teammates and the organization the best chance to win, then I can't be out there doing that. And to be sitting on the sideline just collecting a paycheck, I feel like that would be wrong. So, I stand up here today with that conviction. I understand the magnitude of what I'm doing today. . . . One thing I've always lived by is giving everything you've got today, so, when you look back tomorrow, you won't feel ashamed because you left something on the table. I feel like in my eight years, there was not a day when I didn't give this game everything I had."

During his eight years with the 49ers, Willis recorded a team-record 950 tackles and 733 solo stops, registered 20½ sacks and 60 tackles for losses, intercepted eight passes, which he returned for 131 yards and two touchdowns, forced 16 fumbles, and recovered five others. Leading the 49ers in tackles in each of his first four seasons, Willis finished either first or second in the league in that category on three separate occasions.

Expressing his appreciation to Willis for everything he contributed to the organization, 49ers CEO Jed York said in a prepared statement, "On behalf of the entire San Francisco 49ers organization, my family, and our Faithful fans, I would like to thank Patrick for everything he has brought to this team and our community. Some of the greatest memories in the history of our franchise have come from his passion, dedication, and sacrifice."

49ers head coach Jim Tomsula added, "He redefined his position. That's a different man. Pat changed a lot of lives here. Pat will change a lot of lives. . . . I've never heard Pat Willis complain."

Just two months after Willis retired, he joined Open-Source Storage, a storage and infrastructure company used by other companies, where he currently holds the position of executive vice president for partnerships and serves as a member of the board of directors.

CAREER HIGHLIGHTS

Best Season

Willis performed magnificently his first year in the league, earning Pro Bowl, First-Team All-Pro, and 2007 NFL Defensive Rookie of the Year honors by recording four sacks and a league-leading 174 tackles, including 136 of the solo variety. But Willis had his finest all-around season in 2009, once again gaining Pro Bowl and First-Team All-Pro recognition by leading the league with 152 tackles, registering four sacks, forcing three fumbles, scoring one touchdown on defense, and establishing career-high marks with three interceptions, 13 tackles for loss, and 11 quarterback hits.

Memorable Moments/Greatest Performances

Willis excelled in his first game as a pro, recording 11 tackles and forcing a fumble during a 20–17 win over the Arizona Cardinals in the 2007 regular-season opener.

Willis had another big game against the Cardinals on November 25, 2007, making 18 tackles, including 17 solo stops, during a 37–31 overtime win.

Willis turned in a tremendous all-around effort during a 21–19 victory over Tampa Bay on December 23, 2007, recording two sacks, forcing a fumble, and registering a season-high 20 combined tackles, including 12 of the solo variety.

Willis scored the first points of his career during a 33–30 overtime win over Seattle on September 14, 2008, when he returned his interception of a Matt Hasselbeck pass 86 yards for a touchdown.

Although the 49ers lost to the Patriots by a score of 30–21 on October 5, 2008, Willis performed brilliantly, recording a sack and a season-high 18 tackles, including 14 solo stops.

Willis helped lead the 49ers to a 10–3 victory over the Buffalo Bills on November 30, 2008, by making 14 tackles and forcing a fumble.

Willis contributed to a 35–0 shutout of the St. Louis Rams on October 4, 2009, by recording 2½ sacks and returning his interception of a Kyle Boller pass 23 yards for a touchdown.

Willis earned NFC Defensive Player of the Week honors by recovering a fumble and recording a game-high 12 tackles during a 48–3 mauling of the Tampa Bay Buccaneers on October 9, 2011.

Willis earned that distinction again by intercepting a pass, recording 10 tackles, and anchoring a 49ers defense that surrendered just 45 yards rushing and 145 yards of total offense during a 34–0 win over the Jets on September 30, 2012.

Willis starred during a 34–24 victory over the Atlanta Falcons on December 23, 2013, finishing the game with a season-high 18 tackles, including 15 solo stops.

Notable Achievements

- Scored two defensive touchdowns.
- Recorded more than 100 tackles six times, making more than 150 stops twice.

- Led NFL in combined tackles and solo tackles twice each.
- Finished second in NFL in combined tackles and solo tackles once each.
- Led 49ers in tackles four times.
- Holds 49ers career record for most tackles (950).
- Ranks second in franchise history with 16 forced fumbles.
- Two-time division champion (2011 and 2012).
- 2012 NFC champion.
- Two-time NFC Defensive Player of the Week.
- Member of 2007 NFL All-Rookie Team.
- 2007 NFL Defensive Rookie of the Year.
- Three-time NFL Alumni Linebacker of the Year (2007, 2009, and 2010).
- Two-time 49ers MVP (2007 and 2009).
- Seven-time Pro Bowl selection (2007, 2008, 2009, 2010, 2011, 2012, and 2013).
- Five-time First-Team All-Pro selection (2007, 2009, 2010, 2011, and 2012).
- 2008 Second-Team All-Pro selection.
- NFL 2010s All-Decade Team.

8

FRANK GORE

Known for his extraordinary work ethic and love for the game of football, Frank Gore established himself as the most prolific running back in franchise history during his 10 seasons in San Francisco, gaining more yards on the ground than any other player in team annals. Rushing for more than 1,000 yards eight times and amassing more than 1,000 yards from scrimmage nine times, Gore led the 49ers in rushing in each of his 10 seasons in the City by the Bay, en route to earning team MVP honors on three separate occasions. A five-time Pro Bowler and one-time All-Pro, Gore helped lead the 49ers to two division titles and one NFC championship, accomplishing all he did after suffering two devastating knee injuries in college that nearly brought his football-playing days to an end.

Born in Miami, Florida, on May 14, 1983, Franklin Gore grew up in a crowded one-bedroom apartment that he shared with his mother and 11 siblings and cousins. Getting his start in football at an early age, Gore recalled, "My first year playing Pop Warner football, my mom had to change my birth certificate because I was too young. I was five, I think, and you were supposed to be six."

Playing the game that he loved at every opportunity, Gore added, "My neighborhood, Coconut Grove, we always played in the streets. It was corner against corner. We all had football teams. Different neighborhoods."

Suffering through a difficult childhood, Gore had to overcome dyslexia and his mother's battles with drug addiction and kidney disease to eventually establish himself as one of the nation's most feared running backs at Coral Gables High School. First discovering his mother's dependence on drugs as a teenager, Gore remembered, "I got up to use the bathroom, and I saw her using. That just stayed on my mind. I was probably a sophomore in high school. I sat down with her and said, 'Mom, why?.' . . . That was the day she started working at it. And she got off those drugs. I had to have a real heart-to-heart with her."

Frank Gore gained more yards on the ground than any other running back in 49ers history.
Courtesy of Stu Jossey

Gore continued to display a maturity beyond his years when his mom developed kidney problems shortly thereafter, recalling, "During my junior year, she almost passed away. She was in intensive care. But she made it through. I remember we were playing against Miami Central in the play-offs. Usually, I don't like going to the hospital. But I went up there and saw her with all these tubes coming out of her. I asked her, 'Mom, do you want me to play?' She shook her head like, 'Yes.' So, I went out there and I had a pretty good game."

From that point on, Gore made his mother's health his top priority, ensuring that she attended her regular dialysis appointments by arranging rides for her with one of his coaches and occasionally missing practice.

Having tended to the needs of his mother, Gore began to address his learning disability that his coach at Coral Gables, Joe Montoya, later said "would have prevented him from going to college." With Montoya spearheading an effort to have Gore transferred to a regular curriculum, his protégé worked exceptionally hard to improve his reading and writing, eventually earning a degree that enabled him to pursue his dream of playing football professionally.

At the same time, Gore emerged as a star on the gridiron with the help of Coach Montoya, who he later credited for much of his success, saying, "When I got to Coral Gables High, it felt like I was on a different level. You play Pop Warner, and you're good, and all the top high schools try to get you. So, I felt like I was pretty good. I got over 1,000 yards my sophomore year, but my coach got fired. At that time, I wasn't really working hard. I was good, but I didn't lift weights. This new coach, Joe Montoya, basically called me out in our first team meeting. He didn't give a shit what I had done to that point. He said, 'I don't care what you did before I got here.' He told the guys things were gonna be different, and they better work hard, or they could get out right now. I felt like he called me out. I was about to leave. But then I met with him. He said, 'Listen to what I say, and you'll be a D-1 player.'"

Gore continued, "Good lesson. I listened to him. I got stronger and stronger, and I got faster. I was the first one at practice. I had to be first in every sprint. He had me programmed. I got better. My senior year, I rushed for 1,000 yards in my first four games. I wanted to play major-college football."

Finishing his senior year with a school-record 2,997 yards rushing and 39 touchdowns, Gore turned in his two most memorable performances during the early stages of the campaign, rushing for 377 yards and two TDs against South Miami in the regular-season opener, before gaining 419 yards on the ground and scoring six touchdowns against District 11-6A foe Southwest a few weeks later.

Subsequently named the top prospect in Dade County by the *Miami Herald*, Gore received scholarship offers from many colleges, recalling, "I had offers to go to different places. I committed to Ole Miss. I figured they just lost Deuce McAllister, and they needed a back, and I could play right away in the big conference. Eli Manning was the quarterback. We could win there. I loved the University of Miami, but they had a lot of backs at the time, and I wanted to play right away."

Gore continued, "That backfield at Miami . . . Clinton Portis, Willis McGahee, Najeh Davenport. One day, [Miami wide receivers' coach] Curtis Johnson rolled up in front of my house. He challenged me. 'You scared to compete? You scared of Portis? If you say you're the best, you have to play with the best.' That hit me. The night before signing day, I told my mom I didn't want to go to Ole Miss anymore. She didn't want me to leave anyway. So, I signed with Miami. I wanted to prove something to them. I got there and asked the coaches, 'What do I have to do to play right away?'"

Gore ended up earning *Sporting News* Big East Freshman of the Year honors by rushing for 562 yards and averaging 9.1 yards per carry while serving as a backup to Portis, before missing most of the next two seasons after suffering separate injuries that tore the ACL in both his knees. Recalling how he felt after sustaining his second serious injury in as many seasons, Gore said, "It made me ask, 'Man, is football really for me?'"

Yet, Gore added that his bad luck may well have been a blessing in disguise, saying, "At times, I look back and say if I wouldn't have been hurt, I would probably have been a top-five or 10 player coming out. It didn't go my way. I look at it as God wanted me to go a different route. Before I got injured, football was very easy. I didn't have to work out. I guess he wanted me to work hard and appreciate the game that He blessed me with the talent to do. That's one thing I focus on."

Gore's history of injuries caused his stock to drop considerably heading into the 2005 NFL Draft, with the 49ers ultimately selecting him in the third round, with the 65th overall pick. Following his arrival in San Francisco, Gore attempted to quell any concerns over his ability to remain healthy by putting off surgery on both shoulders until the end of his rookie year, recalling, "My first year, my rookie year at the 49ers, I had two labrum tears. Both shoulders. I had a chance to get the surgery before the season or play ball, and I told my coaches that I wanted to play and then get the surgeries. The reason was, when I came out of college, everybody said I was injury-prone, and I just wanted to show them how tough I was, and how much I love the game. That's what that year was about. I got the surgeries after that first year in San Francisco. Both shoulders."

After rushing for 608 yards and amassing 739 yards from scrimmage in a part-time role his first year in the league, Gore emerged as a full-fledged star in his second season, earning Pro Bowl and Second-Team All-Pro honors by ranking among the NFL leaders with 1,695 yards rushing, 2,180 yards from scrimmage, nine rushing touchdowns, and an average of 5.4 yards per carry. Gore followed that up by surpassing 1,000 yards rushing and 1,400 yards from scrimmage in each of the next three seasons, performing especially well in 2009, when he earned his second trip to the Pro Bowl by gaining 1,120 yards on the ground, amassing 1,526 yards from scrimmage, and scoring a career-high 13 touchdowns. Gore then missed the final five games of the 2010 campaign after fracturing his right hip during a Week 12 win over the Arizona Cardinals, limiting him to "just" 853 yards rushing and 1,305 yards from scrimmage. However, after returning to action the following year, Gore appeared in every game the 49ers played over the course of the next four seasons, compiling the following numbers during that time:

YEAR	YDS RUSHING	RECS	REC YDS	YDS FROM SCRIMMAGE	TDS
2011	1,211	17	114	1,325	8
2012	1,214	28	234	1,448	9
2013	1,128	16	141	1,269	9
2014	1,106	11	111	1,217	5

Although Gore failed to lead the NFL in any major statistical category, his remarkable consistency enabled him to finish in the league's top 10 in rushing all four years, earning him three more Pro Bowl nominations. Meanwhile, the 49ers made the playoffs in each of the first three seasons, winning two division titles and one NFC championship.

Lacking great size and exceptional running speed, the 5'9", 212-pound Gore went about his job in workmanlike fashion, often preventing him from receiving as much notoriety as some of the league's more spectacular backs. Nevertheless, Gore's elusiveness, exceptional balance, and uncanny field vision made him extremely difficult to bring down in the open field. Gore also read his blocks well and possessed a sudden burst that often enabled him to break into the second line of defense.

In discussing the skill set of his former Miami teammate, New York Giants safety Antrel Rolle said, "You really don't get a full grasp of what kind of runner he is until you go against him. I will say it to the day I die, going against him, I still feel he was the best running back to come through the University of Miami before his knee injuries."

Despite his many contributions to the team, the 49ers allowed Gore to become a free agent following the conclusion of the 2014 campaign, after which he signed a three-year, $12 million contract with the Indianapolis Colts. Expressing his displeasure with the 49ers' handling of the situation after inking his deal with the Colts, Gore said, "The only thing I was hurt by was that I thought we could have done it better. Like, no bullshit. Just straight up. I don't know if I even wanted to go back. But I would have felt better if we would have sat down and had a conversation. I mean, I was going to test the market no matter what. Me and the head coach (Jim Tomsula) talked, and he basically told me I'd be in a certain situation. But I wanted to hear it from the GM [Trent Baalke]."

Gore continued, "I mean, you could let us compete. You didn't have to say I was automatically going to take the back seat. Put it on me. I mean, bro, I finished last season with 1,100 yards. Every time I got an opportunity, I did something with it. So, I felt like, 'Fine, if you want to go with the young guy, make him beat me out.' It wasn't like I can't play anymore. If he beats me out, I can handle that. You can't play this game forever. I knew I couldn't be there forever. But I was there 10 years and I played every down the same whether we were winning or not."

Gore, who left San Francisco with career totals of 11,073 yards rushing, 342 receptions, 2,883 receiving yards, 13,956 yards from scrimmage, 64 rushing touchdowns, and 76 total touchdowns, performed well for the Colts over the course of the next three seasons, gaining another 2,953 yards on the ground and amassing a total of 3,742 yards from scrimmage, with his exceptional work ethic making an extremely favorable impression on Indianapolis GM Chris Ballard, who told Peter King of *Sports Illustrated* after the Colts finished just 4-12 in 2017: "I think the world should know what a gift he has been to football. I don't know if I have ever been around a player who has impacted me more than Frank. His love and respect for football are what all personnel people strive to acquire when we draft players. There will never be another player like him. In this hard year, Frank has kept me going and kept everything in perspective. He has taught me that, no matter how hard it gets, you keep working and respecting the game of football. If he is not a first-ballot Hall of Famer, we need to discontinue how we select."

Nevertheless, with the Colts in a rebuilding mode, they chose not to re-sign Gore at the end of 2017, leaving him to test the free-agent market once again. Gore subsequently spent one season in Miami, rushing for 722 yards in 2018, before gaining 599 yards on the ground as a member of the Buffalo Bills the following year. Continuing to defy Father Time, the 37-year-old Gore signed a one-year deal with the New York Jets prior to the start of the 2020 campaign and ended up leading the team with 653 yards rushing and 742 yards from scrimmage, giving him career totals of 16,000 yards rushing and 19,985 yards from scrimmage that place him among the NFL's all-time leaders. Gore has also rushed for 81 touchdowns, caught 18 TD passes, scored once on a fumble recovery, and made 484 receptions for 3,985 yards.

As of this writing, Gore has not yet indicated if he intends to play again in 2021. Whatever he decides, though, Gore plans to retire as a member of the 49ers, once saying, "When I'm done, whenever I feel like I'm done, I'm going to come back and retire as a Niner."

49ERS CAREER HIGHLIGHTS

Best Season

Although Gore had many outstanding seasons for the 49ers, the 2006 campaign proved to be easily his finest as a member of the team. In addition to scoring nine touchdowns, Gore established career-high marks with 1,695 yards rushing, 61 receptions, 485 receiving yards, 2,180 yards from scrimmage, and a rushing average of 5.4 yards per carry, with his 1,695 yards rushing and 2,180 yards from scrimmage both representing single-season franchise records.

Memorable Moments/Greatest Performances

Although the 49ers suffered an embarrassing 52–17 defeat at the hands of the Washington Redskins on October 23, 2005, Gore scored the first touchdown of his career on a 72-yard fourth-quarter run.

Gore gained more than 100 yards on the ground for the first time as a pro in the final game of the 2005 regular season, rushing for 108 yards during a 20–17 overtime win over the Houston Texans.

Gore earned NFC Offensive Player of the Week honors for the first time by rushing for 134 yards and amassing 172 yards from scrimmage during a 34–20 win over the Oakland Raiders on October 8, 2006.

Gore led the 49ers to a 19–13 victory over the Detroit Lions on November 12, 2006, by rushing for 159 yards and one touchdown, which came on a 61-yard run on the game's opening drive.

Gore set a regular-season single-game franchise record by gaining 212 yards on the ground during a 20–14 win over the Seattle Seahawks on November 19, 2006, earning in the process NFC Offensive Player of the Week honors.

Gore contributed to a 26–23 overtime win over the Denver Broncos in the final game of the 2006 regular season by rushing for 153 yards and gaining another 32 yards on two pass receptions.

Just days after losing his mother to kidney disease, Gore led the 49ers to a 17–16 victory over the St. Louis Rams on September 16, 2007, by rushing for two touchdowns, one of which came on a 43-yard run. He finished the game with 20 carries for 81 yards and those two TDs.

Gore earned NFC Offensive Player of the Week honors by amassing 214 yards from scrimmage and scoring two touchdowns during a 37–31 overtime win over the Cardinals on November 25, 2007, gaining 116 of those yards on the ground and the other 98 on 11 pass receptions.

Gore earned that distinction again by rushing for 207 yards and two touchdowns during a 23–10 win over Seattle on September 20, 2009, with his TDs coming on runs of 79 and 80 yards.

Gore helped lead the 49ers to a 24–9 victory over the Cardinals on December 14, 2009, by rushing for 167 yards and one touchdown.

Gore contributed to a 17–9 victory over the Oakland Raiders on October 17, 2010, by rushing for 149 yards, with his longest run of the day being a 64-yard scamper.

Gore gained 127 yards on just 15 carries during a 24–23 win over the Philadelphia Eagles on October 2, 2011, scoring the game-winning touchdown on a 12-yard run with three minutes remaining in regulation.

Gore rushed for a season-high 141 yards and one touchdown during a 25–19 win over the Detroit Lions on October 16, 2011.

Gore led the 49ers to a 13–6 win over Seattle on October 18, 2012, by amassing 182 yards from scrimmage, gaining 131 of those yards on 16 carries and the other 51 on five pass receptions.

Although the 49ers lost Super Bowl XLVII to the Baltimore Ravens by a score of 34–31, Gore scored one touchdown and rushed for a game-high 110 yards.

Gore helped lead the 49ers to a 35–11 victory over the St. Louis Rams on September 26, 2013, by carrying the ball 20 times for 153 yards and one touchdown, which came on a 34-yard run just before halftime.

Gore proved to be the difference in a 26–21 win over the Philadelphia Eagles on September 28, 2014, rushing for 119 yards and scoring a touchdown on a 55-yard catch-and-run.

Gore excelled in his final game with the 49ers, carrying the ball 25 times for 144 yards during a 20–17 win over the Arizona Cardinals in the 2014 regular-season finale.

Notable Achievements

- Rushed for more than 1,000 yards eight times, topping 1,500 yards once.
- Surpassed 50 receptions three times.
- Amassed more than 1,000 yards from scrimmage nine times, topping 1,500 yards three times and 2,000 yards once.
- Scored at least 10 touchdowns twice.
- Averaged more than 5 yards per carry once.
- Finished third in NFL in rushing yards once and rushing average once.
- Led 49ers in rushing 10 times and receptions twice.
- Holds 49ers regular-season single-game record for most yards rushing (212 vs. Seattle on November 19, 2006).
- Holds 49ers single-season records for most yards rushing (1,695 in 2006), yards from scrimmage (2,180 in 2006), all-purpose yards (2,180 in 2006), and rushing touchdowns (10 in 2009).
- Holds 49ers career records for most rushing attempts (2,442) and most yards rushing (11,073).
- Ranks among 49ers career leaders with 13,956 yards from scrimmage (2nd), 13,956 all-purpose yards (2nd), 64 rushing touchdowns (2nd), 76 touchdowns (4th), and 458 points scored (10th).
- Ranks among NFL career leaders with 3,735 rushing attempts (3rd), 16,000 rushing yards (3rd), 19,985 yards from scrimmage (4th), and 19,992 all-purpose yards (5th).
- Two-time division champion (2011 and 2012).
- 2012 NFC champion.
- Five-time NFC Offensive Player of the Week.
- Three-time 49ers MVP (2006, 2007, and 2010).
- Five-time Pro Bowl selection (2006, 2009, 2011, 2012, and 2013).
- 2006 Second-Team All-Pro selection.
- NFL 2010s All-Decade Team.

9

BOB ST. CLAIR

A giant of a man who longtime teammate Joe Perry called the greatest
blocking lineman he ever saw, Bob St. Clair spent virtually his entire
playing career in San Francisco, playing his high school, college, and
pro ball in the City by the Bay. An outstanding run-blocker who also
excelled in pass protection, St. Clair proved to be the most intimidating
offensive lineman of his time, using his size, strength, speed, and genuine
love of hitting to dominate his opponent at the line of scrimmage from his
right tackle position. Playing through several serious injuries that included
a fractured back, separated shoulder, torn Achilles tendon, and at least six
broken noses, St. Clair gained Pro Bowl and All-Pro recognition five times
each, before being further honored in retirement by having his #79 retired
by the 49ers and being inducted into the Pro Football Hall of Fame.

Born in San Francisco on February 18, 1931, Robert Bruce St. Clair
spent much of his youth roaming the streets of his hometown, leading his
own gang, before turning to football as a way of releasing his inner anger.
After getting his start on the gridiron at Polytechnic High School, St. Clair
experienced an extraordinary growth-spurt in his sophomore year that
added six inches and 50 pounds onto his 5'9", 160-pound frame. Standing
well over 6-foot and weighing considerably more than 200 pounds by the
time he enrolled at the University of San Francisco, St. Clair went on to
earn All-Coast honors as a junior in 1951, when he helped the Dons compile a perfect 9-0 record and earn an invitation to a bowl game, which they
declined since their two African American players, Ollie Matson and Burl
Toler, would not have been permitted to play. Transferring to the University
of Tulsa prior to the start of his senior year after USF dropped its football
program due to funding problems, St. Clair ended his college career by
earning All–Missouri Valley Conference honors as a two-way tackle.

Selected by the 49ers in the third round of the 1953 NFL Draft, with
the 32nd overall pick, St. Clair earned a starting job as a rookie, after
which he displayed his ability to play with pain by missing just two games

Bob St. Clair earned Pro Bowl and All-Pro honors five times each.

despite fracturing the transverse process of his back in three places. Healthy by the start of the 1954 campaign, St. Clair gained Second-Team All-Pro recognition for the first of five times by serving as a key blocker for San Francisco's "Million Dollar Backfield" that included quarterback Y. A. Tittle and running backs Joe Perry, Hugh McElhenny, and John Henry Johnson. Continuing his outstanding play over the course of the next two seasons, St. Clair earned Pro Bowl and All-Pro honors once each, before missing seven games in 1957 with a shoulder separation that required surgery, although he amazingly remained on the field for eight minutes after sustaining his injury.

Generally considered to be one of the finest offensive linemen in the game by the mid-1950s, St. Clair, who stood a towering 6'9" and weighed close to 265 pounds, intimidated the opposition with his mere presence, with Hugh McElhenny claiming that his former teammate's unique blend of size and speed made him the league's most feared blocker. In addressing St. Clair's physical gifts, McElhenny stated, "I do recall sitting in my position in the backfield, and about all I would be looking at was Bob's big ass because he was just so tall and high. He was just so much bigger than the rest of the offensive line. And the defensive line, too. He had great speed for his size. He would have made a great tight end today. Many times, I know he gave me a lot of daylight."

St. Clair's toughness and fondness for the physicality of the game added to his mystique, with the ferocity with which he engaged his opponents instilling even more fear in them. In explaining his predilection for the violence that his profession offered, St. Clair stated, "The game is built around roughness. There is a personal thrill out of knocking a man down, really hitting him. It's the only satisfaction a lineman has. . . . The satisfaction we had when he played as offensive lineman is to watch a back like Hugh McElhenny lead you around the end and flatten that defensive back and get up and watch Hugh go all the way for a touchdown. Or Joe Perry slashing through the line after you flatten the middle linebacker."

Equally effective at blocking for the run or protecting his quarterback, St. Clair possessed so much size and athleticism that the 49ers often used him on defense in goal-line situations, with his height also making him a force on special teams, where he blocked 10 field goal and extra-point attempts in 1956 alone. In discussing his ability to block kicks, St. Clair said, "The first couple of times, I would duck my head and plow through the center and run over the top of him with my cleats. The next time, I looked at the snapper, and, instead of him getting turned over backward again and having my cleats running over his chest, he'd go down automatically on all fours. Once they did that, I'd leapfrog over the top of them, and I could jump straight up and usually I could block the field goal, extra point, or punt."

Praising St. Clair for his outstanding athletic ability, former 49ers quarterback Frankie Albert, who retired just before the huge offensive lineman joined the team, said in 1985: "He's one of the few guys from the old teams that could be playing today. He was that good. And he had the size."

Also known for his unusual lifestyle habits that included eating his meat raw, St. Clair acquired the nickname "The Geek," in deference to a character from the 1947 movie *Nightmare Alley* that ate live chickens. In trying to explain his strange obsession, St. Clair revealed, "My grandmother used to feed me raw meat off the kitchen table. I grew to love raw liver and hearts, bird hearts, dove, and quail."

Commenting on his teammate's bizarre practice, Hugh McElhenny stated, "He'd order a steak and have it thrown on the grill to take the chill off. Have it turned over and have it served. That's how he did it. He also ate raw liver. Sometimes, when you were sitting with him and he was eating that . . . it was kind of gross. But, no, we didn't think anything was wrong with him. That was just how he was raised."

St. Clair continued to perform at an elite level for the 49ers until 1963, earning four more Pro Bowl selections and three more All-Pro nominations, although a torn Achilles tendon forced him to miss nearly half of the 1962 campaign. However, after winning the Len Eshmont Award as the Most Inspirational 49er in 1963, St. Clair announced his retirement when he re-injured his Achilles tendon during the following offseason.

St. Clair, who served as mayor of Daly City, California, during the latter stages of his playing career, subsequently became a county supervisor in San Mateo County for nine years and a paid lobbyist for Orange County for two years. He also owned liquor stores in San Francisco and Daly City, served as a marketing coordinator for a San Francisco meat distributor, and worked in insurance and air freight. After retiring to private life, St. Clair lived another two decades, before a broken hip he suffered during a fall in February 2015 resulted in complications that led to his death in Santa Rosa, California, on April 20, 2015, some two months after he celebrated his 84th birthday.

Upon learning of St. Clair's passing, 49ers owner and chairman John York released a statement that read:

> With the passing of Bob St. Clair, the 49ers organization has not only lost an all-time great but one of our most ardent supporters. One of San Francisco's favorite sons, Bob spent the better part of his life at Kezar Stadium and was quite happy to share memories of his high school days or his 49ers tenure in the beloved venue. I always looked at him as an immortal figure that possessed a tremendous joy for life and all things 49ers. We will continue to celebrate the spirit of Bob St. Clair as we remember all that he brought to this franchise and its fans. Our prayers and best wishes are with his family and friends.

CAREER HIGHLIGHTS

Best Season

While St. Clair gained Second-Team All-Pro recognition a total of five times, both the UPI and the NEA accorded him First-Team All-Pro honors in 1955, indicating that he played his best ball for the 49ers that year.

Memorable Moments/Greatest Performances

St. Clair anchored an offensive line that enabled the 49ers to rush for 252 yards and amass 597 yards of total offense during a 45–14 win over the Baltimore Colts in the final game of the 1953 regular season.

St. Clair helped the 49ers amass 539 yards of total offense during a 33–12 victory over the Packers on November 23, 1958, with 256 of those yards coming on the ground.

St. Clair and his line-mates dominated the line of scrimmage once again on October 8, 1961, with the 49ers rushing for 259 yards and amassing 521 yards of total offense during a 35–0 win over the Los Angeles Rams.

St. Clair and the rest of the 49ers' offensive line followed that up with another dominant performance against the Minnesota Vikings one week later, with the Niners gaining 324 yards on the ground and amassing 555 yards of total offense during a 38–24 win.

Yet, St. Clair maintained that he experienced his greatest thrill in pro football during a 38–21 loss to the Giants in the opening game of the 1956 regular season when he prevented a New York touchdown by running down from behind Hall of Fame safety Emlen Tunnell after the latter intercepted a Y. A. Tittle pass and took off for the San Francisco end zone.

Notable Achievements

- Five-time Pro Bowl selection (1956, 1958, 1959, 1960, and 1961).
- Five-time Second-Team All-Pro selection (1954, 1955, 1958, 1960, and 1962).
- NFL 1950s All-Decade Team.
- #79 retired by 49ers.
- Inducted into 49ers Hall of Fame in 2009.
- Elected to Pro Football Hall of Fame in 2008.

10

JOE PERRY

The first member of San Francisco's famed "Million Dollar Backfield" to make our list, Joe Perry combined speed, power, and elusiveness to establish himself as one of the finest running backs of his era. Nicknamed "The Jet" for his electrifying speed, Perry won three rushing titles, becoming in 1954 the first NFL player to gain more than 1,000 yards on the ground in consecutive seasons. The first African American to play for the 49ers, Perry, who rushed for more touchdowns than anyone else in team annals, continues to rank among the franchise's all-time leaders in several offensive categories some 60 years after he donned the Red and Gold for the last time. A three-time Pro Bowler, three-time All-League selection, and one-time league MVP, Perry later received the additional honors of having his #34 retired by the 49ers and being inducted into the Pro Football Hall of Fame.

Born in Stephens, Arkansas, on January 22, 1927, Fletcher Joseph Perry grew up in Los Angeles, California, after his family moved there during the Great Depression. An outstanding all-around athlete, Perry starred in four sports while attending David Starr Jordan High School, excelling in baseball, basketball, football, and track. Denied an athletic scholarship to UCLA, where he hoped to follow in the footsteps of his hero, Jackie Robinson, Perry enrolled at Compton Junior College, for whom he scored 22 touchdowns as a freshman in 1944. Subsequently recruited by UCLA, Perry instead enlisted in the US Navy and spent one year playing football for the Alameda, California, Naval Training Station team, before returning to Compton following his discharge. Picking up right where he left off at Compton, Perry helped lead the Tartars to two straight National Junior College football championships, prompting both the Los Angeles Rams of the NFL and the San Francisco 49ers of the newly formed All-America Football Conference (AAFC) to offer him contracts.

Facing a complex decision when the Rams offered him $9,500 and 49ers owner Tony Morabito presented him with a contract worth only $4,500, Perry, who originally intended to pursue a career in electrical

Joe "The Jet" Perry won three NFL rushing titles as a member of the 49ers.
Courtesy of RMYauctions.com

engineering and turned down scholarships to the University of Oregon, University of Washington, University of Nevada, and Columbia University to play football, recalled years later, "I told him [Morabito], 'They're offering me $5,000 more than you are.' He said, 'Yeah, well, I know.' But he went on and said, 'We've been looking for a black player in San Francisco. I've checked you out on all facets of life and everything, and you're the guy we want. I can't afford to pay you the amount of money the Rams have offered you, but, if you go with me, you'll never regret it.'"

Perry continued, "I mulled it over for a while because $5,000 was a lot of money in 1947. But Tony sold me. He became like a father to me. I never regretted my decision."

Arriving in San Francisco in 1948, Perry did a little bit of everything for the 49ers as a rookie, gaining 562 yards and scoring a league-high 10 touchdowns on the ground, making eight receptions for 79 yards and one TD, scoring a 12th time on an 87-yard kickoff return, and even intercepting one pass on defense. Emerging as a star in his second year as a pro, Perry earned Second-Team All-AAFC honors by leading the league with 783 yards rushing, eight rushing touchdowns, and an average of 6.8 yards per carry, while also placing near the top of the league rankings with 929 yards from scrimmage, 1,266 all-purpose yards, and 11 TDs.

Continuing to perform well after the 49ers joined the NFL in 1950, Perry averaged 683 yards rushing, 789 yards from scrimmage, and six touchdowns over the course of the next three seasons, claiming years later that he saw little difference between the two leagues: "The first year in the NFL, we weren't too successful. We were 3-9. The next two years, we almost won the thing. There wasn't a real big difference. There was one game, though, when we played the Bears that I noticed it. They won 13–7. But they beat the hell out of us physically. We were beat up pretty good. I guess that was the only game where I noticed a difference in the leagues. . . . They could play good defense in the old league too. I remember one game in the AAFC against the New York Yankees. They had a middle linebacker who followed me everywhere."

After establishing himself as one of the NFL's top backs his first three years in the league, Perry turned in the two most dominant performances of his career in 1953 and 1954, posting the following numbers:

YEAR	YDS RUSHING	RECS	REC YDS	YDS FROM SCRIMMAGE	TDS
1953	1,018	19	191	1,209	13
1954	1,049	26	203	1,252	8

In addition to leading the NFL in rushing and yards from scrimmage both years, Perry ranked among the league leaders in all-purpose yards, yards per carry, and touchdowns scored, topping the circuit in the last category as well in 1953. Perry's exceptional play earned him consecutive Pro Bowl and First-Team All-Pro nominations, with United Press International also naming him its league MVP in 1954.

Blessed with great speed, the 6-foot, 200-pound Perry, who posted a personal-best time of 9.5 seconds in the 100-yard dash in 1947, acquired the nickname "The Jet" during his earliest practice sessions with the 49ers when quarterback Frankie Albert exclaimed, "You're like a jet, Joe," after the running back exploded out of his stance so quickly that Albert failed to hand him the football in time. Years later, Y. A. Tittle addressed the validity of Perry's moniker when he said of his former teammate, "He was the fastest player off the ball in the history of the world. You'd take the ball from center and turn, and he was already gone through the hole."

John Madden, who grew up watching Perry, also marveled at the Hall of Fame running back's tremendous acceleration, stating, "He was so quick. . . . From the time the ball was snapped until he hit the hole was a very short and quick time. He was tough to defend because he was so quick, and hard to hand off to because he was so quick."

Primarily a straight-ahead runner when he first turned pro, Perry learned how to make better use of his great speed and quickness by looking for holes in the defense created by his offensive line. Describing his running style to the *Sacramento Bee*, Perry said, "If you saw a hole, you take it. If you didn't, you kept moving until you did. You run with instinct."

Although somewhat small for an NFL fullback, Perry ran with great power, often breaking into the second line of defense by bowling over potential tacklers and then carrying opposing players for additional yards. Yet, even though Perry viewed himself primarily as a power back, he also proved to be extremely elusive, suggesting, "I was more power than evasive, but I had quite a bit of evasiveness that people didn't consider. I could move to the side to sidestep you before you realized anything. I never depended on power all the time, but I utilized the power I had. I had a lot of drive in my legs, and I could run over people. I don't think they thought I could. I looked small, but I ran big, and I fooled a lot of guys."

A solid blocker as well, Perry drew praise for his proficiency in that area from backfield mate Hugh McElhenny, who said, "Perry was an exceptional guy to be with in the backfield. He was such an outstanding team player. Running backs are only as good as the guys in front of them. I don't know how many times he laid a block that sprang me. I'm just proud to say I was in the same backfield as him."

Extremely likeable, Perry got along well with all his teammates despite the differences in their backgrounds, recalling, "I was the 49ers' only black for a long time, and the nucleus of our team in the '40s was Southern boys, but we got along fabulously. We were like one, big, happy family. If one guy got angry, it didn't do any good. He couldn't fight because he'd have to fight all of us. And, hell, I was part of the family."

Yet, things being as they were at the time, Perry still encountered a significant amount of racial prejudice during his playing career, stating, "I was the first black to play football here. It was rough as hell. There were a lot of unpleasant things that happened. Lots of things were said on the field. You could imagine what they were. It was probably worse playing football instead of baseball, like Jackie Robinson did, because football is such a physical game."

Claiming that he often absorbed extra punishment from tacklers due to "slow" whistles by some officials, Perry added, "I can't remember a season when I didn't hear a racial slur. Someone would say, 'Nigger, don't come through here again,' and I'd say, 'I'm coming through again, and you better bring your family.'"

Fortunately for Perry, though, he always received support from his teammates, with Hugh McElhenny once saying, "Joe confers a distinction by letting you line up with him."

Perry continued to excel in the backfield for the 49ers for several more seasons, amassing more than 500 yards from scrimmage each year from 1955 to 1959. Performing especially well in 1958, Perry gained First-Team All–Western Conference recognition by ranking among the league leaders with 758 yards rushing, 976 yards from scrimmage, and an average of 6.1 yards per carry. But, after the 33-year-old Perry assumed the role of a backup in 1960, the 49ers traded him to the Baltimore Colts at season's end for a future draft pick, ending his 13-year stint in the City by the Bay.

Reacting to news of the deal with his typical grace and class, Perry said, "I'm not at all disgruntled. The Colts can rest assured that, when I report, I'll be in tip-top condition, and I'll give them my very best because that's how I play football."

Perry spent the next two years in Baltimore, rushing for a total of 1,034 yards, amassing 1,550 yards from scrimmage, and scoring four touchdowns, before returning to San Francisco for one final season in 1963. After appearing in nine games with the 49ers as a backup, Perry announced his retirement, ending his pro career with 9,723 yards rushing (1,345 in the AAFC and 8,378 in the NFL), 260 receptions, 2,021 receiving yards, 11,744 yards from scrimmage, 12,532 all-purpose yards, 71 rushing touchdowns, 84 total touchdowns, and a rushing average of 5.0 yards per carry, which ranks among the best in NFL history. The holder of 14 different 49ers rushing and scoring records at the time, Perry also retired as the NFL's all-time leading rusher, although Jim Brown surpassed him shortly thereafter.

After retiring from football, Perry competed in the Professional Bowlers Association Tour, posting an average of over 200, before serving as a scout and assistant for the 49ers and, later, a sales representative for E & J Gallo

Winery. Inducted into the Pro Football Hall of Fame in 1969, Perry lived another 42 years, dying at the age of 84 on April 25, 2011, due to complications from dementia.

Upon learning of his passing, 49ers owner John York released a statement that read: "I was deeply saddened to hear about Joe Perry's passing earlier today. He was a dear friend to my family and me and the entire 49ers organization. He was also an intricate part of our rich history. A truly remarkable man both on and off the field, Joe had a lasting impact on the game of football and was an inspirational man to the generations of players that followed him. Our heartfelt sympathy goes out to his wife, Donna, and his entire family. He will be sadly missed by all of us."

Meanwhile, Y. A. Tittle said of his former teammate, "He was a wonderful, big-hearted guy. He was a super team player, one of the greatest players I've ever been around."

49ERS CAREER HIGHLIGHTS

Best Season

Perry had a fabulous year for the 49ers in 1949, amassing 929 yards from scrimmage and a career-best 1,266 all-purpose yards, scoring 11 touchdowns, and leading the AAFC with 783 yards rushing, eight rushing TDs, and an average of 6.8 yards per carry. However, he posted slightly better overall numbers in both 1953 and 1954, concluding the first of those campaigns with an NFL-leading 1,018 yards rushing, 1,209 yards from scrimmage, 10 rushing touchdowns, and 13 TDs, before scoring eight touchdowns and leading the league with 1,049 yards rushing and 1,252 yards from scrimmage the following year. With the UPI according Perry NFL MVP honors in 1954, we'll identify that as the finest season of his career.

Memorable Moments/Greatest Performances

Perry scored the first touchdown of his career the very first time he touched the football as a pro, running 57 yards to paydirt during a 35–14 win over the Buffalo Bills in the 1948 regular-season opener. Recalling his initial carry for the 49ers years later, Perry said, "It was a 38-pitch off a 34-trap fake. They just had no idea the speed I had, and I went for a touchdown the first time I touched the ball in pro football. From there, it just kind of blossomed."

Perry contributed to a 63–40 victory over the Brooklyn Dodgers on November 21, 1948, by returning a kickoff 87 yards for a touchdown.

Perry helped lead the 49ers to a 51–7 rout of the Bills on October 16, 1949, by running for three touchdowns, the longest of which came on a 24-yard scamper.

Perry proved to be a huge factor in a 17–14 win over the Baltimore Colts on October 29, 1950, carrying the ball 16 times for 142 yards.

Perry led the 49ers to a 30–14 victory over the Green Bay Packers in the final game of the 1950 regular season by carrying the ball nine times for 135 yards and two touchdowns, one of which came on a career-long 78-yard run.

Although the 49ers lost to the Los Angeles Rams by a score of 23–16 on November 4, 1951, Perry starred in defeat, gaining 115 yards on only 12 carries, and scoring a touchdown on a 58-yard run.

Perry completed the only touchdown pass of his career when he collaborated with Billy Wilson on a 31-yard scoring play during a 21–17 win over the Lions in the 1951 regular-season finale.

Perry contributed to a 40–16 victory over the Chicago Bears on October 19, 1952, by running for three touchdowns.

Although Perry carried the ball just twice during a 48–21 win over the Dallas Texans on October 26, 1952, one of those carries resulted in a 78-yard touchdown that matched his career-long run.

Perry helped lead the 49ers to a 31–21 victory over the Philadelphia Eagles in the opening game of the 1953 regular season by carrying the ball 16 times for 145 yards.

Perry helped the 49ers overcome a 21–0 first-quarter deficit to Chicago on October 18, 1953, by rushing for 113 yards and three touchdowns during a 35–28 win over the Bears.

Perry proved to be too much for the Packers to handle on November 22, 1953, scoring a touchdown and gaining 153 yards on just 16 carries during a 37–7 49ers win.

Perry led the 49ers to a 45–14 victory over the Baltimore Colts in the final game of the 1953 regular season by rushing for 108 yards and scoring three touchdowns, the longest of which came on a 40-yard run.

Perry starred during a 35–0 win over the Packers on December 5, 1954, carrying the ball 20 times for 137 yards and one touchdown.

Perry helped lead the 49ers to a convincing 38–21 victory over the Lions on October 30, 1955, by carrying the ball 20 times for 149 yards and two touchdowns.

Perry led the 49ers to a come-from-behind victory over the Packers in the final game of the 1957 regular season by rushing for 130 yards and two second-half touchdowns that turned a 20–13 third-quarter deficit into a 27–20 win.

Perry gained 174 yards on just 13 carries during a 24–21 win over the Lions on November 2, 1958, with his 73-yard TD scamper late in the first half representing his longest run of the year.

Perry went over 100 yards rushing for the final time as a member of the 49ers on October 18, 1959, carrying the ball 15 times for 145 yards during a 34–13 victory over the Lions.

Although Perry gained just 11 yards on four carries during a 21–17 win over the Chicago Bears at Kezar Stadium on October 27, 1957, Perry considered that particular contest to be the most memorable of his career, saying years later, "That game stands out for me because it is the game when [49ers owner] Tony Morabito died. I had been hurt for several weeks. At halftime, Chicago was ahead 17–7. We got word that Tony had died. The mood turned pretty somber. You could hear people crying, that's how much people loved the guy. I played the second half, and we all made a great comeback. We ended up winning 21–17."

Notable Achievements

- Rushed for more than 1,000 yards twice.
- Surpassed 1,000 all-purpose yards three times.
- Scored more than 10 touchdowns three times.
- Averaged more than 5 yards per carry seven times.
- Returned one kickoff for a touchdown.
- Led league in rushing attempts twice, rushing yards three times, yards from scrimmage twice, rushing touchdowns three times, touchdowns once, and rushing average once.
- Finished second in league in all-purpose yards twice, rushing attempts once, rushing touchdowns once, touchdowns once, points scored once, and rushing average once.
- Finished third in league in rushing attempts once, rushing yards twice, yards from scrimmage once, all-purpose yards once, rushing touch-downs once, and rushing average twice.
- Led 49ers in rushing eight times.
- Holds 49ers single-season record for most rushing touchdowns (10 in 1948 and 1953).
- Holds 49ers career record for most rushing touchdowns (68).

- Ranks among 49ers career leaders with 1,667 rushing attempts (3rd), 8,689 rushing yards (2nd), 10,194 yards from scrimmage (4th), 10,952 all-purpose yards (4th), 80 touchdowns (3rd), and 489 points scored (8th).
- Ranks eighth in NFL history with career rushing average of 5.0 yards per carry.
- 1954 United Press International (UPI) NFL MVP.
- Three-time Pro Bowl selection (1952, 1953, and 1954).
- Two-time First-Team All-Pro selection (1953 and 1954).
- 1949 Second-Team All-AAFC selection.
- Pro Football Reference All-1950s First Team.
- NFL 1950s All-Decade Team.
- #34 retired by 49ers.
- Inducted into 49ers Hall of Fame in 2009.
- Elected to Pro Football Hall of Fame in 1969.

11

ROGER CRAIG

One of the most versatile running backs in NFL history, Roger Craig spent eight seasons in San Francisco excelling for the 49ers at both fullback and halfback. The first player ever to rush for more than 1,000 yards and amass more than 1,000 receiving yards in the same season, Craig combined speed, power, superior pass-receiving skills, and the ability to lead block and pass protect to establish himself as arguably the league's most complete back, making him an indispensable member of Bill Walsh's West Coast Offense. Gaining more than 1,000 yards on the ground three times and surpassing 60 receptions on five separate occasions, Craig amassed more than 1,000 yards from scrimmage seven times, topping the magical 2,000-yard mark twice. Along the way, Craig helped the 49ers win seven division titles and three Super Bowls, with his brilliant all-around play earning him four Pro Bowl selections, two All-Pro nominations, one NFL Offensive Player of the Year trophy, and a place in the 49ers Hall of Fame.

Born in Preston, Mississippi, on July 10, 1960, Roger Timothy Craig grew up in Davenport, Iowa, where he learned the value of hard work at an early age, recalling, "My mother and father worked really hard for me growing up. I wasn't hurting for anything, but I saw how hard they worked to make things better for us."

One of eight children, Craig often found himself being compared to his older brother, Curtis, remembering, "Everybody was always asking me, 'Are you going to be like your older brother?' I didn't like it, but I set goals for myself to be better than he was at my age. It worked out well for me. It made me a better person and a better athlete."

Excelling in multiple sports at Davenport Central High School, Craig starred as a running back in football, a hurdler in track, and a wrestler, once qualifying for the Iowa State Wrestling Championship Tournament. Experiencing even greater success on the track and gridiron, Craig finished second in the Iowa State Track and Field Championships in both the 110- and

In 1985, Roger Craig became the first player in NFL history to gain more than 1,000 yards on the ground and top 1,000 receiving yards in the same season. Courtesy of George A. Kitrinos

400-meter hurdles as a senior in 1979, with his time of 14.43 seconds in the first event setting a new school record. Meanwhile, Craig earned Prep All-America honors in football his senior year by rushing for 1,565 yards and 27 touchdowns, capping off his brilliant campaign by gaining 353 yards on the ground and scoring four touchdowns during a playoff loss. Amazingly, Craig accomplished all that after breaking his leg the previous season, recalling, "It just made me realize I have to work that much harder. I figure like this: This is six months of football, and this is my job. There's no time to be relaxing. I feel uncomfortable when I don't come in on Tuesday or work out or watch films of other teams."

Subsequently offered an athletic scholarship to the University of Nebraska, Craig spent three seasons starting at running back in head coach Tom Osborne's I-formation option offense, rushing for a total of 2,446 yards and scoring 26 touchdowns. Particularly effective as a junior in 1981, Craig earned All–Big Eight honors by gaining 1,060 yards on the ground and scoring six touchdowns. Although Craig served primarily as a blocker for Heisman Trophy winning halfback Mike Rozier the following year, he accepted his new role without question, later saying, "I was never really caught up in the glamour, as far as trying to be the featured man on the team."

Impressed with the versatility that Craig displayed in college, the 49ers selected him in the second round of the 1983 NFL Draft, with the 49th overall pick, with head coach Bill Walsh saying at the time, "He can do a lot of the same things Franco Harris does."

Although Craig, who stood 6 feet tall, weighed only 214 pounds when he first arrived in San Francisco, he soon found himself manning the full-back position, where he did an outstanding job of blocking for Wendell Tyler as a rookie, helping the tailback gain 856 yards on the ground. Contributing to the 49er offense in many other ways as well, Craig rushed for 725 yards, made 48 receptions for 427 yards, and scored 12 touchdowns. Craig followed that up with another excellent all-around season, rushing for 649 yards, making 71 receptions for 675 yards, and scoring 10 TDs for San Francisco's 1984 NFL championship team, before taking over as the team's primary running threat in 1985, when he began an exceptional five-year run during which he posted the following numbers:

YEAR	YDS RUSHING	RECS	REC YDS	YDS FROM SCRIMMAGE	TDS
1985	1,050	**92**	1,016	2,066	15
1986	830	81	624	1,454	7
1987	815	66	492	1,307	4
1988	1,502	76	534	**2,036**	10
1989	1,054	49	473	1,527	7

In addition to leading the NFL with 92 receptions in 1985, Craig finished second in the league with 2,066 yards from scrimmage and 15 touchdowns, with his 1,050 rushing yards and 1,016 receiving yards making him the first player in NFL history to gain more than 1,000 yards running and receiving in the same season. Since that time, only two other players—Marshall Faulk and Christian McCaffrey—have accomplished the feat. After performing exceptionally well in each of the next two seasons as well, Craig earned NFL Offensive Player of the Year and Newspaper Enterprise Association NFL MVP honors in 1988 by leading the league with 2,036 yards from scrimmage and finishing third in the circuit with 1,502 yards rushing. Craig also gained Pro Bowl and All-NFC recognition in four of those five seasons and made All-Pro twice. More importantly, the 49ers won four division titles and two Super Bowls, with Craig proving to be one of the most significant contributors to both championship teams.

Blessed with speed, strength, and a willingness to take on tacklers, Craig, who gradually added some 10 pounds of muscle onto his frame, employed an aggressive running style, with former teammate Charles Haley saying, "Roger Craig, my God, he punished guys. He had a motor that would just not stop. I can't even get the words to really describe the passion he played with. I just wanted to emulate that."

Running with his knees unusually high, Craig said, "I run to protect myself. The high knees break tackles. They're like a weapon. If my knee hits somebody right, it might go in his chin or head. Guys back off."

Craig added, "As a running back, I would describe myself as a violent runner. A lot of guys, you know, they don't like contact. I loved contact."

Capable of altering his approach depending on the situation, Craig claimed, "I had speed, if I had to turn it up. If I had to run you over, if I had to get the first down, if I had to dive over the top of the pile; I tried to do it all."

Making perhaps his greatest contribution to the 49ers with his ability to catch the ball out of the backfield, Craig fit Bill Walsh's system perfectly, giving Joe Montana another receiving option. And, once he caught the football, Craig excelled at gaining additional yardage, with Eagles personnel director Lynn Stiles stating, "The thing about him is what he does after he catches the ball. If you don't hit him as soon as he catches the ball, he's capable of breaking it."

In discussing that aspect of his game, Craig said, "Joe trusted me. He knew exactly where I was gonna be, and I was there, and I'd always catch it for 10 or 15 yards. My role was to keep the chains moving."

Further expounding upon his role, Craig stated, "Well, the fullback in the West Coast Offense, you have to be able to catch the ball, and you have to play-action fake. If I didn't sell the fake, I felt like I messed up the play. I took pride in it. I took pride in selling the fake. If I get hit, that means I did my job. That's being a team player. . . . It wasn't about stats. It was about what I brought to the table to help my team win."

Expressing his appreciation to Craig for everything he brought to the team, Bill Walsh said, "He's one of the great people in the league and, to me, the most valuable player."

Ronnie Lott added, "What makes Roger Craig so special is his heart. He plays as if he has the heart of a lion."

Unfortunately, Craig's days as an elite player ended in 1990, when he gained just 439 yards on the ground, accumulated only 640 yards from scrimmage, and scored just one touchdown. Unhappy over the 49ers' subsequent decision to include him on their list of Plan B free agents, Craig chose to sign with the Los Angeles Raiders, leaving San Francisco with career totals of 7,064 yards rushing, 508 receptions, 4,442 receiving yards, 11,506 yards from scrimmage, 11,538 all-purpose yards, 50 rushing touchdowns, and 66 touchdowns, with each of those figures placing him among the franchise's all-time leaders.

"Sure, you're going to have resentment after all the hard years you put in, then you get treated that way," Craig said. "But, for me, it's another challenge in life. I'm excited as hell to be with the Raider organization, for them to believe in me. They gave me the opportunity, the chance to redeem myself, to show people that they didn't make a mistake by bringing me here. I don't want to let them down."

Craig ended up spending just one season in Los Angeles, rushing for 590 yards and amassing 726 yards from scrimmage in 1991, before joining the Minnesota Vikings, with whom he assumed a backup role for two seasons, gaining a total of 535 yards on the ground, accumulating 868 yards from scrimmage, and scoring six touchdowns. Announcing his retirement following the conclusion of the 1993 campaign, Craig ended his career with 8,189 yards rushing, 566 receptions, 4,911 receiving yards, 13,100 yards from scrimmage, 13,143 all-purpose yards, 56 rushing touchdowns, 73 total touchdowns, and a rushing average of 4.1 yards per carry.

Since retiring from football, Craig has spent most of his post–playing career working as the VP of business development at TIBCO Software. He is also an avid runner who has participated in over 38 marathons and half-marathons.

49ERS CAREER HIGHLIGHTS

Best Season

It could be argued that the 1985 campaign represented the finest of Craig's career since, in addition to rushing for 1,050 yards, he led the NFL with 92 receptions, amassed 1,016 receiving yards, and established career-high marks with 2,066 yards from scrimmage and 15 touchdowns, with his brilliant all-around play prompting personnel directors around the league to name him the NFL's number two all-purpose back, behind only Walter Payton, in a poll taken by the *Sporting News*. However, we'll opt instead for the 1988 season since Craig earned NFL Offensive Player of the Year honors and his lone First-Team All-Pro nomination by leading the league with 2,036 yards from scrimmage, while also ranking among the leaders with 1,502 yards rushing, 2,068 all-purpose yards, 76 receptions, and nine rushing TDs.

Memorable Moments/Greatest Performances

Craig scored the first TD of his career when he ran the ball in from 1 yard out during a 48–17 pasting of the Vikings on September 8, 1983.

Craig displayed his tremendous versatility by making four receptions for 37 yards and rushing for 71 yards and three TDs during a 35–21 win over Tampa Bay on December 4, 1983.

Although Craig gained only 24 yards on the ground during a 33–0 victory over the Los Angeles Rams on October 28, 1984, he amassed 83 receiving yards and scored two touchdowns, one of which came on a 64-yard catch-and-run on a pass thrown by Joe Montana.

Craig proved to be a huge factor in Super Bowl XIX, rushing for 58 yards and one touchdown, and making seven receptions for 77 yards and two TDs during the 49ers' 38–16 win over Miami.

Although the 49ers lost the opening game of the 1985 regular season to the Vikings by a score of 28–21, Craig starred in defeat, scoring three touchdowns and amassing 150 yards from scrimmage, with 78 of those yards coming on the ground and the other 72 through the air.

Craig followed that up by making six receptions for 77 yards and rushing for 107 yards and two TDs during a 35–16 win over Atlanta, earning in the process NFC Offensive Player of the Week honors.

Although Craig rushed for only 15 yards during a 38–17 victory over Atlanta in the second meeting between the two teams on October 6, 1985, he made 12 receptions for 167 yards and one touchdown, which came on a 46-yard pass from Joe Montana.

Craig helped lead the 49ers to a 28–14 win over the Rams on October 27, 1985, by scoring two touchdowns and accumulating a total of 195 yards from scrimmage, gaining 63 of those yards on 14 carries and the other 132 on six pass receptions.

Craig turned in another excellent all-around effort against New Orleans on December 15, 1985, making eight receptions for 82 yards and rushing for 88 yards and one TD during a 31–19 win.

Craig earned NFC Offensive Player of the Week honors by rushing for 80 yards, amassing 89 receiving yards, and scoring one TD during a 29–24 win over the Patriots on December 14, 1986.

Craig proved to be the difference in a 34–28 win over the St. Louis Cardinals on October 18, 1987, finishing the game with 71 yards rushing, seven receptions for 99 yards, and two TDs.

Craig rushed for 110 yards and gained another 69 yards on nine pass receptions during a 20–17 win over the Giants on September 11, 1988, earning in the process NFC Offensive Player of the Week honors for the third time.

Craig earned that distinction for the fourth and final time by rushing for a career-high 190 yards and three touchdowns during a 24–21 win over the Rams on October 16, 1988, with the longest of his TDs coming on a sensational 46-yard run during which he broke five tackles.

Craig scored another three TDs during a 48–10 rout of the San Diego Chargers on November 27, 1988, scoring two of them on short runs and the other on a 2-yard pass from Joe Montana.

Craig helped lead the 49ers to a 34–9 victory over Minnesota in the divisional round of the 1988 playoffs by rushing for 135 yards and two TDs, one of which came on a career-long 80-yard run.

Craig also came up big for the 49ers during their 20–16 win over Cincinnati in Super Bowl XXIII three weeks later, finishing the game with 71 yards rushing and eight receptions for 101 yards.

Notable Achievements

- Rushed for more than 1,000 yards three times, topping 1,500 yards once.
- Surpassed 60 receptions five times.
- Surpassed 1,000 receiving yards once, topping 500 yards three other times.

- Amassed more than 1,000 yards from scrimmage seven times, topping 2,000 yards twice.
- Scored at least 10 touchdowns four times.
- Led NFL in receptions once and yards from scrimmage once.
- Finished second in NFL in yards from scrimmage once, all-purpose yards once, and touchdowns once.
- Finished third in NFL in rushing attempts once, rushing yards once, all-purpose yards once, and receptions once.
- Led 49ers in rushing five times, receptions four times, and receiving yards once.
- Ranks among 49ers career leaders with 1,686 rushing attempts (2nd), 7,064 rushing yards (3rd), 508 receptions (3rd), 4,442 receiving yards (10th), 11,506 yards from scrimmage (3rd), 11,538 all-purpose yards (3rd), 50 rushing touchdowns (3rd), 66 touchdowns (5th), and 396 points scored (12th).
- Seven-time division champion (1983, 1984, 1986, 1987, 1988, 1989, and 1990).
- Three-time NFC champion (1984, 1988, and 1989).
- Three-time Super Bowl champion (XIX, XXIII, and XXIV).
- Four-time NFC Offensive Player of the Week.
- 1988 NEA NFL MVP.
- 1988 NFL Offensive Player of the Year.
- Four-time Pro Bowl selection (1985, 1987, 1988, and 1989).
- 1988 First-Team All-Pro selection.
- 1985 Second-Team All-Pro selection.
- 1988 First-Team All-NFC selection.
- Three-time Second-Team All-NFC selection (1985, 1987, and 1989).
- Pro Football Reference All-1980s First Team.
- NFL 1980s All-Decade Second Team.
- Inducted into 49ers Hall of Fame in 2011.

12

TERRELL OWENS

Perhaps the most polarizing figure in franchise history, Terrell Owens spent eight tumultuous years in San Francisco, often proving to be his own worst enemy during that time. Self-absorbed and extremely introspective, Owens frequently failed to see how his actions affected others around him, causing him to clash with 49ers management and many of his teammates on numerous occasions. Nevertheless, Owens gave everything he had to the 49ers on the football field, establishing himself as a tremendous offensive force during his time in the City by the Bay. Surpassing 80 receptions four times and 1,000 receiving yards five times, Owens ranks second only to Jerry Rice in team annals in both categories, with his outstanding play earning him four Pro Bowl selections and three All-Pro nominations. A member of 49er teams that won two division titles, Owens later played for two other division championship clubs, with his contributions to those squads and prolific offensive numbers eventually gaining him induction into the Pro Football Hall of Fame.

Born in Alexander City, Alabama, on December 7, 1973, Terrell Eldorado Owens grew up with his three younger siblings under the most unusual of circumstances. Raised by his mother and grandmother, young Terrell did not learn the identity of his father until he turned 12 years of age, when, after befriending a girl who lived across the street, he found himself being confronted by her dad, who warned him that the girl was actually his half-sister.

Often mistreated by his alcoholic grandmother, who tried to prevent him from competing in sports until he reached high school, Owens nevertheless found a way to play baseball, basketball, and football, spending much of his youth trying to emulate his favorite player on the gridiron, Jerry Rice. Developing into an outstanding all-around athlete at Benjamin Russell High School, Owens lettered four times in football and track, three times in basketball, and once in baseball.

Terrell Owens ranks second only to Jerry Rice in franchise history in receptions and receiving yards.
Courtesy of George A. Kitrinos

Drawing little attention from college scouts since he did not start for Benjamin Russell's football team until his senior year, Owens ultimately accepted an athletic scholarship from the University of Tennessee at Chattanooga, where he continued to compete in multiple sports. Displaying his vast array of athletic skills in college, Owens excelled as a forward on the basketball court for three years, anchored the school's 4x100 relay team at the NCAA championship his senior year, and earned All–Southern Conference honors at wide receiver as a junior by making 58 receptions for 836 yards and six touchdowns. Although Owens posted somewhat less impressive numbers his senior year, making 43 receptions for 667 yards and one TD, his impressive size and speed prompted the 49ers to select him in the third round of the 1996 NFL Draft, with the 89th overall pick.

Thrilled to be joining Steve Young and Jerry Rice in San Francisco, Owens gladly accepted a supporting role his first year in the league, catching 35 passes, amassing 520 yards, and scoring four touchdowns in his 10 starts, while also making significant contributions on the kickoff- and punt-coverage units. With Rice missing virtually all of the ensuing campaign with an injury, Owens emerged as the 49ers' primary receiving threat, leading the team with 60 receptions, 936 receiving yards, and eight TD catches. Continuing to perform at an extremely high level after Rice returned to action in 1998, Owens caught 67 passes, amassed 1,097 receiving yards, finished second in the league with 14 TD catches, and scored 15 touchdowns, prompting Rice, who spent a considerable amount of time explaining the nuances of the game to him, to say, "I just feel T.O. is going to carry on the tradition. I feel like my job is done. . . . When I watch T.O. work, I see myself."

Meanwhile, George Stewart, who served as an assistant coach in San Francisco from 1996 to 2002, suggested, "The only thing that will keep Terrell Owens from being the best is Terrell Owens."

After making 60 receptions for 754 yards and four touchdowns in 1999, Owens began an outstanding three-year run during which he posted the following numbers:

YEAR	RECS	REC YDS	TD RECS	TDS
2000	97	1,451	13	13
2001	93	1,412	**16**	16
2002	100	1,300	**13**	14

Ranking among the NFL leaders in every major pass-receiving category all three years, Owens topped the circuit in TD catches twice and finished third the other year, with his exceptional play gaining him Pro Bowl and First-Team All-Pro recognition each season. Meanwhile, after compiling a record of just 6-10 in the first of those campaigns, the 49ers posted a composite mark of 22-10 over the course of the next two seasons, earning in the process two trips to the playoffs and one division title.

Standing 6'3" and weighing close to 225 pounds, Owens possessed an extremely muscular physique that he helped maintain by constantly exercising, even doing push-ups and biceps curls in between shots while playing pool. Knowing how to use his size and strength to his advantage, Owens did an excellent job of positioning himself between the football and his defender, who he invariably outmuscled for the pigskin in close coverage. Commenting on Owens's proficiency in that area, Atlanta Falcons cornerback Ray Buchanan stated, "It's always a mismatch. If you try to get into his body, forget it. He'll just throw you aside."

Saints general manager Randy Mueller suggested, "He's a lot like Michael Irvin. He's a tough matchup for corners because he is 6'3". He's better in the fourth quarter than the first."

Lovie Smith, defensive coordinator of the Rams at that time, said of Owens, "He's big, he can run, and, if you play him one-on-one, he can outjump a defensive back. He's the complete package."

And, once Owens gathered in the football, his size and speed made him extremely difficult to bring down in the open field, as longtime NFL assistant coach George Catavolos noted when he said, "You've got to keep his yardage after the catch limited; that is probably the most important thing. He's a threat short, in the quick passing game. He can break a tackle and go all the way."

In discussing his teammate's running style, 49ers quarterback Jeff Garcia stated, "When he catches the ball and runs, it's like he runs with anger."

An excellent blocker as well, Owens also proved to be an asset in the running game, with St. Louis Rams cornerback Dexter McCleon commenting, "Terrell does it all. He doesn't take plays off. He blocks in the running game. He plays hard the whole game."

Yet, as much as Owens gave of himself to the 49ers on the football field, his temperamental nature and inability to channel his emotions often made him a divisive force on the sidelines and in the locker room. Constantly demanding that the football be thrown to him, Owens frequently screamed at his quarterback and coaches on the sidelines during contests and criticized them afterwards for their inability to get the ball into his hands as much as he would have liked. Owens also enjoyed drawing attention to himself by engaging in elaborate touchdown celebrations, some of which angered even his own teammates.

One such instance occurred during the early stages of the 2000 campaign, when, after scoring a touchdown during a lopsided 41–24 victory over the Cowboys in Dallas, Owens rubbed salt into the wound by sprinting to midfield and placing the football atop the Cowboys logo. Subsequently suspended by the 49ers for one week and fined $24,000 for his immature behavior, Owens became irate, believing that the organization's admonishment of him displayed a lack of support. Owens grew even angrier when many of his teammates expressed their disapproval by avoiding him in the locker room, causing him to isolate himself from the rest of the team.

Entering the 2001 season with a chip on his shoulder, Owens drew the ire of 49ers head coach Steve Mariucci, when, after San Francisco blew a 19-point lead to the Bears in Chicago, he accused Mariucci of trying to protect the job of his good friend, Bears head coach Dick Jauron. Owens made headlines again the following year, when, after making a touchdown reception during a 28–21 win over the Seahawks in Seattle, he pulled a Sharpie out of his sock, signed the football, and handed it to his financial advisor seated in a luxury box behind the end zone. Crucified in the media for his actions, Owens attempted to defend himself by saying, "I'm smart enough to know when I've done something wrong, but I don't understand this. Guys are beating their wives, getting DUIs and doing drugs, and I get national attention for a Sharpie? People are personally attacking me, calling me a classless asshole because I did something creative during a game. Why?"

Owens continued, "The criticism that hurt me most is that I'm dishonoring the game, have no class, no respect. Who is Dennis Green to say that when he couldn't control Randy Moss? I'm disrespecting the game? I'm not the one with the rap sheet. I've never taken a play off or not blocked. I guess walking off the ball and not blocking anyone like Randy is respecting the game, huh?"

Having finally reached a point of no return in San Francisco, Owens agreed with the 49ers to part ways at the end of 2003, a season in which he earned Pro Bowl honors for the fourth straight time by making 80 receptions for 1,102 yards and nine touchdowns. Traded to the Philadelphia Eagles on March 17, 2004, as part of a three-way deal with the Baltimore Ravens, Owens left San Francisco with career totals of 592 receptions, 8,572 receiving yards, 81 TD catches, and 83 touchdowns, all of which place him second only to Jerry Rice in franchise history.

Upon acquiring Owens, Eagles head coach Andy Reid said, "He has a passion for the game, and that's something I like. I don't mind the personality. He understands how we are and how we operate. The No. 1 thing about this guy is his work ethic. That really jumped out at me at the Pro Bowls. You always heard about Jerry Rice's work ethic, but I've heard that Terrell took it to another level."

Meanwhile, Owens stated, "This is a new beginning. It's a fresh start. I have a clean rap sheet right now."

Owens ended up spending two years with the Eagles, helping them win the NFC championship in 2004 by making 77 receptions for 1,200 yards and 14 touchdowns, before differences with quarterback Donovan McNabb prompted the team to release him at the end of 2005. Subsequently signed by the Cowboys, Owens spent three extremely productive years in Dallas, amassing more than 1,000 receiving yards and scoring at least 10 touchdowns each season, with his 81 receptions, 1,355 receiving yards, and 15 TD catches in 2007 earning him Pro Bowl and First-Team All-Pro honors.

Nevertheless, Owens eventually wore out his welcome in Dallas as well, forcing him to split his final two seasons between the Buffalo Bills and Cincinnati Bengals, before leaving the NFL when no team chose to offer him a contract after he tore his ACL during the 2011 offseason. During his 15 years in the league, Owens made 1,078 receptions, amassed 15,934 receiving yards, caught 153 TD passes, and scored 156 touchdowns, with each of those figures placing him among the NFL's all-time leaders.

Owens subsequently spent one season playing for the Allen Wranglers of the Indoor Football League, while also serving as a member of their ownership group. Owens later signed a one-year, $925,000 contract with the Seattle Seahawks, but never appeared in a single game with them, suffering the indignity of being released just three weeks later. After briefly toying with the idea of playing for the Edmonton Eskimos of the Canadian Football League at 45 years of age, Owens failed to come to terms on a contract with them.

Inducted into the Pro Football Hall of Fame in 2018, Owens displayed his displeasure over having to wait until his third year of eligibility to gain enshrinement by skipping the official induction ceremonies in Canton, Ohio, and hosting his own celebration in McKenzie Arena on the campus of the University of Tennessee at Chattanooga. Owens received the additional honor of being inducted into the 49ers Hall of Fame some seven months later, with team CEO Jed York saying at the time, "Over the course of eight seasons, the 49ers Faithful were fortunate to have front row seats to watch Terrell Owens develop into one of the most prolific wide receivers in the history of the NFL. Not only was Terrell one of the most physically gifted athletes to ever play the game, but he was also one of the most competitive. We are so very proud and honored to induct Terrell into the Edward J DeBartolo Sr. San Francisco 49ers Hall of Fame, where he will take his place among the all-time greats in our team's history."

49ERS CAREER HIGHLIGHTS

Best Season

Owens played his best ball for the 49ers from 2000 to 2002, earning three consecutive First-Team All-Pro nominations. Although any of those seasons would make an excellent choice, we'll go with 2001 since, in addition to leading the NFL with a career-high 16 TD catches and placing ninth in the circuit with 93 receptions, Owens finished in the league's top three with 1,412 receiving yards and 16 touchdowns.

Memorable Moments/Greatest Performances

Owens had his breakout game on October 20, 1996, making four receptions for 94 yards and one touchdown during a 28–21 win over the Cincinnati Bengals, with his TD coming on a 45-yard pass from Steve Young.

Although the 49ers lost to the Carolina Panthers by a score of 30–24 on December 8, 1996, Owens topped 100 receiving yards for the first time in his career, finishing the game with five catches for 110 yards and one touchdown, which came on a 46-yard hookup with Steve Young.

Owens contributed to a 31–7 win over the Giants on November 30, 1998, by making five receptions for 140 yards and one touchdown, which came on a 79-yard first-quarter connection with Young.

Owens experienced his most memorable moment as a member of the 49ers when he gave them a dramatic 30–27 victory over the Packers in the 1998 NFC wild card game by gathering in a 25-yard touchdown pass from Steve Young with just eight seconds remaining in regulation. Owens's TD grab subsequently became known as "The Catch II" in 49ers lore.

Owens starred in defeat on October 8, 2000, making 12 receptions for 176 yards and two touchdowns during a 34–28 overtime loss to the Oakland Raiders.

Owens earned NFC Offensive Player of the Week honors by making 20 receptions for 283 yards and one touchdown during a 17–0 win over the Chicago Bears on December 17, 2000, with his 20 catches representing the highest single-game total in franchise history. Meanwhile, Owens's 283 receiving yards represent the third-highest single-game total in team annals.

Owens helped lead the 49ers to a 24–14 win over the Carolina Panthers on October 7, 2001, by making eight receptions for 118 yards and two touchdowns, which came on third-quarter connections of 29 and 20 yards with Jeff Garcia that turned a 14–10 deficit into a 24–14 lead that San Francisco maintained the rest of the way.

Owens proved to be the difference in a 37–31 overtime win over the Atlanta Falcons on October 14, 2001. After making a 17-yard touchdown reception that tied the score at 31–31 with just 17 seconds remaining in regulation, Owens gave the 49ers the victory when he collaborated with Jeff Garcia on a 52-yard touchdown pass nearly nine minutes into the overtime session. Owens finished the game with nine catches for 183 yards and three TDs.

Owens made another dramatic touchdown catch against the Carolina Panthers on November 18, 2001, when his 7-yard TD grab with just one second left in regulation tied the score at 22–22. The 49ers won the game less than five minutes later on a 26-yard field goal by Jose Cortez.

Owens torched the Arizona defensive secondary for eight receptions, 132 receiving yards, and two touchdowns during a 38–28 49ers win on October 27, 2002, with his TDs coming on passes of 21 and 61 yards from Jeff Garcia.

Owens starred during a 23–20 overtime win over the Oakland Raiders on November 3, 2002, making 12 receptions for 191 yards.

Although the 49ers lost to the Chargers in overtime by a score of 20–17 on November 17, 2002, Owens had another big game, making seven receptions for 171 yards and two touchdowns, the longest of which covered 76 yards.

Owens helped lead the 49ers to a 31–27 win over the Cowboys on December 8, 2002, by making 12 receptions for 123 yards and two touchdowns, with his 8-yard TD grab with just 12 seconds remaining in regulation providing the margin of victory.

Owens came up big for the 49ers in the wild card round of the 2002 NFC playoffs, leading them to a 39–38 come-from-behind victory over the Giants by making nine receptions for 177 yards and two touchdowns. After scoring the game's first points on a 76-yard connection with Jeff Garcia, Owens began a memorable comeback that saw the 49ers overcome a 38–14 third-quarter deficit by making a 26-yard TD catch with 2:03 remaining in the third period. The 49ers subsequently went on to score the next 17 points as well, winning the game on a 13-yard touchdown reception by Tai Streets in the final minute of regulation.

Owens contributed to a 30–14 win over the Pittsburgh Steelers on November 17, 2003, by making eight receptions for 155 yards and one touchdown, which came on a 61-yard pass from Tim Rattay.

Owens amassed more than 100 receiving yards for the final time as a member of the 49ers on December 14, 2003, making eight receptions for 127 yards and one touchdown during a 41–38 loss to the Cincinnati Bengals.

Notable Achievements

- Surpassed 80 receptions four times, topping 100 receptions once.
- Surpassed 1,000 receiving yards five times.
- Scored more than 10 touchdowns four times.
- Led NFL in touchdown receptions twice.
- Finished second in NFL in touchdown receptions once and touchdowns once.
- Finished third in NFL in receiving yards once and touchdown receptions once.
- Led 49ers in receptions five times and receiving yards five times.
- Holds 49ers single-game record for most receptions (20 vs. Chicago on December 17, 2000).
- Ranks among 49ers career leaders with 592 receptions (2nd), 8,572 receiving yards (2nd), 8,734 yards from scrimmage (5th), 8,812 all-purpose yards (6th), 81 touchdown receptions (2nd), 83 touchdowns (2nd), and 502 points scored (7th).
- Two-time division champion (1997 and 2002).
- 2000 Week 16 NFC Offensive Player of the Week.
- Four-time Pro Bowl selection (2000, 2001, 2002, and 2003).
- Three-time First-Team All-Pro selection (2000, 2001, and 2002).
- Three-time First-Team All-NFC selection (2000, 2001, and 2002).
- Pro Football Reference All-2000s First Team.
- NFL 2000s All-Decade Second Team.
- Inducted into 49ers Hall of Fame in 2019.
- Elected to Pro Football Hall of Fame in 2018.

13

DAVE WILCOX

Nicknamed "The Intimidator" and called "the Dick Butkus of outside linebackers" by 49ers linebackers coach Mike Giddings, Dave Wilcox established himself as one of the most dominant players at his position over the course of his 11-year NFL career, which he spent entirely in San Francisco. Known for his toughness and strength, Wilcox excelled in every phase of linebacking play, proving to be particularly effective at stuffing the run and blanketing opposing tight ends in pass coverage. A member of 49er teams that won three division championships, Wilcox earned seven Pro Bowl selections and four All-Pro nominations, before being further honored following the conclusion of his playing career by being inducted into the 49ers Hall of Fame and elected to the Pro Football Hall of Fame.

Born in Ontario, Oregon, on September 29, 1942, David Wilcox grew up with his six brothers and one sister on a farm in nearby Vale, a small town near the Snake River on the Oregon/Washington border. After spending his early years helping out on the family farm by milking cows and baling hay by hand while attending classes in a four-room schoolhouse where the hallway doubled as the cafeteria, Wilcox began his football career at Vale Union High School, recalling years later, "Football was really important. The community had a real pride in that. When we were growing up, we were poor, but we were all happy. Nobody knew any different. Everybody worked hard. That probably came from the Depression, all the people who came to that community."

Wilcox continued, "There were 320 kids in our high school, and about 90 of them turned out for football. Football was kind of the whole thing over there. We won the state championship twice in our classification."

In addition to starring on the gridiron as a two-way lineman in high school, Wilcox excelled in baseball and basketball, earning three letters in each sport, before enrolling at Boise Junior College (now Boise State), where he gained junior college All-America recognition as an offensive and defensive lineman, setting a school record one season by blocking

Dave Wilcox proved to be one of the most dominant outside linebackers of his time.
Courtesy of Mike Traverse.

eight kicks. After two years at Boise, Wilcox accepted a scholarship to the University of Oregon, following in the footsteps of his older brother, who had played for the Ducks prior to joining the Philadelphia Eagles in 1960. After initially playing offensive tackle and defensive end at Oregon, Wilcox moved to guard on offense his senior year, later saying, "I didn't know what I was doing. I was a pulling guard for (Mel) Renfro, and he used to run over me."

Following his early struggles, Wilcox eventually settled into his new post, performing so well that he received invitations to play in the Hula Bowl, Coaches' All-America Game, and College All-Star Game.

Subsequently selected by the 49ers in the third round of the 1964 NFL Draft, with the 29th overall pick, and by the Houston Oilers with the 46th overall pick of that year's AFL Draft, Wilcox ultimately chose to sign with the 49ers, who immediately converted him into a linebacker. Proving to be a natural at his new position, Wilcox had a solid rookie season after laying claim to the starting left-outside linebacker job shortly after he arrived in San Francisco.

Nevertheless, with Wilcox experiencing shoulder problems and needing to put on a few pounds, he knew that he needed to do a considerable amount of work prior to the start of the ensuing campaign, recalling, "I weighed around 230 my first two years, but kept having trouble with my shoulders. They ached so bad I couldn't sleep."

After spending his first offseason in the army, Wilcox dedicated himself to the weight room the following year, gradually adding more than 10 pounds of muscle onto his frame. And, once his shoulders began to heal, Wilcox emerged as one of the league's fiercest hitters, developing a reputation before long for his ability to deliver crushing blows to opposing quarterbacks and ball-carriers, with longtime San Francisco journalist Dave Newhouse writing, "Wilcox hit fullbacks and tight ends like a misplaced steer wrestler, grabbing them at the top of both arms, or by the shirt, and flinging them to the ground. A Dave Wilcox tackle starts at the shoulders and hurts all the way down."

After gaining Pro Bowl recognition for the first time in 1966, Wilcox earned that distinction six straight times from 1968 to 1973. He also earned All-NFC and All-Pro honors four times each, gaining First- and Second-Team All-Pro recognition twice each.

Ideally suited, both mentally and physically, to play linebacker, the 6'3", 242-pound Wilcox possessed good speed and unusually long arms that helped make him equally effective against the run and pass. With arms that measured size 39 in sleeve length, Wilcox employed a somewhat unorthodox arm-tackling technique that he described thusly: "My thinking when tackling is that, if I have to leave my feet, I'm doing exactly what the ball carrier wants—for me to extend myself. I try to think his way. He'll put a move on to get you to move so he can make another move around you. I wait until he stops. Usually, you have to reach out some and get him anyway, so I must use my arms somewhat."

Also blessed with exceptional physical strength, Wilcox had a huge upper body and massive triceps that enabled him to easily shed blockers and bring down opposing ball-carriers, once saying, "What I do best is not let people block me. I just hate to be blocked."

In discussing the tremendous power possessed by his longtime team-mate, John Brodie stated, "Dave Wilcox dominated people. I could find a piece of film every week where he'd take a guy and carry him over and lay him on a pile. Who did that with a 265-pound man? And he never knew he was doing these things."

Particularly tough on tight ends, Wilcox refused to allow them off the line of scrimmage, using his long arms and great strength to prevent them from getting into their pass routes, with Brodie recalling, "I can remember John Mackey, as great as he was, all the great tight ends that came into Kezar Stadium, or wherever we'd go, they never caught diddly. They'd beat us every other way, but nobody could get off the line against him."

And, on those rare occasions when opposing tight ends broke down-field against him, Wilcox had the speed to stay with them, recording a total of 14 interceptions over the course of his career.

Even stronger against the run, Wilcox, claimed Mike Giddings, limited opposing teams to 1.1 yards per carry to his side of the field over a six-year period, forcing them to run away from him most of the time. Praising his star linebacker for his exceptional all-around play, former 49ers head coach Dick Nolan once said, "Wilcox has the size to control the tight end and the speed to stay with the backs. And he is the best open-field tackler I have ever seen."

Detroit Lions Hall of Fame linebacker Joe Schmidt, who played and coached against Wilcox, recalled, "He gave us fits. The lead block had to really come out hard to take him on because he was so strong."

Meanwhile, former Rams and Eagles quarterback Roman Gabriel claimed that Wilcox wreaked havoc on opposing offenses when he suggested, "Basically, Dave played the game from his spot as an outside line-backer like Dick Butkus played it for the Bears in the middle, because the rules weren't quite the same. You could hit people anywhere, anytime, in the face, in the neck—whatever it took to make the play, as long as it was aggressive, within the rules."

Though soft-spoken off the field, Wilcox proved to be a ferocious competitor who often took advantage of the rules in effect at the time, once saying, "They didn't fine you on Monday for something you did on Sunday. I always wanted to make sure that the other players knew you were there. I don't think you intentionally tried to hurt anybody, but I wanted to be involved in every play, right in the middle of it."

Identified as one of the 12 toughest men in the league by an informal poll of NFL coaches, players, and scouts taken during the early 1970s for the book *Inside Pro Football*, Wilcox, said the report, "has earned a league-wide reputation as a 'hitter.' He doesn't push or pull and shove. He hits people with hard hammer blows that send them reeling. Tight ends who run patterns across the field are pet targets of the San Francisco defensive star. More than once, Dave has almost decapitated an unwary tight end. Now, most of them look for him before they start across the middle."

Speaking to the accuracy of the survey, John Brodie said, "He's just a right man, at peace with himself. But, if you talk to any tight end that ever played this game, he is the meanest, most ornery guy that ever played the game. I think he is the best outside linebacker that has ever played the game, by a long way."

Former Minnesota Vikings quarterback Joe Kapp expressed similar sentiments when he said, "A lot of linebackers have that same size and speed. I can recall watching Wilcox between plays. He had a way of crossing his legs and looking nonchalant. But the fact is, once that ball was snapped, he brought an intensity, whether it was on a blitz, whether it was on covering a man, or making the tackle, I gotta say that Dave Wilcox played the position as well as anybody that's ever played the position."

Former 49ers offensive line coach Dick Stanfel agreed, once stating, "As far as I'm concerned, Dave is the finest outside linebacker I have ever seen in pro football."

Yet, despite his all-around brilliance, Wilcox often failed to receive the kind of notoriety he deserved because of his quiet off-field demeanor and the lack of overall success the 49ers experienced his first several years in the league, with one NFL observer remarking, "No one played better or was forgotten faster than Dave Wilcox."

Never one to seek the spotlight, Wilcox remained content knowing that he did his job to the best of his ability, saying, "You have to have enough pride to want to be the best. When no one completes a pass on your side or runs your hole, that gives you a better feeling than what someone says about you in a book."

Continuing to excel at outside linebacker for the 49ers after they developed into a contender during the early 1970s, Wilcox earned All-NFC honors four straight times, before undergoing a second surgery on his troublesome right knee prior to the start of the 1974 campaign. Unable to perform at the same lofty level following his operation, Wilcox stated midway through the season, "It's frustrating not being able to do something you normally can because of a restriction you have no control over."

Choosing to announce his retirement at the end of the year, Wilcox ended his career with 14 interceptions, 149 interception-return yards, 12 fumble recoveries, 38½ sacks, two defensive touchdowns, and countless unrecorded tackles. Wilcox also missed just one game his 11 years in the league, appearing in 153 out of 154 contests, 145 of which he started.

Looking back on his playing career, Wilcox, who remains active with his wife in youth athletics through fundraising auctions in his home state of Oregon, says, "I think I was a very fundamentally sound player. . . . Defensively, I had an area, and I did not like people in that area. So, when I prepared to play the game, it was to keep everybody out of that area. Nobody was gonna run in my area, and nobody was gonna pass in my area. This is my spot, and nobody was welcome there, except me."

Wilcox added, "I did what I was asked to do as a player, and, whatever I did, basically, probably did better than anybody. I don't want to sound like I'm bragging at all, but nobody ever ran to our side. If they ran, they would never make many yards. It all kind of comes back to this—this is my spot, and it's kind of like you're king of the hill and nobody's gonna knock you off of it."

CAREER HIGHLIGHTS

Best Season

Wilcox gained consensus First-Team All-Pro recognition in both 1971 and 1972, performing especially well in the second of those campaigns, when he picked off three passes and recovered three fumbles. However, San Francisco's coaching staff, which rated the team's players based on their performance at the end of each season, gave Wilcox the highest grade of his career following the conclusion of the 1973 campaign. With the typical score for a linebacker being 750, Wilcox received a grade of 1,306 after recording 104 solo tackles, 13 tackles for loss, and four forced fumbles, earning in the process NFC Linebacker of the Year honors from the NFL Players Association.

Memorable Moments/Greatest Performances

Wilcox scored the first touchdown of his career when he ran 8 yards to paydirt after recovering a fumble during a 27–21 win over the Detroit Lions on November 14, 1965.

Wilcox helped anchor a 49ers defense that limited the Los Angeles Rams to just 26 yards rushing and 142 yards of total offense during a 21–13 victory on November 6, 1966.

Wilcox and his cohorts turned in another dominant performance on September 24, 1967, with the 49ers recording eight sacks and surrendering just 64 yards rushing and 97 yards of total offense during a 38–7 manhandling of the Atlanta Falcons.

Although the 49ers lost to Atlanta by a score of 21–7 on October 19, 1969, Wilcox picked off two passes in one game for the first time in his career.

Wilcox starred in defeat once again in the 1971 NFC championship game, recording four solo tackles, five assists, two passes defensed, and one sack during a 14–3 loss to the Dallas Cowboys.

Wilcox's superior run-defense helped the 49ers limit New Orleans to just 7 yards rushing and 84 yards of total offense during a 37–2 mauling of the Saints on October 1, 1972.

Wilcox contributed to a 20–6 win over the Packers on November 26, 1973, by recording a pair of interceptions.

Wilcox ended his career in style, clinching a 35–21 victory over the Saints in his final game as a pro on December 15, 1974, by returning his interception of a Bobby Scott pass 21 yards for a touchdown late in the fourth quarter.

Notable Achievements

- Scored two defensive touchdowns.
- Missed just one game entire career, appearing in 153 out of 154 contests.
- Recorded 104 solo tackles in 1973.
- Tied for sixth in franchise history with 12 fumble recoveries.
- Three-time division champion (1970, 1971, and 1972).
- 1973 NFC NFLPA Linebacker of the Year.
- Seven-time Pro Bowl selection (1966, 1968, 1969, 1970, 1971, 1972, and 1973).
- Two-time First-Team All-Pro selection (1971 and 1972).
- Two-time Second-Team All-Pro selection (1967 and 1973).
- Three-time First-Team All-NFC selection (1971, 1972, and 1973).
- 1970 Second-Team All-NFC selection.
- Inducted into 49ers Hall of Fame in 2009.
- Elected to Pro Football Hall of Fame in 2000.

14

JOHN BRODIE

The longest-tenured player in franchise history, John Brodie spent his entire 17-year NFL career in San Francisco, sharing a love/hate relationship with the hometown fans much of the time. After serving primarily as Y. A. Tittle's backup his first few years in the league, Brodie started for the 49ers behind center for more than a decade, bearing the brunt of the blame for the lack of overall success they experienced for most of the 1960s, before leading them to their first three division championships during the early 1970s. Conducting himself with grace and dignity the entire time, Brodie passed for the second-most yards and threw the third-most touchdown passes in team annals, earning in the process two Pro Bowl selections, two All-Pro nominations, and one league MVP trophy. And following the conclusion of his playing career, Brodie received the additional honors of having his #12 retired by the 49ers and being inducted into the team's Hall of Fame.

Born in Menlo Park, California, on August 14, 1935, John Riley Brodie grew up in the Montclair district of Oakland, where he attended Montclair Grammar School, before making a name for himself as a multi-sport star at Oakland Technical High School. A youth tennis champion, Brodie also earned All-City honors in baseball, basketball, and football, prompting Stanford University to offer him an athletic scholarship.

Although Brodie initially planned to compete in several sports at Stanford, he chose to focus exclusively on football and golf when a separated shoulder he sustained in a freshman basketball game forced him to miss both the basketball and baseball seasons. Healthy by the start of his sophomore year, Brodie secured spots on the school's football and golf teams, performing so well in both sports the next three years that he eventually had to make a difficult decision.

Despite being selected by the 49ers with the third overall pick of the 1957 NFL Draft after gaining consensus All-America recognition his senior year by leading the nation in pass completions (139), passing yards

John Brodie led the 49ers to three straight division titles during the early 1970s.
Courtesy of Mike Traverse

(1,633), touchdown passes (12), and completion percentage (.579), Brodie remained uncertain as to whether or not he wished to pursue a career in football, especially after he spent most of his first three seasons in San Francisco sitting on the bench behind Y. A. Tittle. Continuing to compete on the golf course during the offseason, Brodie shot an opening-round 65 at the San Francisco Open, won the Northern California Amateur golf tournament in 1958, and qualified for the US Open in 1959.

Ultimately, though, Brodie chose football over golf, recalling years later, "You talk about pressure. I was always worried that I wasn't going to make the cut. Fact is, there was only one time I was close enough to say I was in competition in the final round. I had to make up my mind. I couldn't be pro in two sports and do justice to either one."

After starting just nine games for the 49ers his first three years in the league, Brodie began to garner more significant playing time in 1960, when he passed for 1,111 yards, threw six touchdown passes and nine interceptions, completed 49.8 percent of his passes, and posted a passer rating of 57.5 while sharing playing time with Tittle. Assuming the starting role the following year after the 49ers traded Tittle to the New York Giants, Brodie performed relatively well his first year as a full-time starter, finishing third in the league with 2,588 yards passing, throwing 14 TD passes and 12 interceptions, completing 54.8 percent of his passes, and posting a passer rating of 84.7. Brodie compiled decent numbers again in 1962, finishing the year with 2,272 yards passing, 18 touchdown passes, 16 interceptions, a pass-completion percentage of 57.6, and a passer rating of 79.0, before missing all but three games the following year after breaking his arm in an automobile accident during the offseason.

Fully recovered by the start of the 1964 campaign, Brodie reclaimed his starting job, after which he went on to pass for 2,498 yards, throw 14 touchdown passes and 16 interceptions, and complete 49.2 percent of his passes for a 49ers team that won just four games. Brodie followed that up with arguably his finest statistical season, earning Pro Bowl and Second-Team All-Pro honors in 1965 by leading all NFL quarterbacks with 3,112 passing yards, 30 TD passes, and a pass-completion percentage of 61.9, while also finishing second in the league with a passer rating of 95.3, with his outstanding play helping the 49ers improve their record to 7-6-1.

Unfortunately, the 49ers posted a winning mark just three other times during the 1960s, never winning more than seven games in any single season. And, although the 49ers' defense consistently ranked in the bottom half of the league in most categories throughout the period, Brodie received much of the blame for the team's failures, with the fans at Kezar Stadium often booing him for his somewhat inconsistent play, which Bob Oates addressed in the *1963 Street & Smith's Yearbook* when he wrote, "John runs well, handles the ball smoothly, and is a clever passer, though his arm may not be the strongest in the league. . . . If he has a glaring weakness, it is that he seems subject to 'off' days, a distinction which is not exactly unique."

Two years later, Oates further expounded upon Brodie's shortcomings when he suggested, "Brodie is a quarterback who can do everything a quarterback has to do pretty well. He can throw short with reasonable accuracy, he can throw far enough, and he scrambles decently. The problem with John is that he isn't great at anything."

Constantly reminding Brodie of any flaws in his arsenal, the hometown faithful often called for his backup to be summoned from the bench and berated him unmercifully as he ran off the field following a loss, frequently hurling projectiles at him and his teammates, with Brodie recalling, "Sometimes, they didn't bother to take the beer out of the cans. Finally, we had to put up a Cyclone fence to protect ourselves from their hardware."

Once asked by a reporter if he heard the boos raining down upon him, Brodie responded, "I'd have heard 'em if I was down at Third and Market . . . I can't turn off my ears."

On another occasion, Brodie expressed the degree to which he empathized with the fans by saying, "All week long, they catch hell from their bosses and, maybe sometimes, from their wives. They get all jammed up. Who could blame them? One day a week, they get out to the game, and all of a sudden, they're my bosses. They can shout whatever they want. Ok, let 'em."

Despite the harsh treatment that Brodie often received from the hometown fans, he chose to remain in San Francisco after the Houston Oilers of the rival American Football League offered him a huge contract following his outstanding performance in 1965. With the 49ers improving their contract offer to him, Brodie agreed to stay in the City by the Bay for several more seasons—a period during which he experienced some of his greatest success.

After posting relatively modest numbers in 1966 and 1967, Brodie led the NFL with 3,020 yards passing and finished second in the league with 22 TD passes and a pass-completion percentage of 57.9 in 1968, although he also threw a league-high 21 picks. Brodie followed that up by passing for 2,405 yards and 16 touchdowns in 1969, even though he missed some playing time after developing tendinitis in his throwing arm. Brodie then reached the apex of his career in 1970, earning Pro Bowl, First-Team All-Pro, and NFL MVP honors by leading the league with 2,941 passing yards, 24 touchdown passes, and a passer rating of 93.8, while also throwing only 10 interceptions, with his exceptional play eliciting the following writeup from a short-lived football magazine called *Pro Quarterback*: "John Brodie always has had a style which impresses people, whether they're teammates, rivals or professional observers. 'If I had an obstacle course for passes,' said one scout, 'where they had to throw a variety of passes, I think Brodie would rank right up there at the top. Maybe behind Joe Namath, but right in there with Unitas and Jurgensen.'"

Meanwhile, legendary Dallas Cowboys head coach Tom Landry stated, "The highest tribute that can be paid a quarterback is to say that he strikes a little fear into whatever defensive team he faces. Brodie does that. I marvel at the way he has now mastered the art of quarterback."

Although Brodie never again performed at the same lofty level, he led the 49ers to two more division titles, before losing his starting job to Steve Spurrier in 1973. Choosing to announce his retirement at season's end, Brodie ended his playing career with 31,548 passing yards, 214 touchdown passes, 224 interceptions, a pass-completion percentage of 55.0, and a passer rating of 72.3. He also gained 1,167 yards on the ground and ran for 22 touchdowns. At the time of his retirement, Brodie ranked third in NFL history in total passing yardage, trailing only Hall of Fame quarterbacks Johnny Unitas and Fran Tarkenton.

After retiring from football, Brodie briefly served as an NFL football and golf analyst for NBC Sports, before spending several years competing as a professional golfer on the Senior PGA Tour. However, after posting one win and 12 top-10 finishes, Brodie had to adopt a more sedentary lifestyle when he suffered a major stroke in 2000 that nearly killed him. Now 85 years of age, Brodie currently resides in La Quinta, California.

Reflecting back on Brodie's playing career, Bill Walsh, who arrived in San Francisco six years after Brodie played his last game for the 49ers, said, "He carried the team through some of the roughest times and some of the best times. What he could do that you don't see much now in football is he had a touch on his passes. He could throw the soft screen pass, or he could throw the ball over someone's head. He could drill the ball if he needed to. He was an absolute technician and an artist. He had the instincts of a great football player, and he was one of the greatest performers at the quarterback position in history."

CAREER HIGHLIGHTS

Best Season

Brodie performed exceptionally well for the 49ers in 1965, leading all NFL quarterbacks with 242 pass completions, 3,112 yards passing, 30 touchdown passes, and a 61.9 pass-completion percentage. However, he had his finest all-around season in 1970, earning First-Team All-Pro and NFL MVP honors by completing 59 percent of his passes and leading the league with 2,941 yards passing, 24 TD passes, and a total quarterback rating of 93.8. Commenting on the outstanding play of his quarterback following the conclusion of the campaign, 49ers head coach Dick Nolan proclaimed,

"Brodie has always been a good quarterback. Last season he was a great one. The 49ers were a better ball club, stronger in almost every department. But it was John's consistency that brought us the division championship."

Memorable Moments/Greatest Performances

Brodie threw the first touchdown pass of his career while serving in a mop-up role during a 31–10 loss to the Detroit Lions on November 17, 1957, collaborating with Billy Wilson on a 20-yard scoring play in the fourth quarter.

Working in relief of Y. A. Tittle, Brodie gave the 49ers a 14–10 win over the Lions on October 9, 1960, by throwing a pair of fourth-quarter touchdown passes to Billy Wilson and R. C. Owens.

Brodie led the 49ers to a lopsided 35–3 victory over the Washington Redskins in the opening game of the 1961 regular season by throwing for 237 yards and four touchdowns, the longest of which went 34 yards to running back J. D. Smith.

Brodie had a big game against the Chicago Bears on November 19, 1961, passing for 322 yards and three touchdowns during a 41–31 49ers' win, with his two TD tosses to split end Aaron Thomas covering 70 and 45 yards.

Brodie led the 49ers to a 22–21 win over the eventual NFL champion Green Bay Packers on December 10, 1961, by throwing for 328 yards and two touchdowns, the longest of which came on a 51-yard connection with Bernie Casey.

Brodie passed for 272 yards and four touchdowns during a 35–12 win over the Minnesota Vikings on December 2, 1962, collaborating three times with Bernie Casey on scoring plays that covered 20, 48, and 40 yards.

Brodie directed the 49ers to a 31–21 victory over the Bears on October 4, 1964, finishing the game with 252 yards passing and three TD passes, the longest of which went 43 yards to Dave Parks.

Brodie had another big day against the Bears in the 1965 regular-season opener, earning NFL Offensive Player of the Week honors for the first of four times by throwing for 269 yards and four touchdowns during a 52–24 win, with the longest of his TD passes being a 59-yard connection with Bernie Casey.

Brodie passed for 209 yards and a career-high five touchdowns during a 45–24 victory over the Minnesota Vikings on November 28, 1965, collaborating twice with John David Crow on scoring plays, and once each with Bernie Casey, Dave Kopay, and Dave Parks.

Brodie led the 49ers to a 27–20 win over the Packers on December 1, 1968, by throwing for 301 yards and three touchdowns, the longest of which went 59 yards to running back Bill Tucker.

Brodie starred during a 20–17 victory over the Baltimore Colts on November 16, 1969, passing for 356 yards and two touchdowns, with his 18-yard TD strike to Jimmy Thomas in the fourth quarter providing the margin of victory.

Brodie gave the 49ers a 34–31 win over the Cleveland Browns on September 27, 1970, when he collaborated once again with Thomas late in the final period, this time from 61 yards out. Brodie finished the game with 277 yards passing and three TD passes.

Brodie had an extremely efficient afternoon against the Bears on November 8, 1970, completing 21 of 28 pass attempts for 317 yards and three touchdowns during a 37–16 Niners' win, with the longest of his TD passes going 79 yards to Gene Washington.

Brodie led the 49ers to a 31–3 win over the Philadelphia Eagles on October 3, 1971, by passing for 262 yards and three touchdowns, the longest of which came on a 42-yard connection with tight end Ted Kwalick.

Coming off the bench to replace an ineffective Steve Spurrier, Brodie led the 49ers to a 20–17 victory over the Minnesota Vikings in the 1972 regular-season finale by completing 10 of 15 passes for 165 yards and two touchdowns, with his 2-yard TD toss to Dick Witcher in the game's closing moments putting the 49ers in the playoffs.

Notable Achievements

- Passed for more than 3,000 yards twice, topping 2,500 yards four other times.
- Threw more than 20 touchdown passes three times, tossing 30 TD passes once.
- Completed more than 60 percent of passes twice.
- Posted touchdown-to-interception ratio of better than 2–1 once.
- Posted passer rating above 80.0 four times, topping 90.0 twice.
- Led NFL in pass completions three times, passing yards three times, touchdown passes twice, pass completion percentage twice, and passer rating once.
- Finished second in NFL in pass completions once, passing yards once, touchdown passes once, completion percentage twice, and passer rating once.

- Finished third in NFL in pass completions twice, passing yards twice, and pass completion percentage twice.
- Holds 49ers record for most seasons played (17).
- Ranks among 49ers career leaders with 201 games played (5th), 4,491 pass attempts (2nd), 2,469 pass completions (2nd), 31,548 passing yards (2nd), and 214 touchdown passes (3rd).
- Three-time division champion (1970, 1971, and 1972).
- Four-time NFL Offensive Player of the Week.
- 1965 NFL Comeback Player of the Year.
- 1970 NFL MVP.
- Two-time Pro Bowl selection (1965 and 1970).
- 1970 First-Team All-Pro selection.
- 1965 Second-Team All-Pro selection.
- 1970 First-Team All-NFC selection.
- #12 retired by 49ers.
- Inducted into 49ers Hall of Fame in 2009.

15

HUGH MCELHENNY

The finest open-field runner of his time, Hugh McElhenny combined with Joe Perry to give the 49ers arguably the NFL's most potent running tandem for much of the 1950s. Nicknamed "The King" for his greatness on the football field, McElhenny possessed outstanding speed, superb vision, and incredible balance—qualities that made him a threat to score every time he touched the football. Surpassing 1,000 yards from scrimmage twice and 1,000 all-purpose yards three times during his nine years in San Francisco, McElhenny continues to rank among the franchise's all-time leaders in several offensive categories some 60 years after he played his last game for the 49ers. A five-time Pro Bowler and five-time All-Pro, McElhenny later received the additional honors of having his #39 retired by the 49ers and being inducted into the Pro Football Hall of Fame.

Born to an Irish father and Canadian mother in Los Angeles on December 31, 1928, Hugh Edward McElhenny Jr. began his football career as a 15-year-old, 125-pound freshman at L.A.'s George Washington High School in 1943. In addition to starring on the gridiron for the Generals over the course of the next four seasons, McElhenny excelled in track, posting a time of 9.8 seconds in the 100-yard dash, while also setting state high school records in the broad jump, high hurdles, and low hurdles.

Recruited by several major colleges, including Alabama, Notre Dame, Navy, Nebraska, UCLA, Oregon, and Kansas, McElhenny recalled, "When I finished high school, I could have gone to any university in the country." After initially accepting a football and track scholarship to USC, McElhenny withdrew from the agreement when the school reneged on its offer to help subsidize him by paying him $65 per month for the ludicrous chore of watering the grass around the Tommy Trojan statue.

A foreign language short of being eligible to participate in college athletics, McElhenny subsequently enrolled at Compton Junior College, where he spent one year starring alongside future NFL teammate Joe Perry in the backfield, helping to lead the Tartars to an undefeated season and a victory

Hugh McElhenny combined with Joe Perry to give the 49ers the NFL's most formidable running tandem for much of the 1950s.
Courtesy of RMYAuctions.com

in the 1948 Junior Rose Bowl. Making an extremely favorable impression on Tom Harmon during his time at Compton, McElhenny drew praise from the former Heisman Trophy winner, who gushed, "I've never seen such a combination of speed and size."

Choosing to accept an athletic scholarship to the University of Washington following his one year at Compton, McElhenny spent the next three seasons starring at fullback for the Huskies, earning All–Pacific Coast Conference honors twice and All-America recognition once by setting then-school records for most rushing yards in a career (2,499) and a season (1,107), while also establishing a single-game school mark that still stands by gaining 296 yards on the ground during a victory over arch-rival Washington State in 1950.

Nevertheless, McElhenny's years in Seattle proved to be highly controversial since rumors abounded that the university paid him $10,000 a year for his services. McElhenny also did not get along well with head football coach Howie Odell, who constantly admonished him for showing up late to practice, ignoring training rules, and drinking too much. While McElhenny later admitted to excessive libation, he defended himself against the first charge by explaining that team practices often conflicted with his class schedule.

Paying very little attention to any allegations made against McElhenny, the 49ers made him the ninth overall pick of the 1952 NFL Draft when they selected him in the first round, after which they paired him with former Compton teammate Joe Perry in their offensive backfield. Excelling at halfback alongside Perry his first year in the league, McElhenny earned Pro Bowl, First-Team All-Pro, and NFL Rookie of the Year honors by rushing for 684 yards, making 26 receptions for 367 yards, accumulating another 680 yards returning punts and kickoffs, scoring 10 touchdowns, finishing second in the league with 1,051 yards from scrimmage, and topping the circuit with 1,731 all-purpose yards and an average of 7.0 yards per carry. McElhenny followed that up with another fine season, once again gaining Pro Bowl and First-Team All-Pro recognition in 1953 by rushing for 503 yards, gaining another 474 yards on 30 pass receptions, scoring five touchdowns, and finishing second in the league with 1,449 all-purpose yards.

A separated shoulder suffered during a 31–27 loss to the Chicago Bears in Week 6 of the 1954 campaign brought McElhenny's season to a premature end, forcing him to miss the final six contests. Sharing playing time with veteran Joe Arenas and rookie Dicky Moegle when he returned to action the following year, McElhenny rushed for only 327 yards and accumulated just 729 yards from scrimmage. However, he rebounded in a big way in 1956, earning Pro Bowl and Second-Team All-Pro honors by amassing a career-high 1,109 yards from scrimmage and finishing third in the league with 916 yards rushing, eight rushing touchdowns, and 1,447 all-purpose yards.

Standing 6'1" and weighing 195 pounds, McElhenny possessed a sculpted body that featured broad shoulders and a 32-inch waist. Blessed with exceptional running speed and extraordinary balance as well, McElhenny posted a personal-best time of 9.6 seconds in the 100-yard dash while in college, which rivaled that of the reigning PCC sprint champion, and regularly defeated Olympic decathlete Bob Mathias in the low and high hurdles during his time at Washington.

McElhenny's explosive speed and tremendous agility forced opposing teams to alter their game plans prior to facing the 49ers, with Los Angeles Rams coach Hampton Pool commenting, "Preparing for a team that lists McElhenny on the roster, you just can't take any chances."

McElhenny's amazing peripheral vision and unique ability to change directions at will also contributed to his ability to navigate his way past opposing defenders, with Joe Perry saying, "Mac was the best open-field runner of our era. He was a will o' the wisp out there. Sayers was a great open-field runner too, but he was different than Mac. It's hard to pinpoint what it was."

Called "the best running back I have seen in a long, long time" by former Bears quarterback Johnny Lujack, McElhenny also received praise for his long, graceful stride from Steve Sabol of NFL Films, who referred to him as "A true artist of the Gridiron, descendant of Grange, ancestor to Payton," and proclaimed, "McElhenny was a Running Back. Almost no one has brought to that calling the same art and bravura that identified his game. They lifted his broken field running to the edge of the concert hall. Somebody said it was the closest approach he's ever seen to ballet on the football field."

Meanwhile, Washington State coach Jim Sutherland marveled at McElhenny's extraordinary peripheral vision, stating, "If you ever watched McElhenny, you'd think he had eyes in the back of his head. I've seen him cut away from a tackler that 99 percent of the backs wouldn't even have seen. It wasn't instinct—he just saw the guy, out of the corner of his eye."

Former 49ers teammate and close friend Billy Wilson addressed another of McElhenny's greatest strengths when he said, "There's no question he could do everything. He could change direction on a dime. He had great cutting ability, where other backs were just slashers."

In discussing the attitude that he brought with him to the playing field, McElhenny revealed, "My attitude carrying the ball was fear, not a fear of getting hurt, but a fear of getting caught from behind and taken down and embarrassing myself and my teammates."

McElhenny continued, "I was never an individual that liked body contact, so I always tried to avoid it as much as I could, and maybe that was the reason that I ran the way that I did."

McElhenny then tried to explain the success he experienced on the football field by saying, "Speed is one ingredient. I had pretty good speed, but I couldn't beat Joe Perry in the 50. I could beat him in the 100, though.

To be a good running back, well, it's just God's gift. It's not something you can teach. I did things by instinct. Running, balance, all of it was instinct. You also have to know where other people are in the field."

McElhenny's instincts and God-given ability helped make him one of the most celebrated players of his time, with former NFL commissioner Bert Bell stating emphatically, "McElhenny is the best runner in the history of the National Football League."

Longtime NFL official Tommy Timlin agreed with Bell's assessment, proclaiming, "Hugh is the best runner of all time, college or pro."

Red Strader, who served as a coach in San Francisco from 1952 to 1955, said, "Hugh McElhenny is the greatest of them all. I played fullback with the old Chicago Bulls against Red Grange. Grange was an elusive but soft runner. McElhenny has better change of pace, is two seconds faster and more than 20 pounds heavier than Grange, which gives Mac a lot more power."

Defensive back Dean Berby, who played with McElhenny in college and against him in the pros, stated, "Jimmy Brown was the greatest running back I ever saw because he was all power. Hugh's biggest thing was acceleration and change of direction . . . Brown was the greatest, but I would put Hugh in the top half-dozen all-time running backs."

McElhenny earned his last two Pro Bowl selections as a member of the 49ers in 1957 and 1958, totaling 929 yards rushing, 1,753 yards from scrimmage, 1,918 all-purpose yards, and 11 touchdowns over the course of those two seasons, before injuries and advancing age forced him to assume a less prominent role the next two years. After McElhenny served them as a part-time player in 1959 and 1960, the 49ers failed to protect him in the 1961 NFL expansion draft, allowing the Minnesota Vikings to claim him. McElhenny left San Francisco with career totals of 4,288 yards rushing, 195 receptions, 2,666 receiving yards, 6,954 yards from scrimmage, 9,100 all-purpose yards, 35 rushing touchdowns, and 51 total touchdowns. He also averaged a robust 4.9 yards per carry during his nine years in the City by the Bay.

McElhenny ended up spending two seasons in Minnesota, earning Pro Bowl honors for the sixth and final time in 1961 by rushing for 570 yards, amassing 853 yards from scrimmage and 1,069 all-purpose yards, and scoring seven touchdowns, one of which came on a spectacular 32-yard run against the 49ers during which he avoided tackles by seven of his former teammates. Later identifying that touchdown as the most satisfying of his career, McElhenny revealed that he wanted to score in the worst way as a means of gaining a measure of revenge against 49ers head coach

Red Hickey, with whom he did not see eye-to-eye during his time in San Francisco.

After reuniting with former 49ers teammate Y. A. Tittle in New York in 1963, McElhenny spent one final season with the Lions, before announcing his retirement following the conclusion of the 1964 campaign with career totals of 5,281 yards rushing, 264 receptions, 3,247 receiving yards, 8,528 yards from scrimmage, 11,375 all-purpose yards, and 60 TDs.

Following his playing days, McElhenny rejoined the 49ers as a color commentator from 1966 to 1972, before becoming vice president of the Washington Transit Authority in Seattle. He also later worked for a local bottling company until retiring to private life in 1995. Just two years later, doctors diagnosed McElhenny as having a rare nerve disorder called Guillain-Barre syndrome, which almost killed him. Temporarily paralyzed from the neck down, McElhenny had to use a walker for a year, during which time he lost nearly one-third of his body weight. Fortunately, McElhenny eventually recovered from his illness and continues to grace us with his presence.

49ERS CAREER HIGHLIGHTS

Best Season

McElhenny had an outstanding year for the 49ers in 1956, finishing third in the NFL with a career-high 916 yards rushing, while also ranking among the league leaders with 1,109 yards from scrimmage, 1,447 all-purpose yards, and eight rushing touchdowns. But he performed even better as a rookie in 1952, earning First-Team All-Pro and NFL Rookie of the Year honors by gaining 684 yards on the ground, placing near the top of the league rankings with 1,051 yards from scrimmage and 10 touchdowns, and leading the NFL with 1,731 all-purpose yards and a rushing average of 7.0 yards per carry, with his exceptional play prompting *Sport Magazine* to identify him as the NFL Player of the Year.

Memorable Moments/Greatest Performances

McElhenny led the 49ers to a 37–14 victory over the Dallas Texans on October 5, 1952, by gaining 170 yards on just seven carries and scoring two TDs, which came on a career-long 89-yard run and a 33-yard pass from Y. A. Tittle.

McElhenny turned in a tremendous all-around effort during a 40–16 win over the Chicago Bears on October 19, 1952, carrying the ball 12 times for 103 yards, gaining another 33 yards on three pass receptions, and returning a punt 94 yards for a touchdown, with his 122 punt-return yards on the day giving him a total of 258 all-purpose yards. Following the conclusion of the contest, 49ers quarterback Frankie Albert paid tribute to McElhenny by entering the locker room, presenting him with the game ball, and telling him, "You're now the King," before turning to Joe Perry and saying, "Joe, you're just the Jet."

McElhenny followed that up with another strong outing, carrying the ball five times for 93 yards and scoring a pair of touchdowns during a 48–21 win over the Texans on October 26, 1952, with one of his TDs coming on an 83-yard run and the other on a 19-yard pass from Frankie Albert.

Although the 49ers lost to the Giants by a score of 23–14 on November 9, 1952, McElhenny made perhaps the most memorable play of his career when he ran half the length of the field without his helmet after making a diving catch of a Y. A. Tittle pass at the San Francisco 35 yard line. More than 60 years later, McElhenny's brilliant 77-yard catch-and-run received a No. 93 ranking from the NFL Network on that station's list of the 100 greatest plays in NFL history.

McElhenny helped lead the 49ers to a 31–24 victory over the Bears on October 17, 1954, by carrying the ball 10 times for 114 yards and two TDs, one of which came on a 47-yard scamper.

McElhenny gained more than 100 yards on the ground again the following week, rushing for 126 yards and one touchdown during a 37–31 win over the Lions on October 24, 1954, with his TD coming on a 60-yard run.

McElhenny provided much of the offensive firepower when the 49ers defeated the Packers by a score of 17–16 on November 18, 1956, carrying the ball 18 times for 140 yards and one touchdown, which came on an 86-yard scamper in the third quarter that represented the longest run in the NFL all year.

McElhenny proved to be a thorn in the side of the Packers once again in the next meeting between the two teams, rushing for 132 yards and one touchdown during a 38–20 49ers win on December 8, 1956.

McElhenny starred during a 17–13 win over the Colts on December 8, 1957, making eight receptions for a career-high 165 yards and one touchdown, which came on a 14-yard pass from John Brodie in the fourth quarter that put the 49ers ahead to stay.

McElhenny contributed to a 33–12 victory over the Packers on November 23, 1958, by carrying the ball 22 times for 159 yards and one touchdown.

Notable Achievements

- Rushed for 916 yards in 1956.
- Amassed more than 1,000 yards from scrimmage twice.
- Amassed more than 1,000 all-purpose yards three times, topping 1,500 yards once.
- Averaged more than 5 yards per carry three times.
- Scored 10 touchdowns in 1952.
- Returned one punt for a touchdown.
- Led NFL with 1,731 all-purpose yards and rushing average of 7.0 yards per carry in 1952.
- Finished second in NFL in yards from scrimmage once and all-purpose yards once.
- Finished third in NFL in rushing yards once, all-purpose yards once, and rushing TDs twice.
- Led 49ers in rushing twice.
- Ranks among 49ers career leaders with 877 rushing attempts (8th), 4,288 rushing yards (7th), 6,954 yards from scrimmage (8th), 1,494 kickoff-return yards (11th), 9,100 all-purpose yards (5th), 35 rushing touchdowns (7th), and 51 touchdowns (9th).
- 1952 NFL Rookie of the Year.
- 1952 *Sport Magazine* NFL Player of the Year.
- Five-time Pro Bowl selection (1952, 1953, 1956, 1957, and 1958).
- Two-time First-Team All-Pro selection (1952 and 1953).
- Three-time Second-Team All-Pro selection (1954, 1956, and 1957).
- Pro Football Reference All-1950s First Team.
- NFL 1950s All-Decade Team.
- #39 retired by 49ers.
- Inducted into 49ers Hall of Fame in 2009.
- Elected to Pro Football Hall of Fame in 1970.

16

Y. A. TITTLE

Although he is perhaps remembered most for leading the New York Giants to three consecutive NFL championship game appearances during the latter stages of his career, Y. A. Tittle previously spent 10 years in San Francisco, serving as the 49ers' primary signal-caller in seven of those. Experiencing many highs and lows during his time in the City by the Bay, Tittle played mostly for mediocre teams, with the 49ers making just one playoff appearance with him starting for them behind center. Nevertheless, the man nicknamed "The Bald Eagle" for his prematurely receding hairline and outstanding leadership ability distinguished himself as a member of the 49ers, earning four Pro Bowl selections, one All-Pro nomination, and one league MVP trophy. And, following the conclusion of his playing career, Tittle received the additional honors of being inducted into both the 49ers' and the Pro Football Hall of Fame.

Born in Marshall, Texas, on October 24, 1926, Yelberton Abraham Tittle grew up idolizing fellow Texan Sammy Baugh, who starred at quarterback for TCU during the 1930s, before embarking on a 16-year Hall of Fame career with the Washington Redskins. After spending much of his youth trying to emulate Baugh by throwing footballs through hanging tires, as he had seen his hero do in newsreels, Tittle began his career on the gridiron at local Marshall High School, which he led to an undefeated record and a trip to the state finals in his senior year.

Subsequently recruited by Louisiana State University and the University of Texas, Tittle elected to attend LSU, where he made a name for himself as a junior by being named MVP of the legendary 1947 Cotton Bowl, which, played during an ice storm, ended in a scoreless tie with Arkansas. Tittle followed that up by earning team MVP honors his senior year, prompting the Detroit Lions to select him with the sixth overall pick of the 1948 NFL Draft. Tittle, though, chose to sign with the Baltimore Colts of the All-America Football Conference, with whom he spent the next two seasons starting at quarterback, throwing for a total of 4,731 yards and 30

Y. A. Tittle's exceptional play behind center in 1957 earned him NFL MVP honors from UPI.
Courtesy of RMYAuctions.com

touchdowns, before competing against NFL players for the first time when the Colts joined the more established league in 1950. However, after the Colts disbanded at the end of the year (a second incarnation of the Colts was born in 1953), Tittle became a member of the 49ers when they selected him with the third overall pick of the 1951 NFL Draft.

After completing just 63 passes for 808 yards and eight touchdowns his first season in San Francisco while serving primarily as Frankie Albert's backup, Tittle began to garner more significant playing time in 1952, when, starting five games behind center, he passed for 1,407 yards and 11 TDs.

However, Tittle didn't become a full-time starter until 1953, when he led the 49ers to a 9-3 record that earned them a close second-place finish in the NFL Western Conference by passing for 2,121 yards, running for six scores, and finishing second in the league with 20 touchdown passes, a pass-completion percentage of 57.5, and a passer rating of 84.1, with his outstanding play gaining him Pro Bowl recognition.

Tittle earned Pro Bowl honors again in 1954 after the 49ers added future Hall of Famer John Henry Johnson to a loaded backfield that already included Joe Perry and Hugh McElhenny. Tittle, who ended up leading the 49ers to a 7-4-1 record by ranking among the league leaders with 2,205 yards passing, a pass-completion percentage of 57.6, and a passer rating of 78.7, recalled years later how playing alongside the other members of San Francisco's "Million Dollar Backfield" made life easy for him, saying, "It made quarterbacking so easy because I just get in the huddle and call anything, and you have three Hall of Fame running backs ready to carry the ball."

Unfortunately, the 49er defense failed to hold up its end, causing the team to plummet to the depths of the Western Conference when Tittle struggled somewhat behind center in 1955. Although Tittle finished second in the NFL with 2,185 yards passing and led the league with 17 touchdown passes, he also topped the circuit with 28 interceptions, completed just 51.2 percent of his passes, and posted a passer rating of just 56.6. Another subpar campaign followed, prompting head coach Frankie Albert to turn briefly to rookie QB Earl Morrall, before reinserting Tittle in the starting lineup toward season's end. Rediscovering his touch in 1957, Tittle earned Pro Bowl, First-Team All-Pro, and league MVP honors from UPI by leading all NFL signal-callers with a pass-completion percentage of 63.1 and ranking among the league leaders with 2,157 yards passing, 13 touchdown passes, and a passer rating of 80.0, with his exceptional performance leading the 49ers to a regular-season record of 8-4 that tied them with the Detroit Lions for the best mark in the Western Conference. However, they subsequently lost a one-game playoff with Detroit, dropping a 31–27 decision that sent the Lions to the NFL championship game, which they won.

In addition to his more famous moniker, the 6-foot, 192-pound Tittle gradually acquired the nickname "Colonel Slick" for his clever ball-handling, sharp play-calling, and ability to read defenses. Also known for his strong throwing arm, Tittle developed a reputation for being the league's best long passer, with journalist and 49ers historian Dave Newhouse saying, "He had a big arm, and he had a big heart. With that bald head, he looked 50 years old, but he could throw the ball."

Tittle's ability to throw the ball deep downfield led to him often collaborating with 49ers wide receiver R. C. Owens on a play that became known as the "alley-oop." With the 6'3" Owens capable of outjumping virtually any defensive back in the league, Tittle frequently threw the ball high in his direction, allowing him to soar in the air and catch it at its highest point.

Although Tittle employed a sidearm, almost underhand motion, he released the ball quickly and delivered it with great accuracy. Exhibiting outstanding "touch" on his shorter passes, Tittle proved to be particularly effective on the screen play, enabling star running backs Perry, McElhenny, and Johnson to frequently pick up huge chunks of yardage.

In discussing his former teammate, Perry said, "Y. A. Tittle was a brainy quarterback. He was a thinker, and he had a strong arm. He would stay in that pocket and wait for the man to get open. He'd wait until he got done what he had to do."

McElhenny stated, "Y. A. was a great player for us, but nobody knew about him back east. When he got to New York, it was like they discovered him."

A perfectionist with a highly competitive spirit and outstanding leadership ability, Tittle never admitted defeat, twice leading all NFL quarterbacks in fourth-quarter comebacks. Praising Tittle for his ability to lead his team back from adversity, Dave Newhouse said, "You always had to worry about Y. A. because he could come back and destroy you."

Newhouse then added, "With those 49er teams, they had to outscore their own defense. If they could have ever drafted a defense instead of all those quarterbacks, Bill Walsh wouldn't have started a legacy. He would have followed one."

Considered one of the finest quarterbacks of his era, Tittle often found himself being compared to the league's other top signal-callers, with Baltimore Colts halfback Lenny Moore, when asked to compare him to teammate Johnny Unitas in 1963, saying, "I played with Tittle in the Pro Bowl two years ago, and I discovered he's quite a guy. . . . He and John, however, are entirely different types . . . Tittle is a sort of 'con man' with his players . . . he comes into a huddle and 'suggests' that maybe this or that will work on account of something he saw happen on a previous play. . . . The way he puts it, you're convinced it's a good idea and maybe it will work. John, now, he's a take-charge guy. . . . He tells you what the other guy's going to do, what he's going to do, and what he wants you to do."

Following his outstanding performance in 1957, Tittle struggled somewhat during the 1958 preseason, causing Frankie Albert to name the much younger John Brodie his starter for the regular-season opener. Although

Tittle ended up starting six contests, he suffered an injury to his right knee ligament during a 35–27 loss to the Colts in Week 10 that brought his season to a premature end. After regaining his starting job in 1959, Tittle spent much of the ensuing campaign sitting on the bench behind Brodie, before being dealt to the Giants for guard Lou Cordileone at season's end. Tittle left the 49ers having passed for 16,016 yards, thrown 108 touchdown passes and 134 interceptions, run for 637 yards and 22 TDs, completed 55.9 percent of his passes, and posted a QBR of 70.0 as a member of the team, leading the Red and Gold to an overall record of 45-31-2 as a starter.

After initially considering retiring rather than switching teams at such an advanced age, the 34-year-old Tittle decided to take a more positive approach to his situation, stating years later, "Throwing a football was the best thing I could do in life, and I had done it since I was in the sixth grade. So, I took my shoulder pads that I'd used for 16 years and went to New York feeling like a rookie trying to make the team for the first time."

Finding new life following his arrival in New York, Tittle ended up becoming the toast of the town after he led the Giants to the Eastern Conference title and an appearance in the NFL championship game three straight times, earning in the process three Pro Bowl selections and two First-Team All-Pro nominations. Tittle also gained recognition as league MVP from United Press International in 1962, before being similarly honored by both the Associated Press and the Newspaper Enterprise Association the following year. Performing especially well those two seasons, Tittle threw for 3,224 yards and a league-leading 33 touchdowns in 1962, before once again topping the circuit with 36 TD passes in 1963, while also passing for 3,145 yards and leading the league with a quarterback rating of 104.8 and a pass-completion percentage of 60.2.

Claiming that Tittle still possessed a strong throwing arm in his mid-30s, Pat Summerall, who played for the Giants from 1958 to 1961, later noted, "We didn't have anybody, nor had we had anybody, who came close to throwing the ball as well as he did. I mean, the ball, you could hear it whistling when he let it go."

Unfortunately for Tittle and the Giants, all three seasons ended in disappointing fashion, with New York losing to Green Bay twice and Chicago once in NFL championship games. And, after age, injuries, and a poor supporting cast caused Tittle to perform poorly in 1964, he announced his retirement at season's end, leaving the game with more passing yards (33,070) and touchdown passes (242) than any other quarterback in pro football history. Tittle also threw 248 interceptions, rushed for 1,245 yards and 39 touchdowns, completed 55.2 percent of his passes, and posted a quarterback rating of 74.3 over the course of his career.

Following his retirement, Tittle, who worked as an insurance salesman in the offseason during his playing days, founded his own company, which he called Y. A. Tittle Insurance & Financial Services. He also spent five seasons serving as a 49ers assistant coach, before leaving the game to focus exclusively on his business, which he developed into a major insurer in the Palo Alto, California, region. After spending his final years suffering from dementia that adversely affected his memory and limited his conversation to a handful of topics, Tittle died of natural causes on October 8, 2017, some two weeks shy of his 91st birthday.

49ERS CAREER HIGHLIGHTS

Best Season

Tittle had arguably his finest statistical season for the 49ers in 1953, when he threw for 2,121 yards and finished second in the NFL with 20 touchdown passes, a pass-completion percentage of 57.5, and a quarterback rating of 84.1. But Tittle earned his lone First-Team All-Pro nomination as a member of the team in 1957 by leading all NFL quarterbacks with 176 pass completions and a pass-completion percentage of 63.1, while also ranking among the league leaders with 2,157 yards passing, 13 TD passes, and a quarterback rating of 80.0, with his outstanding play prompting the UPI to accord him NFL MVP honors.

Memorable Moments/Greatest Performances

Tittle led the 49ers to a 24–14 win over the Chicago Bears on November 1, 1953, by throwing for 304 yards and one touchdown, which came on a 19-yard pass to Billy Wilson.

Tittle followed that up by passing for 301 yards and three touchdowns during a 31–27 win over the Los Angeles Rams on November 8, 1953, with his 17-yard fourth-quarter TD pass to Gordie Soltau providing the margin of victory.

Although Tittle threw only 14 passes during a November 29, 1953, victory over the Baltimore Colts, he completed 10 of them, finishing the game with 220 yards through the air and three TD passes, the longest of which went 61 yards to Billy Wilson.

Tittle concluded the 1953 campaign in style, throwing for 371 yards and four touchdowns during a 45–14 win over the Colts in the regular-season finale, with two of his TD tosses going to Gordie Soltau and the other two to Joe Perry and Billy Wilson.

Tittle directed the 49ers to a lopsided 35–0 victory over the Packers on December 5, 1954, by completing 15 of 18 pass attempts for 233 yards and two touchdowns, one of which came on a 68-yard hookup with Bill Jessup.

Tittle turned in another extremely efficient performance during a 20–17 win over the Colts on December 2, 1956, completing 14 of 18 pass attempts for 284 yards and two touchdowns, the longest of which came on a 77-yard connection with Billy Wilson.

Tittle threw for 268 yards and two touchdowns during a 21–17 win over the Bears on October 13, 1957, with his 7-yard TD toss to R. C. Owens late in the fourth quarter providing the margin of victory.

Tittle and Owens provided further heroics on November 3, 1957, with the two men collaborating on a 41-yard scoring play in the closing moments of a 35–31 victory over the Lions. Tittle finished the game 21-of-28, for 230 yards and two touchdowns.

Tittle continued to be a thorn in the side of the Lions on November 2, 1958, when, with the 49ers trailing by a score of 21–17 and 10 minutes remaining in regulation, he came in to relieve an ineffective John Brodie. After receiving a warm greeting from the nearly 60,000 fans in attendance at Kezar Stadium, Tittle led the 49ers downfield on a scoring drive that culminated with a game-winning 32-yard touchdown pass to Hugh McElhenny.

Tittle led the 49ers to a 33–12 win over the Packers on November 23, 1958, by throwing for 283 yards and three touchdowns, the longest of which went 23 yards to R. C. Owens.

Tittle teamed up with Owens for another big play on October 25, 1959, hitting his favorite receiver with a 46-yard touchdown pass in the final minute of regulation, to give the 49ers a 20–17 win over the Bears.

Notable Achievements

- Passed for more than 2,000 yards four times.
- Threw 20 touchdown passes in 1953.
- Completed more than 60 percent of passes once.
- Posted passer rating above 80.0 twice.
- Led NFL in pass completions once, touchdown passes once, and pass completion percentage once.

- Finished second in NFL in pass completions once, passing yards twice, touchdown passes once, pass completion percentage four times, and passer rating once.
- Finished third in NFL in pass completions twice, passing yards once, touchdown passes once, and passer rating twice.
- Ranks among 49ers career leaders with 2,194 pass attempts (5th), 1,226 pass completions (6th), 16,016 passing yards (5th), and 108 touchdown passes (5th).
- 1957 UPI NFL MVP.
- Four-time Pro Bowl selection (1953, 1954, 1957, and 1959).
- 1957 First-Team All-Pro selection.
- Inducted into 49ers Hall of Fame in 2009.
- Elected to Pro Football Hall of Fame in 1971.

17

GENE WASHINGTON

The 49ers' all-time leader in receiving yards and touchdown receptions at the time of his retirement, Gene Washington proved to be one of the NFL's most dynamic wideouts for much of his career, which he spent almost entirely in San Francisco. A true gamebreaker who possessed good size, outstanding speed, and exceptional leaping ability, Washington led the 49ers in receptions six times and receiving yards eight times, with his career average of 18 yards per catch representing the highest mark in franchise history. One of the first 49ers to amass more than 1,000 receiving yards in a season, Washington continues to rank extremely high in team annals in every major pass-receiving category more than 40 years after he donned the Red and Gold for the last time, with his outstanding play earning him four Pro Bowl selections, three All-Pro nominations, and a spot on the Pro Football Reference All-1970s Second Team.

Born in Tuscaloosa, Alabama, on January 14, 1947, Gene Alden Washington grew up in Long Beach, California, where he starred in football and track while attending Long Beach Polytechnic High School. Offered an athletic scholarship to Stanford University, Washington decided to take full advantage of the school's commitment to integrate minorities into its student body. One of just 25 African American students on a campus of 10,000, Washington spent the next four years serving as a pioneer of sorts, becoming the first black member of the Delta Tau Delta fraternity, while also excelling on the football field for the Cardinals at wide receiver. Originally a quarterback, Washington gradually transitioned to receiver during his time at Stanford, ending his college career with 122 receptions for 1,785 yards and 10 touchdowns. Performing especially well as a senior in 1968, Washington earned All-America honors by setting then-school records for most receptions (71), receiving yards (1,117), and touchdown catches (8) in a single season.

Impressed with Washington's exceptional play at the collegiate level, the 49ers made him the 16th overall pick of the 1969 NFL Draft when

Gene Washington's career average of 18 yards per reception represents the
highest mark in franchise history.
Courtesy of Mike Traverse

they selected him in the middle of the first round, nine spots after they
took Penn State tight end Ted Kwalick with the seventh pick. After earning a starting job during training camp, Washington went on to have an
outstanding rookie season, gaining Pro Bowl and First-Team All-Pro recognition by making 51 receptions for 711 yards and three touchdowns for
a 49ers team that finished just 4-8-2. Performing even better the following
year, Washington helped the 49ers capture the NFC West Division title for
the first of three straight times by leading the NFL with 1,100 receiving
yards and placing near the top of the league rankings with 53 receptions
and 12 TD catches, earning in the process Pro Bowl and First-Team All-Pro
honors once again.

Quickly establishing himself as John Brodie's favorite receiver, Washington developed a special chemistry with his quarterback that he attributed largely to his earlier experiences on the gridiron, saying, "I played quarterback through my junior year at Stanford, so, when I made the switch from quarterback to receiver, as a receiver, I thought the way a quarterback thought. So, often times, a receiver will say to a quarterback, 'I can get open,' but the quarterback can't see the receiver in that particular situation. You might think you're open, but, from my vantage point as a quarterback, you're not open. So, I always thought along the lines of a quarterback, trying to get myself in situations where, not only did I feel that I could maneuver, but the quarterback could see it."

Washington added, "Quarterbacks, they rely on that. They can't wait to see you get open and throw the ball before it's too late. But a lot of receivers don't think about that. All they think about is just their little immediate area. 'Well, I'm here, the defensive back's here, I'm open.' There's a lot more to it than that."

Praising Washington for his ability to see things from his perspective, Brodie stated, "He knew my problems, and he knew how much time he had. He had a little clock in his head, and he took as much as he could, but he didn't take any more. And he knew if I was in trouble, he'd be looking."

Brodie continued, "We saw eye to eye a whole bunch when it came to football. His experience as a quarterback gave him a valuable perspective as a receiver. He knew how the field looked from where I was standing, and that helped him explain to me how the field looked to him, and what worked best for him."

Blessed with a considerable amount of physical talent as well, the 6'2", 185-pound Washington possessed good size, outstanding speed and quickness, and tremendous agility. A precise route-runner who did a superb job of separating himself from his defender, Washington drew praise from longtime NFL head coach George Allen, who said, "Washington was slippery. He was hard to jam. He was a fluid receiver. He'd be on you before you knew it."

John Madden also expressed his admiration for Washington when he compared him to Hall of Fame receiver Lance Alworth in 1970, stating at the time, "He has the same fluidity, the ability to go long or catch the short ones. That's pretty good, comparing a guy to Lance Alworth."

Perhaps bearing an even closer resemblance to Lynn Swann as a receiver, Washington exhibited similar grace and elegance on the playing field, while also displaying the same ability to make diving catches and out-leap defenders for the football. And, once he gathered in the pigskin, Washington used his great quickness to outmaneuver would-be tacklers, making him a threat to score from anywhere on the field.

In addressing Washington's ability to run with the football, Green Bay Packers' perennial All-Pro safety Willie Wood said, "Gene was a great, great receiver. His biggest strength, I think, was running with the ball once he'd catch it. He was almost like a running back in the open field. If the ball was anywhere near him, he was going to get it."

Washington had another outstanding year for the 49ers in 1971, earning his third straight trip to the Pro Bowl by making 46 receptions for 884 yards and four touchdowns, before gaining Pro Bowl and First-Team All-Pro recognition the following year by catching 46 passes, finishing third in the NFL with 918 receiving yards, and leading the league with 12 touchdown receptions.

Although Washington continued to perform at an elite level for another five seasons, he did so in relative obscurity, with the 49ers' failures as a team contributing greatly to the lack of notoriety he received. After advancing to the playoffs three straight times from 1970 to 1972, the 49ers posted a winning mark just once over the course of the next five seasons, a period during which Washington found himself being further hampered by having multiple defenders assigned to him on virtually every play. Nevertheless, Washington remained one of the NFL's most dangerous wideouts, leading the league with an average of 21.2 yards per reception in 1974, before making 44 receptions for 735 yards and nine touchdowns the following year. But, with the 49ers in a rebuilding mode following an embarrassing 2-14 finish in 1978, they traded Washington to the Detroit Lions during the subsequent offseason. Ending his lengthy stint in San Francisco with career totals of 371 receptions, 6,664 receiving yards, and 59 TD catches, Washington ranked either first or second in franchise history in all three categories at the time, with only Billy Wilson having caught more passes.

Washington ended up spending just one season in Detroit, making 14 receptions for 192 yards and one touchdown in 1979, before announcing his retirement. Moving back to California following his playing days, Washington returned to his alma mater, where he spent nearly a decade working in Stanford's athletic department, first in an administrative capacity, and then, as the school's assistant athletic director. Hired as the director of football development for the NFL in 1993, Washington remained in that post for one year, before assuming the position of director of football operations. Functioning in that role for the next 16 years, Washington assumed responsibility for overseeing all aspects of the game, including the on-field conduct of players. Essentially the league's disciplinarian, Washington established codes of conduct that covered everything from post-touchdown celebrations to illegal hits.

When not monitoring players, Washington pursued other interests, including serving on the board of directors of several large companies, including New York Bancorp and Goodrich Petroleum Corporation. Washington also returned to Stanford in 2003 to help their business school create the NFL-Stanford Executive Education Program. Now 74 years of age, Washington has assumed a less-public persona since relinquishing his NFL duties in 2009.

49ERS CAREER HIGHLIGHTS

Best Season

Washington gained First-Team All-Pro recognition in three of his first four seasons, posting the best numbers of his career in 1970, when he led the NFL with 1,100 receiving yards and ranked among the league leaders with 53 receptions and 12 TD catches.

Memorable Moments/Greatest Performances

Washington scored the first two touchdowns of his career during a 27–21 loss to the Los Angeles Rams on October 12, 1969, connecting with John Brodie on pass plays that covered 20 and 33 yards.

Washington topped 100 receiving yards for the first time as a pro almost exactly one year later, making seven receptions for 145 yards and one touchdown during a 20–6 win over the Rams on October 11, 1970, with his TD coming on a 59-yard pass from Brodie.

Washington followed that up with a strong performance against New Orleans, catching four passes for 126 yards and two touchdowns during a 20–20 tie with the Saints on October 18, 1970.

Washington helped lead the 49ers to a 37–16 win over the Bears on November 8, 1970, by making five receptions for 119 yards and two touchdowns, one of which covered 79 yards.

Washington starred against New Orleans once again in the second meeting between the two teams in 1970, making five receptions for 131 yards and three touchdowns during a 38–27 win on December 13, with his TDs coming on passes from John Brodie that covered 30, 37, and 26 yards.

Washington contributed to a 27–10 victory over the New England Patriots on October 31, 1971, by making five receptions for 160 yards and one touchdown, which came on a 71-yard connection with Brodie.

Although Washington made just one reception during the 49ers' 24–20 win over the Redskins in the divisional round of the 1971 playoffs, it went for a 78-yard touchdown.

Washington proved to be a huge factor when the 49ers defeated the San Diego Chargers by a score of 34–3 in the opening game of the 1972 regular season, finishing the day with eight receptions for 140 yards and three touchdowns, the longest of which covered 45 yards.

Washington starred in defeat on November 5, 1972, making six receptions for 164 yards and two touchdowns during a 34–24 loss to the Packers, with his TDs coming on 62- and 34-yard passes from Steve Spurrier.

Washington collaborated with Spurrier on another long pair of scoring plays during a 24–23 win over the Rams on November 9, 1975, with their TD connections covering 42 and 68 yards. Washington finished the game with five receptions for 144 yards and those two TDs.

Washington helped lead the 49ers to a 28–7 victory over the Lions on October 23, 1977, by making four receptions for 112 yards and two touchdowns, which came on passes from Jim Plunkett that covered 32 and 35 yards.

Notable Achievements

- Missed just two games in nine seasons, appearing in 124 of 126 contests.
- Surpassed 50 receptions twice.
- Surpassed 1,000 receiving yards once.
- Scored 12 touchdowns twice.
- Averaged more than 20 yards per reception three times.
- Led NFL in receiving yards once, touchdown receptions once, and yards per reception once.
- Finished second in NFL in touchdown receptions once.
- Finished third in NFL in receiving yards once, touchdown receptions once, and touchdowns once.
- Led 49ers in receptions six times and receiving yards eight times.
- Holds 49ers career record for most yards per reception (18.0).
- Ranks among 49ers career leaders with 371 receptions (8th), 6,664 receiving yards (4th), 6,663 yards from scrimmage (10th), 6,663

all-purpose yards (12th), 59 touchdown receptions (3rd), and 59 touchdowns (7th).

- Three-time division champion (1970, 1971, and 1972).
- Four-time Pro Bowl selection (1969, 1970, 1971, and 1972).
- Three-time First-Team All-Pro selection (1969, 1970, and 1972).
- Four-time First-Team All-NFC selection (1969, 1970, 1971, and 1972).
- Pro Football Reference All-1970s Second Team.

18

BILLY WILSON

One of the NFL's premier receivers for much of the 1950s, Billy Wilson combined soft hands, good speed, tremendous agility, and superior blocking ability to establish himself as the first great wideout in 49ers history. Spending his entire 10-year career in San Francisco, Wilson excelled despite playing in a run-oriented offense, surpassing 50 receptions five times and 800 receiving yards on four separate occasions. Leading the league in pass receptions three times and TD catches once, Wilson earned six Pro Bowl selections and four All-Pro nominations, with his exceptional all-around play also earning him a spot on the Pro Football Reference All-1950s First Team.

Born in Sayre, Oklahoma, on February 3, 1927, William Gene Wilson moved with his family to San Jose, California, at the age of three to escape the Dust Bowl drought that swept through the prairies during the Great Depression. After starring on the gridiron at Campbell Union High School, Wilson enlisted in the US Navy and spent three years serving his country during World War II, before returning to California following his discharge. Wilson subsequently enrolled at San Jose State University, where his strong play over the course of the next three seasons prompted the 49ers to select him in the 22nd round of the 1950 NFL Draft, with the 283rd overall pick, despite his small-college background.

With the 49ers having previously selected six other receivers in that very same draft, Wilson faced long odds in making the team. However, his hard work, dedication, and outstanding play during the preseason ultimately earned him a roster spot, after which he spent his first season in San Francisco assuming a part-time role. Appearing in nine games as a rookie, Wilson made 18 receptions for 268 yards and three touchdowns. Functioning in a similar capacity the following year, Wilson caught 23 passes, amassed 304 receiving yards, and scored another three touchdowns. But, after Wilson joined the starting unit full-time in 1953, he became the first

Billy Wilson led the NFL in pass receptions three times and TD catches once.

49ers' receiver to make a major impact on the NFL, posting the following numbers over the course of the next five seasons:

YEAR	RECS	REC YDS	TD RECS
1953	51	840	10
1954	60	830	5
1955	53	831	7
1956	60	889	5
1957	52	757	6

Ranking among the NFL leaders in receptions and receiving yards all five years, Wilson led the league in the first category three times and finished second another time. He also topped the circuit in TD catches once and amassed the second-most receiving yards in the league twice, with his exceptional play earning him Pro Bowl and All-Pro honors in each of the last four seasons.

Wilson managed to compile the numbers he did even though he played in an offense that predicated much of its success on the running abilities of future Hall of Famers Joe Perry, Hugh McElhenny, and John Henry Johnson. Furthermore, Wilson competed during an era when NFL teams played only 12 games and league rules provided far less protection to quarterbacks and wide receivers.

An outstanding all-around athlete, the lanky Wilson, who stood 6'3" and weighed 190 pounds, possessed good speed, excellent leaping ability, and superb moves, with Don Shula, who played defensive back in the NFL for seven seasons before beginning his Hall of Fame coaching career, recalling, "I remember a play Billy made when he caught a pass, leaped straight up into the air over myself and two other defenders, and ran it in for a touchdown. It was a great play, and he truly was a great receiver. He is one of the few players of another era that would excel today."

Wilson also made an extremely favorable impression on Tom Landry, who once said, "Billy Wilson was almost impossible to cover. He was a great receiver who had a great mind and understanding of the game."

Wilson's greatest assets, though, may well have been his exceptionally soft hands and ability to avoid defenders in the open field, as longtime teammate Bob St. Clair noted when he said, "Billy had hands like glue. His ability to run after the catch was amazing. He is probably one of the most underrated players in NFL history."

Also excelling at wrestling the ball away from defenders and blocking for the team's outstanding stable of running backs, Wilson drew praise from Bill Walsh for his proficiency in both areas, with the legendary 49ers head coach stating, "Billy had speed and incomparable agility. No one could go up for a ball like he could in traffic. He was also one of the best blocking receivers the game has seen."

Known for his fiery disposition and tremendous competitive spirit as well, Wilson, said Y. A. Tittle, was "one of the fiercest competitors I ever played with. He was our #1 receiver. Whenever we needed a big catch, I went to him, because I knew he would make the play."

Fellow 49ers receiver Gordie Soltau expressed similar sentiments when he said of his former teammate, "He was a fierce competitor, fearless, unselfish, a great team player. You couldn't ask for a better teammate."

Soltau then added, "He knew how to go get the ball. Tittle had a lot of confidence in him."

Meanwhile, Hall of Fame safety Emlen Tunnell, when asked to name the toughest receiver he ever faced, said, "Billy Wilson of the 49ers. He's probably the greatest end I ever saw. He gave me more trouble than anybody. Anybody who ever covered him probably would say the same thing."

Continuing to perform at an elite level for two more years, Wilson gained Pro Bowl recognition in 1958 and 1959 by totaling 87 receptions, 1,132 receiving yards, and nine touchdowns over the course of those two seasons, before retiring following the conclusion of the 1960 campaign after being limited by injuries to just four games and three receptions. Ending his career with 407 receptions, 5,902 receiving yards, and 49 TD catches, Wilson retired as the NFL's second-leading all-time receiver, with only Green Bay's Don Hutson having gathered in more passes.

Following his playing days, Wilson spent another 30 years with the 49ers, serving them primarily as a scout or assistant coach during that time. After retiring to private life, Wilson survived a bout with colon cancer in 2004, later saying, "I had two major surgeries and a couple other procedures. I lost a lot of weight, but I'm fine now." Wilson lived another five years, dying of bone cancer at a hospice center in Carlsbad, San Diego, on January 27, 2009, just a few days shy of his 82nd birthday. Upon learning of his passing, 49ers owners Denise and John York released a statement that read: "When you look at what Billy accomplished in his 10 years as a 49ers' player, it's quite remarkable. Considered as one of the greatest wide receivers to ever play the game, Billy's impact on the 49ers organization is far-reaching, not only as a player, but also as a coach and administrator. We are grateful for all of Billy's contributions, and he will be missed."

Despite his many achievements, Wilson has yet to be inducted into the Pro Football Hall of Fame. Stating the belief that he considered Wilson's omission to be a huge oversight, Bill Walsh told the *San Francisco Chronicle* in 2004, "He was the best receiver in the league and led the league in receiving. He was MVP of the Pro Bowl when that game meant something. He was one of the most admired players and respected players in football. . . . I've thought that Billy should have been enshrined years ago. He deserves it as much as a lot of people who have gotten into the Hall of Fame, myself included."

CAREER HIGHLIGHTS

Best Season

Wilson posted outstanding numbers for the 49ers from 1953 to 1956, earning three Second-Team All-Pro nominations by amassing more than 800 receiving yards four straight times, while also recording 60 receptions twice and catching six touchdown passes once. But Wilson had his finest all-around season in 1957, when, in addition to leading the NFL with 52 receptions, he placed near the top of the league rankings with 757 receiving yards and six TD catches, with his exceptional play prompting five different news sources to accord him First-Team All-Pro honors.

Memorable Moments/Greatest Performances

Wilson scored the first touchdown of his career in his very first game as a pro when he gathered in a 25-yard pass from Frankie Albert during a 24–10 win over the Cleveland Browns in the opening game of the 1951 regular season.

Although Wilson made just two receptions for 19 yards during a 19–14 win over the New York Yanks on November 11, 1951, one of those catches went for a 7-yard touchdown in the final minute of regulation that provided the margin of victory.

Wilson helped lead the 49ers to a 23–17 win over the Washington Redskins on November 16, 1952, by making three receptions for 80 yards and one touchdown, which came on a 6-yard pass from Y. A. Tittle in the fourth quarter that provided the margin of victory.

Wilson contributed to a 31–21 win over the Philadelphia Eagles in the 1953 regular-season opener by making three catches for 77 yards and two touchdowns, hooking up with Y. A. Tittle on scoring plays that covered 39 and 37 yards.

Wilson topped 100 receiving yards for the first time in his career later that year, making nine receptions for 127 yards and one TD during a 45–14 win over the Baltimore Colts in the final game of the 1953 regular season.

Wilson helped the 49ers forge a 24–24 tie with the Los Angeles Rams on October 3, 1954, by making 11 receptions for 158 yards.

Although the 49ers lost to the Chicago Bears by a score of 34–23 on October 23, 1955, Wilson had a huge game, making eight receptions for 192 yards and two touchdowns, which came on a pair of long connections with Y. A. Tittle that covered 37 and 72 yards.

Wilson starred in defeat once again on November 27, 1955, catching seven passes for 143 yards and one touchdown during a 26–14 loss to the Baltimore Colts, with his TD coming on a 44-yard hookup with Tittle.

Wilson provided most of the punch the 49ers mustered on offense during a 10–10 tie with the Eagles on November 25, 1956, with his seven receptions for 120 yards accounting for nearly half the yardage (285) they gained on the day.

Wilson came up big for the 49ers on December 2, 1956, making five receptions for 148 yards and two touchdowns during a 20–17 victory over the Colts, with his 77-yard fourth-quarter connection with Y. A. Tittle providing the winning margin.

Although the 49ers lost to the Lions by a score of 31–27 in a one-game playoff to determine the Western Conference champion in 1957, Wilson excelled in his one postseason appearance, finishing the game with nine receptions for 107 yards and one touchdown.

Wilson helped lead the 49ers to a 33–12 win over the hapless Green Bay Packers on November 23, 1958, by making eight receptions for 128 yards and two touchdowns, the longest of which covered 15 yards.

Notable Achievements

- Surpassed 50 receptions five times.
- Surpassed 800 receiving yards four times.
- Scored 10 touchdowns in 1953.
- Led NFL in receptions three times and touchdown receptions once.
- Finished second in NFL in receptions once, receiving yards twice, and touchdowns once.
- Finished third in NFL in receiving yards once and touchdown receptions once.
- Led 49ers in receptions six times and receiving yards six times.
- Ranks among 49ers career leaders with 407 receptions (7th), 5,902 receiving yards (5th), 5,902 yards from scrimmage (11th), 49 touchdown receptions (tied-5th), and 49 touchdowns (tied-10th).
- Six-time Pro Bowl selection (1954, 1955, 1956, 1957, 1958, and 1959).
- 1957 First-Team All-Pro selection.
- Three-time Second-Team All-Pro selection (1954, 1955, and 1956).
- Pro Football Reference All-1950s First Team.

19

NAVORRO BOWMAN

Plagued by injuries that ultimately shortened his career, NaVorro Bowman started only 74 games at inside linebacker for the 49ers over parts of eight seasons. Nevertheless, Bowman combined with Patrick Willis during that time to form one of the most dynamic linebacker tandems in NFL history. Amassing more than 140 tackles in each of his four seasons as a full-time starter, Bowman recorded the fourth-most stops in franchise history, with his exceptional play helping the 49ers win two division titles and one NFC championship. A three-time Pro Bowler, Bowman also gained All-Pro recognition four times, before ending his career with the Oakland Raiders in 2017.

Born in District Heights, Maryland, on May 28, 1988, NaVorro Roderick Bowman began competing in sports at an early age, receiving his introduction to basketball and football at the District Heights Boys and Girls Club. Later developing into an outstanding two-way football player at Suitland High School, Bowman earned First-Team All-State and Maryland Defensive Player of the Year honors his junior year by recording 165 tackles, nine sacks, and three fumble recoveries as a linebacker, while also gaining 1,200 yards on the ground and scoring 22 touchdowns as a running back on offense.

Although Bowman missed most of his senior year with a shoulder injury, he received a scholarship to Penn State University, where, after red-shirting as a freshman, he went on to star for the Nittany Lions at inside linebacker for two seasons despite experiencing great personal loss, with his father, Hillard, dying unexpectedly in June 2008, and his high school coach and good friend, Nick Lynch, losing his life in an automobile accident later that year. Displaying tremendous resolve, Bowman earned First-Team All–Big Ten honors as a junior in 2008 by recording 106 total tackles, 61 solo stops, 16½ tackles for loss, four sacks, two forced fumbles, one fumble recovery, and one interception.

NaVorro Bowman combined with Patrick Willis to form one of the most dynamic linebacker tandems in NFL history.
Courtesy of Jeffrey Beall

Choosing to forgo his final year of college eligibility, Bowman declared himself eligible for the 2010 NFL Draft, where he ended up going to the 49ers in the third round, with the 91st overall pick. Bowman subsequently spent his first season in San Francisco serving the 49ers primarily on special teams, while also seeing a limited amount of duty as a backup on defense, recording a total of 46 tackles over the course of the campaign. Laying claim to the starting left-inside linebacker job in 2011 following the free agent departure of Takeo Spikes during the offseason, Bowman immediately established himself as a force to be reckoned with, earning First-Team All-Pro honors by registering 143 tackles and finishing second in the league with 111 solo stops, with his superb play helping the 49ers compile a regular-season record of 13-3 that earned them their first division title in nearly a decade. Bowman continued to perform at an elite level in each of the next two seasons, gaining Pro Bowl and First-Team All-Pro recognition in both 2012 and 2013 by registering a total of 293 tackles, while also picking off three passes and recording seven sacks.

Combining with Patrick Willis to give the 49ers an elite pair of inside linebackers, Bowman possessed an outstanding combination of speed, quickness, and strength, making him extremely effective in both pass coverage and run defense. Although somewhat undersized at 6'1" and 230 pounds, Bowman made up for whatever he lacked in that area with superior instincts, outstanding pursuit, and sheer tenacity. Capable of engaging blockers at the line of scrimmage or chasing down ball-carriers and receivers in the open field, Bowman, according to 49ers fullback Kyle Juszczyk, possessed "freaky range and deceptive speed for a stockier linebacker."

Meanwhile, in recalling his first encounter with Bowman, 49ers tight end George Kittle revealed that he found himself being totally intimidated by the linebacker's powerful physique, saying, "I was terrified. He's a monster. Are you kidding me? I was a rookie coming from Iowa. Going against a guy like that was . . . I'm pretty sure my entire OTAs, he'd do curls, so he'd look even bigger before practice. Terrifying."

Wide receiver Trent Taylor claimed that he experienced similar feelings when he first arrived in San Francisco, saying of Bowman, "I knew I wasn't trying to get anywhere close to him. He was a scary dude."

Despite their initial trepidation, Bowman's teammates eventually came to embrace his strong work ethic and tremendous determination, with Kittle stating, "He did a really good job of setting the standard. NaVorro always does a great job of high intensity every play. He didn't take plays off and always ran to the ball."

Following his outstanding play during the 2013 regular season, Bowman continued to excel in the playoffs, totaling 21 tackles, forcing a fumble, and recording a sack during victories over the Green Bay Packers and Carolina Panthers, before sustaining a serious injury to his left knee during a 23–17 loss to the Seattle Seahawks in the NFC championship game. Forced to undergo reconstructive surgery to repair a torn ACL, MCL, and PCL, Bowman subsequently missed the entire 2014 campaign, before returning to action the following year, when, despite appearing a step slower in pass coverage, he remained a terror against the run, earning his third Pro Bowl selection and fourth All-Pro nomination by recording a league-leading 154 combined tackles and 116 solo stops.

However, just as Bowman appeared to be returning to top form, he ruptured his Achilles tendon during the early stages of the 2016 campaign, sidelining him for the rest of the year and bringing his days as a dominant defender to an end. Although Bowman returned to the playing field in 2017, he failed to display the same burst he once had and often struggled in pass coverage, lacking his earlier ability to move laterally and break on the football. Displeased with Bowman's overall performance, the 49ers attempted to trade him to another team, but, finding no suitors, they ended up releasing him five games into the campaign, with GM John Lynch subsequently telling the media on October 13, 2017, "He's given his heart and soul for this organization. And I know he's a fan favorite. So, this isn't going to be easy for the fans, but Kyle [Shanahan] and I felt like it was in the best interest of our team, and, so, we've acted accordingly."

Signed by Oakland shortly thereafter, Bowman spent the rest of the year starting at middle linebacker for the Raiders, recording 89 tackles in 10 games, before sitting out the entire 2018 campaign after failing to receive an offer from any team he considered commensurate with his ability. Choosing to announce his retirement prior to the start of the ensuing campaign, Bowman returned to the 49ers' practice facility in Santa Clara on June 4, 2019, to make his decision known to the public, saying at the time: "I was a guy coming from District Heights, Maryland, and this was the organization that chose to let me play in the NFL. . . . I felt like the 49ers is my home. It's the place that loved me from the start. I wanted to come back and retire a Niner, and they welcomed me, so, I'm glad it happened."

Bowman continued, "Guys say, 'You look like you can still play.' I can. But I'm content with it. There's plenty of organizations, but the 49ers are really a historic and well-respected place. I wouldn't want to be anywhere else."

Bowman then added, "I'm enjoying real life. I washed my car for the first time outside my house, and it was the best thing ever. I'm waking up and spending time with my family. I coach my son's 10-and-under basketball team. They were a group of development kids, but, if you see them play now, you'll enjoy the show."

Over parts of eight seasons in San Francisco, Bowman recorded 671 tackles (505 solo), registered 12½ sacks, forced nine fumbles, recovered five others, and intercepted four passes, which he returned for 104 yards and one touchdown.

Looking back on the goal-line play he made against Seattle in the 2013 NFC championship game that resulted in him tearing his knee ligaments, Bowman said, "Yeah. That one play. You want to be a football player. I always say, 'Should I have just let him score?' Then maybe I'll be playing 12, 13 years and be a six-time All-Pro. I don't know. But I was giving everything for my teammates. That's what happens. That's why they say it's a 100 percent injury rate in this game. The fans recognize, and that's why I played the game—to get the love from the fans and the respect from my fellow players."

49ERS CAREER HIGHLIGHTS

Best Season

Bowman had a tremendous year for the 49ers in 2015, leading the NFL with 154 combined tackles and 116 solo stops. He also performed brilliantly in 2011, earning First-Team All-Pro honors for the first of three straight times by recording 143 combined tackles, 111 solo stops, 13 tackles for loss, two sacks, and three fumble recoveries. However, Bowman had the finest all-around season of his career in 2013, when, in addition to ranking among the league leaders with 145 tackles and 120 solo stops, he brought down opposing ball-carriers behind the line of scrimmage nine times, forced six fumbles, recovered two others, registered five sacks, successfully defended eight passes, and recorded two interceptions, one of which he returned for a touchdown.

Memorable Moments/Greatest Performances

Bowman helped lead the 49ers to a 13–8 win over the Cincinnati Bengals on September 25, 2011, by making a game-high 13 tackles.

Bowman contributed to a 27–20 victory over the Giants on November 13, 2011, by recording a season-high 15 tackles, including 11 of the solo variety.

Bowman registered 12 tackles and the first sack of his career during a 19–17 win over the Seattle Seahawks on December 24, 2011.

Although the 49ers lost to the Giants in overtime by a score of 20–17 in the 2011 NFC championship game, Bowman starred in defeat, recording a game-high 14 tackles.

Bowman helped lead the 49ers to a 30–22 win over the Packers in the opening game of the 2012 regular season by recording 11 tackles and his first career interception, which he returned to the Green Bay 23 yard line, thereby setting up a 23-yard touchdown run by Frank Gore.

Although the 49ers suffered a 24–13 defeat at the hands of the Minnesota Vikings on September 23, 2012, Bowman recorded a career-high 18 combined tackles during the contest.

Bowman contributed to a 35–11 win over the St. Louis Rams on September 26, 2013, by recording two sacks and one forced fumble.

Bowman clinched a 34–24 win over the Atlanta Falcons on December 23, 2013, by returning his interception of a Matt Ryan pass 89 yards for a touchdown with just over a minute remaining in regulation. Nicknamed the "Pick at the Stick," Bowman's pick-six assured the 49ers of a victory in the last game they ever played at Candlestick Park.

Bowman followed that up one week later by intercepting a pass, forcing a fumble, recovering another, recording a sack, and registering nine solo tackles during a 23–20 win over the Arizona Cardinals in the final game of the 2013 regular season.

Continuing to excel in the 2013 postseason, Bowman helped lead the 49ers to a 23–20 victory over the Packers in the wild card round of the playoffs by recording 10 solo tackles and forcing a fumble, before making another 11 tackles and registering a sack during a 23–10 win over the Carolina Panthers one week later. And, before injuring his knee during the latter stages of the NFC championship game, Bowman performed brilliantly, recording a game-high 14 tackles, registering a sack, and forcing a fumble.

Notable Achievements

- Scored one defensive touchdown.
- Recorded more than 140 tackles four times.
- Led NFL with 154 combined tackles and 116 solo tackles in 2015.
- Finished second in NFL in combined tackles once and solo tackles twice.
- Finished third in NFL with six forced fumbles in 2013.
- Led 49ers in tackles four times.
- Ranks among 49ers career leaders with 709 tackles (4th) and nine forced fumbles (10th).
- Two-time division champion (2011 and 2012).
- 2012 NFC champion.
- December 2013 NFC Defensive Player of the Month.
- Three-time Pro Bowl selection (2012, 2013, and 2015).
- Four-time First-Team All-Pro selection (2011, 2012, 2013, and 2015).

20
RANDY CROSS

Perhaps the finest interior lineman ever to don the Red and Gold, Randy Cross spent his entire 13-year NFL career in San Francisco, excelling for the 49ers at both center and right guard. Performing equally well at both positions, Cross earned three trips to the Pro Bowl, three All-Pro nominations, and eight All-NFC selections, with his stellar play helping the 49ers win six division titles and three Super Bowls. A member of the Pro Football Reference All-1980s First Team, Cross proved to be one of the NFL's most durable players throughout his career, missing just one non-strike game from 1979 to 1988, en route to appearing in the third-most contests of any offensive lineman in franchise history.

Born in Brooklyn, New York, on April 25, 1954, Randall Laureat Cross grew up in Encino, California, where he starred in football and track and field at Crespi Carmelite High School, winning the CIF California State shotput championship as a senior in 1972 with a throw of 67 feet, 6.5 inches that set school and stadium records that still stand. After accepting an athletic scholarship to UCLA, Cross began to focus almost exclusively on football after he became the Bruins' starting center midway through his sophomore year, recalling, "To me, college football was everything. In my first game as a Bruin, we beat the number one team in the country, Nebraska. And my last game, we beat then number one Ohio State."

Displaying a tremendous amount of versatility during his time at UCLA, Cross manned multiple positions along the offensive line, saying, "I played two positions at UCLA, offensive guard and center. I played guard my junior year, played center my sophomore year, and played both positions my senior year in college."

Cross continued, "We had a rotating offensive line of nine guys my senior year, which paid dividends to my versatility. But I feel that I would have made every consensus All-American team if I played just guard. . . . I made First-Team All-American as a guard, despite playing half the season at center."

Randy Cross excelled for the 49ers at both guard and center.
Courtesy of George A. Kitrinos

Yet, Cross contends that he does not consider his All-America designation to be his greatest accomplishment at UCLA, stating, "Beating Ohio State in the Rose Bowl for the National Championship was my proudest moment in college because the Buckeyes were the number one team in the country, and we really gave it to them that day, beating them 23 to 10."

Cross's outstanding play his senior year, coupled with his ability to play multiple positions, made him extremely confident heading into the 1976

NFL Draft, recalling, "Draft-wise, having the luxury of being exceptional at more than one position was a plus in the scouts' eyes, and that versatility really improved my draft stock."

Revealing that a number of teams expressed interest in him prior to the draft, Cross said, "I initially got a call from the Cleveland Browns, and they asked what I thought about the prospects of playing for them. I quickly responded with apparently the wrong answer when I responded, saying, 'You mean, like playing in Cleveland, Ohio?'"

Ultimately selected by the 49ers in the second round, with the 42nd overall pick, Cross claims that he did not experience much anxiety on draft day, stating, "There was no going to New York City to wait and hear your name called by a team. It was only me sitting at home waiting for the phone to ring. The call came a little later than expected, but the 49ers took me with the 12th pick in the second round since they lost their initial pick in a trade. . . . My draft selection was not bad in my opinion. I was an undersized lineman that never lifted a single weight."

After initially being slated to assume a backup role when he first arrived in San Francisco, Cross joined the starting unit when second-year center Bill Reid suffered a season-ending injury, with Cross recalling, "He blew his knee out the second week of practice, and from there I was given the opportunity to start by default, and I never looked back."

After replacing Reid at center, Cross performed well enough his first year in the league to earn a spot on the NFL All-Rookie Team. Cross continued to man that post for the 49ers for two more years, before shifting over to right guard when he returned to action in 1979 after missing the final seven games of the previous campaign with an injury. Beginning a string of 10 seasons during which he missed just one game, Cross quickly established himself as one of the league's finest players at his position, earning All-NFC honors for the first of eight times in 1980, before gaining Pro Bowl and Second-Team All-Pro recognition the following year. And, as Cross developed into a top-tier lineman, the 49ers emerged as perennial contenders in the NFC, winning six division titles and three Super Bowls from 1981 to 1988.

Although somewhat undersized at 6'3" and 260 pounds, Cross possessed outstanding strength, quickness, and agility, making him an extremely effective pass-protector and run-blocker. One of the league's top pulling guards, Cross proved to be particularly proficient at creating holes downfield for 49er running backs Roger Craig and Wendell Tyler, both of whom rushed for more than 1,000 yards with his help. In discussing what he considered to be his greatest assets, Cross said, "My best attribute as a player was having a really strong work ethic, and my strength paid dividends for me once I actually started lifting weights."

After starting at right guard for the 49ers in each of the previous eight seasons, Cross returned to the center position in 1987, spending his final two years there, before retiring following the conclusion of the 1988 campaign. Recalling that his decision to leave the game proved to be a rather easy one, Cross stated, "I knew it was time to start looking at other things once I reached the age of 34. I was thinking to myself, 'I'm not performing the way I'm accustomed to, and it's not up to my standard.' Plus, my knee had been through enough after just having offseason surgery the season before."

Cross continued, "Super Bowl XXIII was my last game in the NFL, and it ended beautifully with John Taylor catching an unbelievable pass from Joe Montana. After that, I was able to ride off into the sunset, and go be with my three kids and wonderful wife. . . . It was perfect. It's what you dream of being able to do when you're a young kid growing up. That was something out of the movies, you didn't get to go out with a Super Bowl as your final game. It was the perfect time to step away. It was kind of a special feeling to walk off that field and look around that stadium in Miami, soak it in because it was the last time I'd ever do it."

Cross, who began preparing for life after football by doing radio work while still playing for the 49ers, subsequently transitioned seamlessly into a career in broadcasting, serving as an analyst for CBS Sports' coverage of the NFL from 1989 to 1993, before assuming a similar position at NBC from 1994 to 1997. Returning to CBS in 1998, Cross has spent the past two decades reprising his role as a game analyst. He also co-hosts a show on Sirius NFL Radio. When not talking football, Cross can usually be found enjoying himself on the golf course.

Looking back fondly on his years with the 49ers, Cross says, "I was fortunate enough to be on a great team, with great players, and coaches that helped me get three rings in Super Bowls XVI, XIX, and XXIII. I was really proud of the way we ran the ball and executed the west-coast offense. . . . Joe Montana and Jerry Rice were screaming advantages, and the opposing team just knew they couldn't stop them. Jerry caught everything in his direction and won many games for us late with great grabs. And Montana was always poised, a great leader, and very reliable as a passer."

CAREER HIGHLIGHTS

Best Season

Although Cross gained Pro Bowl and Second-Team All-Pro recognition in 1984 as well, he performed slightly better in 1981, when *Pro Football Weekly*, the NEA, and the Pro Football Writers also accorded him First-Team All-Pro honors.

Memorable Moments/Greatest Performances

Cross anchored an offensive line that enabled the 49ers to gain 317 yards on the ground during a 20–16 win over the Minnesota Vikings on November 29, 1976.

Cross helped the 49ers rush for a season-high total of 282 yards during a 20–7 victory over the New Orleans Saints on November 27, 1977.

Cross's superior blocking at the point of attack helped the 49ers amass 527 yards of total offense during a 42–27 win over the St. Louis Cardinals on September 18, 1983.

Cross and his line-mates turned in another dominant performance on December 4, 1983, with the 49ers rushing for 227 yards during a 35–21 victory over the Tampa Bay Buccaneers.

Cross helped the 49ers control the line of scrimmage once again during a 37–31 win over the Redskins on September 10, 1984, with the Niners rushing for 167 yards and amassing 534 yards of total offense.

Cross and the rest of San Francisco's offensive line performed brilliantly in Super Bowl XIX, with the 49ers gaining 211 yards on the ground and amassing 537 yards of total offense during a 38–16 win over the Miami Dolphins.

Notable Achievements

- Six-time division champion (1981, 1983, 1984, 1986, 1987, and 1988).
- Three-time NFC champion (1981, 1984, and 1988).
- Three-time Super Bowl champion (XVI, XIX, and XXIII).
- Member of 1976 NFL All-Rookie Team.
- Three-time Pro Bowl selection (1981, 1982, and 1984).
- Three-time Second-Team All-Pro selection (1981, 1984, and 1986).
- Four-time First-Team All-NFC selection (1980, 1981, 1984, and 1985).
- Four-time Second-Team All-NFC selection (1982, 1986, 1987, and 1988).
- Pro Football Reference All-1980s First Team.

21

KEN WILLARD

A powerful runner once identified by Green Bay Packers Hall of Fame linebacker Ray Nitschke as the hardest-hitting back in the NFL, Ken Willard spent nine seasons in San Francisco, rushing for the fourth-most yards in franchise history during that time. Leaving the City by the Bay at the end of 1973 as the second-leading rusher in team annals, Willard led the 49ers in rushing seven times, gaining more than 800 yards on the ground twice and amassing more than 1,000 yards from scrimmage on five separate occasions. A member of 49er teams that won three consecutive division titles during the early 1970s, Willard earned four Pro Bowl selections and one All-Pro nomination, before spending one final season with the St. Louis Cardinals.

Born in Richmond, Virginia, on July 14, 1943, Kenneth Henderson Willard starred in baseball and football while attending Varina High School in nearby Henrico County, performing so well on the diamond that he received an offer to sign with the Boston Red Sox prior to even graduating. Recalling the decision that faced him at the time, Willard told *Sports Illustrated* in 1965:

> I could have quit high school when I was 17 and signed with Boston to play baseball. I was just about as big then as I am now, and I could hit the long ball often enough. They sent Ted Williams down to Richmond to talk to me, and they offered me a lot of money. I thought about it, but I wasn't sure I would be dedicated enough to my education to go back winters to get my degree. Then I had read somewhere that only about 7% of all baseball rookies ever make it in the major leagues, and I thought about traveling around in buses in the minors, and I hate buses. So, I went to North Carolina on a football scholarship.

Ken Willard amassed more than 1,000 yards from scrimmage five times as a member of the 49ers.
Courtesy of Mike Traverse

Continuing to compete in both sports at UNC, Willard gained Academic All-America recognition by excelling for the Tar Heels at fullback on the gridiron, while also leading the ACC in home runs twice. In fact, Willard is unofficially credited with the longest home run in school history, once driving the ball an estimated 525 feet. But Willard made an even greater name for himself on the football field, leading the Tar Heels in rushing three straight times, with his 835 yards gained on the ground, 1,054 yards from scrimmage, and nine touchdowns scored his senior year earning him Second-Team All-America honors.

Selected by the 49ers with the second overall pick of the 1965 NFL Draft, ahead of future NFL Hall of Famers Dick Butkus and Gale Sayers, after earlier being selected by the Buffalo Bills in a secret draft held by the

rival AFL, Willard wasted little time in signing with the 49ers, later revealing that he never seriously considered playing for the Bills when he said, "I
was picked by Buffalo in a secret draft a week before the 49ers drafted me,
but I wasn't interested in the AFL, and I didn't like the secret draft. I guess
maybe if I had come up to the pros five or 10 years from now, when the
AFL is better established, I might have been interested."

Before reporting to the 49ers, though, Willard chose to play for the
College All-Stars against the NFL champion Cleveland Browns, stating
later that year, "It is a gradual indoctrination. I started with the All-Star
Game in Buffalo, where you play against the best college players. Then I
went to the All-Star camp at Northwestern. We scrimmaged the Chicago
Bears, and I got my first taste of the pros. Then we played the best of the
pros—the Cleveland Browns—in the All-Star Game. So, the transition
from college to professional football was gradual."

Well prepared for the rigors of the NFL by the time he arrived in San
Francisco, Willard ended up earning Pro Bowl and Second-Team All-Pro
honors as a rookie by rushing for 778 yards, amassing 1,031 yards from
scrimmage, and scoring nine touchdowns after laying claim to the starting
fullback job during the preseason. He followed that up with another strong
performance in 1966, gaining Pro Bowl recognition for the second straight
time by finishing fifth in the league with 763 yards rushing, making a
career-high 42 receptions for 351 yards, accumulating 1,114 yards from
scrimmage, and scoring seven touchdowns.

Hampered by a broken arch in his foot he believed at the time to be
nothing more than an excruciatingly painful sprain, Willard subsequently
suffered through a subpar 1967 season during which he rushed for only 510
yards and amassed just 752 yards from scrimmage. Reflecting back on his
injury, Willard said, "I had a very tough time running on it. I couldn't run
on it during the week. We used to shoot it up before games. If you saw my
foot now, you'd understand what I'm talking about."

Fully recovered by the start of the 1968 campaign, Willard had one
of the most productive seasons of his career, earning Pro Bowl honors and
gaining Second-Team All-Pro recognition from two major news sources by
finishing second in the NFL with 967 yards rushing, while also ranking
among the league leaders with 1,199 yards from scrimmage and seven rushing touchdowns. Willard earned his fourth and final trip to the Pro Bowl
the following year by amassing 883 yards from scrimmage and scoring 10
touchdowns, before accumulating more than 1,000 yards from scrimmage
in each of the next two seasons, while also gaining a total of 1,644 yards on
the ground and scoring 15 touchdowns.

Standing 6'1" and weighing close to 220 pounds, Willard had a thick build and the heavy thighs of a power runner that helped make him extremely effective between the tackles. Yet, at the same time, he possessed surprising speed that enabled him to break his runs to the outside when he needed to do so. An outstanding blocker as well, Willard contributed to the success of the 49ers in many ways, proving to be a key figure in the resurgence they experienced during the early portion of the 1970s.

Willard remained in San Francisco until the end of 1973, with knee problems limiting him to just 711 yards rushing, 1,002 yards from scrimmage, and seven touchdowns over the course of his final two seasons with the 49ers. Choosing to join the St. Louis Cardinals prior to the start of the 1974 campaign when the 49ers sought to reduce his salary, Willard spent one year serving the Cardinals as a backup, before announcing his retirement with career totals of 6,105 yards rushing, 277 receptions, 2,184 receiving yards, 8,289 yards from scrimmage, 45 rushing touchdowns, and 17 TD catches. Compiling virtually all those numbers during his time in San Francisco, Willard retired as the NFL's eighth-leading all-time rusher.

Following his playing days, Willard, who attended law school at William & Mary in 1967, spent many years selling life insurance, before retiring to Virginia, where he lives with his wife of nearly 60 years.

Looking back on his playing career, Willard says, "I'm most proud of lasting in the league as long as I did. I missed only one game in the regular season in my nine years in San Francisco. . . . I enjoyed my time in football, but I've also enjoyed my time out of football. When I got through playing, I felt like I did everything I could do in the game. I would've loved to have won a Super Bowl, though. That's the one thing you can accomplish that would change your life."

49ERS CAREER HIGHLIGHTS

Best Season

Although Willard earned his lone All-Pro nomination in 1965 by gaining 778 yards on the ground, amassing 1,031 yards from scrimmage, and scoring nine touchdowns, he posted better overall numbers in 1968, when he established career-high marks with 967 yards rushing, 1,199 yards from scrimmage, and seven rushing touchdowns, ranking among the league leaders in all three categories.

Memorable Moments/Greatest Performances

Willard scored the first touchdown of his career when he gathered in a 20-yard pass from John Brodie during a 52–24 win over the Chicago Bears in the opening game of the 1965 regular season.

Willard went over 100 yards rushing for the first time as a pro during a 45–24 victory over the Minnesota Vikings on November 28, 1965, finishing the game with 18 carries for 113 yards.

Willard helped the 49ers forge a 30–30 tie with the Bears on November 13, 1966, by scoring three times on short TD runs.

Willard starred during a 35–34 loss to the Philadelphia Eagles the following week, rushing for 124 yards, gaining another 60 yards on seven pass receptions, and scoring a pair of touchdowns.

Willard helped lead the 49ers to a convincing 41–14 victory over the Detroit Lions on Thanksgiving Day 1966 by gaining 114 yards on 20 carries.

Willard enabled the 49ers to forge a 20–20 tie with the Los Angeles Rams on November 17, 1968, by carrying the ball 24 times for 128 yards and one touchdown.

Willard followed that up by rushing for 110 yards and two touchdowns during a 45–28 win over the Pittsburgh Steelers on November 24, 1968.

Willard led the 49ers to a 14–12 win over the Atlanta Falcons in the final game of the 1968 regular season by rushing for a season-high total of 162 yards and scoring two touchdowns, one of which came on a career-long 69-yard run.

Willard proved to be a huge factor when the 49ers defeated the Browns by a score of 34–31 on September 27, 1970, rushing for 105 yards and two touchdowns.

Willard contributed to a 24–21 victory over the Jets on November 28, 1971, by carrying the ball 15 times for 129 yards.

Willard gained more than 100 yards on the ground for the final time in his career on December 2, 1973, carrying the ball 15 times for 117 yards during a 38–28 win over the Philadelphia Eagles.

Notable Achievements

- Missed just one game in nine seasons, appearing in 125 out of 126 contests.
- Rushed for more than 800 yards twice.
- Amassed more than 1,000 yards from scrimmage five times.

- Scored 10 touchdowns twice.
- Finished second in NFL with 967 yards rushing in 1968.
- Finished third in NFL with 1,199 yards from scrimmage in 1968.
- Led 49ers in rushing seven times.
- Ranks among 49ers career leaders with 1,582 rushing attempts (4th), 5,930 rushing yards (4th), 8,086 yards from scrimmage (6th), 8,086 all-purpose yards (7th), 45 rushing touchdowns (4th), and 61 touchdowns (6th).
- Three-time division champion (1970, 1971, and 1972).
- Four-time Pro Bowl selection (1965, 1966, 1968, and 1969).
- 1965 Second-Team All-Pro selection.

22

BRYANT YOUNG

The heart and soul of the 49ers' defense for 14 seasons, Bryant Young used his outstanding leadership ability and dominant play at the line of scrimmage to establish himself as one of the most beloved players in franchise history. The winner of more Len Eshmont awards than anyone else in team annals, Young displayed great courage and a tremendous work ethic during his time in San Francisco, with his inspirational play also earning him team MVP and NFL Comeback Player of the Year honors once each. A member of 49er teams that won four division titles and one Super Bowl, Young gained Pro Bowl and All-Pro recognition four times each, before being further honored in 2020 by being inducted into the 49ers Hall of Fame.

Born in Chicago Heights, Illinois, on January 27, 1972, Bryant Colby Young attended local Bloom High School, where he starred on the gridiron, prompting the University of Notre Dame to offer him an athletic scholarship. Excelling at defensive tackle for the Fighting Irish for four years, Young gained Honorable Mention All-America recognition as a junior, before earning First-Team All-America honors his senior year, when, as team captain, he recorded 67 tackles and 6½ sacks.

Selected by the 49ers with the seventh overall pick of the 1994 NFL Draft, Young immediately laid claim to the starting left defensive tackle job, after which he went on to earn a spot on the NFL All-Rookie Team by recording six sacks, 49 tackles, one forced fumble, and one fumble recovery for a 49ers team that ended up winning the Super Bowl. Performing well once again in 1995, Young recorded another six sacks, before posting the best numbers of his career the following year, when he earned Pro Bowl and First-Team All-Pro honors by registering 11½ sacks, 76 tackles (61 solo), one forced fumble, one fumble recovery, and a league-leading two safeties. Although Young subsequently registered just four sacks and 45 tackles in 1997, his ability to occupy multiple blockers on virtually every play helped teammate Dana Stubblefield earn NFL Defensive Player of the Year honors, with David Fucillo of *Niners Nation* later writing, "Dana Stubblefield

Bryant Young proved to be the heart and soul of the 49ers' defense for 14 seasons.
Courtesy of George A. Kitrinos

finished with 15 sacks, was defensive player of the year, and walked away with a huge contract from the Redskins. I still contend Bryant Young should have received commission on that deal because he was a primary reason Stubblefield had so many clear shots."

Teaming up with Stubblefield to form arguably the finest pair of defensive tackles in the league, the 6'3", 291-pound Young combined speed, strength, quickness, and tremendous intensity to establish himself as one of the finest all-around players at his position. Making life miserable for opposing quarterbacks and running backs, Young drew praise from Hall of Fame QB Kurt Warner, who said of his former adversary, "He was just a beast. You always say as a quarterback, the hardest thing to deal with is an interior pass rush. You know, guys who can create quick pressure up the middle against you. And that's who Bryant Young was."

Warner continued, "Probably my greatest rivalry, whether I was with the Rams or the Cardinals, was the 49ers. I remember going against Bryant so many times, and he was just one of those transcendent guys on the interior of the defensive line. You just don't see them very often."

An outstanding teammate and exceptional leader of men as well, Young, said 49ers' linebacker Winfred Tubbs, "has that big heart. He's a real down-to-earth nice guy, and you just don't see that attitude out of defensive linemen of that ability and that talent. You can say he's a mean guy by the way he plays, but, nah . . . he'd do anything to help you. He's just an example-setter for the whole team."

Steve Mariucci, the 49ers' head coach at the time, stated, "When you start talking about Bryant Young, he's as good a football player as you're going to find at any position in the game. He's as hard a worker as you're going to find in any sport. He's a gentleman, he's a good husband, he's a good father, and he's a class act. He's a very unique individual. He's a stud. You can only hope and pray that you can coach guys like BY in your career."

Meanwhile, 49ers defensive coordinator Jim Mora Jr. claimed that Young remained totally unaffected by his success, saying, "He never, ever comes across with an air of a superstar, or a prima donna. You'd never know that he was a superstar. And he is a superstar. Make no mistake about that. He's the premier player at his position in the NFL."

Young performed at an elite level for the 49ers once again in 1998, recording 9½ sacks, 54 tackles (42 solo), and 19 QB pressures in the season's first 12 games, before breaking his leg during a 31–7 victory over the New York Giants in Week 13. Forced to sit out the remainder of the year after having a titanium rod inserted to help repair his broken fibula and tibia, Young subsequently displayed his extraordinary work ethic by engaging in a strenuous offseason workout regimen that amazingly had him ready for the start of the ensuing campaign. Starting all 16 games for the 49ers at his familiar position of left defensive tackle in 1999, Young showed no ill effects from his devastating injury, earning Pro Bowl and Second-Team All-Pro honors by recording a team-high 11 sacks and registering 41 tackles, 19 of which resulted in losses. Also named NFL Comeback Player of the

Year and the winner of the prestigious Len Eshmont Award as the 49ers' most inspirational and courageous player, Young drew praise from martial arts expert and personal trainer George Chung, who said:

> It was absolutely miraculous the way Bryant came back from that to where he is today. I think most people that have an injury like that, it not only devastates them physically, but mentally and spiritually as well. That kind of injury can end a person. That's the kind of injury that ends with people in dark rooms and feeling sorry for themselves, and angry and bitter at their family the rest of their life, you know what I mean? You see movies like that. Bryant overcame that. He never saw that as an option. That's a testament to his character. That's why he's such an inspirational player and person.

Jim Mora Jr. also expressed his admiration for Young when he stated, "To see a guy come from an injury like he had, and just push and push like he did, and also stay positive, people feed off that. He has set a standard for himself, and he never compromises that standard at all. The young guys see that and try to emulate it. That's inspiration."

Claiming that he drew inspiration from his teammate, Winfred Tubbs said, "I don't think he's lost anything since the injury. In fact, he has gained another element that has made him an even more forceful presence on the field and in the locker room. It's his attitude toward the game, his attitude toward each play. Me, going on to that field with that defense, I know I'm not going to loaf, I know I'm not going to see anyone else loaf, because I know BY is not going to loaf. He sets an example for the whole team not to give up at all. Ever."

Young remained a force on the interior of the 49ers' defensive line for another eight years, missing only four more contests during that time and earning another two trips to the Pro Bowl and one more All-Pro nomination, before announcing his retirement following the conclusion of the 2007 campaign. Ending his career with 89½ sacks, 627 tackles, 12 forced fumbles, and seven fumble recoveries, Young ranks among the franchise's all-time leaders in each of the first three categories. Meanwhile, Young's three career safeties and eight Len Eshmont Awards both place him first in franchise history.

After retiring as an active player, Young spent three years serving as a defensive line coach at the collegiate level, before stepping away from the game for a period of time to focus more on his family. Unfortunately, his teenage son, Colby, developed a brain tumor shortly thereafter that made dealing with his illness Young's top priority. Ultimately forced to spend four months in hospice care, Bryant Colby Young Jr. died of pediatric brain cancer at only 15 years of age on October 11, 2016.

Recalling the last conversation that he had with his son, an emotional Young said, "I told him just how much I appreciated his courage and his resilience. And I told him I love him. I told him how much I was proud of him, and for the young man to go through something like that."

Almost two years later, Young returned to coaching as the defensive line coach for the Atlanta Falcons—a position he continues to hold. More recently, Young received the honor of being inducted into the 49ers Hall of Fame, with team CEO Jed York first announcing the team's plans in a statement made on Twitter that read. "You could not ask for someone to be a better 49er and a better human being than Bryant Young. There was no question he was the heart and soul of this team as a player and a person who took great pride in wearing the SF oval. He exemplifies the championship culture we strive for in the game of football and in life."

CAREER HIGHLIGHTS

Best Season

Although Young also performed exceptionally well from 1998 to 2001, he had his finest all-around season in 1996, earning his lone First-Team All-Pro nomination by establishing career-high marks with 11½ sacks, 76 tackles, and two safeties.

Memorable Moments/Greatest Performances

Young recorded the first sack of his career in his first game as a pro when he brought down Jeff Hostetler behind the line of scrimmage during a 44–14 win over the Los Angeles Raiders in the 1994 regular-season opener.

In addition to recording a sack during the 49ers' lopsided 44–15 victory over Chicago in the divisional round of the 1994 playoffs, Young anchored a defense that limited the Bears to just 39 yards rushing on 18 carries.

Young contributed to a 44–20 win over the Miami Dolphins on November 20, 1995, by recording two sacks in one game for the first time in his career.

In addition to anchoring a defense that allowed just 36 yards rushing and 105 yards of total offense during a 34–0 manhandling of the St. Louis Rams on September 8, 1996, Young recorded two sacks, one of which resulted in a safety.

Young earned NFC Defensive Player of the Week honors by recording a career-high three sacks during a 28–11 win over the Rams on October 6, 1996.

Young helped lead the 49ers to a 14–0 victory over the Philadelphia Eagles in the wild card round of the 1996 NFC playoffs by recording two sacks.

Young earned NFC Defensive Player of the Week honors for the second time by registering two sacks and a safety during a 26–7 win over the Atlanta Falcons on December 12, 1999.

Young earned that distinction again by recording three sacks and three tackles for losses during a 28–25 victory over the Rams in the opening game of the 2005 regular season.

Young dominated the St. Louis offensive line once again on September 16, 2007, registering three sacks, seven solo tackles, and one forced fumble during a 17–16 win over the Rams.

Notable Achievements

- Finished in double digits in sacks twice.
- Finished second in NFL with 19 tackles for loss in 1999.
- Led 49ers in sacks four times.
- Tied for first in franchise history with three safeties.
- Ranks among 49ers career leaders with 14 seasons played (tied-6th), 208 games played (tied-3rd), 89½ sacks (3rd), 614 tackles (6th), and 12 forced fumbles (4th).
- Four-time division champion (1994, 1995, 1997, and 2002).
- 1994 NFC champion.
- Super Bowl XXIX champion.
- Three-time NFC Defensive Player of the Week.
- Member of 1994 NFL All-Rookie Team.
- 1999 NFL Comeback Player of the Year.
- 2004 49ers MVP.
- Eight-time Len Eshmont Award winner.
- Four-time Pro Bowl selection (1996, 1999, 2001, and 2002).
- 1996 First-Team All-Pro selection.
- Three-time Second-Team All-Pro selection (1998, 1999, and 2001).
- Three-time First-Team All-NFC selection (1996, 1998, and 2001).
- NFL 1990s All-Decade Second Team.
- Inducted into 49ers Hall of Fame in 2020.

23

DWIGHT CLARK

Permanently etching his name into 49er lore with his game-winning catch in the 1981 NFC championship game, Dwight Clark will always be remembered for making arguably the most significant play in franchise history. Nevertheless, the sure-handed receiver accomplished a great deal more during his nine-year NFL career, which he spent entirely in San Francisco. A key member of 49er teams that won five division titles and two Super Bowls, Clark led the club in receptions three times and receiving yards five times, en route to recording the fourth-most receptions and third-most receiving yards in team annals. A two-time Pro Bowler and one-time All-Pro, Clark later received the additional honors of having his #87 retired by the 49ers and being inducted into the team's Hall of Fame. Continuing to contribute to the success of the organization following his playing days, Clark spent nine years serving the club as a front-office executive, during which time the 49ers won six more division titles and another Super Bowl.

Born in Kinston, North Carolina, on January 8, 1957, Dwight Edward Clark later moved with his family to Charlotte, North Carolina, where he starred in football and basketball while attending Garinger High School. Although basketball remained his first love, Clark accepted a football scholarship from Clemson University, which initially recruited him as a quarterback. However, with the school having a glut of players at that position, Clark soon found himself playing wide receiver, before being moved to strong safety his sophomore year. Unhappy with his new role, Clark briefly considered leaving Clemson and playing basketball for Appalachian State University, before the Tigers' coaching staff switched him back to the offensive side of the ball. Clark subsequently spent his three remaining years at Clemson playing wide receiver, posting unimpressive numbers that included 33 receptions, 571 receiving yards, and three touchdowns.

Looking back on his college career some years later, Clark told the *San Francisco Chronicle*, "If my football future had been decided by what I did in college, I'd be working at Wendy's now."

Dwight Clark led the 49ers in receptions three times and receiving yards five times.
Courtesy of George A. Kitrinos

Fortunately for Clark, 49ers head coach Bill Walsh stumbled upon him quite by accident, with the *Chronicle* reporting, "In 1979, Walsh called to set up a pre-draft workout with Clark's roommate, Clemson quarterback Steve Fuller. Clark, on his way out their apartment door to play golf, picked up the phone. Walsh asked Clark if he could attend the workout to catch Fuller's passes, and Clark, after accepting the invitation, ended up catching everything in sight. 'My whole story,' Clark once said, 'is being in the right place at the right time.'"

Subsequently selected by the 49ers in the 10th round of the 1979 NFL Draft, with the 249th overall pick, Clark spent his first season in San Francisco assuming a backup role, making just 18 receptions for 232 yards and failing to score a touchdown. But, after laying claim to a starting job the following year, Clark emerged as one of the NFL's biggest surprises, placing near the top of the league rankings with 82 receptions, 991 receiving yards, and eight touchdown catches. Proving himself to be much more than just a one-year wonder, Clark earned Pro Bowl and Second-Team All-NFC honors in 1981 by finishing second in the NFL with 85 receptions, amassing 1,105 receiving yards, and scoring four touchdowns during the regular season, before sending the 49ers to their first Super Bowl by making his extraordinary game-winning fingertip touchdown catch in the back of the end zone against Dallas in the closing moments of the NFC championship game.

Continuing to perform well during the strike-shortened 1982 campaign, Clark gained Pro Bowl and First-Team All-Pro recognition by making a league-leading 60 receptions in only nine games, while also finishing second in the circuit with 913 receiving yards and scoring five touchdowns. Clark followed that up with four more extremely productive seasons, averaging nearly 60 receptions and just over 800 receiving yards from 1983 to 1986, while gathering in a total of 26 touchdown passes, with his 10 TD catches in 1985 placing him fourth in the league rankings. Performing especially well in 1983 and 1984, Clark made 70 receptions for 840 yards and eight touchdowns in the first of those campaigns, before catching 52 passes, amassing 880 receiving yards, and scoring six TDs the following year.

Although the 6'4", 212-pound Clark lacked elite speed, he had good moves, outstanding route-running ability, and superb hands, which, along with his large catch-radius, made him a favorite target of Joe Montana, with whom he quickly developed a special rapport, both on and off the playing field. In discussing his former teammate, Montana said, "Everybody talks about The Catch all of the time, but he made so many other catches that we all forget about because of that one. I remember him for a lot more than that because he saved my butt a lot."

An outstanding teammate as well, Clark drew high praise from Roger Craig, who said, "Dwight Clark is the kind of guy that makes you feel special. And he's special. He has this humbleness about him. He's so humble as a human being, and he just always was there to help me when I needed help. If I needed advice from him, he would always be there for me."

Meanwhile, Jerry Rice, who eventually replaced Clark as the 49ers' number one receiver, discussed the degree to which the veteran wideout assisted him when he first arrived in San Francisco, recalling, "When I first came here, I was like a deer in the headlights because I'm looking at Joe Montana, Dwight Clark, Ronnie Lott, all these great players, and I'm saying to myself, 'Where do I fit in here?.' . . . He welcomed me with open arms, and he knew I was coming in to carry on that tradition. I remember he helped me learn how to run this out-route, and, when I first came into the league, I didn't know how to run that route, and it was frustrating, but then, all of a sudden, Dwight just took me out and said, 'Hey, this is how you do it.' And I just copied that from him. Even as a rookie, I credit Dwight Clark with a lot of my success."

Clark spent one more season in San Francisco, making 24 receptions for 290 yards and five touchdowns in a part-time role in 1987, before announcing his retirement. Ending his career with 506 receptions, 6,750 receiving yards, and 48 touchdown catches, Clark continues to rank among the franchise's all-time leaders in all three categories. Extremely durable, Clark never missed a game his entire career, appearing in 134 consecutive non-strike contests.

After the 49ers retired his #87 in 1988, Clark remained away from the game for two more years, before returning to the organization as a front office executive in 1990. Promoted to general manager in 1996, Clark remained in that position until 1998, when he resigned to become the first general manager in the expansion era of the Cleveland Browns. After serving as vice president and director of football operations in Cleveland from 1999 to 2001, Clark handed in his resignation when new head coach Butch Davis requested the right to make all personnel decisions. Clark subsequently returned to North Carolina to run his real estate business, before eventually rejoining the 49ers in a business-operations capacity.

Sadly, after undergoing months of tests and treatments for weakness in his left hand, Clark announced in March 2017 that he had been diagnosed with ALS. Saying at the time that he believed his condition may well have been related to three concussions he sustained during his playing career, Clark stated, "I've been asked if playing football caused this. I don't know for sure. But I certainly suspect it did. And I encourage the National Football League Players Association and the NFL to continue working together in their efforts to make the game of football safer, especially as it relates to head trauma."

Clark added, "I just remember saying when I retired that my life would be complete because I've done so many things that I had no idea I was going to get to do. Be hard to say I've had a bad life even though I got a bad break now."

Some seven months later, on October 22, 2017, the 49ers honored Clark by holding a special ceremony during halftime of their game against the Dallas Cowboys. In addition to presenting a video tribute to the former wide receiver, the 49ers brought back 30 members of the 1981 team to pay their respects to Clark, who then addressed the crowd and expressed his thanks. Former 49ers owner and longtime friend Edward J. DeBartolo Jr. also hosted a reunion early in 2018 that enabled many of Clark's former teammates to reminisce with him and share a final goodbye.

Speaking in depth about living with ALS a few weeks later, Clark said on the 49ers Insider Podcast, "There's nothing stopping it or reversing it. It's just slowing it down, which I guess is the best I can hope for. . . . As an athlete, at least give me something I can fight. I'm fighting with the few little weapons I have. It's very frustrating as it progresses. I used to pick up a cup and take a drink. Now, it's two hands and make sure my fingers are underneath it, so I don't spill it. I drop 50 things a day. . . . What I'm trying to do is, I'm 61, and I'm just trying to make it to 62. And, when I get there, I'll just try to make it to 63."

Dwight Clark died of ALS on June 4, 2018, seven months prior to his 62nd birthday. Upon learning of his passing, the 49ers issued a statement that read:

> The San Francisco 49ers family has suffered a tremendous loss today with the passing of Dwight Clark. We extend our condolences and prayers to Dwight's wife, Kelly, his family, friends, and fans, as we join together to mourn the death of one of the most beloved figures in 49ers history. For almost four decades, he served as a charismatic ambassador for our team and the Bay Area. Dwight's personality and his sense of humor endeared him to everyone he came into contact with, even during his most trying times. The strength, perseverance, and grace with which he battled ALS will long serve as an inspiration to so many. Dwight will always carry a special place in our hearts, and his legacy will live on as we continue to battle this terrible disease.

Expressing his sadness over losing his close friend, Eddie DeBartolo Jr. released his own statement that read:

> My heart is broken. Today, I lost my little brother and one of my best friends. I cannot put into words how special Dwight was to me and to everyone his life touched. He was an amazing husband,

father, grandfather, brother, and a great friend and teammate. He showed tremendous courage and dignity in his battle with ALS, and we hope there will soon be a cure for this horrendous disease.

I will always remember Dwight the way he was—larger than life, handsome, charismatic, and the one who could pull off wearing a fur coat at our Super Bowl parade. He was responsible for one of the most iconic plays in NFL history that began our run of Super Bowl championships, but, to me, he will always be an extension of my family. I love him and will miss him terribly. Our hearts and prayers are with his wife Kelly, his children, and the entire Clark family.

Ronnie Lott also addressed the passing of his former teammate by saying, "He was willing to try harder than any Niner. That's what I loved about him. Think about his story—it's the ultimate of trying. Trying to always give your heart. That's Dwight Clark."

CAREER HIGHLIGHTS

Best Season

Although Clark posted career-high marks in receptions (85) and receiving yards (1,105) in 1981, he played his best ball for the 49ers during the strike-shortened 1982 campaign, earning his lone First-Team All-Pro nomination by making a league-leading 60 receptions and amassing 913 receiving yards in just nine games, with his exceptional play prompting noted *Sports Illustrated* writer Paul Zimmerman to name him his 1982 NFL Player of the Year.

Memorable Moments/Greatest Performances

Clark recorded the first two touchdowns of his career during a 37–27 win over the Jets on September 21, 1980, collaborating with Joe Montana on scoring plays that covered 20 and 7 yards.

Clark went over 100 receiving yards for the first time as a pro during a 38–35 overtime victory over the New Orleans Saints on December 7, 1980, making six receptions for 155 yards and one touchdown, which came on a 71-yard connection with Montana.

Clark proved to be a thorn in the side of the Saints once again on September 27, 1981, making four receptions for 135 yards and one touchdown during a 21–14 49ers win, with his TD coming on a 78-yard hookup with Montana.

Although the 49ers lost to Denver by a score of 24–21 on September 19, 1982, Clark had a big game, making nine receptions for 127 yards and one TD, which covered 24 yards.

Clark starred in defeat once again on December 11, 1982, making 12 receptions for 135 yards and one touchdown during a 41–37 loss to the San Diego Chargers.

Clark helped lead the 49ers to a 34–21 win over the Houston Oilers on October 21, 1984, by making five receptions for 127 yards and one TD, which came on a career-long 80-yard hookup with Joe Montana.

Clark contributed to a 21–10 victory over the Giants in the divisional round of the 1984 playoffs by making nine receptions for 112 yards and one touchdown, hooking up with Montana on a 21-yard scoring play.

Clark experienced easily the most memorable moment of his career in the 1981 NFC championship game, when he gave the 49ers a 28–27 win over the Dallas Cowboys by making a last-minute 6-yard touchdown reception in the back of the end zone. With Dallas holding a 27–21 lead and only 58 seconds remaining on the clock, Clark leaped high in the air to gather in a pass thrown by Joe Montana, bringing the ball in by his fingertips, to tie the score at 27–27. Ray Wersching's subsequent conversion of the extra point gave the 49ers a one-point lead that they refused to surrender, putting them in the Super Bowl for the first time. The play, which became known simply as "The Catch," is generally considered to be one of the greatest in NFL history and the most famous in Bay Area sports history, with Clark later saying, "It's a signature moment for 49er fans that bonds me with them no matter how long I live."

Notable Achievements

- Never missed a game his entire career, appearing in 134 consecutive non-strike contests.
- Surpassed 60 receptions five times, topping 80 catches twice.
- Surpassed 1,000 receiving yards once.
- Scored 10 touchdowns in 1985.
- Led NFL with 60 receptions in 1982.
- Finished second in NFL in receptions once and receiving yards once.
- Finished third in NFL in receptions once.
- Led 49ers in receptions three times and receiving yards five times.

- Ranks among 49ers career leaders with 506 receptions (4th), 6,750 receiving yards (3rd), 6,800 yards from scrimmage (9th), 6,800 all-purpose yards (11th), 48 touchdown receptions (7th), and 48 touchdowns (tied for 12th).
- Five-time division champion (1981, 1983, 1984, 1986, and 1987).
- Two-time NFC champion (1981 and 1984).
- Two-time Super Bowl champion (XVI and XIX).
- Two-time Pro Bowl selection (1981 and 1982).
- 1982 First-Team All-Pro selection.
- 1982 First-Team All-NFC selection.
- 1981 Second-Team All-NFC selection.
- #87 retired by 49ers.
- Inducted into 49ers Hall of Fame in 2009.

24

CHARLIE KRUEGER

One of the longest-tenured players in franchise history, Charlie Krueger spent his entire 15-year NFL career in San Francisco, persevering through the dark days of the 1960s to play a huge role in revitalizing the 49ers during the early 1970s. After playing defensive end his first three seasons, Krueger moved inside to tackle, where he established himself as one of the league's top run-stuffers, helping the 49ers capture three consecutive division titles during the latter stages of his career. A two-time Pro Bowler and two-time All-Pro, Krueger later received the additional honors of having his #70 retired by the 49ers and being inducted into the team's Hall of Fame.

Born in Caldwell, Texas, on January 28, 1937, Charles Andrew Krueger grew up in poverty with his seven siblings, spending much of his spare time working in his father's mattress factory to help make ends meet, with longtime friend Tom Watson remembering, "They were a poor family with a lot of children, and they did whatever they could to make a living. The boys in the family helped out in the mattress factory to make a little extra money. Charlie was a kind person and looked after us little kids."

Gradually developing a love for the game of football, Krueger began his career on the gridiron as a defensive lineman at Caldwell High School, recalling years later, "I was a fat kid in a small town in Texas. If you didn't play sports or you weren't in the band, no one knew who you were. If I could get close enough to hit you, I would. I was squatty as a freshman. By my sophomore year, I was 6'2" and 190 pounds."

Subsequently offered scholarships to Texas A&M, Rice, and Houston, Krueger chose to remain close to home and play for the Aggies and newly hired head coach Paul "Bear" Bryant. Reflecting back on his decision, Krueger said, "Football is a hell of a way to live. It just happened that way for me. When I got out of high school, the easiest thing for me to continue on in school was to accept a scholarship. I wasn't that highly sought after. I received three offers, so I went to school."

Charlie Krueger proved to be one of the NFL's top run-stuffers during his 15 seasons in San Francisco.
Courtesy of Mike Traverse

Developing into a superb two-way lineman at Texas A&M, Krueger earned Southwest Conference Sophomore Lineman of the Year honors in 1955, before gaining All-America recognition in each of the next two seasons. Retaining many fond memories of his college days, Krueger, who served 10 years in the Army Reserve, retiring as captain, later said, "I owe Texas A&M a lot. I received a great education and a military commission."

Selected by the 49ers with the ninth overall pick of the 1958 NFL Draft, Krueger arrived in San Francisco with high expectations surrounding him. However, he ended up missing his entire rookie year after breaking his arm during the preseason. Healthy again by the start of the 1959 campaign, Krueger started every game for the 49ers at right defensive end, beginning in the process a streak of 52 consecutive starts. Establishing himself as one of the league's top players at his position the following year, Krueger earned Pro Bowl and Second-Team All-Pro honors for the first of two times in 1960, before moving inside to left defensive tackle two years later. Remaining at that post for the rest of his career, Krueger proved to be a model of consistency for the 49ers, providing pressure up the middle against the pass and stout run defense, while appearing in 146 out of a possible 154 contests over the course of the next 11 seasons.

Particularly effective against the run, the 6'4", 260-pound Krueger used his strength, quickness, and agility to dominate his opponent at the point of attack, forcing opposing teams to consistently assign him multiple blockers. In discussing the degree to which Krueger excelled at stopping the run, Dallas Cowboys head coach Tom Landry once proclaimed, "No one is able to gain running at Charlie Krueger."

Former Texas A&M Heisman Trophy winner John David Crow, who also played with Krueger in San Francisco, said of his longtime teammate, "He would knock your brains out. He was a very, very tough football player. He wasn't as big when he was playing in college as he was with the 49ers. He was a good teammate, a good guy, and one of the reasons we had a good football team."

Hall of Fame Green Bay Packers guard Jerry Kramer discussed what it was like going up against Krueger, calling his frequent foe "exceptionally strong," and saying, "He beats on you unmercifully."

An outstanding technician, Krueger employed such excellent footwork and used his hands so well that teams around the league often used film of him as an instructional tool for their own young linemen.

In addition to his other attributes, Krueger possessed a strong work ethic and tremendous determination, with former 49ers teammate Len Rohde saying, "How can I describe Charlie? Very, very, very intense. . . . Whatever Charlie did, he did with 110-percent intensity."

Revealing that he never allowed his opponent to distract him on the playing field, Krueger, who rarely spoke to opposing players on gamedays, stated, "Starr and Unitas were as wily as they were good. . . . It's an old trick trying to distract a rusher. They'll say, 'Good move,' or 'How did you get there?' Sometimes, they'll flat out hit you with a compliment. Then you go away thinking what good folks they are and lose your concentration."

Krueger also revealed that he spent his most enjoyable years in San Francisco playing for 49ers head coach Dick Nolan, who led the team to three straight NFC Western Division titles from 1970 to 1972. In discussing his former coach, Krueger said, "Dick Nolan was a very moral sort of person. He might kick you in the butt, but he was fair. You've got to have a certain tenacity as a defensive player, and it worked out for me."

Choosing to announce his retirement after the 49ers finished just 5-9 in 1973, Krueger ended his playing career with one interception, seven fumble recoveries, one touchdown, and three safeties, which ties him for the most in team annals. He also ranks among the franchise's all-time leaders in games played, appearing in a total of 198 contests, 194 of which he started.

After retiring as an active player, Krueger settled in Clayton, California, where he became known for his work with Easter Seals, the March of Dimes, and the Max Baer Heart Fund. Unfortunately, Krueger, who missed just eight games his entire career, experienced significant health problems in retirement due to his willingness to sacrifice his body for the betterment of the team during his playing days, with the June 27, 1988, issue of *Sports Illustrated* revealing that he underwent surgery on his left knee in 1979 that basically left him crippled. As the article says: "After the surgery, it was discovered that for years the 49ers had allowed the sturdy tackle to play though they knew, following an operation on the knee to repair medial collateral ligament damage in '63, that Krueger was missing the anterior cruciate ligament in that knee."

The 49ers' negligence led to a 1988 lawsuit filed by Krueger against the team that resulted in him being awarded more than $2.3 million in damages. Finding that Krueger received repeated anesthetic injections during his NFL career that allowed him to play with badly damaged knees, Judge John Dearman of the California Superior Court in San Francisco handed down a decision that cited "fraudulent concealment" and stated, "Today, Krueger cannot climb, squat, kneel, lift, stoop, run, jog, or even walk or stand for prolonged periods of time. He is in constant pain. . . . He has been forced to live not only with the physical pain, but also with the grievous knowledge that he was betrayed by the very people for whom he sacrificed so much. He suffers from depressive neurosis and its accompanying symptoms—insomnia, restlessness, low self-esteem, and morbidity."

Krueger, who eventually had to rely on a cane to walk after undergoing five knee surgeries, spinal fusion, and shoulder-replacement surgery, continued to be affected mentally by his injuries in his later years, once saying, "I still have bad dreams about football. I get some sleep, but, if I stay still long enough, my body starts hurting. The best way I can explain it is that I lived through so many football seasons."

Krueger added, "Football doesn't have much meaning to me anymore. It's like I worked 20 years in a slaughterhouse. . . . The environment in pro football is such that you play with injuries. If I had an injury, I always went to the doctors. . . . If they said I could play, I played. I played because it was my job. I relied on them to tell me not to play. I relied on the wrong people. . . . Pro football's a hard place to make a living. Maybe that's why they don't send old men to war. Old men know better."

Krueger continued to suffer until February 5, 2021, when he died at the age of 84 from heart and kidney failure. Following his passing, the 49ers released a statement that read: "Charlie was known as the 'Textbook Tackle' for his reputation as a technician and his tremendous strength. He was a tough, resilient and smart player who looked out for his teammates, both on and off the field. We extend our condolences and prayers to his wife, Kris, and the entire Krueger family."

CAREER HIGHLIGHTS

Best Season

Krueger had the finest season of his career in 1960, when he earned Pro Bowl and Second-Team All-Pro honors for one of two times by helping the 49ers surrender the fewest points of any team in the league (205).

Memorable Moments/Greatest Performances

In addition to anchoring a 49ers defense that sacked Detroit quarterbacks Tobin Rote and Earl Morrall a total of eight times during a 33–7 win over the Lions on November 1, 1959, Krueger scored the first points of his career when he tackled Rote in the end zone for a safety.

Krueger recorded the second of his three career safeties when he sacked quarterback Ed Brown in the end zone during a 25–7 win over the Bears on October 30, 1960.

Krueger lit the scoreboard again when he tackled Bart Starr in the end zone for a safety during a 22–21 win over the Packers on December 10, 1961.

Krueger scored the only touchdown of his career when he ran 6 yards to paydirt after recovering a fumble during a convincing 52–24 victory over the Bears in the opening game of the 1965 regular season.

Krueger recorded his only career interception during a 17–17 tie with the Washington Redskins on October 5, 1969.

Notable Achievements

- Scored one defensive touchdown.
- Tied for first in franchise history with three safeties.
- Ranks among 49ers career leaders with 15 seasons played (tied for 4th) and 198 games played (7th).
- Three-time division champion (1970, 1971, and 1972).
- Two-time Pro Bowl selection (1960 and 1964).
- Two-time Second-Team All-Pro selection (1960 and 1965).
- 1970 Second-Team All-NFC selection.
- #70 retired by 49ers.
- Inducted into 49ers Hall of Fame in 2009.

25

JOE STALEY

A tremendous presence on the 49ers' offensive line for 13 seasons, Joe Staley earned the respect and admiration of everyone within the organization with his consistently excellent play, outstanding leadership ability, and total dedication to his profession. Spending his entire career in San Francisco, Staley started a total of 181 games for the 49ers—165 of those at left offensive tackle. One of the team's steadiest performers, Staley helped the 49ers win three division titles and one NFC championship, earning in the process six Pro Bowl selections, three All-Pro nominations, and a spot on the NFL 2010s All-Decade Team. Yet, it is for the influence that Staley had on the other players around him that he will likely be remembered most.

Born in Rockford, Michigan, on August 30, 1984, Joseph Andrew Staley began his career in football as a tight end at Rockford High School, where he caught a total of 24 passes and amassed 559 receiving yards in his three years as a starter. Performing especially well his senior year, Staley earned a spot on the *Grand Rapids Press* Dream Team by making seven touchdown receptions, with his outstanding play prompting both the *Detroit Free Press* and the *Detroit News* to identify him as a top-50 prospect. In addition to excelling on the gridiron at Rockford High, Staley competed in multiple events in track and field, with his school-record time of 21.9 seconds in the 200-meter dash representing the fastest mark ever recorded by a future NFL offensive lineman.

Offered an athletic scholarship to Central Michigan University, Staley spent his freshman season playing tight end, before transitioning to the offensive line after he added 80 pounds onto his 6'5" frame prior to the start of his sophomore year. Excelling at left tackle for the Chippewas the next three seasons, Staley served as a member of an offensive line that helped CMU boast a 1,000-yard rusher each year and quarterback Kent Smith pass for more than 2,000 yards in both 2004 and 2005. Retaining

Joe Staley anchored the 49ers' offensive line from his left tackle position for 13 seasons.
Courtesy of Mike Morbeck

his outstanding footspeed despite his increased weight, Staley posted a time of 4.70 seconds in the 40-yard dash at CMU's junior pro day.

Recalling Staley's move to the offensive line, current Notre Dame head coach Brian Kelly, head man at Central Michigan at the time, said, "His dad was not a fan of moving him to tackle from tight end. I said, 'You've got to trust me on this. I know it doesn't seem like the right move for him, but he's going to make a lot of money in the NFL.' To this day, Mr. Staley and I have a pretty good relationship."

Kelly added, "He was so competitive, so athletic. I'd be hard-pressed to think of anyone who's come close to running a 40-yard dash time at the combine like the speed he did. He ran a 4.7. . . . He just had an incredible physical gift. He was so talented. And he had toughness. He was the consummate gentleman off the field, tough guy on the field."

Selected by the 49ers in the first round of the 2007 NFL Draft, with the 28th overall pick, Staley spent his first season in San Francisco starting at right tackle, before moving to the left side of the offensive line the following year. Starting every game at left offensive tackle for the first of seven times, Staley quickly established himself as one of the league's better players at his position, prompting the 49ers to sign him to a six-year contract extension prior to the start of the ensuing campaign. After missing seven games in both 2009 and 2010, Staley started every contest in each of the next five seasons, gaining Pro Bowl recognition each year, while also being accorded Second-Team All-Pro honors in 2011, 2012, and 2013.

Excelling in San Francisco's run-oriented offense throughout the period, the 6'5", 295-pound Staley used his size, strength, and superior athleticism to help Frank Gore gain more than 1,000 yards on the ground seven times. Meanwhile, Staley's exceptional speed and quickness enabled him to do an excellent job of providing blindside pass protection for 49er quarterbacks Shaun Hill, Alex Smith, and Colin Kaepernick.

An outstanding technician and extremely intelligent player who carefully studied the tendencies of his opponent, Staley said, "I'm going against the one guy every single play. There are things I do in the first quarter trying to set him up for the third or fourth quarter. And the defensive player is doing the same thing to me. . . . I have to anticipate if he's trying to set me up or if he's trying to make me think he's setting me up for something later. I study my ass off. I prepare my ass off physically. You have to be incredibly mentally tough to play offensive line. You have to be physically tough. It's a culmination of so many different aspects of your life you carry over to what you want to be as a man."

Staley added, "I have in-game experience against most of the guys I face, so I watch the games I've gone against them to see what they did. Guys play me different because I am different, not a typical tackle. I'm lighter. More athletic. But after the game, they become people again. I have lots of friends in the league. I think guys respect me because I give respect."

Highly respected by the members of San Francisco's coaching staff as well, Staley drew praise from former 49ers head coach Jim Harbaugh, who said, "He played every game in 2011, 2012, 2013, and 2014. He also threw the greatest block I've ever seen, and that was in the playoffs against New Orleans on Alex Smith's great touchdown run. He's the best offensive lineman I've ever coached."

After missing three games in 2016, Staley started all but one contest over the course of the next two seasons, earning his sixth and final trip to the Pro Bowl in 2017. However, Staley subsequently suffered through an injury-plagued 2019 campaign during which he started just seven games, missing six contests with a fractured fibula and another three with a broken finger. Choosing to announce his retirement on social media on April 25, 2020, Staley said via Twitter, "My body is telling me it's time."

Elaborating further on his physical woes during a podcast interview with "Bussin' with the Boys," Staley stated, "It was a bunch of stingers. It got to the point where in the Super Bowl, I'd make contact with my head with anybody and I'd have—from the base of my head down to my back—I'd have just a zing, and my arm would go numb. I had herniations at a bunch of different levels and really severe stenosis. The doctor was like, 'If you're going to continue to play football, you're probably going to have to have fusion surgery on multiple levels.' I was like, 'I'm 35. I've got kids. I don't want to not be able to turn my neck for the rest of my life.'"

Staley continued, "When I went and saw these doctors, I realized how serious it was. They were like, 'If you continue to play, you're going to really do some long-term damage.'"

Staley later said during another interview, "Last year should have been the pinnacle of my career. We had an absolutely unbelievable team, from the culture to the coaching staff, front office, the players that were around. And it was like that the entire year. But, for me personally, it was really, really difficult because of the injuries. . . . I had the broken leg, which was kind of a weird rehab for that. I had a lot of complications coming back from that. . . . And then I came back and broke the finger, had to have surgery on that. . . . While that happened, I had a back thing, and then I've had the neck stuff that's been going on for a little bit, and it just kind of got worse and worse as the season went on."

Staley added, "I made the decision that, for me, my family, and what my life looks like going forward, it was the right time, I guess—if there is a right time—to step away."

Upon learning of Staley's decision to retire, fellow 49ers offensive lineman Mike McGlinchey said, "I think he's a Hall of Famer without a doubt. It's a no-brainer. Joe was the most complete offensive tackle of his generation."

Meanwhile, George Kittle spoke of the impact that Staley made on him during their time together in San Francisco, stating, "There's not enough that you could say about Joe Staley. He's absolutely incredible in everything that he does. He embodies everything about football that I think football should be about—the hard work, the grit, how much fun he has playing the game, how much better he is at playing that position than a lot of other people in the league. . . . Everything that Joe Staley has done, the things he showed me in the three years I got to play with him, his dedication to it, just reinforced my love for the game of football, and he just always encouraged me to be the best football player I could possibly be."

Kittle then added, "I don't think there's any replacing Joe Staley. What Joe did such a great job of was he instilled a lot of values and virtues with the team. We're all going to have our opportunity to step up and fill the shoes Joe left behind. I don't think any one person can do it, but I think we have a great group of guys who can come together and fill that role."

CAREER HIGHLIGHTS

Best Season

Staley earned All-Pro honors three straight times from 2011 to 2013, with the 2012 campaign being the finest of his career. Anchoring an offensive line that enabled the 49ers to finish fourth in the NFL in yards rushing, Staley helped San Francisco running backs average a robust 5.1 yards per carry.

Memorable Moments/Greatest Performances

Staley scored the only touchdown of his career during a 24–14 win over the Jets on December 7, 2008, when he ran 6 yards to paydirt after recovering a fumble.

Staley helped the 49ers gain a season-high total of 256 yards on the ground during a 23–10 win over the Seattle Seahawks on September 20, 2009.

Staley's superior blocking at the point of attack helped the 49ers rush for 311 yards and amass 621 yards of total offense during a 45–3 rout of the Buffalo Bills on October 7, 2012.

Staley helped the 49ers control the line of scrimmage once again in the divisional round of the 2012 playoffs, with the Niners rushing for 323 yards and amassing 579 yards of total offense during a 45–31 win over the Green Bay Packers.

The signature play of Staley's career occurred during San Francisco's 36–32 victory over New Orleans in the divisional round of the 2011 play-offs when he raced downfield ahead of Alex Smith and delivered a key block against Roman Harper that enabled Smith to cross the goal line from 28 yards out. Recalling Staley's extraordinary effort, Patrick Willis said, "That was one of the biggest games of my career playing with Joe, and to see him throw that block, I remember thinking to myself, 'They're going to throw a flag,' because I felt we were the ones who always got the flag. Low [*sic*] and behold, it was a perfect block and Alex scored. I was so excited for multiple reasons. For one, it was Joe leading the way, then, two, we were winning the game and going to the NFC championship. . . .You got to have those kinds of plays to be remembered. He most definitely is going to have his time with memories."

Notable Achievements

- Three-time division champion (2011, 2012, and 2019).
- 2012 NFC champion.
- 2016 49ers MVP.
- Six-time Pro Bowl selection (2011, 2012, 2013, 2014, 2015, and 2017).
- Three-time Second-Team All-Pro selection (2011, 2012, and 2013).
- NFL 2010s All-Decade Team.

26

CEDRICK HARDMAN

The 49ers' all-time sack leader, Cedrick Hardman spent 10 seasons in San Francisco terrorizing opposing quarterbacks from his right defensive end position. Registering at least 10 sacks in a season seven times, Hardman recorded an unofficial total of 112½ sacks for the 49ers that remains a franchise record more than 40 years after he donned the Red and Gold for the last time. Leading the team in that category on five separate occasions, Hardman earned Pro Bowl and All-NFC honors twice each, with his superior pass-rushing ability helping the 49ers capture three division titles.

Born in Houston, Texas, on October 4, 1948, Cedrick Ward Hardman attended George Washington Carver High School, where he starred on the gridiron at running back, before transitioning to defensive end while in college. Although Hardman eventually developed into an elite pass-rusher at the University of North Texas, he later revealed that he initially had no intention of playing football professionally, recalling, "I was going to school, and I had no intentions of being a football player at the time. I was studying engineering, and I was on the intramural squad. One thing led to another and, the next thing I knew, I was playing football."

Seeing very little action his first two years at North Texas, Hardman remembered, "I came from the back of the pack at North Texas State. I only started two or three games my junior year, but I played next to Mean Joe Greene and got my appetite whetted for getting to the quarterback."

After becoming a member of the starting unit his senior year, Hardman emerged as a tremendous force on defense, recording 30 sacks in just 10 games, with 11 of those coming during a dominant performance against Tulsa. Named First-Team All–Missouri Valley Conference, Hardman subsequently continued his outstanding play in the Blue-Gray Game and the Senior Bowl, earning defensive MVP honors for both contests.

Impressed with Hardman's breakout season, the 49ers made him the ninth overall pick of the 1970 NFL Draft when they selected him in the first round. Hardman subsequently spent most of his rookie season serving

Cedrick Hardman holds franchise records for most sacks and most forced fumbles.
Courtesy of Mike Traverse

the 49ers primarily as a designated pass-rusher and rotational player along the defensive front, before securing a starting job during the latter stages of the campaign. Excelling in his somewhat limited role, Hardman recorded 10 sacks, although he struggled terribly against the run, with 49ers assistant coach Mike Giddings later saying that the team "held a party for Ced after he closed his first trap. The party was in 1972, his third season."

Developing into one of the NFL's premier pass-rushers in 1971, Hardman earned Pro Bowl and Second-Team All-NFC honors by recording 18 sacks, 45 tackles, and five forced fumbles. However, he sustained a serious knee injury during the subsequent offseason that hampered his performance in each of the next two seasons, recalling, "My injury in '72, that was hard. It happened in the offseason, while I was playing basketball."

Failing to give his injury enough time to heal, Hardman rushed back to action far too soon, later admitting, "It was my first major injury, and I didn't understand nature played a part in the healing process. Nature had to take its course, and it hadn't done so. I didn't play up to my best ability again until '74. I think '72 and '73 were nightmares. It was all because it hadn't healed completely, and the strength hadn't come back. I didn't understand that, and a lot of the moves I used to make, I couldn't make because I had to compensate for the weakness in my leg."

Hardman added, "I was very fortunate that I had Coach Nolan. He stuck with me, and he allowed me to get well. I played through it, and boy it hurt, but eventually I got back to normal."

Despite his ailing knee, Hardman recorded a total of 18 sacks for the 49ers from 1972 to 1973, while also registering a career-high 60 tackles in the second of those campaigns. Furthermore, sentiments expressed by 49ers defensive line coach Paul Wiggin would seem to indicate that Hardman may well have been too hard on himself, with Wiggin recalling, "I once watched him completely destroy Art Shell during a preseason game with Oakland. That, in itself, was a feat, but what made it more impressive was that he did it shortly after having major knee surgery. He damaged it in the summer and was supposed to miss the entire year, but he came back and completely manhandled Shell."

Fully healthy by the start of the 1974 season, Hardman recorded 10½ sacks, before gaining Pro Bowl and Second-Team All-NFC recognition for the second time the following year by registering 15 sacks and 41 tackles, while anchoring a defensive line that became known as the "Gold Rush" for its ability to apply pressure to opposing quarterbacks. While fellow Gold Rush members Tommy Hart, Cleveland Elam, and Jimmy Webb also got their fair share of sacks, Hardman instilled more fear in opposing signal-callers than any other member of San Francisco's defensive front, with New Orleans Saints QB Archie Manning saying, "Most times, before I could even set up to throw, Hardman had already made his way into my blind spot, all that speed coming off the corner. It was like being underwater in some rickety shark cage at night; you didn't know when it was coming, but it was coming."

Revealing his intense desire to get to the quarterback on every single down, Hardman stated, "That's what I went to San Francisco to do—sack the quarterback. Sacking the quarterback was my only reason for being in pro football. That was the attraction to me, getting after the quarterback—it consumed my whole life. Every day of my life from 1970 until I stopped, it was about getting after the quarterback."

Although somewhat undersized at 6'3" and 255 pounds, Hardman possessed so much speed and agility that opposing offensive linemen had a difficult time impeding his progress at the line of scrimmage, with Paul Wiggin saying, "When I think of Cedrick Hardman, I think of that incredibly quick first step and burst off the ball. A great space rusher. Cedrick played left end in college, and we moved him to the right side to get him away from the tight end, which really opened up his game."

Extremely confident in his ability to beat any lineman one-on-one, Hardman claimed, "If I got off the ball, then I was gone. I had the philosophy in my head that there was no way a guy could go backwards faster than I could go forward. Whenever I got off the ball, I was gone. It didn't matter what was pre-planned, when I really got off, I just went, and I thought I could beat the guy in front of me and get around him."

Hardman continued, "Most sacks are gotten on the snap count, on the get-off. That's the one thing the rule makers can't take away from you. My main weapon was speed. If I could get off the ball—I mean, really get off the ball—there would be no contact until I reached the quarterback. That offensive tackle would not touch me. I lined up way outside, so much that I changed the way that defensive end was played. In fact, my style of pass-rushing evolved into what eventually became the rush linebacker in the 3-4 defense. Players like Lawrence Taylor and Pat Swilling and Derrick Thomas—those players lined up outside the tackle."

Hardman ended his soliloquy by saying, "I chased and caught quarterbacks—plain and simple, end of story. That was my business. That's what I feel I was put on this earth to do. Ask any of those number 12's or 14's what kind of game I brought on Sunday back in the '70s. I can assure you, my friend, their memories mostly aren't pleasant ones."

Revealing that Hardman forced his team to alter its approach on offense, St. Louis Cardinals quarterback Jim Hart stated, "Hardman was incredibly quick, so the key for us was throwing quickly, a lot of three-step drops. Those kinds of plays can frustrate any great pass rusher. Then, we'd mix in the draw plays, which would often work because he was so aggressive. Then, the play-action passes. The whole operation was focused on keeping him off-balance, to keep him thinking. The last thing I wanted to do was sit back there in a seven-step drop and let Hardman make his statement."

Hardman continued to excel at right defensive end for the 49ers for four more years, recording another 41 sacks from 1976 to 1979, despite missing five games due to various injuries, including a broken fibula that forced him to the sidelines for the final three games of the 1976 season. But, with the 49ers in a rebuilding mode following a 2-14 finish in 1979, they released Hardman, who subsequently signed with the Oakland Raiders. Hardman left San Francisco with unofficial career totals of 112½ sacks, 18 forced fumbles, seven fumble recoveries, and 437 tackles, with the first two figures both representing franchise records.

Serving the Raiders primarily as a situational pass-rusher the next two seasons, Hardman contributed to an Oakland team that defeated Philadelphia in Super Bowl XV. After retiring at the end of 1981, Hardman spent one season serving as a player-coach with the Oakland Invaders in the ill-fated USFL, before retiring for good. Looking back at his brief stint in the USFL, Hardman said, "After the NFL, that was tough. We had a trip to Birmingham, and it was like a whistle-stop. It took 10 hours by airplane. Somewhere over Tennessee, I made up my mind I wouldn't play any more football."

Following his playing days, Hardman began a career in acting, landing roles in the films *Stir Crazy* and *House Party*, and appearing on the television shows *Police Woman* and *The Fall Guy*. Hardman also became involved in a variety of business and coaching ventures, briefly serving as a volunteer training camp assistant with the Baltimore Ravens. Hardman lived until March 8, 2019, when he died of undisclosed causes at the age of 70. In announcing his passing, the 49ers released a statement that read, "We are truly saddened by the loss of one of the all-time great 49ers, Cedrick Hardman. During his 10-year career in red and gold, he anchored the vaunted 'Gold Rush' defensive line with a nonstop motor that put fear in the minds of opposing quarterbacks. As a football player, Cedrick's accomplishments were many. As a man, his impact on the lives of others was just as impressive. Our condolences and prayers go out to the Hardman family and all who are mourning the passing of Cedrick."

49ERS CAREER HIGHLIGHTS

Best Season

Hardman played his best ball for the 49ers in 1971, when, in addition to recording an unofficial and career-high total of 18 sacks, he forced five fumbles and registered 45 tackles, earning in the process Pro Bowl and Second-Team All-NFC honors. Years later, Hardman revealed that, according to former *Oakland Tribune* sportswriter Dave Newhouse, he actually registered 21 sacks, claiming, "Newhouse kept up with my sacks—he knew I had 21." Hardman then added, "That year, we played the Cowboys, and I had five on Roger Staubach in the NFC championship game. We lost 14–3, so it didn't matter, but that was what our coach Dick Nolan expected of me."

Memorable Moments/Greatest Performances

Hardman scored his only points as a member of the 49ers when he sacked quarterback Bobby Scott in the end zone for a safety during a 40–0 mauling of the Saints on October 21, 1973.

Hardman contributed to San Francisco's 17–14 win over Minnesota in the divisional round of the 1970 NFC playoffs by sacking quarterback Gary Cuozzo twice.

Hardman proved to be a huge factor when the 49ers recorded a 24–20 victory over Washington in the divisional round of the 1971 postseason tournament. After preventing the Redskins from increasing their seven-point lead in the closing moments of the first half by throwing wide receiver Roy Jefferson for a 12-yard loss on a flanker reverse from deep in 49ers territory, Hardman helped preserve the victory by sacking quarterback Billy Kilmer on the game's final play.

Although the 49ers lost to the Cowboys by a score of 14–3 in the 1971 NFC championship game one week later, Hardman recorded 3½ of the five sacks they registered against Roger Staubach.

Hardman once again starred in defeat against Dallas in the divisional round of the 1972 NFC playoffs, recording another 3½ sacks during a 30–28 loss.

Notable Achievements

- Finished in double digits in sacks seven times.
- Led 49ers in sacks five times.
- Holds 49ers "unofficial" career records for most sacks (112½) and forced fumbles (18).
- Three-time division champion (1970, 1971, and 1972).
- Two-time Pro Bowl selection (1971 and 1975).
- Two-time Second-Team All-NFC selection (1971 and 1975).

27
JOHN TAYLOR

A study in perseverance, John Taylor overcame the death of his mother, an inauspicious beginning to his NFL career, and a drug suspension to establish himself as one of the league's most dangerous wide receivers. Despite spending his entire time in San Francisco playing second fiddle to Jerry Rice, Taylor surpassed 50 receptions three times and 1,000 receiving yards twice, ending his nine-year stay in the City by the Bay as one of the franchise's all-time leaders in both categories. An outstanding performer on special teams as well, Taylor amassed the second-most punt-return yards in team annals, with his varied skill set making him a key contributor to 49er teams that won eight division titles and three Super Bowls. A two-time Pro Bowler and one-time All-Pro, Taylor received the additional honor of being named to the NFL 1980s All-Decade Second Team for his abilities as a punt-returner.

Born in Pennsauken, New Jersey, on March 31, 1962, John Gregory Taylor received his introduction to sports at a local graveyard that he and his childhood friends used as a makeshift playground. Preferring baseball over football during his early years, Taylor fared much better on the diamond than he did on the gridiron at Pennsauken High School, with one of the school's football coaches, Mike Colombo, later saying, "He was a nonentity here as an athlete. I'm telling you, he may have caught the winning pass against the Bengals in the Super Bowl, but, if you wanted to go back and see him play as a senior, you'd have to wade through 40 cans of film to find him."

Weighing barely 140 pounds when he graduated from Pennsauken High, Taylor received just one scholarship offer to play baseball in college, which he rejected, choosing instead to work at a liquor warehouse. Taylor spent the next several months driving a liquor truck, until a mugging in Atlantic City prompted him to turn in his dolly and union card, with Colombo recalling that Taylor told him afterwards, "My life isn't worth a couple of bottles of booze."

John Taylor excelled for the 49ers on both offense and special teams.
Courtesy of George A. Kitrinos

Taylor subsequently assumed numerous odd jobs the next few months, before a growth spurt that added three inches and 20 pounds onto his frame convinced him to give college sports a try. After competing in baseball for one year at tiny Johnson C. Smith University in Charlotte, North Carolina, Taylor transferred to Delaware State University, where he spent the next three seasons excelling on the gridiron as a wide receiver and return man, ending his college career with 100 receptions, 2,426 receiving yards, 33 TD catches, and 42 touchdowns. Performing especially well as a senior in 1985, Taylor gained recognition as the Mid-Eastern Athletic Conference (MEAC) Offensive Player of the Year and earned All-MEAC First-Team honors for the second straight time by setting new single-season conference records for most touchdowns (15) and TD catches (13).

Selected by the 49ers in the third round of the 1986 NFL Draft, with the 76th overall pick, Taylor arrived in San Francisco unprepared to compete at the pro level, with former 49ers receivers coach Denny Green recalling, "He could run two patterns when he got here—go short and go long." Further hampered by a back strain he sustained during training camp, Taylor spent his first year in the league on injured reserve, before making only nine receptions for 151 yards upon his return to the active list in 1987. Nevertheless, Bill Walsh remained optimistic about Taylor's future, constantly praising him for his athletic ability and toughness after the catch.

Unfortunately, Taylor suffered another setback just prior to the start of the 1988 regular season when the NFL suspended him for violating the league's substance abuse policy, causing him to miss the first four games of the campaign. Looking back on his transgression some years later, Taylor said, "Drugs were all around me growing up at home, at college, and even once I got here. I cannot believe it when people say they haven't done this, or there is no way they will do that. When you're young, you're dumb. I came here in 1986 and two years later I made a mistake. I used cocaine."

Taylor continued, "I failed a drug test in training camp. I was warned, and I got the message. And then they took two more tests before the first game of the season, one for the 49ers and one for the league. The one here came out negative and the one by the league was positive. I asked for a new test, but the league said no. I was suspended, out of the box for 30 days. And then the league came back long after it was all over and said they had made a mistake. I would miss the first game, against New Orleans. I would miss four games in all, but I promised myself I was not going to be another black man that became a miserable statistic. I promised myself I would come back better, stronger."

Taylor did indeed come back better and stronger, earning Pro Bowl and First-Team All-NFC honors in 1988 by leading the league with 556 punt-return yards, two punt-return TDs, and an average of 12.6 yards per punt-return, making 14 receptions for 325 yards and two touchdowns, and amassing 1,106 all-purpose yards. Taylor then punctuated his outstanding season by gathering in a 10-yard TD pass from Joe Montana in the closing moments of Super Bowl XXIII, to give the 49ers a dramatic 20–16 victory over the Cincinnati Bengals. Taylor followed that up with a banner year in 1989, gaining Pro Bowl and Second-Team All-Pro recognition by accumulating 468 yards on special teams and making 60 receptions for 1,077 yards and 10 touchdowns after joining the starting offensive unit.

Claiming that the improvement in Taylor's play did not surprise him in the least, Roger Craig said that he knew his teammate had the ability to succeed in the NFL the first time he saw him at training camp in 1987, recalling, "The things that he was doing in practice were unbelievable. I'm just happy they started throwing more to him."

Meanwhile, Bill Walsh addressed Taylor's rise to prominence by saying, "John came to the 49ers as a wide receiver from Delaware State. He had great physical talent, but not a lot of background in playing sophisticated football. We simply miscalculated how long it would take John to be ready to play in the NFL. Consequently, we were disappointed in him. John was not adapting well to the competition, he appeared confused and frustrated, and he had lost his enthusiasm. . . . But instead of giving up on him, we took a longer term, more patient approach. We waited an extra year to allow him to mature and grow into this level of competition and into the role we wanted him to play. Now he is an All-Pro and one of the great receivers in the game."

In addition to his physical gifts, which included outstanding speed and superb leaping ability, the 6'1", 185-pound Taylor possessed soft hands, good moves, and the ability to break tackles, making him extremely dangerous once he got his hands on the football. One of the league's top deep threats, Taylor averaged more than 17 yards per reception three times, recording seven touchdown catches of at least 70 yards over the course of his career. Taylor also returned two punts for touchdowns, with one of those covering 95 yards.

Yet, even as Taylor emerged as one of the NFL's better receivers, he retained inside of him a certain amount of bitterness toward the media for its handling of his drug suspension, which he believed contributed to the death of his mother from an aneurysm nearly one year later. Complex, moody, and somewhat introverted, Taylor did not speak to anyone in the press for a long period of time, explaining his actions by saying: "The press had written that I was suspended for drugs and alcohol when I had not ever been asked about it, and when they didn't even know the full story. Nobody bothered to dig and find out. They just wrote what they thought. Sure, it hurt me, but it hurt my family even more. Especially my mom. And less than a year later, she died. . . . I blamed them for it. She went to her grave never knowing the full truth. I promised myself I would never forgive them for that."

Although doctors later explained to Taylor that his mother's aneurysm was solely responsible for her passing since it had gone undetected for quite some time, he continued his practice of not speaking to the media, later saying, "By then, it was established, John Taylor does not talk to the press. And things were working out for me. So, I figured, if it ain't broke, don't fix it."

Taylor remained a significant contributor to the 49ers on offense for six more years, recording more than 50 receptions and 900 receiving yards another two times from 1990 to 1995. Performing especially well in 1991 and 1993, Taylor caught 64 passes, amassed 1,011 receiving yards, scored nine touchdowns, and accumulated 1,278 all-purpose yards in the first of those campaigns, before making 56 receptions for 940 yards and five touch downs two years later. But, after seeing his production fall off somewhat in 1995, Taylor announced his retirement when the 49ers released him, ending his career with 347 receptions, 5,598 receiving yards, 1,517 punt return yards, 7,448 all-purpose yards, 43 TD catches, and 46 touchdowns.

Since retiring from football, Taylor has remained mostly out of the spotlight, once owning his own trucking company, before taking a job as a staff member in San Jose juvenile detention.

CAREER HIGHLIGHTS

Best Season

Although Taylor amassed a single-season franchise record 556 punt-return yards in 1988, he had his finest all-around season in 1989, earning his lone All-Pro nomination by making 60 receptions and establishing career-high marks with 1,077 receiving yards, 1,083 yards from scrimmage, 1,551 all-purpose yards, and 10 touchdowns.

Memorable Moments/Greatest Performances

Taylor scored the first touchdown of his career when, after recovering a fumble on offense, he ran the ball in from 26 yards out during a 48–0 dismantling of the Los Angeles Rams in the final game of the 1987 regular season.

Taylor contributed to a 20–13 victory over the Detroit Lions on October 2, 1988, by returning a punt 77 yards for a touchdown.

Taylor made the first TD reception of his career when he collaborated with Steve Young on a 73-yard scoring play during a 24–21 win over the Minnesota Vikings on October 30, 1988.

Taylor recorded the longest punt return in franchise history when he returned a punt 95 yards for a touchdown during a 37–21 win over the Washington Redskins on November 21, 1988.

Although Taylor made just one reception in Super Bowl XXIII, it proved to be a big one, with his 10-yard TD grab with just 34 seconds remaining in regulation giving the 49ers a 20–16 victory over the Cincinnati Bengals.

Taylor went over 100 receiving yards for the first time in his career during a 38–28 win over the Philadelphia Eagles on September 24, 1989, finishing the game with six catches for 136 yards and one touchdown, which came on a 70-yard connection with Joe Montana.

Taylor helped lead the 49ers to a 24–20 win over New Orleans on October 8, 1989, by gathering in a pair of fourth-quarter touchdown passes from Joe Montana, with his 32-yard grab during the latter stages of the final period providing the margin of victory.

Taylor torched the Atlanta defensive secondary for five receptions, 162 receiving yards, and one touchdown during a 23–10 win on December 3, 1989, with his TD coming on a 38-yard pass from Steve Young.

Taylor followed that up with an extraordinary effort, earning NFC Offensive Player of the Week honors by making 11 receptions for 286 yards and two touchdowns during a 30–27 victory over the Rams on December 11, 1989, with his 286 receiving yards representing a single-game franchise record. Taylor, who collaborated with Joe Montana on scoring plays that covered 92 and 95 yards, also returned three punts for 35 yards, giving him a total of 321 all-purpose yards.

Taylor contributed to a 26–13 win over Washington on September 16, 1990, by making eight receptions for 160 yards and one TD, which came on a 49-yard hookup with Joe Montana.

Taylor proved to be the difference in a 24–21 victory over the Houston Oilers on October 7, 1990, catching four passes for 132 yards and two touchdowns. After gathering in a 78-yard TD pass from Joe Montana earlier in the contest, Taylor scored the game-winning touchdown in the final period when he collaborated with Montana again, this time from 46 yards out.

Taylor provided further late-game heroics when he hooked up with Steve Young on a 34-yard scoring play in the closing minutes of a 20–17 win over Minnesota in the final game of the 1990 regular season.

Although the 49ers ended up losing the 1990 NFC championship game to the Giants by a score of 15–13, Taylor recorded the only touchdown of the contest in the third quarter when he gathered in a 61-yard pass from Joe Montana.

Taylor accounted for both 49er touchdowns during a 17–14 loss to Atlanta on November 3, 1991, with one of his TDs coming on a 97-yard reception that remains the longest in franchise history.

Taylor earned NFC Offensive Player of the Week honors by making seven receptions for 113 yards and one touchdown during a 24–22 win over the Seattle Seahawks on December 8, 1991, with his 15-yard TD grab in the closing moments providing the margin of victory.

Taylor had a big game against the Rams on November 28, 1993, making six receptions for 150 yards and one touchdown during a 35–10 49ers win, with his TD coming on a 76-yard pass from Steve Young.

Notable Achievements

- Returned two punts for touchdowns.
- Surpassed 50 receptions three times.
- Surpassed 1,000 receiving yards twice.
- Surpassed 1,000 all-purpose yards three times, topping 1,500 yards once.
- Scored 10 touchdowns in 1989.
- Averaged more than 20 yards per reception once.
- Recorded longest punt return in NFL in 1988 (95 yards).
- Recorded longest reception in NFL in 1991 (97 yards).
- Led NFL in punt-return yards, punt-return touchdowns, and punt-return average in 1988.
- Holds 49ers single-season record for most punt-return yards (556 in 1988).
- Ranks among 49ers career leaders with 347 receptions (tied-9th), 5,598 receiving yards (7th), 43 touchdown receptions (tied-8th), 1,517 punt-return yards (2nd), and 7,448 all-purpose yards (9th).
- Eight-time division champion (1987, 1988, 1989, 1990, 1992, 1993, 1994, and 1995).
- Three-time NFC champion (1988, 1989, and 1994).
- Three-time Super Bowl champion (XXIII, XXIV, and XXIX).
- Two-time NFC Offensive Player of the Week.
- Two-time Pro Bowl selection (1988 and 1989).
- 1989 Second-Team All-Pro selection.
- 1988 First-Team All-NFC selection.
- NFL 1980s All-Decade Second Team.

28

BRUCE BOSLEY

Once referred to as the best center in the game by Detroit Lions Hall of Fame middle linebacker Joe Schmidt, Bruce Bosley spent 13 seasons in San Francisco excelling for the 49ers at both center and guard. Earning Pro Bowl honors at both positions, Bosley appeared in four league All-Star games, while also gaining All-Pro recognition once and All–Western Conference recognition twice. One of the league's most durable players, Bosley missed just three games from 1958 to 1968, at one point appearing in every contest the 49ers played for six consecutive seasons. And, although the 49ers failed to earn a playoff berth with Bosley starring for them up front, his outstanding blocking at the point of attack helped them consistently rank among the NFL leaders in points scored and total offense.

Born in Fresno, California, on November 5, 1933, Bruce Lee Bosley moved with his family at an early age to Green Bank, West Virginia, where he starred on the gridiron at fullback while attending Green Bank High School. Looking back at the time the two young men spent together at Green Bank, longtime friend Gary McPherson, who went on to play basketball at the collegiate level, recalled, "Bruce was two years ahead of me, but we played football together two years, and his stretch was really impressive. I didn't know anyone stronger in the area before consolidation. Bruce was the strongest guy around. . . . I was only 6'1½" and about 162 pounds during my two years in high school. Bosley was so much bigger and stronger. He was about 6'2" and 250 pounds. He could run over people. . . . He really had a body on him. He would be driving down High Steer in Morgantown with one arm and holding a piece of lumber outside the car with the other arm."

After earning Third-Team Class B All-State honors at Green Bank, Bosley received a football scholarship to West Virginia University, where he spent his college career starring for head coach Art "Pappy" Lewis as a two-way tackle. A four-year letter winner at WVU, Bosley combined brute strength with the agility of a much smaller man to be named to 12

Bruce Bosley earned Pro Bowl honors for the 49ers as both a center and a guard.
Courtesy of Mike Traverse

All-America teams, with his stellar play on both sides of the ball helping to lead the Mountaineers to an overall record of 31-7. Performing especially well as a senior in 1955, Bosley earned consensus All-America honors, prompting the 49ers to select him in the second round of the 1956 NFL Draft, with the 15th overall pick.

Inserted at left defensive end immediately upon his arrival in San Francisco, Bosley spent his first NFL season starting for the 49ers at that post, before moving to guard the following year. Plagued by injuries in 1957, Bosley appeared in only six games, before beginning a four-year run during which he started all but four contests for the 49ers at left guard. Establishing himself as one of the league's top players at that position, Bosley earned Second-Team All-Pro and First-Team All–Western Conference honors in

1959. Although Bosley failed to gain official All-Pro recognition from the Associated Press the following year, three major news sources named him to their All-Pro squads, with the Newspaper Enterprise Association (NEA), *New York Daily News*, and United Press International (UPI) all according him Second-Team honors.

Continuing to excel after the 49ers moved him to center in 1962, Bosley anchored the interior of San Francisco's offensive line for the next seven seasons, missing just one contest and earning three more trips to the Pro Bowl during that time, while also garnering another All-Pro nomination from the *New York Daily News* in 1966.

Standing 6'2" and weighing close to 250 pounds, Bosley used his superior size, strength, and intelligence to dominate his opponent in the trenches, helping the 49ers' offense gradually emerge as one of the best in the NFL, with their 421 points scored and 5,270 yards of total offense in 1965, both leading the league. Also blessed with outstanding quickness and athleticism, Bosley became one of the first centers to play in the shotgun formation, which 49ers head coach Red Hickey began implementing in 1961. An outstanding leader as well, Bosley spent two seasons serving as a team captain.

Dealt to the Atlanta Falcons following the conclusion of the 1968 campaign, Bosley spent one final season in Atlanta, starting nine games for the Falcons at center, before announcing his retirement. Ending his 14-year playing career having missed a total of just nine games, Bosley started 156 of the 175 contests in which he appeared.

Following his retirement, Bosley, who opened a home restoration business during his playing days, continued to manage the operation and worked tirelessly in several civic endeavors, serving on the board of directors for the San Francisco Annex for Cultural Arts and the San Francisco Council for the Performing Arts. He also served as president of the NFL Alumni Association and volunteered much of his time to the San Francisco Film Festival and the San Francisco Ballet.

Commenting on Bosley's many philanthropic contributions to the community, *Vallejo Independent Press* sports editor Dave Beronio once wrote, "As a newsman of more than 40 years, I have found very few 'Bruce Bosleys,' those willing to contribute and participate during and after their days as stars. It would be difficult for me to believe that I will see his equal again in our area."

Yet, even though Bosley spent nearly 40 years of his life in Northern California, he never forgot his West Virginia roots, once telling *Charleston*

Daily Mail sports editor Bill Smith, "Things may change, and your career may take you away in a different direction, but there are things you never forget. I've never left my roots. They are in West Virginia."

Bosley remained active in the San Francisco community until April 26, 1995, when he died of a heart attack at 61 years of age while attending the United Way's annual awards dinner at the Westin St. Francis Hotel. Stricken just as some 500 guests were being seated in the hotel ballroom, Bosley failed to regain consciousness after having cardiopulmonary resuscitation administered to him by paramedics. Describing the incident shortly thereafter, Hosea Martin, the United Way's associate vice president for marketing, said, It was a traumatic experience. Some tears were being shed. There was a feeling of helplessness."

Upon learning of his onetime teammate's passing, former 49ers wide receiver R. C. Owens said, "Bruce was a great, great football player and a great character, both on and off the field. I'm really going to miss him."

49ERS CAREER HIGHLIGHTS

Best Season

It could be argued that Bosley played his best ball for the 49ers in 1965, when he earned one of his four trips to the Pro Bowl, with his outstanding play prompting Pro Football Reference to assign him an "Approximate Value" of 10 that represented the highest grade of his career. However, Bosley gained All-Pro recognition for the only time in 1959, with the *Sporting News* awarding him a spot on its First Team and the Associated Press according him official Second-Team honors.

Memorable Moments/Greatest Performances

Bosley helped the 49ers amass 407 yards of total offense during a 34–13 win over the Detroit Lions on October 18, 1959, with 299 of those yards coming on the ground.

Bosley's superior blocking at the point of attack helped the 49ers rush for 218 yards and gain a total of 536 yards on offense during a 41–31 win over the Chicago Bears on November 19, 1961.

Bosley dominated his man at the line of scrimmage once again on November 18, 1962, with the 49ers rushing for 207 yards and amassing

470 yards of total offense during a 24–17 victory over the Los Angeles Rams.

Bosley anchored an offensive line that enabled the 49ers to amass 487 yards of total offense during a 41–14 manhandling of the Lions on November 24, 1966, with 214 of those yards coming on the ground.

Notable Achievements

- Played in every game in 10 of 13 seasons, at one point appearing in every contest for six straight seasons.
- Four-time Pro Bowl selection (1960, 1965, 1966, and 1967).
- 1959 Second-Team All-Pro selection.

29

LEN ROHDE

A teammate of his immediate predecessor on this list for nine seasons, Len Rohde spent 15 years in San Francisco, appearing in more games during that time than any other offensive lineman in team annals. Starting every game that the 49ers played from 1963 to 1974, Rohde never missed a game his entire career, appearing in a franchise-record 208 consecutive contests. A pillar of strength for the 49ers at left offensive tackle, Rohde provided ample pass protection for John Brodie and created huge holes in the running game, with his consistently excellent play making him a key contributor to teams that won three division championships.

Born in Palatine, Illinois, on April 16, 1938, Leonard Emil Rohde acquired a strong work ethic at an early age, helping out on his family's dairy farm while also attending a one-room country school that, in his own words, had "one teacher, eight grades, and 24 kids all in the same place." Left with little time to pursue outside interests, Rohde did not compete in sports until his sophomore year at Palatine Township High School, recalling years later that he did so at the urging of his freshman English teacher, Charles Feutz, who doubled as the school's football coach. Recounting how he began his career on the gridiron, Rohde said, "I come in and I'm bigger than most of the kids, and Mr. Feutz says, 'Have you ever thought about going out for football?' I told him, 'No, not really. We've got work on the farm. I've got work after school.'"

Revealing that Feutz remained determined to recruit him for the football team, Rohde continued, "He was pretty creative. He told the other guys on the team, 'Listen, if you ever see that big hayseed guy around school, you ought to befriend him, see if he'd be interested in trying out for football.' By the end of the year, a lot of the guys I hung around with were guys on the football team. So, the next year I joined them."

After spending his sophomore year learning the intricacies of offensive and defensive line play, Rohde missed most of his junior year due to a knee injury. However, he established himself as a standout two-way lineman as

Len Rohde appeared in a franchise-record 208 consecutive games for the 49ers.
Courtesy of Mike Traverse

a senior, while also winning the Illinois state heavyweight wrestling championship. Subsequently spurning several offers to wrestle in college, Rohde instead chose to attend Utah State University on a football scholarship, recalling, "Actually, most of my offers from colleges were to wrestle. Yet I really wanted to play football. I really didn't care that much about wrestling. Utah State gave me a shot as a football player, and that's where I went."

Rohde ended up starting for the Aggies at offensive tackle and defensive end for three years, gaining All–Skyline Eight recognition twice, and being named team captain his senior year, when he also earned team MVP honors.

Selected by the 49ers in the fifth round of the 1960 NFL Draft, with the 59th overall pick, Rohde chose to play in the NFL, rather than join the

Buffalo Bills, who also selected him in that year's AFL Draft. Rohde then spent his first two seasons in San Francisco serving primarily as a backup to starting right tackle Bob St. Clair, before a strong preseason showing at right defensive end in 1962 convinced him that he had found a new home, with Rohde saying years later, "A few weeks before the season started, we'd played the New York Giants at Kezar in an exhibition game. Y. A. Tittle was playing against the 49ers for the first time since he'd been traded to the Giants the year before. I was playing against him as a defensive end and got a couple sacks on him. Then Leo Nomellini blocked a punt. I fell on it in the end zone for a touchdown. I thought I was going, man. Things were taking off for me."

But, after being installed as the starting right defensive end for the regular-season opener, Rohde struggled terribly, prompting the coaching staff to move him back to the offensive side of the ball. Rohde finally received his big break later that year, though, when St. Clair tore his Achilles tendon, allowing Rohde to start the final six contests at right tackle. After holding his own against Rams Hall of Fame defensive end Deacon Jones, Rohde became the 49ers' starting left tackle the following year, a role he maintained for the next 12 seasons.

Starting 168 consecutive contests from 1963 to 1974, the 6'4", 250-pound Rohde remained a fixture at left tackle for a 49ers offense that often ranked among the most potent in the NFL. Performing his job in unspectacular fashion, Rohde did not excel in any particular aspect of offensive line play. But he gradually established himself as one of the league's steadiest and most reliable linemen, doing an outstanding job of protecting the blindside of quarterback John Brodie, while also providing excellent lead blocking for running backs Ken Willard and J. D. Smith, each of whom ranks among the franchise's all-time leading rushers. Finally recognized for his consistently strong play in 1970, Rohde earned Pro Bowl honors for the only time in his career by helping the 49ers capture the division title for the first of three straight times.

Displaying tremendous grit and determination through the years, Rohde played through several injuries, the most serious of which nearly caused his string of consecutive starts to come to an end in 1974, with Rohde remembering, "We played the New York Jets, and I had a bad knee injury, so I wrapped it up. Then, we were going to play the Kansas City Chiefs the next Monday. I didn't play a whole lot, but I did play a couple of downs. Fortunately, I recovered quickly and finished the game out."

Presented with the Len Eshmont Award as the team's most courageous and inspirational player at season's end, Rohde discussed his streak years later, saying, "It's one of those things that creeps up on you and you don't realize. You don't set out to do something like that, you take things one at a time and, all of a sudden, you realize you've got a string going. And then you hope you can hang on."

Rohde hung on until the end of 1974, when a bad back and a conversation with head coach Dick Nolan prompted him to announce his retirement. Recalling the events that transpired at the time, Rohde said, "I was getting to the point where my back was bothering me quite a bit. Almost every practice had become a struggle, but I hadn't definitely said, 'Hey, this is it.' I had my streak going, and I thought I was still playing pretty well."

Rohde continued, "Coach Nolan treated me well. He pulled me in one day and said, 'You've been a good team guy all these years and you could really help us a lot.' And I said, 'How can I do that?' And he said, 'If you retire.' I said, 'I think I got the message.'"

Following his playing days, Rohde opened several restaurants in the San Francisco Bay Area, at one point owning nine Burger King and six Applebee's franchises. Eventually retiring to private life, Rohde helped raise money for children every year through his involvement with the NFL Alumni golf tournament. Rohde lived until May 13, 2017, when he passed away nearly one month after celebrating his 79th birthday, with the cause of death not made public.

Looking back on his playing career several years earlier, Rohde said, "As an offensive tackle, there aren't too many individual stats you can hang your hat on. But I guess playing in 208 games, winning the Len Eshmont, the NFC West, and going to the Pro Bowl aren't bad."

Particularly proud of the NFL sack record he helped the 49ers set in 1970, Rohde stated, "We allowed eight sacks in an entire season, and that was an NFL record. The record earned us the nickname, 'The Protectors,' and it's one of the things I'm most proud of when I look back on my career."

Rohde continued, "I had a long career. The first two, three years, it was survival: get me to the end of the day. Get me to the end of the week, and there were quite a few years like that, though I got in the Pro Bowl one year. . . . Maybe I wasn't where I ultimately would like to be—one of the top players and in the Hall of Fame and all that. I wasn't quite at that level, but I was at a level where they weren't looking to replace me all the time. I was there, and I was doing my job."

Rohde then added, "I probably wouldn't have gone to college without football. I owe an awful lot to the game, and I was around people who had a great influence on me. I feel pretty grateful for the opportunities, and I wouldn't trade them for anything."

CAREER HIGHLIGHTS

Best Season

Rohde had the finest season of his career in 1970, when he earned his only trip to the Pro Bowl by helping the 49ers finish first in the NFL in total offense, with the team's impenetrable offensive line allowing just eight sacks of John Brodie all year.

Memorable Moments/Greatest Performances

Rohde anchored an offensive line that enabled the 49ers to amass 517 yards of total offense during a 38–7 win over the Atlanta Falcons on September 24, 1967, with 180 of those yards coming on the ground.

Rohde and his line-mates dominated Atlanta's defense at the point of attack once again on December 10, 1972, with the 49ers gaining a season-high total of 210 yards on the ground during a 20–0 win.

Rohde helped the 49ers rush for 203 yards and amass 424 yards of total offense during a 40–0 mauling of the New Orleans Saints on October 21, 1973.

Notable Achievements

- Never missed a game his entire career, appearing in franchise-record 208 consecutive contests.
- Ranks among 49ers career leaders with 15 seasons played (tied for 4th) and 208 games played (tied for 3rd).
- Three-time division champion (1970, 1971, and 1972).
- 1970 Pro Bowl selection.

30

MATT HAZELTINE

One of the most overlooked and underappreciated players in franchise history, Matt Hazeltine spent 14 seasons in San Francisco, appearing in more games during that time than any other linebacker in team annals. The first truly outstanding player to man that position for the 49ers, Hazeltine spent most of his time lining up on the right side of San Francisco's defense, where he proved to be strong against both the run and the pass, recording 12 interceptions and recovering 16 fumbles, with the second figure placing him among the team's all-time leaders. Although the 49ers made just one playoff appearance during his lengthy stay in the City by the Bay, Hazeltine earned the respect of everyone around the league with his consistently excellent play, gaining Pro Bowl and All-Pro recognition twice each.

Born just north of San Francisco, in the small town of Ross, California, on August 2, 1933, Matthew Emory Hazeltine Jr. attended Tamalpais High School in nearby Mill Valley, where he emerged as a two-way star on the gridiron, playing center on offense and linebacker on defense for the school's football team. Continuing to excel at both positions after accepting an athletic scholarship to the University of California–Berkeley, Hazeltine established himself as a top prospect by gaining Freshman All-America recognition in 1951, before being accorded All-America honors following both his junior and senior years.

Selected by the 49ers in the fourth round of the 1955 NFL Draft, with the 45th overall pick, Hazeltine arrived in San Francisco expecting to play center. But, with veteran Bill Johnson still holding down that position, the 49ers needing much more help on the defensive side of the ball, and Hazeltine having intercepted 10 passes during his college career, the coaching staff decided to employ him at linebacker instead. After earning a starting job during training camp, Hazeltine acquitted himself extremely well as a rookie, while splitting his time between both outside linebacker positions in San Francisco's new 4-3 defense (most teams at that time were

Matt Hazeltine appeared in more games for the 49ers than any other linebacker in franchise history.
Courtesy of Footballcardgallery.com

in the process of transitioning from a 5-2 alignment). Hazeltine then spent the next two seasons assuming a similar role, before finally settling in at right-side linebacker in 1958, where he remained for the rest of his career.

Gradually establishing himself as one of the better outside linebackers in the game, Hazeltine earned First-Team All–Western Conference honors for the first of two times in 1959, when he ranked among the league leaders with three fumble recoveries, which he returned for a total of 42 yards and one touchdown. Hazeltine also gained Pro Bowl and Second-Team All-Pro recognition in both 1962 and 1964, recording an "unofficial" total of 11½ sacks in the second of those campaigns.

Although somewhat undersized at 6'1" and 220 pounds, Hazeltine compensated for whatever he lacked in that area with his quickness, intelligence, and superb instincts. An extremely cerebral player, Hazeltine did an outstanding job of studying his opponents and breaking down their tendencies, allowing him to consistently be in the right place at the right time. As a result, Hazeltine typically was among the first 49ers defenders to arrive at the football, even though the unavailability of tackling statistics for that period makes it impossible to determine just how many times he brought down opposing ball-carriers. Nevertheless, Hazeltine's 12 interceptions, 16 fumble recoveries, and three defensive touchdowns serve as testaments to his playmaking ability. An excellent team leader as well, Hazeltine served as a 49ers team captain for five seasons.

Hazeltine's greatest strengths, though, may well have been his consistency and durability. Although not particularly flamboyant, Hazeltine proved to be one of the 49ers most reliable and dependable players, performing his job in an understated, but extremely effective manner. Meanwhile, he earned the nickname "Iron Man" by starting every game the 49ers played 11 times from 1955 to 1968, appearing in 176 out of a possible 184 contests during that 14-year period. Just as outstanding off the field, Hazeltine later had a team award named after him, with the Matt Hazeltine Award being presented annually to the team's "most courageous and inspirational defensive player."

However, Father Time eventually began to catch up with Hazeltine, and, with the 36-year-old linebacker already showing signs of slowing down, his days as a starter in San Francisco came to an end in 1969, when he sustained a series of injuries that kept him out the entire year. But, feeling that he still had something left to offer, Hazeltine signed with the Giants prior to the 1970 campaign, with his wisdom and leadership helping them nearly advance to the playoffs. Proving to be particularly influential in the development of young defensive end Fred Dryer, who went on to stardom as a member of the Los Angeles Rams, Hazeltine later drew praise from his onetime pupil, who called him his "Rock of Gilbraltar" and credited him for helping maximize his abilities.

Choosing to announce his retirement after one year in New York, Hazeltine, who opened an insurance agency in Los Altos, California, during his playing days, transitioned seamlessly into a career in business, spending the next several years expanding his operation, before contracting amyotrophic lateral sclerosis (ALS), also known as Lou Gehrig's disease, in 1981. After being confined to a wheelchair for more than a year, Hazeltine lost his battle with the dreaded disease on January 13, 1987, passing away at only

53 years of age, with his death coming just one month after former 49er running back Gary Lewis lost his life to the same illness.

Some 30 years later, after Dwight Clark announced that he, too, faced a similar fate, Hazeltine's widow, Deborah, spoke of her husband's final days, saying, "Matt knew what Dwight Clark learned: There is no cure, and the body is going to give out."

She then added, "Getting hit time and time and time again, God knows how many concussions that man suffered."

49ERS CAREER HIGHLIGHTS

Best Season

Hazeltine gained Pro Bowl and All-Pro recognition in both 1962 and 1964, playing the best ball of his career in the second of those campaigns, when he recorded an unofficial total of 11½ sacks.

Memorable Moments/Greatest Performances

Hazeltine scored the first of his three career touchdowns during a 35–27 loss to the Baltimore Colts on November 30, 1958, when he returned his interception of a Johnny Unitas pass 13 yards for a TD that gave the 49ers a 27–7 lead late in the first half.

Hazeltine lit the scoreboard again when he returned a fumble 40 yards for a touchdown during a 34–13 win over the Detroit Lions on October 18, 1959.

Hazeltine crossed the opponent's goal line for the final time in his career when he returned a fumble 22 yards for a TD during a 21–10 win over the eventual Super Bowl champion Green Bay Packers on October 9, 1966.

Notable Achievements

- Scored three defensive touchdowns.
- Recorded "unofficial" total of 11½ sacks in 1964.
- Ranks among 49ers career leaders with 14 seasons played (tied for 6th) and 16 fumble recoveries (2nd).
- Two-time Pro Bowl selection (1962 and 1964).
- Two-time Second-Team All-Pro selection (1962 and 1964).

31

CHARLES HALEY

A versatile defender who excelled at both linebacker and defensive end during his NFL career, Charles Haley established himself as one of the league's premier edge rushers during his time in San Francisco. A member of 49er teams that won five division titles and two Super Bowls, Haley led the club in sacks six straight times, earning in the process three Pro Bowl selections, one All-Pro nomination, and one NFC Defensive Player of the Year trophy. Yet, in addition to gaining widespread recognition as one of the league's most dominant defenders over the course of those six seasons, Haley developed a reputation for being a malcontent whose volatile temperament and dour disposition frequently caused him to clash with teammates and coaches alike. As a result, the 49ers ended up trading Haley to the Dallas Cowboys, with whom he spent five years tormenting his former team, before returning to San Francisco for a second tour of duty.

Born in Gladys, Virginia, on January 6, 1964, Charles Lewis Haley attended William Campbell High School in nearby Naruna, where he spent three years playing linebacker and tight end, earning All–Region III, All–Group AA, and Defensive Player of the Year honors as a senior by leading his team to the Seminole District championship. Failing to receive scholarship offers from any major colleges, Haley enrolled at James Madison University in Harrisonburg, Virginia, where he registered a school-record 506 tackles over the course of the next four seasons while shuttling back and forth between linebacker and defensive end, with his exceptional play at both positions earning him Division I-AA All-America honors twice.

Selected by the 49ers in the fourth round of the 1986 NFL Draft, with the 96th overall pick, Haley performed well as a situational pass-rusher his first year in the league, earning a spot on the NFL All-Rookie Team by recording 59 tackles and finishing second among first-year players with 12 sacks. Manning a hybrid "Elephant" position, which allowed him to line up on either side of the defensive line based on the strength of the offensive formation, Haley later drew praise from 49ers defensive line coach Bill

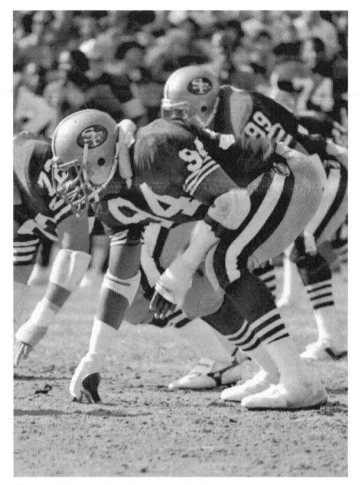

Charles Haley led the 49ers in sacks six straight times.
Courtesy of George A. Kitrinos

McPherson, who said, "He was really quick off the ball, had great hands for pass rush, and was really smart. We worked him as a pass-rusher and he really bought into it. He could go out there, if you wanted him to, and line up at any defensive position. Charles had great quickness and those hands got a lot of sacks. He buried the quarterback a lot."

After recording another 6½ sacks as a designated pass-rusher the following year, Haley moved to left-outside linebacker full-time in 1988. Excelling at that post for the next four seasons, Haley brought down opposing quarterbacks behind the line of scrimmage a total of 45 times, with his outstanding play earning him three trips to the Pro Bowl and one

First-Team All-Pro nomination. Performing especially well in 1988 and 1990, Haley recorded 11½ sacks and a career-high 69 tackles in the first of those campaigns, before gaining NFC Defensive Player of the Year recognition from the UPI two seasons later by registering 16 sacks.

Blessed with tremendous all-around ability, the 6'5", 255-pound Haley used his strength, speed, and agility to wreak havoc on opposing offenses, with former 49ers defensive coordinator and head coach George Seifert saying, "I think what really made Charles Haley a great player is that he was one of those guys that could run over you, or he was so fast that he could run around you. I think that really made him unique. He just caused havoc on the football field. This guy could take over the ball game, and there aren't that many guys as a defensive player that could take over the game like that. It was hard for offensive linemen to really block him because they didn't know if he was going to bull-rush them, or if he was going to use his finesse to get around them."

Seifert added, "Charles was the ultimate player. He was not just about rushing the quarterback, though. I think as an offensive coordinator, you had to prepare for this guy in a very unique way, and there's not that many guys, maybe Lawrence Taylor, that were so dominant on the line of scrimmage."

Roger Craig also spoke highly of his former teammate, saying, "He was the kind of guy that would just put fear into your heart when he was on the field. He was just a relentless defensive lineman that would irritate you while he was out on the field. He could go around you, he could go through you, and he could jump over your head. He was so athletic that you just couldn't block him."

Joe Montana discussed the degree to which Haley contributed to the success of the 49ers when he stated, "Charles Haley was one of the biggest impact players on the 49ers defense. He was not only a big reason for the 49ers' success on defense, but the team's success also. Just ask the Cowboys what he meant to their defense when he arrived!"

Former 49ers owner Eddie DeBartolo expressed his admiration for Haley when he said, "I don't know if there was a player that was as dominant or as scary as Charles Haley."

Yet, despite his exceptional play, which helped the 49ers win five division titles and back-to-back NFL championships in 1988 and 1989, Haley gradually began to wear out his welcome in San Francisco with his disruptive and antagonistic behavior that included locker room tirades and assaults on teammates, of both a verbal and physical nature. Two incidents, in particular, changed his relationship with the team forever, with Haley claiming that the first of those occurred after he confided in a 49ers official about some personal problems, only to discover at a later date that the official subsequently disclosed the content of their conversations to several of Haley's teammates.

Haley further distanced himself from the rest of the team by confronting quarterback Steve Young in the locker room following a 1991 loss to the Raiders and Haley's close friend, Ronnie Lott, who the 49ers allowed to leave via free agency during the previous offseason. Angered by the outcome of the contest, Haley moved aggressively toward Young before teammates intervened. In explaining his version of events, Haley stated, "It's been said that I charged at Steve Young over throwing an interception. That wasn't what happened. I was so mad. The reasons were that I wanted to beat Ronnie Lott and the Raiders so bad, and we needed the win very much to make the playoffs, which we eventually did not do. I smashed my hand through a glass door. So, I screwed up. The main thing is I'm one of the worst in the world at accepting losing."

Haley continued, "That was the situation that changed my relationship in San Francisco for good. I felt they treated me after that without any respect. The thing that got me was that different things like that happened there all the time with other players, and no one said anything. Yet, they wanted to make a spectacle of me. Sure, we had talks after that, but the whole thing was they didn't listen. They looked right past me. They looked at me like I was stupid, and they thought of me as stupid. . . . It's always been negative somewhere, and I've always been a misfit. I've fought that all my life. It's been me against the world. You get tired."

Haley also claimed that his anger over losing Ronnie Lott as a teammate ultimately led to his departure. Revealing that he took out much of his frustration on 49ers head coach George Seifert, Haley said, "I just picked on him. I couldn't let it go. That ended up with me getting out of there. I didn't realize that we all get cut at some point. My vision was short term. All I could see was my best friend hurting, and I wanted to take the anger out on the people that made it."

Haley finally received his ticket out of town on August 26, 1992, when the 49ers traded him to the Dallas Cowboys for a 1993 second-round draft pick and a 1994 third-round selection. Admitting years later that he displayed poor judgment by dealing Haley to Dallas, Eddie DeBartolo said, "As an owner, the worst and biggest mistake that I ever made—ever made!—was to go ahead and agree to trade Charles. It was a fiasco. I knew it was going to come back to haunt us. . . . It was just a horrible trade. They talk about the trade that made Dallas a contender when they made that big trade with Minnesota for Herschel Walker. I don't think that's anything compared to when they stole Charles Haley from us. It still haunts me to this day."

Meanwhile, Cowboys owner Jerry Jones looked back far more favorably on the deal that brought Haley to Dallas, recalling, "I was keenly aware that Charles had issues in San Francisco. Most were. I called [49ers GM] Carmen Policy and asked him what it would take to get Haley. . . . No one would have thought we could have made the trade with San Francisco, a competitor and a rival. I was sure happy they let us make the trade with him. [Oakland Raiders owner] Al Davis called me after it was announced and said, 'You know, you just won the Super Bowl.'"

The arrival of Haley in Dallas ended up shifting the balance of power in the NFC, with the Cowboys winning three of the next five Super Bowls with Haley starting for them at right defensive end. In addition to earning two Pro Bowl selections and one All-Pro nomination in his five years with the Cowboys, Haley brought an intensity to the Dallas defense that did not previously exist, with Emmitt Smith saying, "He came in with something different. He brought in this different kind of edge. It made everybody better."

Former Dallas defensive lineman Tony Casillas discussed the manner with which Haley interacted with his new teammates when he recalled, "He was not a nice guy. He was hard on people. I think some people took that personally. There were times he pushed the envelope too much. And you were like, 'Charles, I had enough of your [butt] today.' And he would keep poking you and poking you. I would be the first to tell you there were a lot of guys who didn't like him, but everybody respected him."

Casillas then added, "There were times I would see the guy, and he could barely walk in the locker room before the game. And literally be the last guy to get dressed. You had to respect that. He played injured. He played hurt a lot."

In attempting to explain why he treated his teammates the way that he did, Haley said years later, "I had one standard in my life: to be great. I had one standard when I stepped on the field: I kick butt, and I never turn that standard down. I'm going to step on toes. I'm going to step on feet. . . . I will step on your neck if I have to. If you look like Tarzan and play like Jane, I'm going to tell you. When you step on people's toes and you push them, either they are going to fight, or they are going to cower. You are going to see what you are dealing with. I only want warriors around me. I was trying to win."

After helping the Cowboys win the NFL championship in 1995 by recording a team-high 10½ sacks, Haley missed most of the ensuing campaign with a ruptured disc in his back that brought his days as a dominant pass-rusher to an end. Choosing to announce his retirement at the end of the year, Haley sat out the entire 1997 season, before Bill Walsh and Eddie DeBartolo convinced him to return to San Francisco, with Haley later saying, "When Bill asked me to come back, I just felt such loyalty to him and to Mr. DeBartolo. They did so much for my family. Mr. D, he taught me what family was all about, the sacrifice, and the commitment."

Haley ended up spending two more years in San Francisco, recording another three sacks in a backup role, before retiring for good following the conclusion of the 1999 campaign. Ending his career with 100½ sacks, 503 tackles, 26 forced fumbles, eight fumble recoveries, two interceptions, and one touchdown, Haley recorded 66½ sacks, 331 tackles, 14 forced fumbles, seven fumble recoveries, one interception, and his lone TD as a member of the 49ers. Meanwhile, Haley's five Super Bowl victories place him second only to Tom Brady all-time.

Following his retirement, Haley, who gained induction into the Pro Football Hall of Fame in 2015, spent two years serving the Detroit Lions as an assistant defensive coach, before becoming a special advisor for both the 49ers and Cowboys in their rookie mentoring programs. Treated with daily medication since being diagnosed with bipolar disorder, Haley now expresses mixed feelings about how he conducted himself during his playing days, saying during a 2016 interview:

> I have regrets, a whole bunch of regrets, about the way I treated my teammates, my coaches, my family, and people in general during my playing career, but, as far as winning, as far as maximizing my team's opportunity for success, I have zero. But it required a lot of sacrifice. I sacrificed my back, my knees. I've been parking in handicapped spaces for almost 10 years now. It takes me a while to get around, and I just turned 52 this past January. I'm not exactly an old man, but let me tell you, my body is old. We won Super Bowls and we made the fans happy, I mean, when it comes to playing in the NFL, that's Mount Olympus, where the football gods reside. That's why we all play, so I'm okay with how it all turned out, and I'm paying the price with my body every waking hour.

As for how he dealt with his emotional disorder, Haley says, "I never felt like I belonged. That brought about a lot of anger and stuff. My problem was I never asked for help. Maybe if I did, a lot of things wouldn't have transpired. . . . When I came into the league, I had a 10-year-old,

12-year-old inside me screaming for help. But I was afraid to ask for help. I didn't get help until after I was done with football. I always wanted help but was afraid to ask for help."

Haley added, "I'm bipolar. I knew something was wrong—everybody was telling me something was wrong. But I just thought everybody was putting me down. Instead of dealing with the problem, I ran from it. I pushed everyone away."

Identifying Bill Walsh as someone who refused to give up on him, Haley said, "Bill Walsh followed me my whole career. I got a chance to call him and talk to him. Two days before he died, he called me and asked, 'How can I help you?' I've never understood why he cared about me. To this day, it mystifies me. I didn't know what I did, but he was always there for me."

49ERS CAREER HIGHLIGHTS

Best Season

Haley turned in his most dominant performance as a member of the 49ers in 1990, when he earned First-Team All-Pro honors by finishing third in the NFL with a career-high 16 sacks, forcing three fumbles, and recording 58 tackles, with the UPI subsequently naming him its NFC Defensive Player of the Year.

Memorable Moments/Greatest Performances

Haley recorded the first sack of his career when he brought down Steve Bartkowski behind the line of scrimmage during a 16–13 loss to the Los Angeles Rams on September 14, 1986.

Haley followed that up by registering two sacks during a 26–17 win over the New Orleans Saints on September 21, 1986.

Haley recorded three sacks in one game for the first time as a pro during a 20–0 win over the Atlanta Falcons on November 23, 1986.

Although the 49ers lost to the Bears by a score of 10–9 on October 24, 1988, Haley sacked Jim McMahon three times, with one of his sacks resulting in a safety.

Haley contributed to the 49ers' 20–16 victory over the Cincinnati Bengals in Super Bowl XXIII by sacking Boomer Esiason twice.

Haley recorded three of the nine sacks the 49ers registered against Ken O'Brien during a 23–10 win over the Jets on October 29, 1989.

Haley scored the only touchdown of his career when he returned a fumble 3 yards for a TD during a 45–3 rout of the Falcons on November 12, 1989.

Haley earned NFC Defensive Player of the Week honors by sacking Warren Moon twice during a 24–21 win over the Houston Oilers on October 7, 1990.

Notable Achievements

- Scored one defensive touchdown.
- Finished in double digits in sacks four times.
- Finished second in NFL with four forced fumbles in 1986.
- Finished third in NFL with 16 sacks in 1990.
- Led 49ers in sacks six times.
- Ranks among 49ers career leaders with 66½ sacks (4th) and 14 forced fumbles (3rd).
- Five-time division champion (1986, 1987, 1988, 1989, and 1990).
- Two-time NFC champion (1988 and 1989).
- Two-time Super Bowl champion (XXIII and XXIV).
- 1990 Week 5 NFC Defensive Player of the Week.
- Two-time NFC Defensive Player of the Month.
- Member of 1986 NFL All-Rookie Team.
- 1990 UPI NFC Defensive Player of the Year.
- Three-time Pro Bowl selection (1988, 1990, and 1991).
- 1990 First-Team All-Pro selection.
- Two-time First-Team All-NFC selection (1988 and 1990).
- Inducted into 49ers Hall of Fame in 2015.
- Elected to Pro Football Hall of Fame in 2015.

32

FORREST BLUE

A key contributor to 49er teams that won three straight division titles during the early 1970s, Forrest Blue spent seven seasons in San Francisco, establishing himself during that time as one of the finest centers in the game. Starting at that post for the Red and Gold for six years, Blue served as the anchor of an outstanding unit that helped the 49ers consistently rank among the NFL leaders in total offense, with his dominant play up front earning him four trips to the Pro Bowl, three All-Pro nominations, and four All-NFC selections.

Born in Marfa, Texas, on September 7, 1945, Forrest Murrell Blue Jr. grew up in Tampa, Florida, where his family moved following the retirement of his father, a US Army captain. Starring in multiple sports while attending Chamberlain High School, Blue excelled in baseball, basketball, football, and track, while also making the National Honor Society for his outstanding performance in the classroom.

After accepting an athletic scholarship to Auburn University, Blue spent one year playing baseball and football for the Tigers, before concentrating exclusively on football his final three seasons. Starting at center for Ralph "Shug" Jordan's squad in each of those years, Blue distinguished himself as a senior in 1967 by being named team captain and gaining All-America recognition.

Subsequently selected by the 49ers in the first round of the 1968 NFL Draft, with the 15th overall pick, Blue spent his first season in San Francisco backing up veteran Bruce Bosley at the center position, before laying claim to the starting job the following year after the 49ers traded Bosley to the Atlanta Falcons. Remaining at that post for the next six seasons, Blue started all but two games for the 49ers from 1969 to 1974, a period during which he established himself as arguably the NFL's top center. In addition to earning Pro Bowl and First-Team All-NFC honors four straight times from 1971 to 1974, Blue gained All-Pro recognition on three separate occasions, being named to the First Team in 1971, 1972, and 1973.

Forrest Blue earned four Pro Bowl selections and three All-Pro nominations during his time in San Francisco.
Courtesy of Mike Traverse

Big, strong, and quick, Blue, who stood 6'6" and weighed more than 260 pounds, possessed more size and strength than most players who manned his position at that time, with former 49ers tight end Ted Kwalick saying of his onetime teammate, "Forrest was big back then, for that era. He was a big center, and he did a great job. I think he was really dominant. You take a guy like Forrest Blue or John Matuszak, who I played with on the Raiders, and these guys were 270, 280 pounds. But they didn't have bellies. That was unheard of back then."

Former 49ers linebacker Frank Nunley expressed similar thoughts when he said of Blue, "He was huge. He was 6-foot-6. He was fast and strong."

Blessed with an unusual combination of size and mobility, Blue possessed enough strength to handle the nose tackle without help, enough quickness to engage the middle linebacker at the next level, and enough speed to lead 49er running backs downfield on screen passes. Particularly well suited, because of his size and strength, to block one-on-one whoever lined up over him, Blue drew praise from San Diego Chargers defensive tackle Ron East for his proficiency in that area, with East saying, "You can't get around him. And you don't go over him. There's really not much to say."

Extremely intelligent, competitive, and versatile as well, Blue contributed to the success of the 49ers in many ways, also serving as their long snapper on punts, field goals, and extra points. Meanwhile, Blue's leadership and unselfish attitude helped bring continuity to a 49ers' offensive line that did a tremendous job of protecting John Brodie, with Blue combining with fellow linemen Len Rohde, Cas Banaszek, Randy Beisler, and Woody Peoples in 1970 to allow a mere eight sacks of the veteran quarterback. And, with the 49ers also leading the NFL in points scored that year, they captured the NFC West Division title for the first of three straight times.

One of the league's most durable players, Blue started every game for the 49ers for five straight seasons, before finally missing two contests during the latter stages of the 1974 campaign after being kicked in the face by an opposing player during a 27–0 victory over the Atlanta Falcons in Week 11. Originally diagnosed with just a broken nose, Blue ended up having reconstructive surgery on his face, telling a reporter for the *San Francisco Chronicle*, "The doctors here took one look at me and told me to forget about football. But I'd like to play this week. They treat us like normal people. They don't have to do what we do on Sundays."

After remaining on the sidelines for the next two weeks, Blue returned to action for the final game of the regular season, which resulted in a 35–21 win over the New Orleans Saints. Ironically, that turned out to be Blue's last appearance in a 49ers uniform since the team traded him to the Baltimore Colts during the subsequent offseason. Blue spent the next four years in Baltimore, helping the Colts win three AFC East Division titles, before announcing his retirement due to a degenerative disc in his back following the conclusion of the 1978 campaign.

After retiring from football, Blue settled with his family in the Sacramento area, where he became a general contractor and founded a construction company that he called Forrest Blue Properties. However, Blue soon began behaving irrationally, in both his business and personal lives. Although he never acted violently toward anyone in his family, Blue occasionally became belligerent and aggressive, with his former wife Anne recalling, "I thought he was going through a depression from getting out of football."

Blue's erratic behavior caused his marriage to end in 1986, although he later married and divorced twice more. Yet, through all his trials and tribulations, Blue remained close to his daughters, who later revealed that his condition continued to worsen, claiming that he often spoke of "bad dreams" and hallucinated that he saw fairies. Growing increasingly paranoid, Blue began mistaking a Kleenex box for a listening device and took to barricading his bedroom at night with dresser drawers.

No longer able to care for himself after being diagnosed with early-onset dementia likely brought on by his career in football, Blue moved into the home of one of his daughters, where he attacked and wrecked a treadmill after mistaking it for an intruder. Later admitted to a nursing home, Blue spent several years there, before finally entering an assisted living facility in Carmichael, California, in 2009, where, according to his daughter Brittney, he often talked about "little people that lived in the walls" and expressed the belief that people were using his contracting license to perform illegal work. Blue remained at the facility for nearly two years, before dying of chronic traumatic encephalopathy (CTE) at 65 years of age, on July 16, 2011.

49ERS CAREER HIGHLIGHTS

Best Season

Blue played his best ball for the 49ers from 1971 to 1973, earning First-Team All-Pro honors three straight times. Since the 49ers finished third in the NFL in yards gained in 1971, with San Francisco running backs averaging a robust 4.3 yards per carry, we'll identify that as the finest season of Blue's career.

Memorable Moments/Greatest Performances

Blue anchored an offensive line that enabled the 49ers to rush for 202 yards and amass 510 yards of total offense during a 31–3 win over the Philadelphia Eagles on October 3, 1971.

Blue scored the only points of his career four weeks later, when he returned a fumbled punt 25 yards for a touchdown during a 27–10 win over the Patriots on October 31, 1971.

Blue helped the 49ers gain a season-high total of 263 yards on the ground during a 24–21 victory over the Jets on November 28, 1971.

Although Blue suffered horrendous facial damage during a 27–0 shutout of the Atlanta Falcons on November 24, 1974, his tremendous blocking at the point of attack helped the 49ers gain 202 yards on the ground.

Notable Achievements

- Missed just two games in seven seasons, appearing in 96 out of 98 contests.
- Scored one touchdown.
- Three-time division champion (1970, 1971, and 1972).
- Four-time Pro Bowl selection (1971, 1972, 1973, and 1974).
- Three-time First-Team All-Pro selection (1971, 1972, and 1973).
- Four-time First-Team All-NFC selection (1971, 1972, 1973, and 1974).

33

DWIGHT HICKS

One of the key figures in the 49ers' road to prominence during the early
1980s, Dwight Hicks joined Ronnie Lott, Eric Wright, and Carlton
Williamson in forming arguably the NFL's finest defensive secondary
from 1981 to 1985. Starting at free safety for the 49ers for seven seasons,
Hicks led the team in picks three times, ending his career as one of the
franchise's all-time leaders in interceptions and interception-return yards.
A hard-hitter and sure tackler as well, Hicks contributed in many ways to
49er teams that won three division titles and two Super Bowls, with his
outstanding all-around play earning him four trips to the Pro Bowl, two
All-NFC selections, and one All-Pro nomination.

Born in Mount Holly, New Jersey, on April 5, 1956, Dwight Hicks
starred on the gridiron at Pennsauken High School, leading his team to a
9-1 record and a number two ranking in South Jersey in 1972, while splitting his time between the safety and cornerback positions. After accepting
a scholarship to the University of Michigan, Hicks established himself as
one of the nation's top safeties, gaining All–Big Ten Conference recognition
twice and earning All-America honors in 1977, when he also led the Big
Ten with 161 punt-return yards.

Selected by the Detroit Lions in the sixth round of the 1978 NFL
Draft, with the 150th overall pick, Hicks failed to earn a roster spot during
training camp, prompting him to sign with the Canadian Football League's
Toronto Argonauts, with whom he spent the 1978 campaign. Returning
to the States after being released by the Argonauts at season's end, Hicks
joined the Philadelphia Eagles, who cut him during the 1979 preseason.
Hicks then spent the next several weeks working in the stock room of a
health food store in Detroit, before being signed by the 49ers. Arriving in
San Francisco at midseason, Hicks ended up appearing in eight games and
recording a team-high five interceptions, which he returned for a total of
57 yards.

Dwight Hicks ranks among the 49ers career leaders in interceptions and interception-return yards.
Courtesy of Mearsonlineauction.com

After laying claim to the starting free safety job the following year, Hicks established himself as the only reliable member of a porous defensive secondary that ranked next-to-last in the league in pass defense. Seeking to improve themselves in that area, the 49ers selected Ronnie Lott, Eric Wright, and Carlton Williamson in the first three rounds of the 1981 NFL Draft, leaving the 25-year-old Hicks as the most experienced member of an extremely talented but young group of defensive backs.

Assuming a leadership role within the unit, Hicks imparted his knowledge to the other members of the 49ers' young, hard-hitting defensive secondary, which soon became known as "Dwight Hicks and his Hot Licks." Hicks also performed exceptionally well on the playing field, earning Pro Bowl and Second-Team All-Pro honors in 1981 by finishing third in the NFL with nine interceptions and leading the league with 239 interception-return yards, which established a new single-season franchise record (later broken by Deion Sanders). Continuing to perform at an elite level in each of the next three seasons, Hicks earned three more trips to the Pro Bowl by totaling eight interceptions, two of which he returned for touchdowns. Meanwhile, Hicks's outstanding leadership ability prompted his teammates to name him defensive captain from 1983 to 1985.

Although the 6'1", 190-pound Hicks lacked elite running speed, his intelligence and superb instincts enabled him to do an excellent job of covering receivers deep downfield. Even more effective against the run, Hicks developed a reputation as one of the league's hardest-hitting defensive backs, combining with teammate Ronnie Lott to instill fear into opposing receivers and running backs. Revealing the aggressive attitude that he brought with him to the playing field, Hicks stated prior to Super Bowl XIX against Miami, "No one is going to get a reputation off me. On the field, it's like a different world. It's like a war, really."

Hicks spent one more season in San Francisco, recording four interceptions in 1985, before being released by the 49ers prior to the start of the ensuing campaign. Ending his seven-year stint in the City by the Bay with 30 interceptions, 586 interception-return yards, three touchdown interceptions, four defensive touchdowns, 14 fumble recoveries, and one sack, Hicks continues to rank among the franchise's all-time leaders in all but the last category.

Unable to find work for several months following his release by the 49ers, Hicks admitted during a 1986 interview that his prior use of cocaine likely prevented several teams from contacting him. Claiming that he began using the substance in 1981, Hicks revealed that he continued to use it for the next five years, before abandoning the practice in the summer of 1985. Also saying that "cocaine is completely out of my life now and has been since early this summer," Hicks added, "I never got strung out on cocaine. I was never a big user, and I stopped using it when I started reading up on it after those deaths [of Maryland basketball star Len Bias and Cleveland Browns' safety Don Rogers]. . . . There are people using it occasionally throughout the world. And people who abuse it. I was not an abuser. I've experimented with it before. But, as far as abusing something, where I'm out of my mind or couldn't make rational decisions, or that I needed help, that was not the case at all. . . . I've come to my senses about cocaine. The little bit I did use, I felt stupid that I used it."

Hicks also stated that his use of cocaine never affected his on-field performance, saying, "I have to make split-second decisions when I play free safety. You have to make calls, then react to things that come your way."

Claiming that the 49ers became aware of Hicks's drug use in "late 1983 or possibly 1984," Bill Walsh said that he "personally did everything I could to help Dwight Hicks," revealing that he even offered him a new two-year contract in the summer of 1986. Walsh added, "The fact that I personally left training camp to visit with him in August is an indication that the 49ers have his best interests in mind."

However, Hicks chose not to accept Walsh's offer, saying during his interview, "People have told me it was better than nothing. But for the things I'd accomplished, most other guys are rewarded for. It just seems a shame I wasn't given my just due. I don't feel that offer was what I was worth."

But Hicks also conceded during that same interview, "I want to get back into the game. If that's what it took (the same offer today), I think I'd probably take it."

Hicks eventually signed with the Indianapolis Colts, for whom he appeared in nine games in 1986, before retiring at season's end. Following his playing days, Hicks began a career in acting, appearing in such films as *The Rock* and *Armageddon*, as well as a number of television shows, including *How I Met Your Mother*, *Castle*, *Body of Proof*, and *The X-Files*.

Discussing his divergent careers some year later, Hicks said, "It's funny how life works. When you find a passion and put effort into it, things will fall into your lap. You never know when opportunity comes. You have to find your passion. . . . I consider myself to be very fortunate in life. I found one passion, had a great career, and I embraced another one."

49ERS CAREER HIGHLIGHTS

Best Season

Hicks had the finest season of his career in 1981, when he earned his lone All-Pro nomination by finishing third in the NFL with nine interceptions, leading the league with 239 interception-return yards, recovering four fumbles, which he returned for a total of 80 yards, recording 76 tackles and 14 pass deflections, and scoring a pair of touchdowns on defense.

Memorable Moments/Greatest Performances

Hicks recorded his first career interception during a 38–28 loss to the Denver Broncos on November 18, 1979.

Hicks contributed to a 23–7 victory over the Tampa Bay Buccaneers on December 9, 1979, by picking off Doug Williams twice.

Hicks helped lead the 49ers to a 30–17 win over the Washington Redskins on October 4, 1981, by recording a pair of interceptions, which he returned for a total of 104 yards and one touchdown, and recovering a fumble, which he returned 80 yards for a score.

Hicks intercepted another two passes during a 17–14 win over the Atlanta Falcons on November 8, 1981, returning his two picks a total of 37 yards.

Hicks capped off his exceptional 1981 campaign by making a key play in Super Bowl XVI, when he thwarted an early scoring opportunity for the Cincinnati Bengals by intercepting a Ken Anderson pass, which he subsequently returned 27 yards to the San Francisco 32 yard line. After scoring on the ensuing drive, the 49ers built a 20–0 halftime lead, before holding on in the second half to record a 26–21 victory over their AFC counterparts.

Hicks contributed to a 30–24 win over the Los Angeles Rams on December 2, 1982, by picking off Vince Ferragamo twice.

Hicks scored his third career touchdown when he ran 40 yards to paydirt after intercepting a Neil Lomax pass during a 42–27 victory over the St. Louis Cardinals on September 18, 1983.

Hicks crossed the opponent's goal line for the fourth and final time when he returned an interception 62 yards for a touchdown during a 32–13 win over the Saints on October 16, 1983.

Hicks helped the 49ers earn a trip to the playoffs as a wild card in 1985 by intercepting a pass and recovering a fumble during a 31–16 victory over the Dallas Cowboys in the regular-season finale, with his outstanding play earning him NFC Defensive Player of the Week honors.

Notable Achievements

- Scored four defensive touchdowns.
- Recorded at least five interceptions twice.
- Amassed more than 100 interception-return yards twice, topping 200 yards once.
- Led NFL with 239 interception-return yards in 1981.

- Led NFL with two touchdown interceptions in 1983.
- Finished second in NFL with 80 fumble-return yards in 1981.
- Finished third in NFL with nine interceptions in 1981.
- Led 49ers in interceptions three times.
- Ranks among 49ers career leaders with 30 interceptions (6th), 586 interception-return yards (3rd), three touchdown interceptions (tied-2nd), and 14 fumble recoveries (tied-3rd).
- Three-time division champion (1981, 1983, and 1984).
- Two-time NFC champion (1981 and 1984).
- Two-time Super Bowl champion (XVI and XIX).
- 1985 Week 16 NFC Defensive Player of the Week.
- Four-time Pro Bowl selection (1981, 1982, 1983, and 1984).
- 1981 Second-Team All-Pro selection.
- Two-time First-Team All-NFC selection (1981 and 1984).

JUSTIN SMITH

Nicknamed "Cowboy" for his Missouri roots and blue collar mentality, Justin Smith provided leadership and consistently excellent play along the 49ers' defensive front for seven seasons, serving as a key contributor to teams that won two division titles and one NFC championship. Excelling for the 49ers at multiple positions, Smith starred at both end and tackle, becoming in 2011 the first player ever to be accorded First- and Second-Team All-Pro honors at different positions in the same season. A two-time team MVP, Smith recorded at least seven sacks three times and led 49ers defensive linemen in tackles seven straight times, with his outstanding all-around play earning him five Pro Bowl selections and three All-Pro nominations.

Born in Jefferson City, Missouri, on September 30, 1979, Justin Smith grew up some seven miles northeast, in the small city of Holts Summit. A star football player at Jefferson City High School, Smith led the Jefferson City Jays to the Class 5A state championship as a senior in 1997, earning in the process All-District and All-State honors. Subsequently offered an athletic scholarship to the University of Missouri, Smith continued to excel on the gridiron in college, earning Big-12 Defensive Freshman of the Year honors in 1998 by recording 3½ sacks and 86 tackles, before registering 97 tackles, 24 tackles for loss, and 11 sacks two years later, with his exceptional play his junior year gaining him All–Big 12 and First-Team All-America recognition.

Choosing to forgo his final year of college eligibility, Smith declared himself available for the 2001 NFL Draft, where the Cincinnati Bengals selected him with the fourth overall pick. Laying claim to the starting right defensive end job immediately upon his arrival in Cincinnati, Smith performed well his first year in the league, securing a spot on the NFL All-Rookie Team by recording 8½ sacks, 54 tackles, and two interceptions. Establishing himself as one of the most consistent players at his position over the course of the next six seasons, Smith started 96 consecutive games

Justin Smith starred for the 49ers at both defensive end and tackle.
Courtesy of Mike Morbeck

for the Bengals, registering another 35 sacks and amassing more than 70 tackles three times. But, with Smith becoming a free agent at the end of 2007 and the 49ers seeking to improve their porous defense, the two sides agreed on a six-year, $45 million contract that brought the big defensive end's time in Cincinnati to an end.

Continuing his solid play for the 49ers, Smith averaged seven sacks and 64 tackles from 2008 to 2011, earning in the process three Pro Bowl selections and one All-Pro nomination. Particularly effective in the last of those campaigns, Smith received All-Pro recognition as both a defensive end and defensive tackle, playing end in the 49ers' 3-4 base defense and moving to tackle when they switched to their 4-2 nickel defense.

Blessed with outstanding speed and tremendous strength, the 6'4", 285-pound Smith exploded off the football, making him extremely effective at batting down passes, applying pressure to opposing quarterbacks, and containing the opponent's running game. Often assigned multiple blockers, Smith also contributed to the success of the players around him with the havoc he created at the line of scrimmage.

Known for his signature "chop-to-bull" move, one in which he chopped an opponent's arm and drove his shoulder into him before violently shoving him back, Smith made a lasting impression on 49ers offensive lineman Alex Boone with that particular maneuver, with Boone stating, "When he wants to hit the jets, you'd better be ready for it. He's very famous for the chop-to-bull, which kills everybody. Once you set your hands on him, you've got to be very firm with him, as opposed to another defensive end, where you just kind of put your hands on him. . . . If you watch the film, he gets everybody with it. It's pretty impressive. You know it's coming, but he still gets you on it somehow. It's unbelievable."

Former NFL quarterback and NFL analyst Ron Jaworski discussed Smith's ability to dominate his opponent when he said, "There are always three or four plays every game where he just knocks the socks off somebody. Sometimes we don't give him enough credit for being a great player. We always talk about his effort, but he has great skill."

Smith's defensive line coach in San Francisco, Jim Tomsula, expressed similar sentiments when he stated, "We laugh a lot because we talk about how he's a high-motor guy. A lot of times you hear high-motor guy and that's a guy that's maybe not real talented, but he works really hard. Let's not forget this guy comes out and he's a phenomenal athlete. We're always laughing when everybody busts his chops, 'high motor, high motor.' He's high motor, but he puts it with a whole lot of ability, and then you put a mindset to it."

Vic Fangio admitted that he did not realize the full extent of Smith's talent until he became the 49ers' defensive coordinator in 2011, saying, "I knew Justin Smith was a good player but, until I got here and was actually involved in coaching him and seeing him play day to day and game to game, he's better than my perception was. He's probably having his best year he's ever had. No. 1, he's got great talent and, 2, he's tenacious. He loves to play the game of football the right way."

More than just an outstanding player, Smith helped create a winning culture in San Francisco with his exceptional leadership ability and total dedication to the team and his profession. In discussing Smith's tremendous work ethic, former 49ers cornerback Eric Davis described a scene he witnessed at the team's practice facility during the bye week in 2011: "Most of the players aren't around. You go outside to where the outdoor weight equipment is set up. It's a cold morning. And through the fog and the mist you see this one character out there. Of course, it's Cowboy. He's blowing steam like a Brahma bull. Just getting in his workout. He won't stop. That's just how he is, and that's how he is on the field. He's relentless."

Aldon Smith described the manner in which his fellow Missouri alum took him under his wing when he first arrived in San Francisco in 2011, recalling, "From the time I stepped into the NFL, he was a guy who helped me out with everything. I worked out with him during the lockout, and he helped me a lot just coming in my rookie year. Then, on the field, we just work well with each other. We feed off each other. We have a rhythm that we just developed together."

Admired and respected by everyone within the organization, Smith won the Len Eshmont Award twice for the inspiration he provided to his teammates and received the Hazeltine Iron Man Award on four separate occasions, with that trophy going to the team's most courageous and dedicated defensive player as selected by the coaching staff.

After starting the previous 185 contests, dating back to his time in Cincinnati, Smith missed the final two games of the 2012 regular season with a torn triceps he suffered during a 41–34 win over the Patriots on December 16. However, he returned for the postseason, which ultimately ended with a 34–31 loss to the Baltimore Ravens in Super Bowl XLVII. Smith then signed a two-year contract extension with the 49ers during the subsequent offseason, with GM Trent Baalke saying at the time, "Justin consistently sets a standard of excellence, serving as an example for everyone within our organization. This contract allows Justin to finish his career as a 49er!"

After fulfilling the terms of his contract, Smith announced his retirement on May 18, 2015, saying that he based his decision largely on a lingering shoulder injury he sustained during the 2013 campaign that prevented him from playing up to his full capabilities. Smith added, "There's arthritis build up, wear and tear . . . it's a young man's game. . . . They all want you to keep playing, and I want to keep playing as well, but, when you get on the bald tires, you're on the bald tires."

Commenting on Smith's decision to retire when he did, Jim Tomsula said, "People are going to compare him to everybody else. He compares himself to himself. That's the bar he sets. . . . I've always known with Justin that, if he didn't feel like health-wise he can play at the level he wants to, he's not going to do it."

Meanwhile, Vic Fangio told the *Sacramento Bee*, "I think the one thing that defines him is that he's just a true warrior in the truest sense of the word. He played a whole season last year with half an arm. There are a lot of guys that wouldn't have even gone out there. But the guy loves football, loves playing, loves competing. He's definitely in my personal top three or five Hall of Fame players that I've been around."

Ending his career with 87 sacks, 884 tackles, 16 forced fumbles, 10 fumble recoveries, and three interceptions, Smith recorded 43½ sacks, 414 tackles (300 solo), 64 tackles for loss, 10 forced fumbles, five fumble recoveries, and one interception in his seven seasons with the 49ers. Smith also missed just two games his entire career, starting 110 out of a possible 112 contests during his time in San Francisco.

Upon learning of Smith's retirement, 49ers CEO Jed York described him as "tough, physical, durable, hard-working, dedicated, and selfless," adding, "Justin embodies each of those qualities and brought even more with him to work each and every day. Whether it was chasing down a wide receiver and forcing a fumble to seal a win, or driving a tackle back into the quarterback's chest, he gave everything he had every play. Justin has earned the respect of the entire NFL community, and he will always be remembered as one of the 49ers' all-time greats."

Jim Tomsula also had high praise for Smith, saying, "As a football coach, you will always be searching for the next Justin Smith, knowing full well you will never find a player quite like him. Everybody knows about his toughness, durability, and instincts, but his greatest attribute does not get the attention it deserves. Justin never concerned himself with personal accomplishments—his unselfish nature made that impossible. People like to say, 'They broke the mold with him,' but there was never a mold. Justin Smith is a hand-crafted football player."

49ERS CAREER HIGHLIGHTS

Best Season

Smith had an outstanding season for the 49ers in 2010, recording a career-high 8½ sacks, while also registering 70 tackles, 12 tackles for loss, and 17 hits on opposing quarterbacks. But he performed slightly better in 2011, earning his lone First-Team All-Pro nomination and a third-place finish in the NFL Defensive Player of the Year voting by registering 7½ sacks, forcing three fumbles, making 58 tackles, and recording 20 quarterback hits.

Memorable Moments/Greatest Performances

Smith acquitted himself extremely well in his debut with the 49ers, recording seven tackles and a sack during a 23–13 loss to the Arizona Cardinals in the 2008 regular-season opener.

Smith contributed to a 31–13 victory over the Detroit Lions on September 21, 2008, by recording a sack, forcing a fumble, and intercepting a pass.

Smith helped lead the 49ers to a 28–6 win over the St. Louis Rams in the final game of the 2009 regular season by recording eight solo tackles and a career-high 3½ sacks.

Smith turned in another outstanding performance in the 2010 regular-season finale, recording three sacks, 10 tackles, and one forced fumble during a 38–7 win over the Cardinals.

Smith made perhaps his biggest play as a member of the 49ers on October 2, 2011, when he helped preserve a 24–23 victory over Philadelphia by forcing a late turnover that allowed the 49ers to run out the clock. With the Eagles in possession of the football near midfield and needing only a field goal to take the lead with just over two minutes remaining in the fourth quarter, Michael Vick delivered a short pass in the flat to Jeremy Maclin that the wide receiver took all the way down to the 49ers' 32 yard line before being chased down from behind by Smith, who punched the ball away, resulting in a fumble that teammate Dashon Goldson recovered. The 49ers subsequently ran out the clock, giving them a win in a game they once trailed by 20 points. Commenting on Smith's extraordinary effort following the conclusion of the contest, 49ers defensive coordinator Vic Fangio stated, "That's a defensive equivalent of 'The Catch.' Now, 'The Catch' happened in an NFC Championship Game, which added to the luster. This was the fourth regular season game, but it was a tremendous effort. . . . For him to have that type of energy and hustle at that time of the game, knowing how his body had to be feeling at that point, speaks volumes about what he is as a person."

Notable Achievements

- Missed just two games in seven seasons, starting 110 out of 112 contests.
- Recorded at least seven sacks three times.
- Recorded at least 70 tackles twice.
- Led 49ers with 8½ sacks in 2010.

- Led 49ers' defensive linemen in tackles seven times.
- Ranks among 49ers career leaders with 43½ sacks (9th) and 10 forced fumbles (tied-7th).
- Two-time division champion (2011 and 2012).
- 2012 NFC champion.
- Two-time 49ers MVP (2008 and 2011).
- Five-time Pro Bowl selection (2009, 2010, 2011, 2012, and 2013).
- 2011 First-Team All-Pro selection.
- Two-time Second-Team All-Pro selection (2012 and 2013).

35

MERTON HANKS

A versatile defender who manned three different positions in the 49ers' defensive secondary, Merton Hanks used his superb instincts and outstanding range to establish himself as one of the NFL's top playmakers on that side of the ball, recording at least five interceptions on three separate occasions. Originally a cornerback, Hanks spent most of his time in San Francisco at free safety, ending his eight-year stint in the City by the Bay with the fourth-most picks in franchise history. A member of 49er teams that won five division titles and one Super Bowl, Hanks earned Pro Bowl, All-Pro, and All-NFC honors four times each while wearing the Red and Gold, before spending one final season with the Seattle Seahawks.

Born in Dallas, Texas, on March 12, 1968, Merton Edward Hanks grew up with his five older siblings in a single-parent household after losing his father as an infant to a senseless shooting. As the baby of the family, young Merton often found himself being pampered, with his mother saying years later, "He was just kind of sheltered and spoiled. We say he's cocky and a little bit selfish, but we sort of made him that way."

Spending much of his time at the homes of his two best friends, Doug Adams and D'Wayne Tanner, Hanks made a similar impression on his two closest companions, with Tanner stating, "Mert thought he was God's gift to women. In high school, I wrote an article about him for our neighborhood paper, and the headline was *CONFIDENCE OR COCKINESS?*"

Starring in multiple sports at Lake Highlands High School, Hanks excelled on the gridiron and in track, where he earned district championship honors as a sprinter. Subsequently offered an athletic scholarship to the University of Iowa, Hanks spent his college career playing cornerback for the Hawkeyes, recording a total of 10 interceptions in his four years as a starter, with his four picks as a senior in 1990 earning him All–Big Ten honors.

After declaring himself eligible for the 1991 NFL Draft, Hanks posted an unimpressive time of 4.74 seconds in the 40-yard dash at the scouting

Merton Hanks ranks fourth in franchise history with 31 career interceptions.
Courtesy of George A. Kitrinos

combine, ultimately causing him to fall considerably on draft day. However, Hanks's poor time proved to be the least of his worries, since he and his wife, Marva, lost their prematurely born baby boy just two weeks before the draft because of undeveloped lungs and kidneys. Later expressing regrets about how he handled himself in the days that followed, Hanks said, "I wasn't very mature about the situation. I initially didn't grieve with Marva, and she felt like she was by herself."

Hanks's woes continued to mount on draft day, when the first four rounds passed without his name being called. But after 49ers defensive backs coach Ray Rhodes and scouting director Tony Razzano pleaded with head coach George Seifert to select Hanks, the team finally claimed him in the fifth round, with the 122nd overall pick. Recalling his feelings at the time, Hanks later said, "Quite frankly, I was disgusted. I was a first-round talent that slid to the fifth round because I had a poor combine. I remember telling Ray Rhodes that I'd be better than a lot of players picked ahead of me in my rookie year. Everybody kind of laughed and giggled and thought it was more sour grapes from being picked in the fifth round, but my prediction pretty much proved out true."

After former 49ers standout cornerback Eric Wright took him under his wing upon his arrival in San Francisco, Hanks performed well as a nickel-back his first year in the league, before moving to strong safety the following year, when, despite starting just five contests, he recorded two interceptions and 64 tackles. Replacing an injured Dana Hall at free safety during the early stages of the 1993 campaign, Hanks found a permanent home, taking to his new position so well that the 49ers ultimately traded Hall to the Cleveland Browns. Beginning a string of 94 consecutive starts at that post, Hanks registered 67 tackles and picked off three passes, which he returned for 104 yards and one touchdown. Emerging as one of the NFL's best players at his position the following year, Hanks earned Pro Bowl, All-Pro, and All-NFC honors for the first of four straight times by finishing fourth in the league with seven interceptions, while also making 72 tackles, and recovering two fumbles. Continuing his outstanding play in each of the next three seasons, Hanks picked off another 15 passes and scored three more touchdowns on defense, enabling him to develop a reputation as one of the league's top playmakers.

In discussing Hanks's ability to create turnovers, former 49ers teammate Jerry Rice said, "He just had a knack for the football. He knew how to find the football in that he would always be around the ball to make a play."

Long and lean at 6'2" and 185 pounds, Hanks made up for whatever he lacked in size with great instincts, tremendous closing speed, superior ball skills, and an ability to break quickly on the football, with Steve Young stating, "Mert covers more ground than anyone else at his position, and his quick changes of direction surprise a lot of quarterbacks."

Meanwhile, Jerry Rice claimed that Hanks hit harder than most people thought, saying, "He's like a smaller Ronnie Lott. He doesn't mind sticking his head in there."

Admitting that he underestimated Hanks's abilities heading into the 1991 NFL Draft, George Seifert stated, "He was bright, competitive, had great range. He probably exceeded our expectations as a player. He was very good."

Former 49ers executive John McVay spoke to Hanks's consistency when he called him a "good, solid, strong player," and claimed, "He never made a mistake. I don't think he ever made a mistake in a game."

Brett Favre had high praise for Hanks prior to the 1995 NFC semifinal playoff game between the 49ers and Packers, saying, "I think Merton Hanks is a great player and probably one of the greatest safeties in the league—if not the best safety."

Supremely confident in his own abilities, Hanks expressed no such doubts, stating, "I'm just absolutely convinced I'm the best free safety in the league. I guess you're not really supposed to 'pub' yourself like that, but I look at the film—and it's the truth."

Hanks then added, "I have a confidence in myself that borders on arrogance, but I know when I need to learn something, and I'm open to learning it."

Not afraid to draw attention to himself on or off the playing field, Hanks punctuated every big play he made with an elaborate celebratory dance he first introduced in 1995 when he picked up a Michael Irvin fumble and returned it for a touchdown during a 38–20 victory over the Dallas Cowboys. From that point on, every time Hanks intercepted a pass or recovered a fumble, he engaged in what became known as the "Chicken Dance," strutting in an exaggerated fashion with his arms waving and his long "chicken neck" bopping up and down like a pogo stick.

Revealing the inspiration for his dance, Hanks said, "It came from watching Bert and Ernie on *Sesame Street* with my daughters. We were playing around with it and then one day it made its way to the practice field, then it popped up on game day. That's the long and short of it."

Recalling the consternation that he felt every time he saw Hanks employ his dance, George Seifert stated, "We all remember the neck. He used to scare the heck out of me when he would bobble that neck. I was always afraid he was gonna get hurt, that he would be out, and we would lose him for games."

Hanks remained in San Francisco until the end of 1998, when he signed with the Seattle Seahawks as a free agent after recording 31 interceptions, amassing 380 interception-return yards, registering 474 tackles, forcing three fumbles, recovering 10 others, and scoring five touchdowns in his eight years with the 49ers, with one of his TDs coming on a 48-yard punt return. Hanks ended up spending just one season in Seattle, picking off another two passes as a member of the Seahawks in 1999, before announcing his retirement.

After a few years away from the game, Hanks returned to the NFL in 2003, serving as the league's assistant director of operations from 2003 to 2011, before assuming the position of NFL vice president of football operations in charge of player conduct for the next five years. Handing in his resignation in 2016, Hanks became the senior associate commissioner of Conference USA, a role in which he is responsible for managing all of the league's operations for football and baseball, including officiating, scheduling, game operations, player conduct, and player safety.

49ERS CAREER HIGHLIGHTS

Best Season

Hanks played his best ball for the 49ers from 1994 to 1997, gaining Pro Bowl and All-Pro recognition four straight times, with his five interceptions, 63 tackles, two fumble recoveries, and one touchdown scored on defense in 1995 earning him his lone First-Team All-Pro selection. However, Hanks had his finest all-around season in 1994, when he established career-high marks with 72 combined tackles, 65 solo stops, and seven interceptions, which he returned a total of 93 yards.

Memorable Moments/Greatest Performances

Hanks recorded the first interception of his career during a 34–31 loss to the Buffalo Bills on September 13, 1992.

After intercepting a pass earlier in the game, Hanks punctuated a 41–3 rout of the Atlanta Falcons on November 9, 1992, by returning a punt 48 yards for a touchdown in the fourth quarter.

Hanks earned NFC Defensive Player of the Week honors for the first of five times by intercepting two passes during a 42–7 win over the New Orleans Saints on November 22, 1993, returning one of his picks 67 yards for a touchdown.

Hanks earned that distinction again for his performance during a 27–21 win over the Lions on October 9, 1994, finishing the game with six tackles, one fumble recovery, and one interception, which he returned 38 yards to the Detroit 7 yard line to help set up a 49ers touchdown.

Hanks again laid claim to NFC Defensive Player of the Week honors by recording a pair of interceptions during a 21–14 victory over the Dallas Cowboys on November 13, 1994.

Hanks contributed to a 28–3 win over the Patriots on September 17, 1995, by picking off Drew Bledsoe twice.

Hanks helped lead the 49ers to a 38–20 win over the Cowboys on November 12, 1995, by recording an interception and recovering a fumble, which he returned 38 yards for a touchdown.

Hanks scored again on a 38-yard fumble return during a 24–12 win over the Philadelphia Eagles on November 10, 1997.

Hanks crossed the opponent's goal line again during a 34–17 victory over the Denver Broncos on December 15, 1997, when he returned his interception of a John Elway pass 55 yards for a TD.

Notable Achievements

- Scored four defensive touchdowns.
- Returned one punt for a touchdown.
- Recorded at least five interceptions three times.
- Amassed more than 100 interception-return yards twice.
- Led 49ers in interceptions four times.
- Ranks among 49ers career leaders with 31 interceptions (tied-4th), 380 interception-return yards (8th), and 474 tackles (10th).
- Five-time division champion (1992, 1993, 1994, 1995, and 1997).
- 1994 NFC champion.
- Super Bowl XXIX champion.
- Five-time NFC Defensive Player of the Week.
- Four-time Pro Bowl selection (1994, 1995, 1996, and 1997).
- 1995 First-Team All-Pro selection.
- Three-time Second-Team All-Pro selection (1994, 1996, and 1997).
- Three-time First-Team All-NFC selection (1994, 1995, and 1997).
- 1996 Second-Team All-NFC selection.

36

TOMMY HART

Although Tommy Hart spent most of his 10 seasons in San Francisco being overshadowed by his more celebrated line-mate, Cedrick Hardman, he proved to be nearly as effective at applying pressure to opposing quarterbacks. Starting opposite Hardman at left defensive end for eight years, Hart recorded almost as many sacks, while also doing a much better job of defending against the run. Second on the 49ers' all-time sack list, Hart finished in double digits in that category on five separate occasions, earning in the process Pro Bowl and All-Pro honors once each. A member of 49er teams that won three straight division titles, Hart later returned to the organization as an assistant coach to help lead the 49ers to seven more division titles and three NFL championships.

Born in Macon, Georgia, on November 7, 1944, Tommy Lee Hart attended Ballard High School, where he starred on the gridiron as a two-way lineman. Growing up in the segregated South, Hart drew little interest from the region's major universities, prompting him to ultimately accept a football scholarship from Morris Brown College, a historically black institution located some 90 miles northwest, in the city of Atlanta. Excelling in multiple sports at Morris Brown, Hart earned four letters in football as an offensive guard, offensive tackle, and defensive tackle, and another three in track as a sprinter and shotputter, posting a personal-best time of 9.7 seconds in the 100-yard dash. Particularly proficient on the gridiron, Hart gained all-conference recognition three times and received the additional distinction of being named a Second-Team NAIA All-American his senior year.

Selected by the 49ers in the 10th round of the 1968 NFL Draft, with the 261st overall pick, Hart saw very little action as a rookie, appearing in only five games while serving as a backup to starting defensive ends Stan Hindman and Clark Miller. Although Hart assumed a somewhat expanded role the following year, appearing in all 14 games as a situational pass-rusher and special teams player, he continued to function primarily as a backup,

Tommy Hart ranks second on the 49ers' all-time sack list.
Courtesy of Mike Traverse

before finally joining the starting unit in 1970, when he started every game for the 49ers at left defensive end for the first of eight straight seasons.

Combining with Cedrick Hardman during that time to give the 49ers one of the most formidable pass-rushing duos in the NFL, Hart amassed more than 100 sacks, with some sources crediting him with an average of 15 per season. Performing especially well in 1972 and 1976, Hart recorded 16 sacks in the first of those campaigns, gaining in the process honorable-mention All-NFC recognition. Four years later, Hart earned Pro Bowl, All-Pro, and All-NFC honors by registering a team-high 17 sacks, in helping the 49ers set a single-season franchise record by bringing down opposing quarterbacks behind the line of scrimmage a total of 61 times. Hart also won the prestigious Len Eshmont Award both years as the player who best exemplified the "inspirational and courageous play" of former 49er Len Eshmont, who died of infectious hepatitis at only 39 years of age in 1957.

Hart's tremendous quickness allowed him to excel as a pass-rusher despite his somewhat smallish 6'4" 245-pound frame. He also possessed outstanding strength and a nonstop motor, both of which helped make him effective against the run as well. But even though Hart proved to be a more complete player than Cedrick Hardman, causing most teams to run away from him and toward his fellow "Gold Rush" member, he received less notoriety due to the understated manner with which he carried himself. Far more reserved than the outspoken Hardman, Hart rarely drew attention to himself, on or off the field, preferring to let his play do his talking for him. Yet, Hart's consistently excellent play at left defensive end made him one of the most significant contributors to 49ers teams that won three consecutive division titles during the early 1970s.

Hart remained in San Francisco until 1978, when the 49ers traded him to the Chicago Bears prior to the start of the regular season. Unofficially credited with 106 sacks and 608 solo tackles as a member of the 49ers, Hart continues to rank among the franchise's all-time leaders in both categories. He also intercepted two passes, recovered eight fumbles, recorded one safety, and scored two touchdowns during his time in San Francisco.

After leaving the 49ers, Hart spent two seasons in Chicago, before ending his playing career with the New Orleans Saints in 1980. Although estimates vary, it is believed that Hart registered more than 130 sacks during his 13 years in the league.

Returning to San Francisco following his retirement, Hart spent another 11 years with the 49ers, serving as an assistant defensive coach from 1983 to 1991 and a scout from 1992 to 1993. He later spent 10 seasons with the Dallas Cowboys, coaching the team's defensive ends in 1996 and 1997, and scouting for them from 1998 to 2005, before retiring to private life.

49ERS CAREER HIGHLIGHTS

Best Season

Hart performed exceptionally well for the 49ers in 1972, recording 65 tackles and a team-high 16 sacks. However, he had his finest all-around season in 1976, earning his lone Pro Bowl and All-Pro nominations by making 73 tackles, registering a career high 17 sacks, and forcing three fumbles.

Memorable Moments/Greatest Performances

Hart recorded the first of his two career interceptions during a 20–6 victory over the Los Angeles Rams on October 11, 1970.

Hart scored the first points of his career when he returned a fumble 63 yards for a touchdown during a 26–14 win over the St. Louis Cardinals on October 24, 1971.

Hart picked off his second pass as a pro during a lopsided 37–2 win over the New Orleans Saints on October 1, 1972.

Hart contributed to a 31–3 victory over the Bears on November 16, 1975, by returning a fumble 10 yards for a touchdown.

Hart turned in a dominant performance against the Rams on October 11, 1976, forcing three fumbles and recording six of the 10 sacks the 49ers registered against quarterback James Harris during a 16–0 win. Hart's six sacks set a single-game franchise record that has since been equaled only by Fred Dean.

Hart led the defensive charge when the 49ers recorded seven sacks and limited the New Orleans offense to just 95 total yards during a 33–3 man-handling of the Saints on October 17, 1976.

Hart and his defensive mates once again dominated the opposition the following week, with the 49ers recording eight sacks and surrendering a total of just 44 yards to Atlanta's offense during a 15–0 shutout of the Falcons on October 23, 1976.

Notable Achievements

- Scored two defensive touchdowns.
- Started every game in each of last eight seasons, at one point appearing in 126 consecutive contests.
- Finished in double digits in sacks five times.
- Finished second in NFL with 69 fumble-return yards in 1971.
- Led 49ers in sacks twice.
- Holds share of 49ers single-game record for most sacks (6 vs. L.A. Rams on October 11, 1976).
- Ranks among 49ers career leaders with 106 sacks (2nd) and 608 tackles (7th).
- Three-time division champion (1970, 1971, and 1972).
- 1976 Pro Bowl selection.
- 1976 Second-Team All-Pro selection.
- 1976 First-Team All-NFC selection.

37

KERMIT ALEXANDER

An outstanding defensive back who excelled for the 49ers at both cornerback and safety, Kermit Alexander spent seven seasons in San Francisco, during which time he recorded the third-most interceptions in franchise history. Leading the team in that category on six separate occasions, Alexander intercepted at least five passes five times, once finishing second in the league with nine picks. Starring for the 49ers on special teams as well, Alexander consistently ranked among the NFL leaders in kickoff- and punt-return yards, amassing more than 1,000 all-purpose yards twice and returning two punts for touchdowns. Nevertheless, Alexander has been most closely associated through the years with his hit on Gale Sayers that helped bring the Hall of Fame running back's career to a premature end.

Born in New Iberia, Louisiana, on January 4, 1941, Kermit Joseph Alexander moved with his family at a very young age to the state of California, where he grew up in the projects of South-Central Los Angeles. The oldest of 11 children, Alexander spent his early years roaming the streets with his friends, recalling many years later how his life may have headed down a different path had a young policeman named Tom Bradley, who later became mayor of Los Angeles, not confronted him for stealing from a corner store. Recounting that Bradley asked him if he wanted to amount to something or to nothing, Alexander chose to work hard and educate himself at local Mount Carmel High School, where he also began his career on the gridiron.

Subsequently offered an athletic scholarship to UCLA, Alexander starred for the Bruins in multiple sports, winning the NCAA championship in the triple jump in track, while also earning All-America honors as a defensive back in football. Displaying his versatility while in college, Alexander also spent some time at running back, gaining 708 yards on the ground, amassing 1,216 yards from scrimmage, and scoring eight touchdowns in his three years of varsity play.

Kermit Alexander excelled for the 49ers at cornerback, safety, and on special teams.
Courtesy of Mike Traverse

Selected by the 49ers with the eighth overall pick of the 1963 NFL Draft and by the Denver Broncos with the fifth overall pick of that year's AFL Draft, Alexander chose to sign with the 49ers, for whom he performed exceptionally well at left cornerback as a rookie, leading the team with five interceptions, while also ranking among the NFL leaders with 638 kickoff-return yards and an average of 26.6 yards per kickoff return. Moved to free safety in 1964, Alexander continued his strong play at that post the next two seasons, recording a total of eight interceptions. Performing even better on special teams, Alexander accumulated 672 yards returning kickoffs and punts in the first of those campaigns, before amassing 1,028 all-purpose yards in 1965, with his 741 kickoff-return yards leading the NFL.

Shifted to right cornerback prior to the start of the 1966 campaign, Alexander spent the next four seasons starting opposite Jimmy Johnson, giving the 49ers one of the top pair of cover corners in the NFL. Recording a total of 23 interceptions during that time, Alexander performed especially well in 1968, when he earned a trip to the Pro Bowl and Second-Team All-Pro honors from UPI by finishing second in the league with nine interceptions, which he returned for a total of 155 yards. Continuing to excel on special teams as well, Alexander amassed a career-high 1,269 all-purpose yards in 1966, with his 1,182 kickoff- and punt-return yards leading the league.

The speedy Alexander, who stood 5'11" and weighed 187 pounds, played the game with reckless abandon, earning the respect of teammates and fans alike with his willingness to sacrifice his body for the betterment of the team. A hard-hitter, Alexander often hurled his body at opposing receivers and running backs, with his most notable hit coming against Gale Sayers in 1968, when he delivered a rolling tackle to the runner's right knee that ended up shortening the career of the future Hall of Famer. Yet, despite his violent style of play, Alexander missed just four games in his seven seasons with the 49ers, at one point appearing in 83 out of 84 contests.

Further endearing himself to his teammates with his willingness to fight for what he believed in, Alexander served as president of the NFL Players Association and stood up to 49ers management during contract negotiations, a practice that gradually spread to the rest of the team, with noted sportswriter Tom Friend stating in his *Outside the Lines* piece, "players to this day . . . thank him for their nest eggs."

Alexander remained in San Francisco until the end of 1969, when the 49ers traded him to the Los Angeles Rams. Leaving the City by the Bay with career totals of 36 interceptions, 499 interception-return yards, 23 fumble recoveries, 4,579 all-purpose yards, and four touchdowns, Alexander subsequently spent two seasons in Los Angeles, recording another seven interceptions and scoring two more touchdowns, before ending his career as a backup with the Philadelphia Eagles in 1973.

Following his playing days, Alexander, who spent his offseasons working in San Francisco as a probation officer, continued in that capacity on a full-time basis until 1984, when he experienced a life-changing event that he detailed many years later in his book entitled *The Valley of the Shadow of Death: A Tale of Tragedy and Redemption.* Alexander's book, which he co-authored with San Francisco State University criminal justice professors Alex Gerould and Jeff Snipes, describes the events surrounding the senseless murder of his mother, sister, and two nephews during a home invasion by three members of the Rollin 60's Neighborhood Crips, whose intended victims lived two doors away.

Revealing the tremendous impact that the incident made on his life, Alexander writes, "That morning, the killers did not just take my family, they killed me. Any Kermit that lived before that day died that morning. All that he carried with him, trust, joy, hope, went with his relatives to their graves."

Alexander goes on to say that he embarked on a one-man vigilante mission, talking to the streets at night, working his old contacts from the neighborhood, trying to track down the killers himself. Although the LAPD eventually caught those responsible for the fatal shootings, the damage had been done to the psyche of Alexander, who subsequently found himself being consumed with feelings of guilt, often saying to himself, "You should have been there, you could have stopped what happened."

His marriage and family life having fallen apart, Alexander recalls, "I had no motivation. I no longer saw possibilities. I just couldn't visualize a future, or anything that could bring peace or contentment. I couldn't imagine deliverance."

Many years passed before a renewed relationship with his current wife, Tami, and the adoption of five young Haitian children helped Alexander find a new purpose in life. Recalling the first time he laid eyes on one of the children, a boy named Clifton, Alexander writes, "And that was the moment, the first glimpse at a second chance. The Path was lit. I could see a way out of the Valley. Shed the ghosts of Watts in the Land of High Mountains."

Now 80 years old, Alexander lives with his family in Riverside, California, where he does charity work, holding annual Super Bowl parties that raise thousands of dollars to help fight child abuse. Alexander and his wife also founded Operation Windmill International, which is dedicated to lighting up the lives of children through the use of wind and solar technology in third world countries.

49ERS CAREER HIGHLIGHTS

Best Season

Although Alexander performed brilliantly on special teams from 1964 to 1966, he had his finest all-around season for the 49ers in 1968, earning his lone Pro Bowl nomination by ranking among the NFL leaders with nine interceptions and 155 interception-return yards, while also scoring one touchdown on defense and accumulating a total of 447 yards returning kickoffs and punts.

Memorable Moments/Greatest Performances

Alexander recorded the first interception of his career when he picked off a Fran Tarkenton pass during a 45–14 loss to the Minnesota Vikings on September 29, 1963.

Alexander scored his first career touchdown when he ran 70 yards to paydirt after fielding a punt during a 24–14 win over the Packers on November 15, 1964.

Alexander turned in a tremendous all-around effort during a 41–14 victory over the Bears on December 11, 1966, intercepting a pass and scoring a pair of touchdowns on a 14-yard return of a fumble recovery and a 44-yard punt return, with his fabulous performance earning him NFL Defensive Player of the Week honors.

Alexander contributed to a 34–28 win over the Atlanta Falcons on December 10, 1967, by picking off two passes in one game for the first time in his career.

Alexander recorded another pair of interceptions during a 45–28 win over the Pittsburgh Steelers on November 24, 1968, subsequently returning one of his picks 66 yards for a touchdown.

Yet, Alexander has been remembered more than anything through the years for his tackle of Gale Sayers during a 27–19 loss to the Chicago Bears on November 10, 1968, that helped shorten the career of the star running back. With Sayers looking to turn the corner on an end sweep, Alexander delivered a rolling tackle to his right knee that forced him to undergo season-ending surgery, robbing him of much of his extraordinary quickness in the process. Recalling the incident years later, Alexander said, "Sayers' teammates all went back to the huddle, and he was lying there all messed up. I helped him over to the sidelines, and the coach came running up, ranting and raving, cursing me out. I looked him right in the eye and said, 'You need to bring in another running back—this one is all used up.'"

Notable Achievements

- Returned two punts for touchdowns.
- Scored two defensive touchdowns.
- Amassed more than 1,000 all-purpose yards twice.
- Recorded at least five interceptions five times.
- Amassed more than 100 interception-return yards once.
- Led NFL in fumble recoveries twice, kickoff-return yards once, and kickoff- and punt-return yards once.

- Finished second in NFL in interceptions once, kickoff-return yards once, and kickoff- and punt-return yards once.
- Finished third in NFL with 155 interception-return yards in 1968.
- Led 49ers in interceptions six times.
- Holds 49ers career record for most fumble recoveries (23).
- Ranks among 49ers career leaders with 36 interceptions (3rd), 499 interception-return yards (5th), 3,271 kickoff-return yards (5th), and 782 punt-return yards (10th).
- 1966 Week 14 NFL Defensive Player of the Week.
- 1968 Pro Bowl selection.

38

BRENT JONES

Born and raised in the Bay Area, Brent Jones spent his entire 11-year NFL career playing close to home, excelling at tight end for the 49ers from 1987 to 1997. A key member of one of the league's most potent offenses, Jones contributed significantly to teams that won nine division titles and three Super Bowls with his superior pass-catching and blocking skills. Ranking among the franchise's all-time leaders in every major pass-receiving category, Jones earned four trips to the Pro Bowl, two All-Pro nominations, and two All-NFC selections, before gaining the additional distinction of being named to the Pro Football Reference All-1990s Second Team.

Born in San Jose, California, on February 12, 1963, Brent Michael Jones grew up in a football family, receiving his introduction to the sport at an early age from his father, former San Jose State quarterback and high school football coach Mike Jones. Looking back at his childhood, Jones said, "My dad used to play a game with my brother and myself called '100 Catches.' Before we could go to bed, we had to catch a hundred passes in a row, and there were several times you'd catch 80 or 90, and then you'd drop one and have to start again all the way back at zero. So, there were some nights where you'd stay up late."

An outstanding all-around athlete, Jones played baseball and football at Leland High School, actually performing better as a catcher on the diamond than he did as a wide receiver on the gridiron, recalling, "The fact is, I never thought about becoming an NFL tight end. As a young person growing up in San Jose, I had aspirations of playing pro baseball. In high school, I made First-Team All-League on the diamond and was a second-string football player. . . . After I graduated, I went to Santa Clara University on a baseball/football scholarship, and it was there that my football skills blossomed. I was First-Team All-Conference for three years, earned conference Player of the Year honors as a senior, and became an AP, *Football News*, and Kodak All-American."

Brent Jones played for 49er teams that won nine division titles and three Super Bowls.
Courtesy of George A. Kitrinos

Gradually transitioning from wide receiver to tight end during his time at Santa Clara, Jones ended up making 137 receptions for 2,267 yards and 24 touchdowns, with his excellent play prompting the Pittsburgh Steelers to select him in the fifth round of the 1986 NFL Draft, with the 135th overall pick. However, just five days later, Jones sustained a neck injury in an automobile accident that prevented him from competing for a spot on the team.

Recalling the events, Jones said, "I got in a car accident. Me and my wife, Dana, my fiancée at the time. We were a couple of houses away from my house in San Jose. I herniated a disk in my neck and was out for several months. The Steelers were good about it at the time. The situation was they felt like I could be their tight end, but I wasn't able to practice there for a while. They said they were going to have patience with me. It was going pretty well. Then, about a month into the season, they had some cost-cutting going on, and they felt like, 'Hey, your neck might not get better.'"

After being released by the Steelers, Jones eventually signed with the 49ers, later saying, "I signed with the 49ers because of the class of the organization and because I was born and raised in the Bay area, and I thought that was going to be my chance to make an impact right where I was born and raised, and hopefully have an opportunity, and I knew the way the organization treated people they were very fair, and at least I'd get a fair shot this time around."

Recalling that he faced long odds in making the team when he first arrived in San Francisco in 1987, Jones said, "I was eighth-string. There were Russ Francis, Ron Heller, John Frank, and Cliff Benson, to name only four."

Nevertheless, Jones ended up earning a roster spot, after which he spent his first two seasons playing mostly on special teams, making a total of just 10 receptions in extremely limited duty on offense. But, following the retirement of John Frank at the end of 1988, Jones laid claim to the starting tight end job, which he retained for the remainder of his career.

Performing well in his first year as a full-time starter, Jones helped the 49ers win their fourth straight division title and second consecutive NFL championship by making 40 receptions for 500 yards and four touchdowns during the regular season, before catching another eight passes and scoring three TDs in the postseason. Jones followed that up with an extremely productive 1990 campaign, finishing the year with 56 receptions, 747 receiving yards, and five TD catches. After being limited by knee problems to just 10 games, 27 receptions, and no touchdowns in 1991, Jones rebounded in a big way the following year, earning Pro Bowl honors for the first of four straight times by making 45 receptions for 628 yards and four touchdowns. Compiling those numbers while playing through muscle spasms, a strained hamstring, battered ribs, and a bruised knee, Jones also gained unofficial First-Team All-Pro recognition from the Newspaper Enterprise Association. Performing even better the next two seasons, Jones earned consecutive All-Pro and All-NFC selections by catching 68 passes, amassing 735 receiving yards, and scoring three touchdowns in 1993, before making 49 receptions for 670 yards and a career-high nine TDs the following year.

In discussing his teammate and close friend's rise to prominence, Steve Young stated, "He's one of those guys, the ultimate hard worker. They made a spot for him, and now he's in the Pro Bowl. He could have easily never played football. It was against the odds. I think he made himself a player. I don't think anyone knew. He was the only one who had an inkling."

Proving to be the perfect complement to standout wide receivers Jerry Rice and John Taylor, the 6'4", 230-pound Jones did an exceptional job of finding holes in the opposing defense, with Young saying, "I don't know how a quarterback can do it without having a tight end who can find holes inside, against zones. Brent is just the best in the league in finding holes and seams. And he catches every ball. To me, there's Jerry's greatness and everything else, but I don't think you have a great offense unless you have a great tight end."

Jones also drew praise from former Dallas Cowboys and Minnesota Vikings linebacker Jack Del Rio, who said of his frequent foe, "He's a guy that knows how to get open. He's a very smart player. Extremely, extremely good hands, and people don't think that he's as fast as he is. He does a good job of coming open in zones."

Identifying Jones as the key to the 49er offense, Green Bay quarterback Brett Favre suggested, "Brent Jones means to San Francisco's offense what Reggie White means to our defense. I mean, he has been like the pivotal force in them scoring a lot of points and getting to the Super Bowl. Jerry Rice, of course, is a great receiver, but Brent Jones is a guy who really makes it tick for them."

Asked to describe his role in the offense, Jones stated, "I think the 49er offense revolves around having a tight end that can get down the middle of the field with speed, that can catch the ball, that can block, that's really a versatile performer, and I think I've been able to step in and define that position within the 49ers system. I think that's probably been my biggest contribution to the 49er offense and the 49ers as well."

Meanwhile, in addressing his gradual development into one of the league's better blocking tight ends, Jones said, "I've really come a long way. I was generally a wide receiver coming into the league. I've gotten to the point where I think I'm pretty good at it."

After Jones earned his fourth consecutive Pro Bowl selection in 1995 by recording 60 receptions, amassing 595 receiving yards, and scoring three touchdowns, injuries forced him to miss significant playing time in each of the next two seasons, prompting him to announce his retirement following the conclusion of the 1997 campaign. However, before retiring, Jones was named the winner of the AIA Bart Starr Award, which is presented annually to the NFL player who best exemplifies outstanding character and leadership in the home, on the field, and in the community. Ending his playing career with 417 receptions, 5,195 receiving yards, and 33 touchdown catches, Jones continues to rank among the 49ers' all-time leaders in all three categories.

Transitioning seamlessly into a career in broadcasting following his playing days, Jones worked as an analyst for the *NFL on CBS* from 1998 to 2005, before leaving the program to focus on his business, Northgate Capital, a venture capital and private equity investment firm that currently boasts nearly $5 billion in assets. Jones, who co-founded the company with former teammates Steve Young, Mark Harris, and Tommy Vardell in 2000, initially served as the corporation's managing director and founding partner, before gradually transitioning into the role of founder and senior advisor.

CAREER HIGHLIGHTS

Best Season

Jones had a very solid season for the 49ers in 1990, finishing the year with 56 receptions for 747 yards and five touchdowns. However, he earned All-Pro honors for the only two times in his career in 1993 and 1994, concluding the first of those campaigns with an NFC-leading 68 catches for 735 yards and three touchdowns, before making 49 receptions, amassing 670 receiving yards, and scoring nine TDs the following year. It's an extremely close call, but Jones's nine touchdown catches in 1994 made that the most impactful season of his career.

Memorable Moments/Greatest Performances

Jones scored his first career touchdown when he gathered in a 3-yard pass from Steve Young during a 24–23 loss to the Phoenix Cardinals on November 6, 1988.

Although Jones made just one reception for 7 yards during a 55–10 manhandling of the Denver Broncos in Super Bowl XXIV, it went for a touchdown that gave the 49ers a 13–3 lead late in the first quarter.

Jones went over 100 receiving yards for the first time as a pro during a 19–13 win over the Atlanta Falcons on September 23, 1990, finishing the game with five catches for 125 yards and one TD, which came on a 67-yard connection with Joe Montana.

Jones contributed to the 49ers' 28–10 victory over the Washington Redskins in the divisional round of the 1990 playoffs by making four receptions for 103 yards.

In a game the 49ers ended up winning by a score of 21–20, Jones helped them overcome a 20–7 fourth-quarter deficit to New Orleans on November 15, 1992, by hooking up with Steve Young on touchdown passes that covered 14 and 8 yards, with his second TD coming in the closing moments of regulation.

Although Jones made just one reception during a 37–22 win over Washington on November 6, 1994, it went for a career-long 69-yard touchdown.

Jones excelled during a 27–17 loss to the Packers in the divisional round of the 1995 playoffs, making eight receptions for 112 yards.

The final game of Jones's career proved to be a memorable one for him. Although the 49ers ended up losing the 1997 NFC championship game to the Packers by a score of 23–10, Jones earned the respect and admiration of players on both sides by competing in the contest with a badly injured leg, saying afterwards:

> I really thought I wasn't going to be able to play today. I was pretty down the last day or two. I spent a lot of time just trying to be honest, because I thought it was all over. It didn't end the way I wanted it to, but at least I was out on the field. For me, the most painful thing in the world would have been to have to watch from the sidelines. . . . It hurts an awful lot. I had the expectation of going to the Super Bowl and walking off the field in San Diego. We prepared all year for this game, and it didn't happen for us. I really didn't think about it being my last game until the last couple of minutes when guys were coming up to me saying, 'Great career.' Guys from the other team were coming over, and that made it pretty emotional.

Commenting on his teammate's heroic effort, Steve Young said, "It was a miraculous thing that he was able to play today. He couldn't walk last night. He was on crutches this morning. He got some shots and just decided to play regardless. I give him a lot of respect for showing up and playing. He's one of the 49er greats."

Notable Achievements

- Surpassed 50 receptions three times.
- Surpassed 700 receiving yards twice.
- Scored nine touchdowns in 1994.
- Ranks among 49ers career leaders with 417 receptions (6th), 5,195 receiving yards (8th), and 33 touchdown receptions (10th).
- Nine-time division champion (1987, 1988, 1989, 1990, 1992, 1993, 1994, 1995, and 1997).
- Three-time NFC champion (1988, 1989, and 1994).
- Three-time Super Bowl champion (XXIII, XXIV, and XXIX).
- Four-time Pro Bowl selection (1992, 1993, 1994, and 1995).
- Two-time Second-Team All-Pro selection (1993 and 1994).
- Two-time First-Team All-NFC selection (1993 and 1994).
- Pro Football Reference All-1990s Second Team.

39

ABE WOODSON

An outstanding defensive back and sensational performer on special teams, Abe Woodson spent seven seasons in San Francisco establishing himself as the premier return-man of his time. En route to setting franchise records for most kickoff-return yards and kickoff-return touchdowns, Woodson amassed more than 1,000 all-purpose yards four times and led the NFL in kickoff-return average twice, with his career average of 28.7 yards per return placing him among the league's all-time leaders. Excelling for the 49ers in the defensive secondary as well, Woodson recorded a total of 15 interceptions as a member of the team, with his brilliant all-around play earning him five Pro Bowl selections and three All-Pro nominations.

Born in Jackson, Mississippi, on February 15, 1934, Abraham Benjamin Woodson grew up in Chicago, Illinois, where he attended Austin High School. After excelling in multiple sports in high school, Woodson received an athletic scholarship to the University of Illinois, where, in addition to starring at running back for the school's football team, he distinguished himself as a sprinter in track, twice tying the 50-yard indoor high hurdle world record and narrowly missing an Olympic berth in 1956, when he finished fourth at the trials. Meanwhile, Woodson gained All-America recognition for his performance on the gridiron as a senior in 1956, when he rushed for 599 yards, amassed 856 yards from scrimmage, and scored two touchdowns.

Selected by the 49ers in the second round of the 1957 NFL Draft, with the 15th overall pick, Woodson arrived in San Francisco one year later after fulfilling a military commitment. Seeing limited playing time as a rookie in 1958, Woodson appeared in nine games, intercepting one pass as a cornerback on defense, while returning seven punts and 11 kickoffs for a total of 292 yards. Assuming a far more prominent role the following year, Woodson earned First-Team All-Pro honors and the first of his five consecutive trips to the Pro Bowl by finishing second on the 49ers with four interceptions, amassing a total of 525 yards on special teams, and scoring

Abe Woodson holds franchise records for most kickoff-return yards and kickoff-return touchdowns.
Courtesy of Footballcardgallery.com

the first touchdown of his career on a 105-yard kickoff return. After gaining First-Team All-Pro recognition again in 1960 by picking off two passes, leading the league with 672 kickoff- and punt-return yards, and finishing second in the circuit with an average of 29.3 yards per kickoff return, Woodson established himself as the NFL's top return-man over the course of the next three seasons, scoring six times on special teams, amassing more than 1,000 all-purpose yards each year, and leading the league in kickoff-return yards once, kickoff- and punt-return yards twice, and kickoff-return average twice. Performing especially well in 1962 and 1963, Woodson amassed a total of 2,495 all-purpose yards, averaged close to 32 yards per kickoff return, returned four kicks for touchdowns, and intercepted five passes on defense, one of which he returned for a TD.

Woodson's great speed, tremendous acceleration, and superior open-field running ability made him the most dangerous return-man of his time, with only Philadelphia's Timmy Brown rivaling him for much of his career. Capable of altering the outcome of games by providing the 49ers with exceptional field position, Woodson drew praise from former teammate R. C. Owens, who said, "He was a spectacular kick returner who always got us in good position. He was a Big Ten hurdles champ. You'd always see him hurdling over people. We were always in it with Abe because he would get us good field position."

Former Chicago Bears running back Ronnie Bull also expressed his admiration for Woodson when he stated, "You have respect for everyone you play against, and I just had mutual admiration for Woodson. He always gave his best all the time. He was an outstanding kick returner, and he was willing to do it, too . . . I respected guys like Woodson because, if you didn't respect them, they would beat your butt."

A solid cover corner as well, the 5'11", 188-pound Woodson recorded 19 interceptions over the course of his career (15 with the 49ers), which he returned for a total of 206 yards.

Commenting on Woodson's strong defensive play, Bears wide receiver Johnny Morris, who accumulated more yards through the air than anyone else in the history of that franchise, said, "I played against him, and, of course at Illinois he was mostly on offense, and he was really good. He was one of the best defensive backs that I faced. I had just started at wide receiver (after playing halfback), and so it was a learning process for me."

Morris then added, "He was a nice guy. We did a commercial together out in Kezar Stadium during the off-season. That was the first time I had really ever talked to him. He never said anything to you out on the field, hardly. A lot of defensive backs like Herb Adderley would jabber at you one way or another. I remember guys like Johnny Sample would jabber at you. But Abe just seemed to play the game."

Woodson spent one more year in San Francisco, intercepting two passes, amassing 1,014 all-purpose yards, and ranking among the league leaders with 1,013 kickoff- and punt-return yards and an average of 27.5 yards per kickoff return in 1964, before being traded to the St. Louis Cardinals for running back John David Crow at season's end. Woodson left San Francisco having amassed 949 punt-return yards, 4,873 kickoff-return yards, and 6,131 all-purpose yards, scored a total of seven touchdowns on special teams, and averaged 29.4 yards per kickoff-return. He also returned his 15 interceptions a total of 159 yards, gained 39 yards on 20 carries, and made eight receptions for 74 yards.

Woodson ended up spending two seasons in St. Louis, intercepting four more passes and amassing 719 more all-purpose yards, before announcing his retirement following the conclusion of the 1966 campaign with more kickoff-return yards (5,538) than any other player in NFL history at that time. Following his playing days, Woodson worked for many years as a life insurance salesman and a volunteer chaplain for the Nevada prison system. After retiring to private life in 2001, Woodson lived until February 8, 2014, when he passed away just one week before what would have been his 80th birthday.

49ERS CAREER HIGHLIGHTS

Best Season

Woodson's outstanding play on defense and special teams earned him First-Team All-Pro honors in both 1959 and 1960. In addition to recording a career-high four interceptions in the first of those campaigns, Woodson returned one kickoff for a touchdown and amassed a total of 545 all-purpose yards, before leading the league with 672 kickoff- and punt-return yards the following year. However, Woodson made a greater overall impact in 1962 and 1963, establishing himself as arguably the league's foremost return-man over the course of those two seasons. In addition to picking off two passes in 1962, Woodson returned a fumble for a touchdown, scored again on a punt return, and led the NFL with 1,157 kickoff-return yards, 1,336 kickoff- and punt-return yards, and an average of 31.3 yards per kickoff return. Woodson followed that up by recording three interceptions in 1963, while also returning three kickoffs for touchdowns, finishing third in the league with 1,030 kickoff- and punt-return yards, and topping the circuit with an average of 32.2 yards per kickoff return. It's a close call but, since Woodson gained All-Pro recognition for the third and final time in his career in 1963, we'll identify that as his finest season.

Memorable Moments/Greatest Performances

Woodson scored the first touchdown of his career when he returned a kickoff 105 yards for a TD during a 24–16 win over the Los Angeles Rams on November 8, 1959. Woodson's 105-yard return remains the longest in franchise history.

Woodson starred during a 49–0 rout of the Detroit Lions on October 1, 1961, picking off a pass on defense and returning the second-half kickoff 98 yards for a touchdown.

Woodson scored again on special teams when he returned a punt 80 yards for a touchdown during a 20–20 tie with the Lions on November 5, 1961.

Woodson turned in an exceptional all-around effort during a 34–27 win over the Bears on October 14, 1962, returning five kickoffs a total of 157 yards, intercepting a pass, and recovering a fumble, which he returned 37 yards for a touchdown.

Woodson scored the 49ers' only touchdown during a 31–13 loss to the Packers on October 21, 1962, when he returned a punt 85 yards early in the third quarter.

Although the 49ers lost to the Lions by a score of 38–24 on November 11, 1962, Woodson set a single-game franchise record by amassing a total of 210 yards on six kickoff returns.

Woodson scored the 49ers' first points of the 1963 campaign when he returned the opening kickoff of the regular-season opener 103 yards for a touchdown against the Vikings. Unfortunately, the 49ers went on to lose the game by a score of 24–20.

Woodson excelled in defeat once again on September 29, 1963, intercepting a Fran Tarkenton pass and returning a kickoff 95 yards for a touchdown during a 45–14 loss to the Vikings.

Woodson scored the final touchdown of his career when he returned a kickoff 99 yards for a TD during a 48–14 loss to the Giants on November 17, 1963.

Notable Achievements

- Scored one defensive touchdown.
- Returned two punts and five kickoffs for touchdowns.
- Amassed more than 1,000 all-purpose yards four times.
- Led NFL in punt-return yards once, kickoff-return yards once, kickoff- and punt-return yards three times, and kickoff-return average twice.
- Finished second in NFL in kickoff-return yards twice and kickoff-return average twice.
- Holds 49ers single-game record for most kickoff-return yards (210 vs. Detroit on November 11, 1962).
- Holds 49ers single-season record for most kickoff-return touchdowns (3 in 1963).

- Holds 49ers career records for most kickoff-return yards (4,873), most kickoff-return touchdowns (5), and highest kickoff-return average (29.4).
- Ranks seventh in franchise history with 949 punt-return yards.
- Ranks among NFL career leaders with five kickoff-return touchdowns (tied-9th) and 28.7-yard kickoff-return average (4th).
- Five-time Pro Bowl selection (1959, 1960, 1961, 1962, and 1963).
- Two-time First-Team All-Pro selection (1959 and 1960).
- 1963 Second-Team All-Pro selection.

40

ERIC WRIGHT

One of just five men who played on all four of San Francisco's Super Bowl championship teams during the 1980s, Eric Wright combined with Ronnie Lott for five seasons to form arguably the finest cornerback tandem in the NFL. An outstanding cover corner who typically lined up against opposing wide receivers one-on-one, Wright spent his entire 10-year NFL career in San Francisco, helping the 49ers win a total of eight division titles, with his exceptional play earning him Pro Bowl and All-Pro honors twice each. Yet, Wright is largely remembered for making a key play in the closing moments of the 1981 NFC championship game that sent the 49ers to their first Super Bowl.

Born in St. Louis, Missouri, on April 18, 1959, Eric Cortez Wright attended East St. Louis Assumption High School, where he starred on the gridiron, prompting the University of Missouri to offer him an athletic scholarship. Spending his college career excelling at safety under head coach Warren Powers, Wright helped the Tigers earn three bowl appearances, gaining in the process All–Big Eight Conference recognition twice. Later named to Missouri's All-Century Team, Wright equaled a single-game school record by recording three interceptions during a 45–15 victory over San Diego State in 1979.

Subsequently selected by the 49ers in the second round of the 1981 NFL Draft, with the 40th overall pick, Wright arrived in San Francisco the same year as cornerback Ronnie Lott and safety Carlton Williamson, who the team selected in the first and third rounds, respectively. With all three men immediately earning starting jobs and Dwight Hicks firmly entrenched at the free safety position, the 49ers moved Wright to right cornerback, where he found himself starting opposite Lott. Performing well his first year in the league, Wright helped the 49ers capture the division title by picking off three passes and recovering two fumbles for a vastly improved San Francisco defense. Continuing his strong play in the postseason, Wright helped preserve a 28–27 win over Dallas in the NFC championship game

Eric Wright's tackle of Drew Pearson in the 1981 NFC championship game helped preserve the 49ers' victory over Dallas.

by making a game-saving tackle of Cowboys wide receiver Drew Pearson in the final minute of regulation.

After playing well once again in 1982, Wright earned First-Team All-NFC honors for the first of three straight times the following year by recording seven interceptions and leading the league with 164 interception-return yards. Wright then gained Pro Bowl and All-Pro recognition in each of the next two seasons, despite picking off just three passes during that time.

Although Wright often found himself being overlooked in favor of Ronnie Lott, he proved to be at least the equal of his more heralded teammate in terms of his ability to blanket opposing wide receivers. Blessed with exceptional speed and a rangy 6'1", 183-pound frame, Wright gained widespread acclaim as one of the finest man-to-man defenders in the league, with opposing quarterbacks rarely throwing the ball in his direction, often choosing to challenge Lott instead. Revealing the respect that Wright garnered from other teams, John Madden said during the telecast of the 1984 NFC championship game between the 49ers and Chicago Bears, "Eric Wright is one of the most underrated guys on this team. I know [Bears head coach] Mike Ditka was saying, 'Of all their defensive players, the guy that I respect most is Eric Wright. He's their best player.'"

Unfortunately, injuries prevented Wright from ever again performing at an elite level after 1985. After starting just four games over the course of the next two seasons, Wright returned to action full-time in 1988 to help the 49ers win their third Super Bowl of the decade. Nevertheless, he found himself being hampered by a serious groin injury that lingered into the next two seasons, forcing him to assume a part-time role. Choosing to announce his retirement following the conclusion of the 1990 campaign, Wright ended his playing career with 18 interceptions, 256 interception-return yards, five fumble recoveries, and two defensive touchdowns.

Remaining in San Francisco for three more years after retiring as an active player, Wright served the 49ers as assistant defensive backs coach from 1991 to 1993, before returning to the University of Missouri, where he spent two seasons coaching Tigers wide receivers. Wright later accepted the position of defensive secondary coach at Menlo College in Atherton, California, before taking a job in the lumber industry. He also serves as an alumni coordinator for the 49ers, saying during a 2017 interview, "I sell lumber every day and, as the alumni coordinator for the 49ers, it's part of my job description to stay in touch with the alumni. It's something I enjoy a great deal, and it keeps me in touch with the team. I work the home games every Sunday, and, so, I'm still involved."

CAREER HIGHLIGHTS

Best Season

Although Wright gained First-Team All-Pro recognition for the only time in 1985, he had the finest all-around season of his career in 1983, when he picked off seven passes and led the NFL with 164 interception-return yards and two touchdown interceptions.

Memorable Moments/Greatest Performances

Wright contributed to a 21–14 win over the New Orleans Saints on September 27, 1981, by recording the first interception of his career, which he returned 26 yards.

Wright turned in a memorable performance during a 48–17 win over the Minnesota Vikings on September 8, 1983, recording three interceptions, one of which he returned 60 yards for a touchdown.

Wright lit the scoreboard again when he returned his interception of a Gary Hogeboom pass 48 yards for a touchdown during a 42–17 victory over the Cowboys in the final game of the 1983 regular season.

Wright earned NFC Defensive Player of the Week honors by recording an interception and doing an expert job of blanketing standout wide receivers Lonzel Hill and Eric Martin during a 30–17 win over the New Orleans Saints on December 11, 1988.

An outstanding big-game performer, Wright recorded three interceptions in postseason play, with the first of those coming in Super Bowl XVI, when he picked off a Ken Anderson pass during a 26–21 win over the Cincinnati Bengals.

Wright recorded another interception during the 49ers' convincing 38–16 victory over the Dolphins in Super Bowl XIX, snuffing out a Miami scoring threat late in the third quarter by picking off a Dan Marino pass at the San Francisco 1 yard line.

However, Wright is remembered most for a play he made during the latter stages of the 1981 NFC championship game that helped preserve a 28–27 win over the Dallas Cowboys. The play, which ranks among the most important in franchise history, occurred in the final minute of regulation, just moments after Dwight Clark gave the 49ers a one-point lead with his famous TD catch in the back of the end zone. With the Cowboys in possession of the football at their own 20 yard line and needing only a field goal to win the game, Dallas quarterback Danny White hit Drew Pearson with a pass deep over the middle that the receiver gathered in just short of midfield with a lot of open territory in front of him. But, just as Pearson appeared to be heading toward paydirt, Wright reached out with one arm and brought him down with a back-of-the-shoulder-pad tackle that likely would be penalized today. When White fumbled on the very next play, the 49ers laid claim to their first conference championship, after which they went on to defeat Cincinnati in Super Bowl XVI. Looking back at Wright's game-saving tackle years later, Ronnie Lott said, "I think Eric

Wright making 'The Play' to save the game, to pull down Drew Pearson from not scoring, to keep them out of field goal range, was probably one of the biggest plays of the game. History could have definitely been different if Eric doesn't make that play."

Notable Achievements

- Scored two defensive touchdowns.
- Led NFL with 164 interception-return yards and two touchdown interceptions in 1983.
- Led 49ers with seven interceptions in 1983.
- Eight-time division champion (1981, 1983, 1984, 1986, 1987, 1988, 1989, and 1990).
- Four-time NFC champion (1981, 1984, 1988, and 1989).
- Four-time Super Bowl champion (XVI, XIX, XXIII, and XIV).
- 1988 Week 15 NFC Defensive Player of the Week.
- Two-time Pro Bowl selection (1984 and 1985).
- 1985 First-Team All-Pro selection.
- 1984 Second-Team All-Pro selection.
- Three-time First-Team All-NFC selection (1983, 1984, and 1985).

41

— GEORGE KITTLE —

The finest all-around tight end in the NFL today, George Kittle has excelled in every aspect of the game since joining the 49ers in 2017, drawing widespread acclaim for his ability to catch the football, gain additional yardage after the catch, and create holes in the running game.

In his four years with the 49ers, Kittle has already surpassed 80 receptions and 1,000 receiving yards twice each, while further separating himself from the other top players who man his position by establishing himself as the best blocking tight end in the league. Kittle's superior pass-receiving skills and willingness to take on defenders at the line of scrimmage have contributed greatly to the success of 49er teams that have won one division title and one NFC championship, earning him in the process Pro Bowl and All-Pro honors twice each.

Born in Madison, Wisconsin, on October 9, 1993, George Kittle moved with his family to Iowa at the age of seven, beginning his career on the gridiron at Iowa City West High School, before moving to Norman, Oklahoma, where he graduated from Norman High School. Offered an athletic scholarship to the University of Iowa, Kittle spent four seasons playing under head coach Kirk Ferentz, greatly altering his mindset during that time.

Seeing very little action his first three years at Iowa, Kittle later accepted full responsibility for his lack of playing time, saying, "I didn't really play a lot in college my first three years; that was 100 percent my fault. I wasn't really 100 percent all-in on football. Because I'd lived in Iowa City for six years, I had a whole bunch of friends there, so when I came back for college, it was a big party. I had a good time. And I knew something was gonna have to change."

Recalling Kittle's lack of dedication to his craft, Iowa assistant coach LeVar Woods claimed, "George was a wiry, explosive, fast kid and—to be truthful—a little bit of a pain in the ass. What most people would say is,

George Kittle has surpassed 80 receptions and 1,000 receiving yards in two of his first four seasons with the 49ers.
Courtesy of Stu Jossey

he didn't take things seriously. He was more worried about the things that go with college . . . what we call a 'Joe College.'"

Woods continued, "As linebackers' coach, I saw George from the other side his first few years. Frankly, we used to get mad at our guys if they got beat by Kittle. We'd say, 'You got beat by that guy?' But as he started to mature and get more serious about the game, he became a really good football player."

After gradually adding some 50 pounds onto his frame, Kittle developed into an adept run-blocker, saying, "I used to be so soft in high school. I avoided contact. I played free safety in a Cover-1 and was back all the time. It was my decision to change that. I realized if I kept playing soft, I was never going to the see the field."

Recalling the change that he noticed in his teammate prior to the start of his senior year, former Iowa fullback Steve Manders stated, "He was an animal in spring ball, and that's kind of what got him his starting spot. He was out there pancaking guys. He was relentless. It didn't matter who it was."

Although Kittle assumed a far more prominent role in his final season at Iowa, the Hawkeyes' run-heavy offense limited him to just 22 receptions, 314 receiving yards, and four touchdowns, drawing him only a moderate amount of interest from pro scouts heading into the 2017 NFL Draft. Nevertheless, 49ers head coach Kyle Shanahan grew increasingly impressed while watching a tape of Kittle, remembering, "We couldn't believe how good of a run blocker he was. Then we realized that everyone was calling him a run blocker because he didn't have the passing stats. We were impressed with how all-around he was."

With the 49ers planning to work out Hawkeyes signal-caller C. J. Beathard, they sent quarterbacks coach Rich Scangarello to Iowa City, instructing him to take a look at Kittle as well. Recalling the events that subsequently transpired, Scangarello said, "It was the day before they were going on spring break and Kittle and C.J. were best friends who lived together. Kittle had gone big the night before, and he was trying to get out of town on spring break. And I told C.J., 'He has to be there,' which I don't think made George super happy. . . . Well, it was a legendary workout. I probably made him run 80 routes. I mean, I just grinded him. And he was sweating, looking hungover, and he was just completely gassed. And yet, he was just out there going crazy, diving for balls and getting after it. He's just a special guy."

Kittle's exceptional effort, 4.52 speed in the 40-yard dash, and 35-inch vertical leap convinced the 49ers to select him in the fifth round, with the 146th overall pick. However, after Kittle arrived in San Francisco, it took him some time to adjust to life in the NFL, with Scangarello saying, "Let me tell you a story about Kittle: He had a lot of drops his rookie year. It was awful. You watch the Redskins game [a 26–24 Washington victory in Week 6], he dropped two wide-open balls that were huge plays and might have cost us the game. He hurt his ankle and just lost confidence."

Although Kittle ended up posting decent numbers, finishing the year with 43 receptions for 515 yards and two touchdowns, his inconsistent play prompted Scangarello and Shanahan to map out an offseason training program for him, with Scangarello recollecting, "Kyle said, 'You've gotta get this stuff handled . . . you've gotta get him to catch the ball naturally, run through the ball or whatever.' George was moving to Nashville over the offseason, where C.J. lived, and [fellow backup QB] Nick [Mullens] was going to come and work out with them, too. We gave the quarterbacks all these drills to do with him, and he went out and did them. To his credit, it's made him what he is."

Claiming that the practice sessions made a huge impact on his overall conditioning, Kittle said, "I learned how to train differently; I started doing speed and agility workouts I'd never done before. And on top of that, I had C.J., a quarterback who's in my offense, kind of teach me, . . . He sits in the meeting room with Kyle Shanahan every single day, so he was able to tell me, 'Hey, look, on these routes, you should be looking like this instead of this, because this is what Coach Shanahan wants.' And it clicked."

Noticing a maturation in Kittle as well when he returned to the team the following year, 49ers GM John Lynch later noted, "George was hit or miss his rookie year. After that, I think he made a decision: 'I can be pretty good at this.' But he watched some guys that were successful around here and had been pros for a while, and he saw their work ethic and routine, and all of a sudden, he became that guy. You could clearly see that he was becoming more focused and more committed."

Emerging as the 49ers' top offensive weapon in 2018, Kittle earned Pro Bowl and All-Pro honors for the first of two straight times by making 88 receptions for 1,377 yards and five touchdowns, with his 1,377 receiving yards setting a new single-season NFL record for tight ends (since broken). Kittle followed that up with another brilliant performance in 2019, catching 85 passes, amassing 1,053 receiving yards, and scoring five touchdowns despite missing two games with ankle and knee injuries.

Rivaling Kansas City's Travis Kelce as the finest pass-receiving tight end in the league, Kittle possesses soft hands, good speed, and outstanding athleticism that enables him to assume any number of roles in the 49er offense, as Jaguars linebacker Joe Schobert noted when he said, "He can make all the plays. He lines up at receiver, he runs receiver routes. He scored a touchdown on a seam-ball. He lines up in the backfield—he ran a jet-sweep. You don't really see tight ends running jet-sweeps. He got about a 20 or 30-yard gain. . . . You don't see a tight end in the NFL take over games like that since, I think, Rob Gronkowski in his prime."

An exceptional runner after the catch, the 6'4", 250-pound Kittle very much resembles a runaway locomotive once he gathers in the football, with 49ers fullback Kyle Juszczyk saying, "Once he gets the ball, there's nobody who's better than him. He just runs mean and aggressive."

Cardinals linebacker De'Vondre Campbell said of Kittle, "Once the ball is in his hands, he's like a running back, and he's faster than you think."

Expressing his admiration for his fellow tight end, Evan Engram of the Giants stated, "He's just a savage—never goes down on the first hit."

In discussing Kittle's attitude once he begins running with the football, former 49ers wide receiver Dante Pettis suggested, "His mindset is not, 'I'm going to score,' or, 'I want to get as many yards as possible.' It is, 'I want to destroy whoever is in front of me.' That's why he stiff-arms and runs people over. He wants to destroy whoever is in his path."

Kittle provided some insight into his philosophy of doling out punishment to would-be tacklers when he said, "I'm going to *make* them tackle me, and, if they want to tackle me, I'm going to make it as hard as I possibly can on them to see if they want to keep tackling me. . . .You can tell if a guy is running full speed at you at a downhill angle. Yeah, he's going to bring it on me, and I'll lower my shoulder, and we'll see who wins."

Commenting on his teammate's toughness, former 49ers tight end Garrett Celek stated, "There are times when a receiver flinches before he's about to be hit. George never does that. He never flinches. He's never afraid to put himself in a vulnerable position to make a play. George is a savage."

49ers tight ends coach Jon Embree added, "I just had the sense that people were going to struggle to tackle him. There is something in him that makes people not want to tackle him."

Yet, as well as Kittle catches and runs with the football, it is his willingness to contribute to pass or run protection that makes him the most respected tight end in the game today, with Bengals safety Vonn Bell saying, "You've gotta bring your lunchbox with him. He can really sustain a block on the defensive end, and it's not just a chip block. He actually gets in there with the offensive linemen, gets his nose in there, and I guess that's what separates him."

Saints defensive end Cameron Jordan said of Kittle, "I love his play just because he wants to block, and it's rare for a tight end to want to block."

Revealing the pleasure that he derives out of delivering a successful block, Kittle says, "When you pancake a guy, and you feel their breath exhale, to me, that's their soul leaving their body."

Meanwhile, Kyle Shanahan spoke of the tremendous impact that Kittle's blocking has on the 49ers offense when he suggested, "Kittle allows us to do stuff in the run game we haven't done before because of how much he can handle on his own, whether it's gap schemes or outside zone schemes."

49ers run game coordinator Mike McDaniel added, "You're telling me one of the better players in the NFL, at any position, likes run-blocking?

That is a win for every coach. And it's not only what he's doing while block-ing; it's the energy he brings on a constant basis. When your best player is always excited and goes to extra meetings and does sled work before every practice, it's not hard ultimately to win more than you lose. He sets the standard, and other players follow suit."

Kittle's outstanding blocking at the point of attack proved to be a huge factor when the 49ers rushed for 285 yards and threw the ball just eight times during a 37–20 victory over the Packers in the 2019 NFC cham-pionship game. Commending Kittle for the selfless attitude he displayed throughout the contest, John Lynch said, "A lot of guys would be frustrated if we only threw it eight times. Kittle is screaming to the sideline, 'Run it! Run it! They can't stop us.' In many ways, even though he's a young guy, he's a leader of this team because he makes everybody better."

Extremely popular with his teammates for the energy and enthusiasm he brings with him to work each day, Kittle drew praise from Emmanuel Sanders, who said, "I love being around that guy, man. Even when he's not trying to be funny, he's funny."

Rick Scangarello added, "He's got a screw loose, but it's in a special way. He's bigger than life. There are just a few guys in the league that are transcendent players that have this crazy *It* Factor, and he's one of them."

Limited to just eight games in 2020 by a knee injury and a broken bone in his foot, Kittle made only 48 receptions for 634 yards and two touchdowns. However, a return to full health in 2021 should allow Kittle to reclaim his place among the NFL's elite. Kittle, who will not turn 28 until shortly after the 2021 campaign gets under way, will enter the season with 265 career receptions, 3,579 receiving yards, and 14 touchdowns—totals he figures to add to significantly in the coming years.

CAREER HIGHLIGHTS

Best Season

Kittle had a tremendous year for the 49ers in 2019, when, despite being plagued by a torn labrum in his right shoulder and missing two games with ankle and knee injuries, he made 85 receptions for 1,053 yards and five touchdowns, earning in the process his lone First-Team All-Pro nom-ination. But Kittle compiled slightly better overall numbers the previous season, gaining Second-Team All-Pro recognition in 2018 by catching 88 passes, scoring five touchdowns, and amassing 1,377 receiving yards, with

870 of those coming after the catch, the NFL's highest total since at least 2010, when the league began keeping track of the statistic.

Memorable Moments/Greatest Performances

Although the 49ers ultimately lost to the Indianapolis Colts in overtime by a score of 26–23 on October 8, 2017, Kittle sent the game into OT by scoring the first touchdown of his career on a 5-yard pass from Brian Hoyer with just 20 seconds left in regulation. He finished the game with seven receptions for 83 yards and that one TD.

Kittle topped 100 receiving yards for the first time as a pro by making four receptions for 100 yards during a 34–13 win over the Los Angeles Rams in the 2017 regular-season finale.

Kittle starred in defeat on September 30, 2018, making six receptions for 125 yards and one touchdown during a 29–27 loss to the San Diego Chargers, with his TD coming on an 82-yard connection with C.J. Beathard.

Kittle helped lead the 49ers to a 20–14 win over Denver on December 9, 2018, by making seven receptions for a career-high 210 yards and one TD, which came on an 85-yard catch-and-run.

Although the 49ers suffered a 48–32 defeat at the hands of the Super Bowl bound Los Angeles Rams in the 2018 regular-season finale, Kittle had a huge game, making nine receptions for 149 yards and one touchdown, closing out the scoring late in the final period with a 43-yard TD grab.

Kittle contributed to a 37–8 victory over the Packers on November 24, 2019, by making six receptions for 129 yards and one touchdown, which came on a 61-yard connection with Jimmy Garoppolo.

Kittle experienced the signature moment of his young career during a 48–46 win over the Saints on December 8, 2019, when, with the 49ers trailing by a score of 46–45 and only 39 seconds left in the final period, he gathered in a short pass from Jimmy Garoppolo on fourth down and dragged multiple defenders with him down the sideline for a 39-yard gain, despite having one of them tugging at his facemask for the final 20 yards. The 49ers won the game moments later when Robbie Gould converted a 30-yard field goal with just two seconds remaining in regulation. When asked about his extraordinary effort, Kittle said, "I caught the ball and turned upfield. I ran at the guy, and he slowed down instead of coming at me. So, I knew he was just going to try to push me out of bounds and not be very physical at it. So, I ran at him and then just kinda ran past him. He's lucky he got my face mask. He got lucky he held on. Cause I was going to throw him to the ground."

After sitting out the previous two games with a knee injury, Kittle performed magnificently during a 25–20 loss to the Philadelphia Eagles on October 4, 2020, making a career-high 15 receptions for 183 yards and one touchdown.

Notable Achievements

- Has surpassed 80 receptions and 1,000 receiving yards twice each.
- Has led 49ers in receptions and receiving yards twice each.
- 2019 division champion.
- 2019 NFC champion.
- 2018 49ers MVP.
- Two-time Pro Bowl selection (2018 and 2019).
- 2019 First-Team All-Pro selection.
- 2018 Second-Team All-Pro selection.

42

DANA STUBBLEFIELD

An intimidating presence at right defensive tackle, Dana Stubblefield combined with Bryant Young to form a deadly tandem on the interior of the 49ers' defensive line for much of the 1990s. An outstanding pass-rusher who led the 49ers in sacks three times, Stubblefield also defended against the run extremely well, with his excellent all-around play making him a significant contributor to San Francisco teams that won five division titles and one Super Bowl. The 1997 NFL Defensive Player of the Year, Stubblefield also earned three trips to the Pro Bowl, two All-Pro nominations, and four All-NFC selections during his two tours of duty with the 49ers that covered a total of seven seasons.

Born in Cleves, Ohio, on November 14, 1970, Dana William Stubblefield grew up just outside Cincinnati in a single-parent household. Eventually emerging as a multi-sport star at Taylor High School, Stubblefield excelled in football and wrestling, before suddenly finding himself faced with the prospect of having to transfer to another school his senior year when his mother expressed an interest in moving into the city. With Stubblefield dreading the idea of switching schools, Martha Heath, a family friend and teacher at Taylor, suggested that he come live with her family on their farm. Agreeing to the arrangement, Stubblefield subsequently drew a considerable amount of criticism from his friends for his willingness to move in with a white family, recalling years later, "A lot of people were concerned why I was doing it and how they were treating me. Especially with my friends who lived in the area. They were concerned, like, 'Why are you living with this family? You could have asked me.' But the case was, they didn't make an offer to me. I could see some animosity, jealousy, especially now that I'm in the situation I'm in now. Even today, when I go back and visit those friends, there's still some jealousy and animosity."

Although Stubblefield admitted that he lost many of his friends over his decision, he said that the experience helped him a great deal in learning how to deal with people.

Dana Stubblefield earned NFL Defensive Player of the Year honors in 1997.
Courtesy of George A. Kitrinos

After completing his senior year at Taylor High, Stubblefield attended the University of Kansas on Proposition 48 status, failing to qualify for an athletic scholarship due to his struggles in the classroom, with longtime *Lawrence* (Kansas) *Journal-World* sports editor Chuck Woodling saying, "He didn't do very well on the books, but he was a smart guy. He was a classic example of why they would have Prop 48. He screwed up in high school, but he could do the work."

Eventually establishing himself as a mainstay of the Jayhawk defense, Stubblefield recorded 19 sacks, 168 tackles, and 30 tackles for losses in his three years as a starter, with his outstanding play earning him All–Big Eight honors twice and All-America recognition his senior year.

Selected by the 49ers during the latter stages of the first round of the 1993 NFL Draft, with the 26th overall pick, Stubblefield made an immediate impact his first year in the league after laying claim to the starting left defensive tackle job during the preseason. In addition to leading the 49ers with 10½ sacks, Stubblefield recorded 64 tackles and forced one fumble, earning in the process NFL Defensive Rookie of the Year honors. Performing well once again in 1994 after being moved to right tackle following the arrival of Bryant Young, Stubblefield gained Pro Bowl and Second-Team All-NFC recognition by recording 8½ sacks, 38 tackles, and two forced fumbles, with his strong play up front helping the 49ers capture the division title and the NFL championship.

Somewhat less effective the next two years, Stubblefield totaled only 5½ sacks and 67 tackles, although he still managed to earn Pro Bowl and Second-Team All-Pro honors in 1995. Returning to top form in 1997, Stubblefield gained Pro Bowl, First-Team All-Pro, and NFL Defensive Player of the Year recognition by finishing second in the league with 15 sacks, while also forcing three fumbles and registering 61 tackles.

Extremely strong, the 6'2", 300-pound Stubblefield possessed the ability to apply inside pressure to opposing quarterbacks by discarding blockers at the point of attack. Also blessed with outstanding quickness, Stubblefield did an excellent job of plugging up holes at the line of scrimmage and pursuing ball-carriers in space, making him a solid run-defender as well.

A free agent at the end of 1997, Stubblefield chose to sign with the Redskins, with whom he experienced a precipitous decline in overall production over the course of the next three seasons, prompting Washington to release him at the end of 2000. Opting to return to San Francisco, Stubblefield subsequently signed a six-year deal with the 49ers. However, he ended up spending just two more years in the City by the Bay, before being cut by the 49ers following the conclusion of the 2002 campaign after registering just seven sacks the previous two seasons. Stubblefield then spent one final season with the Oakland Raiders, before announcing his retirement after sustaining an injury the following preseason. Ending his playing career with 53½ sacks, 434 tackles, eight forced fumbles, five fumble recoveries, and two interceptions, Stubblefield recorded 46½ sacks, 301 tackles, seven forced fumbles, two fumble recoveries, and both of his interceptions while playing for the 49ers.

Unfortunately, Stubblefield has run afoul of the law on multiple occasions since retiring as an active player. After serving two years' probation for lying to federal investigators about his involvement in the BALCO steroids scandal during his time in Oakland, Stubblefield received a 90-day jail sentence in December 2010 for stealing his former girlfriend's mail by way of fraudulent submission of a change-of-address form. More recently, Stubblefield was charged with raping a 31-year-old developmentally disabled woman at his home in Santa Clara on April 9, 2015, after she arrived to apply for the position of nanny for his two young children. Stubblefield subsequently denied all allegations, with his lawyer saying, "He is 100 percent innocent, this is nothing more than an attempt to take advantage of Mr. Stubblefield." Stubblefield's trial, which finally began on March 3, 2020, nearly four years after the charges were initially made, ended on July 27, 2020, with the former NFL star being convicted of rape and sentenced to 15 years to life in prison.

49ERS CAREER HIGHLIGHTS

Best Season

Although Stubblefield also gained Pro Bowl recognition in 1994 and 1995, he had easily the finest season of his career in 1997, earning NFL Defensive Player of the Year honors by finishing second in the league with 15 sacks, recording 61 tackles, and forcing three fumbles.

Memorable Moments/Greatest Performances

Stubblefield excelled in his first game as a pro, recording two sacks during a 24–13 win over the Pittsburgh Steelers in the opening game of the 1993 regular season.

Stubblefield contributed to a 44–10 victory over the St. Louis Rams on October 22, 1995, by recording the first of his two career interceptions.

Stubblefield earned NFC Defensive Player of the Week honors by sacking Troy Aikman twice during a 17–10 win over the Dallas Cowboys on November 2, 1997.

Stubblefield followed that up by recording a career-high four sacks during a 24–12 victory over the Philadelphia Eagles on November 10, 1997, with his strong performance enabling him to repeat as NFC Defensive Player of the Week.

Notable Achievements

- Finished in double digits in sacks twice.
- Recorded more than 60 tackles twice.
- Finished second in NFL with 15 sacks in 1997.
- Led 49ers in sacks three times.
- Ranks seventh in franchise history with 46½ career sacks.
- Five-time division champion (1993, 1994, 1995, 1997, and 2002).
- 1994 NFC champion.
- Super Bowl XXIX champion.
- Two-time NFC Defensive Player of the Week.
- November 1997 NFC Defensive Player of the Month.
- Member of 1993 NFL All-Rookie Team.
- 1993 NFL Defensive Rookie of the Year.
- 1997 NFL Defensive Player of the Year.
- Three-time Pro Bowl selection (1994, 1995, and 1997).
- 1997 First-Team All-Pro selection.
- 1995 Second-Team All-Pro selection.
- Two-time First-Team All-NFC selection (1995 and 1997).
- Two-time Second-Team All-NFC selection (1994 and 1996).

43

GUY MCINTYRE

A member of 49er teams that won eight division titles and three Super Bowls, Guy McIntyre spent 10 seasons in San Francisco, appearing in every game the 49ers played from 1988 to 1993. Doing an outstanding job of creating holes in the running game and providing pass protection for quarterbacks Joe Montana and Steve Young from his left guard position, McIntyre earned five trips to the Pro Bowl, three All-NFC nominations, and one All-Pro selection. Yet, the extremely mobile and athletic McIntyre is largely remembered today for being one of the first offensive linemen used as a blocking back in short-yardage situations.

Born in Thomasville, Georgia, on February 17, 1961, Guy Maurice McIntyre got into trouble with the law at an early age, being placed on probation after authorities caught him breaking school windows with rocks. Struggling in the classroom as well, McIntyre recalled, "I didn't love school, and I was not an A student; but I knew I had to go in order to participate in sports."

Eventually developing into a standout athlete, McIntyre starred on the gridiron for Thomasville High School, before accepting a football scholarship to the University of Georgia. Weighing only 225 pounds when he first arrived on the Georgia campus, McIntyre saw part-time duty at tight end his freshman year, before transitioning to the offensive line, where he spent his last three seasons playing center and guard. Hindered by back problems for much of his college career, McIntyre suffered from a narrowing of the vertebra that likely caused several teams to lose interest in him prior to the 1984 NFL Draft. However, the 49ers decided to take a chance on him, selecting him in the third round with the 73rd overall pick, with Bill Walsh later saying, "There was a reason why he was still available for us. There was some gamble in drafting him."

Recalling how he learned of his selection by the 49ers, McIntyre said, "I was on the phone with the Detroit Lions at the time when my agent said, 'Hang up. The 49ers just took you.'"

Guy McIntyre earned five Pro Bowl selections and one All-Pro
nomination during his time in San Francisco.
Courtesy of George A. Kitrinos

McIntyre added, "There was some speculation about how long I would
even last in the NFL because I had flat feet and bunions."

McIntyre subsequently spent his first four seasons in San Francisco
serving as a backup and playing mostly on special teams, starting a total of
only eight games during that time. While languishing on the bench, McIntyre also experienced problems off the playing field, later admitting that he

battled drug addiction during the early stages of his career. In discussing his problem, McIntyre stated, "I was thinking I was getting away with it, but I didn't get away. Something has happened in your life. I know it wasn't good; but you have to let it go and not let it ruin your life."

Although McIntyre saw very little playing time his first four years in the league, he gained a measure of notoriety in the 1984 NFC championship game when he helped punctuate a convincing 23–0 victory over the Chicago Bears by working out of the offensive backfield as a blocker in multiple short-yardage situations. In fact, the strategy employed by Bill Walsh during that contest motivated Bears head coach Mike Ditka to use the same formation during a lopsided victory over the 49ers the following year, with William Perry assuming the role of blocking back for Chicago.

Finally becoming a regular member of the starting unit in 1988, McIntyre manned the right guard position for one season, before moving to the left side of the offensive line the following year. Starting every game for the 49ers at left guard in each of the next five seasons, McIntyre emerged as one of the league's finest players at that position, earning five consecutive trips to the Pro Bowl and three All-NFC nominations. Reflecting back on his first Pro Bowl selection, McIntyre said, "You know, after earning the first one, I can remember asking Ronnie Lott, 'How do I act?' It's not that I didn't want it. My goal when I came here was to earn the respect of my peers, to work hard, and play whatever role I could to be a champion."

A regular at the Pro Bowl from that point on, McIntyre served as the prototype guard for Bill Walsh's West Coast Offense. Although somewhat undersized at 6'3" and 275 pounds, McIntyre possessed good strength, outstanding quickness, and superior intelligence, enabling him to do an outstanding job of blocking defenders larger than himself. Equally effective as a run-blocker or pass-protector, McIntyre excelled at using his quickness and athleticism in both roles, with his size and fleetness afoot also allowing Walsh to occasionally employ him as a blocking back in the team's "Angus" short-yardage formation.

With McIntyre having earned his fifth straight Pro Bowl selection in 1993, he turned down the contract offer the 49ers made to him during the subsequent offseason, choosing instead to sign with the Green Bay Packers as a free agent. Commenting on his decision years later, McIntyre said, "I felt different about what they wanted to pay me. I got a little bold and brash, and things didn't turn out the way I thought they would."

McIntyre added, "I apologized to Mr. DeBartolo several years later. He had invested a lot in me, and I was grateful that he gave me an opportunity to prove myself and support my family."

McIntyre ended up spending just one season in Green Bay, starting 10 games for the Packers in 1994, before joining the Philadelphia Eagles, with whom he spent the final two years of his career. After announcing his retirement following the conclusion of the 1996 campaign, McIntyre began a brief career in coaching, serving as offensive line coach with the Rhine Fire of the World League in 2002 and Menlo College from 2004 to 2006, before returning to the 49ers in 2007 as the team's director of player development. While fulfilling that role, McIntyre once said, "These players have to come to realize that, even if they last 20 years in the game, which, of course, very few players will, they're still going to be young when they retire, and they're going to want to do something with their lives." Transitioning into the role of director of alumni relations in 2010, McIntyre continues to serve the 49ers in that capacity.

49ERS CAREER HIGHLIGHTS

Best Season

McIntyre had the finest season of his career in 1992, when he earned All-Pro honors for the only time by helping the 49ers lead the NFL in points scored and total yards gained, with San Francisco running backs averaging a robust 4.8 yards per carry.

Memorable Moments/Greatest Performances

McIntyre scored the first of his two career touchdowns when he recovered a fumble in the Detroit end zone on special teams during a 23–21 loss to the Lions on October 20, 1985.

McIntyre lit the scoreboard again when he gathered in a 17-yard touchdown pass from Joe Montana during a 34–17 loss to the Atlanta Falcons on September 18, 1988.

McIntyre helped the 49ers amass 580 yards of total offense during a 38–7 win over the Seattle Seahawks on September 25, 1988, with 239 of those yards coming on the ground.

McIntyre's strong blocking at the point of attack helped the 49ers rush for 203 yards and amass 475 yards of total offense during a 48–10 manhandling of the San Diego Chargers on November 27, 1988.

McIntyre helped the 49ers control the line of scrimmage once again on November 12, 1989, with the Niners rushing for 235 yards and amassing 515 yards of total offense during a 45–3 rout of Atlanta.

Notable Achievements

- Appeared in 96 consecutive games from 1988 to 1993.
- Eight-time division champion (1984, 1986, 1987, 1988, 1989, 1990, 1992, and 1993).
- Three-time NFC champion (1984, 1988, and 1989).
- Three-time Super Bowl champion (XIX, XXIII, XXIV).
- Five-time Pro Bowl selection (1989, 1990, 1991, 1992, and 1993).
- 1992 Second-Team All-Pro selection.
- Three-time First-Team All-NFC selection (1990, 1991, and 1992).

44

FRANKIE ALBERT

The first in a long line of outstanding quarterbacks to don the Red and Gold, Frankie Albert starred behind center for the 49ers during their formative years, serving as their primary signal-caller the first seven years of their existence. Known as "the T-Formation Wizard" for his passing accuracy and exceptional ball-handling ability, Albert guided the 49ers to four consecutive second place finishes and one All-America Football Conference championship game appearance before the league folded, with his 88 touchdown passes from 1946 to 1949 representing an AAFC record. An extremely versatile performer, Albert also played defensive back and averaged 43 yards per punt during his seven seasons in San Francisco, with his outstanding all-around play earning him one trip to the Pro Bowl, three All-AAFC selections, and one league MVP trophy. Albert accomplished all he did after serving in the US Navy for four years during World War II.

Born in Chicago, Illinois, on January 27, 1920, Frank Cullen Albert grew up in the Los Angeles suburb of Glendale, California, where he attended Glendale High School. Starring on the gridiron in his one season of varsity football at Glendale High, Albert earned CIF High School Player of the Year honors in 1937, prompting Stanford University to offer him an athletic scholarship.

After beginning his college career as a tailback in the then-prevalent single wing, Albert, who barely weighed 155 pounds during his time at Stanford, moved to quarterback when T-formation innovator Clark Shaughnessy left the University of Chicago to become head coach of the Cardinals in 1940. With Shaughnessy installing the T-formation, which had been used only occasionally many years earlier before being revived for the pro game by George Halas's Chicago Bears, Stanford became a national power his first year in charge, going a perfect 9-0 during the regular season, before recording a 21–13 victory over Nebraska in the Rose Bowl. Meanwhile, Albert, who became the first college T-formation quarterback

Frankie Albert threw more touchdown passes than any other quarterback in the brief history of the AAFC.
Courtesy of RMYAuctions.com

in modern football history, gained All-America recognition in both 1940 and 1941.

Excelling in an offense that rewarded deception instead of the power blocking of the single wing, Albert proved to be the key man in a superb backfield that also included future pro running backs Norm Standlee and Hugh Gallarneau, with Shaughnessy calling him "a magician with the ball." In discussing his former quarterback with *Esquire* magazine in 1943, Shaughnessy also said, "He was neither strong nor fast. His talents were primarily those of a faker."

Although the Chicago Bears selected Albert with the 10th overall pick of the 1942 NFL Draft, Albert didn't turn pro for another four years, remaining away from the game while serving in the navy as an aircraft officer in the Pacific during World War II. After returning to action as a member of the Los Angeles Bulldogs of the Pacific Coast Football League in 1945, Albert signed with the 49ers of the newly formed All-America Football Conference prior to the start of the 1946 campaign.

Establishing himself as one of the infant league's top stars before long, Albert gained Second-Team All-AAFC recognition in each of his first two seasons by leading the 49ers to a pair of second place finishes and an overall record of 17-9-2. After ranking among the league leaders with 1,404 passing yards, 14 touchdown passes, a pass-completion percentage of 52.8, and a passer rating of 69.8 in 1946, Albert improved upon those numbers the following year, throwing for 1,692 yards, tossing 18 TD passes, completing 52.9 percent of his passes, and posting a passer rating of 74.3. Albert then reached the zenith of his career in 1948, when he led the 49ers to a record of 12-2 by passing for 1,990 yards and finishing first in the AAFC in three different categories, with his league-leading 29 TD passes remaining a 49er single-season record until John Brodie threw for 30 touchdowns in 1965. Albert's exceptional performance earned him All-AAFC honors from three different news sources and co–league MVP honors, a distinction he shared with Cleveland QB Otto Graham.

Albert, who stood just 5'9" and weighed only 166 pounds, hardly looked like a professional football player. He also did not possess the strongest of arms. But the left-handed-throwing Albert made up for whatever he lacked in height and arm strength with passing accuracy, guile, outstanding mobility, and tremendous ball-handling ability. Particularly effective on rollouts, Albert is often credited with inventing the bootleg play, in which the quarterback fakes a handoff and then runs wide with the ball hidden on his hip. Usually looking for star wide receiver Alyn Beals in such instances, Albert recalled years later, "Beals was my main receiver. Boy, did he have some great moves! He was a good faker. I can remember several times setting up to pass and watching the defensive back fall down after Alyn put a fake on him. The back would trip over his own feet. I'd look at the defensive man lying on his butt while Alyn was wide open."

Quite proficient himself at deceiving the enemy, Albert often frustrated his opponents with his trickery, with Los Angeles Rams linebacker Don Paul likening him to Fran Tarkenton when he told the *Los Angeles Times*, "At least with Tarkenton, those guys knew Francis had the ball. With

Frankie Albert, we weren't always sure. Then, he would stand there and laugh at you."

A capable runner, Albert rushed for 1,272 yards and 27 touchdowns during his time in San Francisco, scoring as many as eight TDs on the ground one season. But Albert's greatest strength lay in his ball-handling skills, a fact that he acknowledged when he stated, "I guess my ability to handle the ball made me effective. I was pretty good on a bootleg. I could hide the ball and run it if I had to."

Meanwhile, Joe Perry discussed his former teammate's daring and football acumen when he said, "Frankie Albert was like a riverboat gambler. He had a sharp mind and did the unexpected. He was unpredictable. But, if you gave him something, he would run the same play 20 times until you stopped it. He used to throw a quick pass to [running back Johnny] Strzykalski. One game he threw the same pass over and over for about five yards. We marched right down the field and scored."

Contributing to the 49ers on defense and special teams as well, Albert occasionally served as a member of the team's defensive secondary and ranked among the finest punters of his time, once leading the AAFC with an average of 48.2 yards per kick. Expressing the enjoyment that he derived out of trying to match wits with opposing quarterbacks as a defender, Albert stated, "I enjoyed playing defense. I didn't do it as often as I would have liked. I played back there in some of the important games, like against the Browns."

Albert remained the 49ers' full-time starting quarterback for two more years, throwing for 1,862 yards and leading the AAFC with 27 touchdown passes in 1949, before earning a trip to the Pro Bowl the following year, after the 49ers joined the NFL, by passing for 1,767 yards and 14 touchdowns. However, Albert injured his throwing shoulder during the early stages of the 1951 season, after which he spent the remainder of the year sharing playing time with Y. A. Tittle. With the two signal-callers competing for playing time once again in 1952, Albert chose to announce his retirement following the conclusion of the campaign, ending his career with 10,795 yards passing, 115 touchdown passes, 98 interceptions, a 53.1 pass-completion percentage, and a quarterback rating of 73.5. Albert also amassed a total of 1,376 all-purpose yards, gaining 1,272 of those on the ground and the other 104 on special teams.

After leaving the NFL, Albert subsequently returned to the playing field as a member of the Canadian Football League's Calgary Stampeders in 1953, before retiring for good at season's end. He then rejoined the 49ers, with whom he spent the next two seasons serving as an assistant coach and scout, before assuming the role of head coach from 1956 to 1958. After guiding the 49ers to an overall record of 19-16-1, Albert left football and spent the next several years working in real estate and raising his three daughters with his wife, Martha. Eventually retiring to Palo Alto, California, Albert lived until September 4, 2002, when he died at a nursing home in Menlo Park from complications of Alzheimer's disease at the age of 82.

CAREER HIGHLIGHTS

Best Season

Albert had easily the finest season of his career in 1948, when, in addition to running for 349 yards and eight touchdowns, he threw for 1,990 yards and led the AAFC with 29 touchdown passes, a completion percentage of 58.2, and a total quarterback rating of 102.9. Accorded unofficial All-AAFC honors by the UPI, the *Sporting News*, and the *New York Daily News* at season's end, Albert received the additional distinctions of being named Pro Football Player of the Year by *Sport Magazine* and sharing league MVP honors with Cleveland Browns Hall of Fame quarterback Otto Graham.

Memorable Moments/Greatest Performances

Albert led the 49ers to a 32–13 win over the Brooklyn Dodgers on September 22, 1946, by running for one score and completing touchdown passes of 35 yards to Len Eshmont and 43 yards to Alyn Beals.

Albert threw three touchdown passes in one game for the first time in his career during a 34–20 win over the Cleveland Browns on October 27, 1946, with two of his TD tosses going to Alyn Beals and the other to Don Durdan.

Albert led the 49ers to a 48–7 rout of the Los Angeles Dons in the final game of the 1946 regular season by running for one score and throwing three touchdown passes, the longest of which went 40 yards to Beals.

Albert made good use of his legs during a 41–24 win over the Buffalo Bills on September 28, 1947, running for three touchdowns.

Albert helped the 49ers forge a 28–28 tie with the Baltimore Colts on October 5, 1947, by throwing three touchdown passes, with his TD tosses of 45 yards to Johnny Strzykalski and 62 yards to Earle Parsons in the fourth quarter bringing his team back from a 28–14 deficit.

Albert threw four touchdown passes in one game for the first time as a pro during a 26–16 victory over the Los Angeles Dons on November 2, 1947, with his longest TD pass of the day going 37 yards to Alyn Beals.

Albert led the 49ers to a 36–20 win over the Dodgers on September 5, 1948, by running 25 yards for one score and throwing three touchdown passes, the longest of which went 49 yards to Beals.

Albert duplicated that effort the following week, scoring himself on a 17-yard run and completing three touchdown passes during a 41–0 rout of the New York Yankees on September 12, 1948.

Albert continued his string of exceptional performances one week later, running for one TD and passing for three others during a 36–14 win over the Los Angeles Dons on September 19, 1948.

Albert punctuated his banner year by throwing four touchdown passes and running for two scores during a 63–40 win over the Dodgers on November 21, 1948.

Albert ran for one touchdown and passed for two others during a 42–14 victory over the Dons on September 18, 1949, with one of his TD tosses being a career-long 75-yard connection with Eddie Carr.

Although Albert threw four interceptions during a 56–28 win over the Cleveland Browns on October 9, 1949, he also completed a career-high five touchdown passes.

Albert led the 49ers to a 41–24 victory over the Dons on November 13, 1949, by throwing for 220 yards and four TDs, the longest of which came on a 57-yard connection with Joe Perry.

Notable Achievements

- Threw more than 25 touchdown passes twice.
- Posted passer rating above 100.0 once.
- Posted touchdown-to-interception ratio of better than 2–1 once.
- Ran for eight touchdowns in 1948.
- Averaged more than 44 yards per punt four times.
- Led league in touchdown passes twice, pass completion percentage once, passer rating once, and yards per punt once.
- Finished second in league in pass completions once, touchdown passes once, pass completion percentage once, passer rating three times, total punt yardage once, and yards per punt twice.
- Finished third in league in pass completions twice, passing yards twice, touchdown passes once, and pass completion percentage three times.

- Ranks among 49ers career leaders with 1,564 pass attempts (8th), 831 pass completions (8th), 10,795 passing yards (8th), 115 touchdown passes (4th), and 27 rushing touchdowns (7th).
- 1950 Pro Bowl selection.
- 1948 *Sport Magazine* Pro Football Player of the Year.
- 1948 AAFC co-MVP.
- Three-time Second-Team All-AAFC selection (1946, 1947, and 1949).

45

KEENA TURNER

Perhaps the most underrated member of San Francisco's championship teams of the 1980s, Keena Turner excelled for the 49ers at right-outside linebacker throughout the decade, making significant contributions to teams that won eight division titles and four Super Bowls. Although sometimes criticized for not being aggressive enough or not excelling in one particular aspect of the game, Turner proved to be one of the NFL's most complete linebackers from 1980 to 1990, earning one Pro Bowl selection and three All-NFC nominations with his strong all-around play. And, since retiring as an active player some 30 years ago, Turner has parlayed the many intangible qualities he exhibited during his playing days into a successful career as a front-office executive.

Born in Chicago, Illinois, on October 22, 1958, Keena Turner grew up in a crime-ridden section of the city ruled by gangs named the Disciples and the Rangers. Managing to skirt the dangers that surrounded him by adhering to the wishes of his parents, who demanded to know his whereabouts at all times, Turner drew inspiration from his grandmother, who spent more than 20 years working in a car wash, before taking a job at a local daycare center. In discussing the matriarch of the family, Turner once said, "She's a hard-working lady, and she has in her mind that, if she stopped working, she'd die. I think she's where I get my determination from."

Spending much of his free time competing in sports, Turner developed into an outstanding all-around athlete at Chicago Vocational High School, proving to be particularly proficient on the gridiron, where he performed well enough to earn a scholarship to Purdue University. After playing defensive end for the Boilermakers for three years, Turner entered the 1980 NFL Draft, where the 49ers selected him in the second round, with the 39th overall pick.

Turner ended up spending his first year in San Francisco serving the 49ers primarily on special teams, although he also intercepted two passes in the four games that he started for them at outside linebacker. Inserted into the starting lineup full-time the following year, Turner helped the 49ers

Keena Turner excelled for the 49ers at outside linebacker throughout the 1980s.
Courtesy of George A. Kitrinos

capture their first NFC championship by recording one interception and recovering three fumbles, before gaining unofficial Second-Team All-Pro recognition from the Newspaper Enterprise Association (NEA) for the first of two times in 1982. Continuing his outstanding play over the course of the next four seasons, Turner earned Second-Team All-NFC honors three times, with his career-high four interceptions in 1984 also earning him a trip to the Pro Bowl.

One of the league's fastest linebackers, the 6'2" Turner spent most of his career playing at close to 215 pounds, although the 49ers listed him in their media guide as being some 20 pounds heavier. Turner's outstanding speed enabled him to do an excellent job of tracking down opposing ball-carriers and covering tight ends and running backs coming out of the backfield, with Bill Walsh recalling, "Keena was just a great, great player for many years. He was the best all-around linebacker in the league for a 10-year period. He could do it all. He was a great blitzer, he tackled well, and was tremendous in pass coverage. Keena was a key to those championship teams."

Yet, despite his outstanding all-around play, Turner often found himself being overlooked for postseason honors, in part because he used finesse over sheer brute force, giving others the impression that he lacked the intensity of some of the league's other top linebackers. The soft-spoken Turner also failed to draw attention to himself by displaying any histrionics on the playing field, choosing instead to conduct himself in an extremely professional manner. Furthermore, Turner had the misfortune of playing at the same time as a number of other extraordinary outside linebackers, with Lawrence Taylor, Wilber Marshall, Otis Wilson, Carl Banks, Pat Swilling, and Rickey Jackson heading the list of exceptional players against whom he had to compete for individual honors.

Nevertheless, Turner proved to be a multitalented, game-changing linebacker who came to exemplify the standard of excellence the 49ers set during the 1980s, once saying, "Anything I have my name on, I want to be good. I watch myself on film, and I get embarrassed when I don't do something right. People ask me if I'm a perfectionist, but I have too many flaws to consider myself perfect. I just feel everything I do is a direct reflection of me personally, and I take everything I do personally. You can't separate yourself and say this is private, this is fun, this is business. It's all the same."

Further expressing the pride that he took in his play, Turner revealed that individual accolades meant little to him when he said, "In my career, I've always tried to work to where I was respected. That's not something you get one time and then, period, that's it. Every season, every game, every play is a challenge, and, when it's over, you add it all up. I know that two weeks after I retire, someone else will be wearing #58 and that people will forget Keena Turner. What's important then is not the way you've been viewed, but what you did. That's not to say I don't think about the way I'm viewed. It's just that it's not that important anymore."

Turner continued, "The two most important things to me are us winning and me making the plays. I think I've always thought this way, but, in the past, it was only natural and human to want to be recognized and noticed for the things you were doing. But, even if you're not recognized and noticed, it doesn't mean you're not doing them."

Commenting further on his lack of notoriety years later, Turner said, "Would I have wanted more accolades or awards? I guess you want that. But I didn't have a problem with the guys who were making it—Rickey Jackson, Hugh Green, and Lawrence Taylor—I respected the hell out of those guys."

Turner continued to excel at outside linebacker for the 49ers for four more years, contributing greatly to teams that won four more division titles and another two Super Bowls, before announcing his retirement following the conclusion of the 1990 campaign. In addition to recording 11 interceptions, amassing 134 interception-return yards, recovering eight fumbles, registering 19½ sacks, and scoring one touchdown during his time in San Francisco, Turner proved to be one of the team's most durable players, missing just two games his first six years in the league, and appearing in every contest the 49ers played six times.

Following his playing days, Turner spent three seasons coaching linebackers at Stanford University under head coach Bill Walsh, before returning to the 49ers, with whom he has spent the last 25 years functioning in a number of roles. After initially serving as a color analyst for 49ers preseason games, Turner moved into the front office in 2001, where he has assumed the positions of player development director, alumni coordinator, director of alumni coordinators, and, most recently, vice president and senior advisor to the general manager. Expressing his appreciation to Turner for everything he brings to the organization, 49ers GM John Lynch stated, "I don't think there's a person in our building who understands the 49er way more than Keena." Turner has also been a constant supporter of Family House in San Francisco for over 30 years, and he has spent the last 25 years hosting The Keena Turner Boys and Girls Clubs Golf Tournament, a charitable cause that has raised more than $5 million.

CAREER HIGHLIGHTS

Best Season

Turner had an outstanding season for the 49ers in 1985, earning one of his three Second-Team All-NFC nominations by recording a career-high six sacks and recovering two fumbles, one of which he returned for a touchdown. But he performed slightly better the previous year, earning his lone trip to the Pro Bowl in 1984 by registering two sacks and a career-best four interceptions.

Memorable Moments/Greatest Performances

Turner recorded his first career interception when he picked off a David Woodley pass during a 17–13 loss to Miami on November 16, 1980.

Turner contributed to a 38–24 victory over the Giants in the divisional round of the 1981 playoffs by recording a sack and recovering a fumble.

In perhaps his most memorable performance, Turner recorded a sack of quarterback Ken Anderson during the 49ers' 26–21 win over Cincinnati in Super Bowl XVI, despite entering the game with a severe case of chicken pox that first hit him the Thursday before the NFC championship game. Recalling how he felt at the time, Turner said, "It was miserable. I couldn't eat, so I lost 10 to 15 pounds between the NFC Championship Game and the Super Bowl. I was sick as a dog."

Turner helped lead the 49ers to a 24–20 win over Atlanta on September 25, 1983, by recording two of the eight sacks they registered against quarterback Steve Bartkowski.

Turner turned in another strong performance against the Falcons on December 2, 1984, recording an interception and a sack during a 35–17 49ers win.

Turner scored the only touchdown of his career when he ran 65 yards to paydirt after recovering a fumble during a 35–8 win over the Washington Redskins on December 1, 1985.

Turner helped lead the 49ers to a 23–12 victory over the Packers on December 6, 1987, by sacking Green Bay quarterback Randy Wright twice.

Notable Achievements

- Scored one defensive touchdown.
- Finished third in NFL with 65 fumble-return yards in 1985.
- Tied for team lead with four interceptions in 1984.
- Eight-time division champion (1981, 1983, 1984, 1986, 1987, 1988, 1989, and 1990).
- Four-time NFC champion (1981, 1984, 1988, and 1989).
- Four-time Super Bowl champion (XVI, XIX, XXIII, XXIV).
- 1984 Pro Bowl selection.
- Two-time NEA Second-Team All-Pro selection (1982 and 1985).
- Three-time Second-Team All-NFC selection (1984, 1985, and 1986).

46

GARRISON HEARST

Although injuries limited his period of dominance to just a few short seasons, Garrison Hearst made a tremendous overall impact during his relatively brief stay in San Francisco, leading the 49ers to two division titles and rushing for the fifth-most yards in franchise history. Gaining more than 1,000 yards on the ground in three of his five seasons in the City by the Bay, Hearst set multiple single-season franchise records that Frank Gore later broke, with his excellent play earning him two Pro Bowl selections, one All-NFC nomination, and one NFL Comeback Player of the Year award. An outstanding team leader, Hearst inspired his teammates with his strong work ethic and total dedication to his profession that once prompted fellow 49er Derrick Deese to say, "I can't imagine any player meaning as much to a team."

Born in Lincolnton, Georgia, on January 4, 1971, Gerald Garrison Hearst grew up in a small town just outside Atlanta that had only three traffic lights and one grocery store. Knowing that he wanted to pursue a career in football at a very young age, Hearst, recalled his mother, "was an athletic kid, but he knew very early what he wanted to do. He wrote a paper in fourth grade in which he said he wanted to be a professional football player."

Beginning his career on the gridiron at Lincoln County High School, Hearst starred at running back, breaking numerous school records, en route to earning All-State honors. Recruited by several major Southern colleges, Hearst received scholarship offers from Auburn, Georgia, and South Carolina, revealing that the Tigers would have been his first choice had they approached him earlier when he said, "I was an Auburn fan. Bo Jackson was the baddest man I have ever seen. I was an Auburn fan. But Auburn didn't recruit me until the day before the state championship game my senior year. I was mad when they finally called me by then. I was like, 'Don't call me now,' but that's when they finally started to recruit me."

Garrison Hearst rushed for more than 1,000 yards three times as a member of the 49ers.

Hearst continued, "I wanted to play my freshman year. So, whatever school I was talking to, my biggest thing was I didn't want to redshirt. I wanted to play. Florida State was a school that I visited, but I knew that I wasn't going to play right away there."

Ultimately narrowing his choice down to either Georgia or South Carolina, Hearst decided to remain in his home state, explaining, "Georgia recruited me harder because they recruited me longer. They started recruiting me as a freshman."

Hearst ended up spending three years starring for the Bulldogs at halfback, finishing his college career with 3,232 yards rushing, 3,934 all-purpose yards, and 33 rushing touchdowns. Performing especially well as a junior in 1992, Hearst rushed for 1,547 yards, amassed 1,871 yards from scrimmage, and set a new SEC record by scoring 21 touchdowns, with his magnificent play earning him First-Team All-America honors and a third-place finish in the Heisman Trophy voting. Hearst also gained SEC Player of the Year recognition and won the Doak Walker award, presented annually to the top collegiate running back in the nation.

In comparing his star running back to some of the previous greats that manned that position at Georgia, Bulldogs head coach Ray Goff stated, "He's a little bit like Rodney Hampton—a pure runner with great vision. He's got good hands like Keith Henderson and is a physical runner like Herschel [Walker] and Lars Tate. I've said many times that Hearst is the most complete back we've ever had at Georgia. One of the most impressive things about him is watching him when he's supposed to block a linebacker on a blitz. The guy will go out just as fast as he came in."

Choosing to forgo his final year of college eligibility, Hearst entered the 1993 NFL Draft, where the Phoenix Cardinals selected him with the third overall pick. Hearst's pro career got off to an inauspicious start, though, when he tore the medial collateral ligament in his left knee during the early stages of the 1993 campaign, forcing him to miss most of his first two seasons. Appearing in a total of just 14 games, Hearst rushed for only 433 yards and scored just two touchdowns, prompting him to later say, "If I had to do it over, I would stay for my senior year. That's knowing what I know now. I tell kids today that, if you are going to make it in the pros, then you are going to make it. There's no better time in your life than in college."

Fully recovered by the start of the 1995 season, Hearst finally began to live up to his enormous potential by rushing for 1,070 yards, amassing 1,313 yards from scrimmage, and scoring two touchdowns. Nevertheless, the Cardinals cut Hearst prior to the start of the ensuing campaign, allowing the Cincinnati Bengals to claim him off waivers. Hearst subsequently spent one season in Cincinnati, gaining 847 yards on the ground in 1996, before signing with the 49ers when the Bengals released him at the end of the year.

Proving to be a tremendous pickup for the 49ers, Hearst helped lead them to a 13-3 record and the division title in 1997 by rushing for 1,019 yards, amassing 1,213 yards from scrimmage, and scoring six touchdowns, before earning Pro Bowl and First-Team All-NFC honors the following year by finishing third in the league with 1,570 yards rushing, placing fourth in the circuit with 2,105 yards from scrimmage, and scoring nine touchdowns, with his 1,570 yards rushing and 2,105 yards from scrimmage setting new single-season franchise records (since broken).

Combining with quarterback Steve Young and wide receivers Jerry Rice and Terrell Owens to give the 49ers one of the NFL's most potent offenses in 1998, the 5'11", 215-pound Hearst displayed a rare skill set that included the ability to hit holes quickly, tremendous acceleration once he broke into the open field, superior pass-receiving skills, and a willingness to sacrifice his body for the team by picking up blitzers. Also blessed with the ability to avoid tacklers at and beyond the line of scrimmage, Hearst drew praise from Lynn Swann for his excellence in that area, with the Hall of Fame receiver commenting, "He has so many moves that, if you blink twice, you might miss four or five of them and he'll be in the end zone."

However, after performing so brilliantly during the 1998 regular season, Hearst suffered a gruesome injury against Atlanta in the divisional round of the playoffs that suddenly put his career in jeopardy. In attempting to spin away from Falcons defensive end Chuck Smith on the very first play from scrimmage, Hearst broke his ankle when he caught his foot in the Georgia Dome turf. Hearst subsequently ran into complications after undergoing surgery to repair the ankle, developing a rare form of bone necrosis that caused the talus bone in his foot to die. Forced to undergo five more operations over the course of the next two years, Hearst spent most of his time in rehab, before amazingly returning to action in 2001, making him the first NFL player ever to resume his career after suffering avascular necrosis.

Mounting a stirring comeback, Hearst gained 1,206 yards on the ground, amassed 1,553 yards from scrimmage, and scored five touchdowns, becoming in the process the only player in league history to rush for more than 1,000 yards after a two-year layoff. Named to the Pro Bowl and awarded NFL Comeback Player of the Year honors for the second time in his career, Hearst received high praise from 49ers head coach Steve Mariucci, who said, "It's the best story of the year, and the best story around here for a while. He means a whole lot to this team in the locker room, on the practice field, in the games. He's a leader and an inspiration to everybody."

Teammate Ray Brown expressed similar sentiments when he stated, "G is probably the most popular person in this locker room. He galvanizes this team. When we see what he puts his body through just to practice, our aches and pains don't seem so significant."

Garnering a significant amount of respect from his opponents as well, Hearst, said Miami Dolphins linebacker Zach Thomas, "is one of those guys you want to hit hard and then help up with a smile. We respect a guy who's fought his way back after sitting out two years, and he came back better than before."

Providing a glimpse into the tremendous determination that helped him persevere through two years of rehabilitation, Hearst stated, "I never thought I wouldn't play again. One specialist I saw a few months after the injury told me to start preparing for life after football, and I know a lot of people around here thought I was through. But those people didn't know what was inside of me."

Hearst remained in San Francisco for another two years, helping the 49ers capture another division title in 2002 by rushing for 972 yards, amassing 1,289 yards from scrimmage, and scoring nine touchdowns, before signing with the Denver Broncos after the 49ers released him following the conclusion of the 2003 campaign. Before leaving the City by the Bay, though, Hearst ruffled some feathers, offending many with remarks he made after learning that former NFL defensive lineman Esera Tuaolo had come out as gay. Quoted in an October 27, 2002, article that appeared in the *Fresno Bee*, Hearst said, "Aww, hell no! I don't want any faggots on my team. I know this might not be what people want to hear, but that's a punk. I don't want any faggots in this locker room."

Hearst later apologized for his remarks, saying, "First of all, I want to apologize for the comments that I made, and to the gay community. I didn't realize it would be so harmful. . . . Being an African American, I know that discrimination is wrong, and I was wrong for saying what I said about anybody—any race, any religion. I want to apologize to the San Francisco 49ers organization, the City of San Francisco for the comments that I made, and to my teammates for bringing this distraction upon us. I hope that everyone can accept my apology. Thank you." Nevertheless, Hearst received a considerable amount of criticism in the media, with his previously pristine reputation suffering irreparable damage.

Hearst ended up spending just one season in Denver, gaining only 81 yards on the ground as a backup in 2004, before announcing his retirement with career totals of 7,966 yards rushing, 229 receptions, 2,065 receiving yards, 10,031 yards from scrimmage, 30 rushing touchdowns, and 39 total TDs. In his five years with the 49ers, Hearst rushed for 5,535 yards, gained another 1,604 yards on 174 pass receptions, amassed 7,139 yards from scrimmage, and scored 33 touchdowns, with 26 of those coming on the ground and the other seven through the air.

After retiring as an active player, Hearst returned to his home state of Georgia, where he has spent the last decade-and-a-half enjoying life with his wife and three children.

49ERS CAREER HIGHLIGHTS

Best Season

Hearst had an outstanding year for the 49ers in 2001, earning NFL Comeback Player of the Year honors by rushing for 1,206 yards, amassing 1,553 yards from scrimmage, scoring five touchdowns, and averaging 4.8 yards per carry. But Hearst reached the apex of his career in 1998, when he earned his lone First-Team All-NFC nomination by ranking among the league leaders with 1,570 yards rushing and 2,105 yards from scrimmage, scoring nine touchdowns, and finishing first in the NFL with a rushing average of 5.1 yards per carry.

Memorable Moments/Greatest Performances

Hearst helped lead the 49ers to a 15–12 win over the St. Louis Rams in just his second game as a member of the team on September 7, 1997, by rushing for 92 yards and one TD, which came on a 35-yard run early in the fourth quarter.

Hearst earned NFC Offensive Player of the Week honors by rushing for 141 yards and one touchdown during a 34–21 win over the Carolina Panthers on September 29, 1997.

Hearst earned that distinction again by rushing for 187 yards and two touchdowns during a 36–30 overtime victory over the New York Jets in the opening game of the 1998 regular season, with his 96-yard TD run some four minutes into the overtime session giving the 49ers the win.

Hearst followed that up in Week 2 by rushing for 138 yards and one touchdown during a 45–10 rout of the Washington Redskins.

Hearst contributed to a 31–20 win over the New Orleans Saints on November 22, 1998, by rushing for 90 yards and scoring a touchdown on an 81-yard catch-and-run.

Hearst put the finishing touches on a convincing 31–7 victory over the Giants on November 30, 1998, by running 70 yards for a touchdown in the fourth quarter. He finished the game with 166 yards rushing and that one TD.

Hearst led the 49ers to a 31–28 win over the Carolina Panthers on December 6, 1998, by rushing for 139 yards and one touchdown, which came on a 71-yard run.

Hearst followed that up by carrying the ball 24 times for a career-high 198 yards and one touchdown during a 35–13 win over the Detroit Lions on December 14, 1998.

Hearst helped lead the 49ers to a 28–27 victory over the Saints on November 11, 2001, by gaining 145 yards on just 17 carries.

Hearst earned NFC Offensive Player of the Week honors for the third and final time by carrying the ball 12 times for 106 yards and two touchdowns during a 40–21 win over the Indianapolis Colts on November 25, 2001, with his TD runs covering 28 and 43 yards.

Hearst proved to be the difference in a 31–24 victory over the Seattle Seahawks on December 1, 2002, rushing for 124 yards and three touchdowns, all of which came on short runs.

Notable Achievements

- Rushed for more than 1,000 yards three times, topping 1,500 yards once.
- Surpassed 500 receiving yards once.
- Amassed more than 1,000 yards from scrimmage four times, topping 2,000 yards once.
- Led NFL with rushing average of 5.1 yards per carry in 1998.
- Finished third in NFL with 1,570 yards rushing in 1998.
- Finished fourth in NFL with 2,105 yards from scrimmage in 1998.
- Led 49ers in rushing four times.
- Ranks among 49ers career leaders with 1,189 rushing attempts (5th), 5,535 rushing yards (5th), 7,139 yards from scrimmage (7th), 7,139 all-purpose yards (10th), and 26 rushing touchdowns (tied for 9th).
- Two-time division champion (1997 and 2002).
- Three-time NFC Offensive Player of the Week.
- 2001 NFL Comeback Player of the Year.
- Two-time Pro Bowl selection (1998 and 2001).
- 1998 First-Team All-NFC selection.

47

STEVE WALLACE

The prototype for the modern day left offensive tackle, Steve Wallace did a superb job of protecting the blindsides of quarterbacks Joe Montana and Steve Young during his 11 seasons in San Francisco. Starting at that post for the 49ers from 1988 to 1996, Wallace used his elite athleticism and nasty disposition to establish himself as one of the NFL's top tackles, contributing greatly to teams that won nine division titles and three Super Bowls. A one-time All-Pro and two-time All-NFC selection, Wallace also served as a precursor to the big-money tackles of today by becoming the first player at his position to sign a contract worth $10 million.

Born in Atlanta, Georgia, on December 27, 1964, Barron Steven Wallace attended Chamblee High School, where he excelled in both football and basketball. Pursued by several major colleges for his prowess on the gridiron, Wallace drew special interest from Auburn University, the University of Georgia, and Florida State University. Ultimately narrowing his choice down to either Auburn or Georgia, Wallace remained uncertain as to which school to attend until Tigers head football coach Pat Dye convinced him to sign with Auburn prior to the start of a Chamblee basketball game, with Wallace recalling, "It was a week after signing day and I had a basketball game. Pat Dye was on one side of the gym and Vince Dooley was on the other. You had a Georgia guy coaching at Auburn and an Auburn guy coaching at Georgia. . . . Coach Dooley said, 'You belong at Georgia.' Coach Dye said, 'If you can hit, you can play for me.' He said a lot of things like that. We really saw eye to eye."

After enrolling at Auburn, Wallace went on to star for the Tigers at offensive tackle, serving as a key member of their 1983 SEC championship team, which also featured future Heisman Trophy winner Bo Jackson. Named All-SEC as a senior in 1985, Wallace subsequently entered the 1986 NFL Draft, where the 49ers selected him in the fourth round, with the 101st overall pick, two rounds later than he expected to be taken.

Steve Wallace did an outstanding job of protecting the blindsides of quarterbacks Joe Montana and Steve Young during his time in San Francisco.
Courtesy of George A. Kitrinos

Looking back on his draft day experience, Wallace remembered, "Draft day, that's a funny story within itself. The 49ers and Denver Broncos had said they were very interested in me. It's kind of funny when I think about it now, but they gave me a call late in the first round saying, 'We're going to pick you up early in the second round.' . . . Next thing I know, the 49ers make their pick in the second round, and then they made three picks in the third round, and I'm sitting there and my stomach's really starting to boil. So, I was getting ticked off, thinking 'How interested is this team?'"

Wallace continued, "When I first went to San Francisco, I was ticked off and had an attitude. Bill Walsh was the first guy I saw when I went in, and I was hot about that draft pick. There was a big difference between the second and fourth round in terms of pay. I went to see him, and he said, 'Hey, we're glad to have you.' I didn't smile or anything, and then he said, 'I know you're mad, but it's all part of the business.' He shrugged his shoulders, and nothing else was said about it. We both kind of laughed about it and moved on."

Assuming a backup role his first two seasons in San Francisco, Wallace started only four games while trying to get his weight under control. Recalling his early struggles in that area, Wallace said, "Back then, Coach Walsh had a deal with Bubba Paris and me. He said, 'Either I give you money every week, or you give me money every week.' I didn't like the idea of me giving him a grand every week, and I probably wasn't even making that as a rookie."

With Paris's increased bulk making it difficult for him to block some of the league's swifter edge-rushers, Wallace replaced him as the starter at left tackle in 1988, after which he went on to help the 49ers win the NFL championship. Looking back at his first year as a full-time starter, Wallace said, "The most exciting thing for me was to start every game that year, and the thought of winning the Super Bowl. I can remember a lot of parts of that ride, going against talented defensive ends like Chris Doleman, Richard Dent, Kevin Greene, Lawrence Taylor, and all the other All-Pros. I just found a way to shut them out, one-by-one."

Doing so without much assistance, Wallace often found himself being left out on an island, having to assume full responsibility for blocking many of the league's top pass-rushers. Recalling the faith that the 49ers coaching staff placed in him, Wallace said, "The one thing I started noticing was that Bill Walsh started leaving out the tight end and the running back to help me and kept them on their own assignments. His thing was, 'You block that guy,' and nothing else was said about it. The funny thing about it in looking back was that most teams had to have that extra protector over there, but I didn't know any better."

Wallace added, "Bill Walsh's greatest fear was Lawrence Taylor. But I could slow him down. In eight games I had against him, he had 1½ sacks."

Although insecurity about his abilities during the early stages of his career often caused him to engage in fisticuffs with other players, the 6'4", 285-pound Wallace eventually learned to better control his emotions.

Nevertheless, he retained his fierce competitive spirit and angry demeanor on the playing field, with John Madden describing his style of play as "nasty, tenacious, and mean," and suggesting that he "played with a defensive player's mentality." Wallace also possessed outstanding quickness and a relentless motor, making him that much more of a difficult matchup for anyone he faced on Sundays.

Unfortunately, Wallace suffered a broken ankle just three plays into Super Bowl XXIII, preventing him from fully enjoying the postgame celebration. Yet, Wallace still holds many fond memories of his first Super Bowl appearance, saying, "The first one is really important because that was the one that I cried. I never imagined being there. Everything hit me all at once. How much work I had done, and all that I had overcome. Then, they started playing, 'We are the Champions,' and it all hit me, we were World Champs."

After sitting out most of the 1989 campaign while his ankle fully healed, Wallace reclaimed his starting job the following year, beginning in the process a string of seven seasons during which he started all but five games at left tackle. Helping the 49ers win five more division titles and another Super Bowl during that time, Wallace earned one trip to the Pro Bowl, one All-Pro nomination, and two All-NFC selections, prompting the 49ers to reward him with a five-year, $10.7 million contract in 1995 that made him easily the league's highest paid player at his position.

Meanwhile, as Wallace further cemented himself as one of the NFL's finest offensive tackles, he took to wearing a Styrofoam and rubber ½" cushioned helmet atop his normal helmet to help reduce the impact he felt upon collision. Speaking of the special equipment he used, Wallace, who suffered several concussions during his career, said, "It was a double helmet, and it was heavy, but that thing was like having a rubber cushion. . . . It worked. I never had another concussion. I truly believed that, if I had another one, I wouldn't have played again. They were bad. I got one in one game and played the next week. People were running around me, and I didn't know where I was. It wasn't until the final five minutes that things settled down and I felt like Steve Wallace again."

Plagued by a partially torn right rotator cuff in 1995, Wallace performed poorly, resulting in him being released by the 49ers in March 1996 due to salary cap constraints. But, after failing to earn a roster spot in Philadelphia, Wallace returned to the 49ers for the league minimum of $275,000 when Kirk Scrafford, his replacement in San Francisco, severely sprained his foot during training camp.

Surprising everyone with his exceptional play upon his return to the City by the Bay, Wallace ended up starting every game at his familiar position of left tackle, with 49ers center Jesse Sapolu commenting, "He went to Philadelphia and the coach there tried to teach him something new, and, after Philadelphia, I don't think anybody gave him a chance to help anybody else."

In explaining the improvement in his performance, Wallace said, "I'm really playing better in a lot of respects. Sometimes you feel you have a lot to prove. There were a lot of false accusations going on about me. When a guy's hurt, it's hard to evaluate him and be fair about it. . . . I did all I could to help this team win the championship, but I got a lot of flack for coming back and playing injured when a lot of guys wouldn't have played with an injury like that. People looked at that in the wrong way."

Yet, despite Wallace's outstanding play, the 49ers released him once again at season's end, bringing to a close his 11-year stay in San Francisco. Wallace subsequently signed with the Kansas City Chiefs, with whom he assumed the role of a backup in 1997, before announcing his retirement at the end of the year. Amazingly, in his 21 years of playing football, dating back to his days in middle and high school, Wallace never experienced a losing season.

After retiring as an active player, Wallace returned to Atlanta, where he began a career as a motivational speaker, delivering speeches to children in both urban and rural areas. Wallace also contributes to the youth of America through his Steve Wallace Everyday Championship Foundation.

49ERS CAREER HIGHLIGHTS

Best Season

Wallace anchored an offensive line that helped the 49ers finish first in the NFL in both points scored and total yards gained in 1992, with his stellar play at left tackle gaining him All-Pro recognition for the only time in his career.

Memorable Moments/Greatest Performances

Wallace helped the 49ers amass 505 yards of total offense during a lopsided 35–3 victory over the Detroit Lions on October 20, 1991, with 233 of those yards coming on the ground.

Wallace provided ample blindside pass protection for Steve Young during a 52–14 rout of Chicago in the final game of the 1991 regular season, with the Bears failing to record a single sack of Young, who threw for 338 yards and three touchdowns.

Although the 49ers lost to Buffalo by a score of 34–31 on September 13, 1992, Wallace did an excellent job of bottling up Bruce Smith, holding the Hall of Fame defensive end to no sacks.

Wallace and his line-mates controlled the line of scrimmage during a 56–17 manhandling of the Atlanta Falcons on October 18, 1992, with the 49ers amassing 590 yards of total offense and Steve Young passing for 399 yards and three touchdowns.

Wallace's strong blocking at the point of attack helped the 49ers amass 565 yards of total offense during a convincing 55–17 victory over the Lions on December 19, 1993, with Steve Young throwing for 354 yards and four touchdowns.

Wallace did an outstanding job of blocking Lawrence Taylor one-on-one during the 49ers' 44–3 rout of the Giants in the divisional round of the 1993 playoffs, with Taylor failing to record a single sack of Steve Young.

Wallace turned in another outstanding postseason performance the following year, dominating six-time Pro Bowl defensive end Leslie O'Neal during a 49–26 win over the San Diego Chargers in Super Bowl XXIX. Looking back on his exceptional effort, Wallace said, "After watching the tapes prior to the game, I heard [TV color commentator] Phil Simms saying, 'The San Diego Chargers should beat the San Francisco 49ers, and this is the reason they should beat them right here: Leslie O'Neal, the six-time Pro Bowler should dominate Steve Wallace.' All my friends, I had about 10 phone calls immediately asking, 'Did you see that?' I'm sitting in my room by myself thinking, 'My God.' But I believed in myself, and I knew that I'd be ready to battle. . . . By the end of the day, he had no tackles, no assists, nothing."

Notable Achievements

- Missed just seven non-strike games in 11 seasons, appearing in 166 out of 173 contests.
- Nine-time division champion (1986, 1987, 1988, 1989, 1990, 1992, 1993, 1994, and 1995).
- Three-time NFC champion (1988, 1989, and 1994).
- Three-time Super Bowl champion (XXIII, XXIV, and XXIX).
- 1992 Pro Bowl selection.
- 1992 Second-Team All-Pro selection.
- 1992 First-Team All-NFC selection.
- 1994 Second-Team All-NFC selection.

48

KEN NORTON JR.

The only man in NFL history to play for teams that won three straight Super Bowls, Ken Norton Jr. accomplished the feat from 1992 to 1994, earning his first two rings as a member of the Dallas Cowboys, before completing his trifecta with the 49ers in 1994. Splitting his career almost equally between the Cowboys and 49ers, Norton spent six seasons in Dallas and seven in San Francisco, excelling for the 49ers at both middle and right-outside linebacker from 1994 to 2000. Starting every game that the 49ers played during that time, Norton led the team in tackles six straight times, ending his seven-year stint in the City by the Bay with the fifth most stops in franchise history. Along the way, Norton helped lead the 49ers to three division titles and their fifth NFL championship, with his consistently excellent play earning him two trips to the Pro Bowl and one All-Pro nomination.

Born in Lincoln, Illinois, on September 29, 1966, Kenneth Howard Norton Jr. grew up in Los Angeles, California, where his father, future heavyweight boxing champion Ken Norton, moved the family shortly after he turned pro in 1967. Taking after his dad, who also starred in football and track in high school and college, Norton Jr. developed into an outstanding all-around athlete as a teenager, excelling at tailback for local Westchester High School. After averaging 8.8 yards per carry his senior year, Norton accepted an athletic scholarship to UCLA, where he gradually transitioned to linebacker. Starting at that post for the Bruins for two seasons, Norton recorded 106 tackles in 1986 and another 125 stops the following year, ending his college career with a total of 339 tackles that places him sixth in school history. Named team MVP, an All-American, and a finalist for the Butkus Award as the nation's top linebacker in 1987, Norton subsequently entered the 1988 NFL Draft, where the Dallas Cowboys selected him in the second round, with the 41st overall pick.

After missing most of his rookie season with a broken thumb, Norton joined the Cowboys' starting defensive unit in 1989, after which he went

Ken Norton led the 49ers in tackles six straight times.
Courtesy of George A. Kitrinos

on to record more than 100 tackles in three of the next five seasons, with his 159 stops in 1993 gaining him Pro Bowl and All-Pro recognition for the first time in his career. A significant contributor to Cowboy teams that won Super Bowls XXVII and XXVIII, Norton led the club in tackles both years, recording a total of 279 stops over the course of those two seasons.

Nevertheless, with the NFL instituting the salary cap following the conclusion of the 1993 campaign, the Cowboys chose not to offer Norton a long-term contract, allowing him to become a free agent. The 27-year-old linebacker subsequently signed with the 49ers, with whom he spent the rest of his career.

Beginning his time in San Francisco at right-outside linebacker, Norton performed well for the 49ers in 1994, recording a team-high 86 tackles during the regular season, before making another 19 stops during the postseason, which culminated with a 49–26 victory over the San Diego Chargers in Super Bowl XXIX. Continuing his outstanding play the following year after being moved inside to middle linebacker, Norton earned Pro Bowl and First-Team All-Pro honors by registering 96 tackles and a career-high three interceptions, two of which he returned for touchdowns. Norton had another outstanding season in 1996, recording 127 tackles, including 106 solo, before moving back to his original position of right-outside linebacker in 1997, when he earned his final trip to the Pro Bowl by making 96 tackles.

Blessed with outstanding physical talent and superior intelligence, Norton possessed all the qualities needed to excel at either middle or outside linebacker. Standing 6'2" and weighing 254 pounds, Norton had the size and strength to ward off blockers at the point of attack. Norton also had the quickness and athleticism to run down opposing ball-carriers and cover backs coming out of the backfield. Meanwhile, Norton's intelligence and enthusiasm made him a huge comfort to Steve Mariucci in 1997, with the 49ers' new head coach leaning heavily on him to provide leadership to his teammates and make any necessary defensive adjustments at the line of scrimmage. A no-nonsense type of player, Norton rarely took part in elaborate on-field celebrations, with his only true indulgence being his trademark punching of the goalposts or the air following a good play as a way of paying tribute to his father. Extremely durable as well, Norton failed to appear in just four games his last 12 years in the league, starting the final 160 contests of his career.

Norton remained in San Francisco for three more seasons, averaging close to 100 tackles from 1998 to 2000, before announcing his retirement after the 49ers finished just 6-10 in the last of those campaigns. Over the course of 13 NFL seasons, Norton recorded 1,272 tackles, 12½ sacks, 12 forced fumbles, 13 fumble recoveries, five interceptions, and two touchdowns. In his seven years with the 49ers, he made 693 stops (549 solo), registered 5½ sacks, forced six fumbles, recovered seven others, and picked off four passes, which he returned for 102 yards and both his TDs.

After retiring as an active player, Norton briefly served as a radio and television football analyst, before beginning a lengthy career in coaching that began in 2004 with a five-year stint as linebacker coach at USC. Since that time, Norton has served as an assistant on the coaching staffs of the Seattle Seahawks (2010–2014 and 2018–2021) and the Oakland Raiders (2015–2017). As defensive coordinator of the Raiders, Norton helped develop outside linebacker Khalil Mack into one of the league's most dominant defensive players. Meanwhile, prior to assuming the same role in Seattle in 2018, Norton proved to be instrumental in the development of perennial All-Pro linebacker Bobby Wagner in an earlier stint as linebacker coach for the Seahawks. Extremely active off the field as well, Norton is a huge contributor to Big Brothers, the Pediatric Aids Foundation, and the Special Olympics.

49ERS CAREER HIGHLIGHTS

Best Season

Although Norton recorded more tackles for the 49ers in three other years, he had his finest all-around season for them in 1995, earning Pro Bowl and First-Team All-Pro honors by making 96 tackles, forcing one fumble, registering one sack, and recording a career-high three interceptions, which he returned for a total of 102 yards and two touchdowns.

Memorable Moments/Greatest Performances

Norton starred during a 44–10 win over the St. Louis Rams on October 22, 1995, scoring a pair of touchdowns on interception-returns of 21 and 35 yards, with his brilliant play earning him NFC Defensive Player of the Week honors.

Norton contributed to a 38–22 victory over the Minnesota Vikings in the divisional round of the 1997 playoffs by returning his interception of a Randall Cunningham pass 23 yards for a touchdown that put the 49ers ahead by a score of 21–7 in the second quarter.

Notable Achievements

- Never missed a game in seven seasons, starting 112 consecutive contests.
- Scored two defensive touchdowns.

- Amassed 102 interception-return yards in 1995.
- Recorded more than 100 tackles three times.
- Led 49ers in tackles six times.
- Ranks fifth in franchise history with 695 tackles.
- Three-time division champion (1994, 1995, and 1997).
- 1994 NFC champion.
- Super Bowl XXIX champion.
- 1995 Week 8 NFC Defensive Player of the Week.
- October 1995 NFC Defensive Player of the Month.
- Two-time Pro Bowl selection (1995 and 1997).
- 1995 First-Team All-Pro selection.
- 1995 First-Team All-NFC selection.

49

BRUNO BANDUCCI

The last original member of the 49ers to play in the NFL, Bruno Banducci spent nine years in San Francisco excelling at right guard, after beginning his career with the Philadelphia Eagles in 1944. Serving as a key blocker for the "Million Dollar Backfield," Banducci starred for the 49ers in both the AAFC and the NFL, helping to lead them to six second-place finishes and one championship game appearance. Along the way, Banducci gained All-League recognition four times, before being further honored by being named to the NFL 1940s All-Decade Team.

Born in Tassignano, Italy, in the province of Lucca, Tuscany, on November 11, 1921, Bruno Banducci immigrated to the United States with his mother and older brother at 10 months of age, arriving in New York City aboard the ship *Argentina* on September 1, 1922. Eventually settling in the suburbs of Richmond, California, in the San Francisco Bay Area, Banducci attended a school run by Catholic nuns, before enrolling at Richmond High School, where he excelled in the classroom and on the football field. Offered an athletic scholarship to Stanford University, Banducci spent three years starring on both sides of the ball for the Cardinals, who he helped lead to a 21–13 victory over Nebraska in the Rose Bowl and a runner-up finish in the national rankings in 1941.

Selected by the Philadelphia Eagles in the sixth round of the 1943 NFL Draft, with the 42nd overall pick, Banducci, who played offensive tackle in college, moved to guard, where he helped pave the way for star running back Steve Van Buren to rush for a league-leading 832 yards in 1945. But, presented with an opportunity to return to the Bay Area the following year when the newly formed All-America Football Conference placed a team in San Francisco, Banducci signed with the 49ers, who he helped lead to an overall record of 38-14-2 over the course of the next four seasons and an appearance in the 1949 AAFC championship game, which they lost to the Cleveland Browns by a score of 21–7. Performing especially well in 1946 and 1947, Banducci earned All-AAFC honors both years, being named to

Bruno Banducci earned a spot on the NFL 1940s All-Decade Team with his outstanding play at right guard for the 49ers.

the First and Second Teams once each. Continuing to excel after the 49ers joined the NFL in 1950 following the collapse of the AAFC, Banducci gained All-Pro recognition in both 1952 and 1954, despite competing with future Hall of Fame guards Lou Creekmur, Dick Stanfel, and Dick Barwegen for postseason honors each year.

Although Banducci stood just 5'11" and weighed only 216 pounds, he used his quickness and tenacity to establish himself as one of the league's best run-blockers. Capable of pulling off the line of scrimmage or engaging his opponent at the point of attack, Banducci proved to be equally effective as an in-line and downfield blocker, with his superior blocking helping the 49ers lead the league in rushing six times. Meanwhile, teammate Joe Perry gained more yards on the ground than any other back in the league in both 1953 and 1954. Extremely competitive, Banducci never gave up on a play, continuing to fight until the referee blew his whistle. And, even though Banducci displayed a tendency to get high in his pass blocking, occasionally allowing his opponent to knock him off balance or toss him aside, he did an effective job of protecting his quarterback from onrushing defenders, enabling Frankie Albert to lead the AAFC in passing once and touchdown passes twice.

After being named team captain in 1953, Banducci, who spent most of his time in San Francisco serving as one of the club's most prominent figures in the locker room and on the playing field, held that title for one more year, before leaving the 49ers following the conclusion of the 1954 campaign when they failed to offer him a new contract. Banducci subsequently played one final season with the Canadian Football League's Toronto Argonauts, before announcing his retirement. After retiring as an active player, Banducci remained in the game for several more years, serving as an assistant on the coaching staffs of the 49ers and the Philadelphia Eagles, while also coaching at the high school level. Banducci later taught high school math at Marin Catholic High School in Kentfield, California, and Sonoma Valley High School in Sonoma, California, before suffering a heart attack that claimed his life on September 15, 1985, at 63 years of age.

49ERS CAREER HIGHLIGHTS

Best Season

Banducci earned First-Team All-AAFC honors in 1947, when he helped the 49ers finish fourth in the conference in points scored and second in total yards gained. However, he missed four games due to injury. On the other hand, Banducci started all but one contest for the 49ers in 1954, when he gained consensus First-Team All-Pro recognition. With the 49ers placing near the top of the NFL rankings in points scored (4th) and yards gained (2nd), we'll identify the 1954 campaign as the finest of Banducci's career.

Memorable Moments/Greatest Performances

Banducci helped the 49ers gain a season-high total of 265 yards on the ground during a 30–14 win over the Brooklyn Dodgers on November 24, 1946.

Banducci anchored an offensive line that enabled the 49ers to amass 416 yards of total offense during a 17–14 victory over the Los Angeles Dons on September 7, 1947, with 262 of those yards coming on the ground.

Banducci and his line-mates dominated the opponent at the point of attack once again on October 24, 1948, with the 49ers rushing for 390 yards and amassing 494 yards of total offense during a 21–10 win over the Baltimore Colts.

Banducci and his cohorts turned in another dominant performance on November 21, 1948, with the 49ers gaining 328 yards on the ground and amassing 547 yards of total offense during a 63–40 win over the Brooklyn Dodgers.

Banducci helped the 49ers amass 490 yards of total offense during a 38–21 victory over the Los Angeles Dons in the final game of the 1948 regular season, with 369 of those yards coming on the ground.

Although the 49ers lost to the Chicago Bears by a score of 32–20 on September 24, 1950, Banducci scored the only touchdown of his career when he gathered in an 11-yard pass from quarterback Frankie Albert.

Notable Achievements

- 1954 Pro Bowl selection.
- 1947 First-Team All-AAFC selection.
- 1946 Second-Team All-AAFC selection.
- 1954 First-Team All-Pro selection.
- 1952 Second-Team All-Pro selection.
- NFL 1940s All-Decade Team.

50

JEFF GARCIA

Following in the footsteps of a legend is never easy. But following in the footsteps of two legends is even more difficult, as Jeff Garcia learned when he assumed the role of starting quarterback in San Francisco in 1999. Trying to live up to the extraordinarily high standards previously set by Hall of Fame signal-callers Joe Montana and Steve Young, Garcia initially struggled behind center, causing others to doubt his ability to succeed in the NFL. But, after being benched for a few games, Garcia went on to establish himself as one of the league's better quarterbacks, leading the 49ers to one division title and passing for more than 3,000 yards three times and 30 touchdowns twice, with his strong play earning him three trips to the Pro Bowl. Forever the underdog, Garcia accomplished all he did after spending five years in the Canadian Football League, after earlier being bypassed by all 28 teams in the 1994 NFL Draft.

Born in the agricultural community of Gilroy, California, on February 24, 1970, Jeffrey J. Garcia grew up on a farm some 60 miles south of San Francisco, where he suffered through a difficult childhood. The grandson of Mexican immigrants, Garcia lost two of his younger siblings before his ninth birthday, with his six-year-old brother, Jason, drowning during a family vacation in Mammoth Lakes, California, on Mother's Day 1977, and his five-year-old sister, Kimberly, dying a little over one year later from massive internal injuries sustained when she fell out of the back of a dump truck used in the family's gravel business.

Recalling how his early losses impacted him during his formative years, Garcia said, "For a long time, I felt like I was robbed of childhood experiences. I thought I had missed out on those special moments that siblings share. Who knows? Maybe my brother would've been one of my receivers in high school."

Turning to football as a way of healing his wounds, Garcia received help from his father, who served as both his coach and mentor at Gilroy High School. Performing exceptionally well at quarterback for Gilroy,

Jeff Garcia passed for a franchise-record 4,278 yards in 2000.
Courtesy of Mearsonlineauctions.com

Garcia later drew praise from former Mustang teammate Clint Wheeler, who stated, "That guy has always worked hard and always been a guy who people were never confident in. He always proved everybody wrong. . . . He was always confident in himself. He was never the fastest guy, never had the strongest arm, but he was a late bloomer. He kept getting stronger and stronger."

Receiving little interest from major college programs, Garcia enrolled at local Gavilan Junior College, where he spent one year playing for his father. But, after earning junior college honorable mention All-America honors in

1989 by passing for 2,038 yards, throwing 18 touchdown passes, and rushing for 584 yards and four TDs, Garcia accepted a full scholarship to nearby San Jose State University. After redshirting as a freshman, Garcia started behind center for the Spartans for three seasons, gaining All-America recognition from UPI his junior year, and ending his college career as the school's all-time leader in total offense.

Yet, despite Garcia's outstanding play at San Jose State, his smallish 6'1", 200-pound frame and lack of elite arm strength caused him to go undrafted by all 28 teams in the 1994 NFL Draft, prompting him to travel north of the border, where he began his pro career as a third-string quarterback with the Calgary Stampeders of the Canadian Football League. Gradually working his way up the depth chart, Garcia ended up starting for four years, earning four CFL All-Star selections, and leading the Stampeders to the 1998 Grey Cup.

Claiming that he basically tried to make the best of a bad situation in Calgary, Garcia said, "I got to the point in Canada in the Canadian Football League with Calgary, even after that fifth season where we won the Grey Cup, I was MVP of the game and had been a four-time CFL All-Star. I pretty much believed the NFL just was not going to happen. I was going to have a life in the Canadian Football League. And, if that was how it was, I was going to make the most of it. I wasn't going to pout about it, I wasn't going to say, 'I should be down south.'"

Nevertheless, Garcia retained deep within a burning desire to play in the NFL, with former CFL and NFL quarterback Doug Flutie recalling, "I remember him asking me about it when his contract came up [in Canada]. I told him he had to take a shot at the NFL because the guys down here were no different from him or me. It's just that they got a shot, and we didn't."

Fortunately for Garcia, Bill Walsh, who had seen him perform while serving as head coach at Stanford from 1992 to 1994, held him in high esteem, once saying, "He could do things that were really out of the ordinary. He can move, he can avoid, he can find receivers. He had great instincts." And, with Walsh having returned to the 49ers early in 1999 as the team's general manager and vice president, he gave Garcia the opportunity he craved, signing him as a free agent to be Steve Young's backup, with Garcia later saying, "I really thought he [Young] was going to be my mentor. I really believed he'd be the guy I'd get to learn from that year and maybe another year before I would step onto the field, which was what I did in Canada with Doug Flutie being our starting quarterback."

However, a career-ending concussion suffered by Young just three games into the 1999 campaign forced Garcia to take the field far earlier than he expected, thrusting him into a pressure-filled situation. Recalling his thoughts at the time, Garcia stated, "What's going through my mind? It's not so much that I'm not physically prepared, it's am I mentally prepared? Do I know the game plan? Am I going to spit the plays out in the huddle? Am I going to execute the plays correctly?"

Revealing that Garcia's 49er teammates picked up on his insecurities, fullback Fred Beasley remembered, "When Jeff got in the huddle, his actions basically said, 'If you don't know what you're doing, don't ask me, because I'm learning here, too.'"

Meanwhile, Terrell Owens suggested, "Jeff had so many expectations on him that, in the little time he had, he was trying to make everyone see he could play. He had a lot of pressure on him. We were losing, and he was trying to pick up where Steve left off."

After leading the 49ers to just one victory in his first four starts, Garcia struggled terribly during a 27–6 loss to Pittsburgh on November 7, prompting head coach Steve Mariucci to replace him behind center with journeyman signal-caller Steve Stenstrom. Revealing that Mariucci's decision caused him to question his ability, Garcia said, "It made me really doubt if I belonged in the NFL."

But, after the 49ers scored a total of just 16 points in the next three games with Stenstrom guiding their offense, Garcia reclaimed his starting job, bringing with him a different mentality, recalling, "It took a benching and watching another quarterback struggle as well for me to realize it's more than just a quarterback. You can't put it all on your shoulders. You've gotta do your best, but you gotta get the guys around you involved as well. I came back for those last five games, and I was a far different quarterback."

Although the 49ers won just one of their final five contests, Garcia performed much better, throwing for more than 300 yards three times, and displaying far more confidence on the playing field and in the locker room. Noticing the change in his quarterback, Bill Walsh remembered, "Jeff was so apologetic initially because he was replacing Steve Young. He would admit his mistakes. You never apologize as a quarterback. Even if you are wrong, never say it, because, once you go public, that's when the trouble starts. With Jeff, it was just a matter of his overcoming the Joe-Steve history, and to do that he had to play."

Assuming the mantle of leadership in San Francisco the following year, Garcia had an outstanding 2000 campaign, earning Pro Bowl honors for the first of three straight times by ranking among the league leaders with 4,278 yards passing, 31 touchdown passes, a pass-completion percentage of 63.3, and a passer rating of 97.6, while also running for 414 yards and four touchdowns. Commenting on his excellent play, Garcia said, "I know people didn't expect this out of me, but I also know that wherever I've been, I've found a way to scratch and claw my way to being one of the better quarterbacks."

Performing extremely well in each of the next two seasons as well, Garcia led the 49ers to one division title and consecutive playoff appearances by throwing for more than 3,000 yards and 20 touchdowns each year, with his 32 TD passes in 2001 making him the first quarterback in team history to throw for more than 30 touchdowns in back-to-back seasons.

Making up for whatever he lacked in size and arm strength with superb instincts, an ability to move well in and out of the pocket, and outstanding leadership ability, Garcia possessed many intangible qualities that enabled him to perform better than most people expected him to, saying, "Because I look so average, people sometimes think I don't have it in me to be above average."

Those within the 49ers organization, though, came to fully appreciate everything Garcia brought to the team, with Bill Walsh saying, "Jeff Garcia does not play for the money, although obviously, that's important. He plays because he loves the game. He wants to play. He wants to succeed. This is an art form for Jeff."

Steve Mariucci stated, "If you know Jeff and you know his family, and you know their background and their history of all the tragedies that they've been through, you can realize and understand why throwing an interception is something that he can shake off real fast. It's not the worst thing that's ever happened to him. He's very resilient."

Meanwhile, Garrison Hearst expressed the confidence he had in his teammate by saying, "If we are going to win a Super Bowl, Jeff Garcia is going to be the quarterback to take us there. That's the way we see it."

Despite missing three games in 2003, Garcia had another solid season, passing for 2,704 yards, completing 57.4 percent of his passes, and throwing 18 touchdown passes and 13 interceptions. But, with the 49ers finishing just 7-9, they decided to go in a different direction at the end of the year, releasing Garcia when the two sides failed to agree on a contract restructuring. During his time in San Francisco, Garcia passed for 16,408 yards, threw 113 touchdown passes and 56 interceptions, compiled a passer rating of 88.3, completed 61.4 percent of his passes, and ran for 1,571 yards and 21 touchdowns.

After leaving the 49ers, Garcia split the next three seasons between the Cleveland Browns, Detroit Lions, and Philadelphia Eagles, experiencing a moderate amount of success during that time as a part-time starter/

backup, before joining the Tampa Bay Buccaneers in 2007. Starting behind center for the Buccaneers for two seasons, Garcia earned the last of his four Pro Bowl selections in 2007 by passing for 2,440 yards and throwing 13 touchdown passes and only four interceptions. After another solid season in Tampa Bay, Garcia returned to Philadelphia, where he appeared in just one game for the Eagles in 2009, before signing with the Omaha Nighthawks of the United Football League at season's end. After one year in Omaha, Garcia returned to the NFL with the Houston Texans. However, after failing to make a single appearance in 2011, Garcia announced his retirement, ending his NFL career with 25,537 yards passing, 161 touchdown passes and 83 interceptions, a pass-completion percentage of 61.6, and a passer rating of 87.5. Garcia also ran for 2,140 yards and 26 touchdowns.

Following his retirement, Garcia joined the advisory board for the now defunct United States Football League. Two years later, in August 2014, Garcia accepted the position of quarterbacks coach for the Montreal Alouettes of the CFL. After fulfilling that role for one season, Garcia spent one year serving the Los Angeles Rams as an offensive assistant. Since leaving that position, Garcia has remained close to the game by providing color commentary for the American Flag Football League.

49ERS CAREER HIGHLIGHTS

Best Season

Although Garcia posted excellent numbers in 2001, concluding the campaign with 3,538 passing yards, 32 touchdown passes, a pass-completion percentage of 62.7, and a quarterback rating of 94.8, he performed even better in 2000, passing for 4,278 yards, throwing 31 TD passes and only 10 interceptions, completing 63.3 percent of his passes, and posting a quarterback rating of 97.6, with his 4,278 passing yards setting a single-season franchise record that still stands.

Memorable Moments/Greatest Performances

Performing extremely well in his first pro start, Garcia led the 49ers to a 24–22 win over the Tennessee Titans on October 3, 1999, by running for one score and completing 21 of 33 pass attempts for 243 yards and two touchdowns, with his 22-yard TD pass to Terrell Owens with just under seven minutes remaining in regulation providing the margin of victory.

Although the 49ers lost to Cincinnati by a score of 44–30 on December 5, 1999, Garcia had a huge game, throwing for 437 yards and three touchdowns, two of them to Jerry Rice.

Garcia starred in defeat once again on October 8, 2000, passing for 336 yards and four touchdowns during a 34–28 overtime loss to the Oakland Raiders.

Garcia led the 49ers to a 17–0 win over the Bears on December 17, 2000, by completing 36 of 44 pass attempts for 402 yards and two touchdowns.

Garcia gave the 49ers a dramatic 37–31 victory over the Atlanta Falcons on October 14, 2001, by hitting Terrell Owens with a 52-yard touchdown pass with 6:16 remaining in overtime, putting the finishing touches on an afternoon in which he threw for 332 yards and three TDs.

Garcia earned NFC Offensive Player of the Week honors by passing for 252 yards and four touchdowns during a 28–27 win over the New Orleans Saints on November 11, 2001, with the longest of his TD tosses going 61 yards to Kevan Barlow.

Garcia's deft passing and running enabled the 49ers to overcome a 24-point third-quarter deficit to the Giants in the 2002 NFC wild card game, with the Niners emerging victorious by a score of 39–38. Garcia, who ran 14 yards for one score and threw three touchdown passes, finished the game with 60 yards rushing and 331 yards passing.

Garcia earned NFC Offensive Player of the Week honors by running for two scores and throwing for four others during a 50–14 rout of the Arizona Cardinals on December 7, 2003.

Notable Achievements

- Passed for more than 3,000 yards three times, topping 4,000 yards once.
- Threw more than 30 touchdown passes twice.
- Completed more than 60 percent of passes four times.
- Posted touchdown-to-interception ratio of better than 2–1 three times.
- Posted passer rating above 90.0 twice.
- Ran for 414 yards in 2000.
- Ran for seven touchdowns in 2003.
- Finished second in NFL in pass completions once, passing yards once, and touchdown passes once.
- Finished third in NFL in touchdown passes once, pass completion percentage once, and passer rating once.

- Holds 49ers single-season records for most pass completions (355 in 2000) and passing yards (4,278 in 2000).
- Ranks among 49ers career leaders with 2,360 pass attempts (4th), 1,449 pass completions (4th), 16,408 passing yards (4th), 113 touchdown passes (5th), 61.4 pass completion percentage (5th—minimum 500 attempts), and 88.3 passer rating (5th—minimum 500 attempts).
- 2002 division champion.
- Two-time NFC Offensive Player of the Week.
- November 2001 NFC Offensive Player of the Month.
- Three-time Pro Bowl selection (2000, 2001, and 2002).

SUMMARY
AND HONORABLE MENTIONS
(THE NEXT 25)

Having identified the 50 greatest players in San Francisco 49ers history, the time has come to select the best of the best. Based on the rankings contained in this book, the members of the 49ers' all-time offensive and defensive teams are listed below. Our squads include the top player at each position, with the offense featuring the three best wide receivers and the two best running backs, tackles, and guards. A third-down back has been included as well. Meanwhile, the defense features two ends, two tackles, two outside

OFFENSE		DEFENSE	
Player	Position	Player	Position
Joe Montana	QB	Tommy Hart	LE
Frank Gore	RB	Leo Nomellini	LT
Joe Perry	RB	Bryant Young	RT
Roger Craig 3rd-Down	Back	Cedrick Hardman	RE
Brent Jones	TE	Dave Wilcox	LOLB
Jerry Rice	WR	Patrick Willis	MLB
Terrell Owens	WR	NaVorro Bowman	ROLB
Gene Washington	WR	Jimmy Johnson	LCB
Joe Staley	LT	Ronnie Lott	S
Bruce Bosley	LG	Dwight Hicks	S
Forrest Blue	C	Kermit Alexander	RCB
Randy Cross	RG	Andy Lee	P
Bob St. Clair	RT	John Taylor	PR
Ray Wersching	PK		
Abe Woodson	KR		

linebackers, one middle linebacker, two cornerbacks, and a pair of safeties. Special teams have been accounted for as well, with a placekicker, punter, kickoff returner, and punt returner also being included. The placekicker and punter were taken from the list of honorable mentions that will soon follow.

Although I limited my earlier rankings to the top 50 players in 49ers history, many other fine players have worn a Niners uniform over the years, some of whom narrowly missed making the final cut. Following is a list of those players deserving of an honorable mention. These are the men I deemed worthy of being slotted in positions 51 to 75 in the overall rankings. Where applicable and available, the statistics they compiled during their time in San Francisco are included, along with their most notable achievements while playing for the 49ers.

51—TIM MCDONALD (DB; 1993–1999)

George A. Kitrinos

49ers Numbers

20 Interceptions, 325 Interception-Return Yards, 544 Tackles, 7 Sacks, 4 Forced Fumbles, 9 Fumble Recoveries, 4 Touchdowns.

Notable Achievements

- Missed just one game in seven seasons, starting 111 out of 112 contests.
- Amassed more than 100 interception-return yards once.
- Recorded more than 90 tackles twice.
- Recorded four sacks in 1998.
- Led NFL with two touchdown interceptions in 1995.
- Finished fourth in NFL with 135 interception-return yards in 1995.
- Tied for team lead with four interceptions in 1998.
- Ranks among 49ers career leaders in touchdown interceptions (tied for 2nd) and tackles (9th).
- Four-time division champion (1993, 1994, 1995, and 1997).
- 1994 NFC champion.
- Super Bowl XXIX champion.
- 1995 Week 13 NFC Defensive Player of the Week.

- Three-time Pro Bowl selection (1993, 1994, and 1995).
- Two-time Second-Team All-Pro selection (1993 and 1995).
- 1993 First-Team All-NFC selection.
- Three-time Second-Team All-NFC selection (1994, 1995, and 1996).

52—HARRIS BARTON (OT; 1987–1996)

George A. Kitrinos

Notable Achievements

- Appeared in 89 consecutive games from 1987 to 1992.
- Eight-time division champion (1987, 1988, 1989, 1990, 1992, 1993, 1994, and 1995).
- Three-time NFC champion (1988, 1989, and 1994).
- Three-time Super Bowl champion (XXIII, XXIV, and XXIX).
- Member of 1987 NFL All-Rookie Team.
- Finished second in 1987 NFL Offensive Rookie of the Year voting.
- 1993 Pro Bowl selection.
- Two-time First-Team All-Pro selection (1992 and 1993).
- Two-time First-Team All-NFC selection (1992 and 1993).
- 1988 Second-Team All-NFC selection.

53—VERNON DAVIS (TE; 2006–2015)

Mike Morbeck

49ers Numbers

441 Receptions, 5,640 Receiving Yards, 5,655 Yards from Scrimmage, 55 Touchdown Receptions.

Notable Achievements

- Surpassed 50 receptions five times, topping 70 catches once.
- Surpassed 900 receiving yards twice.
- Scored 13 touchdowns twice.
- Led NFL with 13 touchdown receptions in 2009.
- Finished third in NFL with 13 touchdown receptions in 2013.
- Led 49ers in receptions and receiving yards twice each.
- Ranks among 49ers career leaders in receptions (5th), receiving yards (6th), touchdown receptions (4th), and touchdowns (8th).
- Two-time division champion (2011 and 2012).
- 2012 NFC champion.
- Two-time Pro Bowl selection (2009 and 2013).
- 2013 Second-Team All-Pro selection.

54—HOWARD MUDD (G; 1964–1969)

Mike Traverse

Notable Achievements

- Appeared in 70 consecutive games from 1964 to 1968.
- Three-time Pro Bowl selection (1966, 1967, and 1968).
- 1968 First-Team All-Pro selection.
- NFL 1960s All-Decade Team.

55—RAY WERSCHING (PK; 1977–1987)

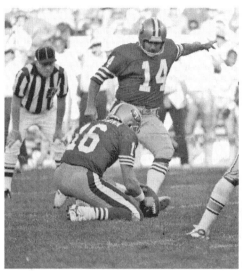

George A. Kitrinos

49ers Numbers

190 Field Goals Made, 409 Extra Points Made, 979 Points Scored, 72.8 Field Goal Percentage.

Notable Achievements

- Scored more than 100 points three times, topping 120 points twice.
- Converted more than 80 percent of field goal attempts twice.
- Led NFL with 131 points scored in 1984.
- Finished second in NFL in field goals made once and field goal percentage twice.
- Finished third in NFL in points scored once.
- Holds 49ers career records for most field goals made and extra points made.
- Ranks second in franchise history in points scored.
- Five-time division champion (1981, 1983, 1984, 1986, and 1987).
- Two-time NFC champion (1981 and 1984).
- Two-time Super Bowl champion (XVI and XIX).
- 1986 Second-Team All-NFC selection.

56—ALYN BEALS (WR; 1946–1951)

Jack McGuire

Career Numbers

211 Receptions, 2,951 Receiving Yards, 49 Touchdown Receptions.

Notable Achievements

- Surpassed 40 receptions four times.
- Surpassed 500 receiving yards four times.
- Scored at least 10 touchdowns four times.
- Led AAFC in receptions once, touchdown receptions four times, touchdowns once, and points scored once.
- Finished second in AAFC in receiving yards once, touchdowns twice, and points scored once.
- Finished third in AAFC in receptions twice, receiving yards once, yards per reception once, and points scored once.
- Led 49ers in receptions and receiving yards four times each.
- Ranks among 49ers career leaders in touchdown receptions (tied for 5th) and touchdowns (tied for 10th).
- Holds AAFC records for most touchdowns (46) and points (278) scored.
- 1946 First-Team All-AAFC selection.
- Three-time Second-Team All-AAFC selection (1947, 1948, and 1949).

57—ANDY LEE (P; 2004–2014)

Jeffrey Beall

49ers Numbers

43,468 Yards Punting, Average of 46.2 Yards Per Punt.

Notable Achievements

- Recorded two punts of more than 80 yards.
- Averaged more than 50 yards per punt once, topping 47 yards per kick five other times.
- Led NFL in total punt yardage twice and average yards per punt once.
- Finished second in NFL in total punt yardage twice and average yards per punt twice.
- Recorded longest punt in NFL twice.
- Holds 49ers single-game records for most total punt yardage (543 vs. Seattle on September 30, 2007) and most yards per punt (57.2 vs. Pittsburgh on September 23, 2007).
- Holds 49ers single-season records for most total punt yardage (4,968 in 2007) and most yards per punt (50.9 in 2011).
- Holds 49ers career records for most punts (941), most total punt yardage (43,468), and most yards per punt (46.2).
- Two-time division champion (2011 and 2012).
- 2012 NFC champion.
- Three-time NFC Special Teams Player of the Week.
- Three-time Pro Bowl selection (2007, 2009, and 2011).
- Three-time First-Team All-Pro selection (2007, 2011, and 2012).
- 2009 Second-Team All-Pro selection.

58—KEITH FAHNHORST (OT; 1974–1987)

Notable Achievements

- Missed just three non-strike games from 1974 to 1986, appearing in 190 out of 193 contests.
- Five-time division champion (1981, 1983, 1984, 1986, and 1987).
- Two-time NFC champion (1981 and 1984).
- Two-time Super Bowl champion (XVI and XIX).
- 1984 Pro Bowl selection.
- 1984 First-Team All-Pro selection.
- Two-time First-Team All-NFC selection (1983 and 1984).
- Two-time Second-Team All-NFC selection (1982 and 1985).

59—GORDY SOLTAU (WR/PK; 1950–1958)

Career Numbers

249 Receptions, 3,487 Receiving Yards, 25 Touchdown Receptions, 70 Field Goals Made, 284 Extra Points Made, 644 Points Scored, 50.4 Field Goal Percentage.

Notable Achievements

- Surpassed 50 receptions twice.
- Surpassed 700 receiving yards twice.
- Scored more than 100 points once.
- Led NFL in points scored twice.
- Finished second in NFL in receptions once, receiving yards once, field goals made once, and field goal percentage once.
- Finished third in NFL in receptions once, field goals made once, and field goal percentage twice.
- Led 49ers in receptions twice and receiving yards twice.
- Ranks fifth in franchise history in points scored.
- Three-time Pro Bowl selection (1951, 1952, and 1953).
- 1952 First-Team All-Pro selection.
- Inducted into 49ers Hall of Fame in 2012.

60—TOMMY DAVIS (P/PK; 1959–1969)

Mike Traverse

Career Numbers

22,833 Yards Punting, Average of 44.7 Yards Per Punt, 130 Field Goals Made, 348 Extra Points Made, 738 Points Scored, 47.1 Field Goal Percentage.

Notable Achievements

- Averaged more than 45 yards per punt six times.
- Recorded one punt of more than 80 yards.
- Recorded longest punt in NFL three times.
- Scored more than 100 points once.
- Led NFL with 19 field goals made in 1960.
- Led NFL with average of 45.6 yards per punt in 1962.
- Finished second in NFL in field goals made once, total punt yardage twice, and punting average once.
- Finished third in NFL in field goals made once, total punt yardage twice, and punting average five times.
- Ranks among 49ers career leaders in total punt yardage (2nd), field goals made (2nd), extra points made (2nd), and points scored (3rd).
- Two-time Pro Bowl selection (1962 and 1963).

61—FRED DEAN (DE; 1981–1985)

MearsonlineAuctions.com

49ers Numbers

40 Sacks, 2 Fumble Recoveries.

Notable Achievements

- Finished in double digits in sacks twice.
- Recorded six sacks in one game twice (vs. Dallas Cowboys on October 11, 1981, and vs. New Orleans Saints on November 13, 1983).
- Recorded five sacks vs. Los Angeles Rams on October 25, 1981.
- Finished second in NFL with 17½ sacks in 1983.
- Led 49ers in sacks three times.
- Ranks 10th in franchise history in sacks.
- Three-time division champion (1981, 1983, and 1984).
- Two-time NFC champion (1981 and 1984).
- Two-time Super Bowl champion (XVI and XIX).
- 1981 UPI NFC Defensive Player of the Year.
- Two-time Pro Bowl selection (1981 and 1983).
- 1981 First-Team All-Pro selection.
- 1981 First-Team All-NFC selection.
- 1983 Second-Team All-NFC selection.
- Inducted into 49ers Hall of Fame in 2009.
- Inducted into Pro Football Hall of Fame in 2008.

62—MICHAEL CARTER (NT; 1984–1992)

George A. Kitrinos

Career Numbers

22½ Sacks, 1 Interception.

Notable Achievements

- Recorded more than six sacks twice.
- Seven-time division champion (1984, 1986, 1987, 1988, 1989, 1990, and 1992).
- Three-time NFC champion (1984, 1988, and 1989).
- Three-time Super Bowl champion (XIX, XXIII, and XXIV).
- 1988 Week 1 NFC Defensive Player of the Week.
- Three-time Pro Bowl selection (1985, 1987, and 1988).
- 1987 First-Team All-Pro selection.
- Two-time Second-Team All-Pro selection (1985 and 1988).
- Three-time First-Team All-NFC selection (1986, 1987, and 1988).

63—WOODY PEOPLES (G; 1968–1977)

Mike Traverse

Notable Achievements

- Three-time division champion (1970, 1971, and 1972).
- Two-time Pro Bowl selection (1972 and 1973).
- Two-time Second-Team All-NFC selection (1971 and 1972).

64—J. D. SMITH (RB/KR; 1956–1964)

49ers Numbers

4,370 Yards Rushing, 121 Receptions, 1,109 Receiving Yards, 5,479 Yards from Scrimmage, 882 Kickoff-Return Yards, 6,361 All-Purpose Yards, 37 Rushing TDs, 5 TD Receptions, 42 TDs, 4.3 Rushing Average.

Notable Achievements

- Rushed for more than 1,000 yards once.
- Amassed more than 1,000 yards from scrimmage three times.
- Averaged more than 5 yards per carry twice.
- Finished second in NFL in rushing yards once and rushing TDs once.
- Finished third in NFL with eight rushing touchdowns in 1961.
- Finished fourth in NFL with 1,169 yards from scrimmage and 11 touchdowns in 1959.
- Led 49ers in rushing five times.
- Ranks among 49ers career leaders in rushing yards (6th) and rushing touchdowns (tied for 5th).
- Two-time Pro Bowl selection (1959 and 1962).
- 1959 Second-Team All-Pro selection.

65—JESSE SAPOLU (C/G; 1983–1984, 1987–1997)

George A. Kitrinos

Notable Achievements

- Started 96 consecutive games from 1988 to 1993.
- 11-time division champion (1983, 1984, 1987, 1988, 1989, 1990, 1992, 1993, 1994, 1995, and 1997).
- Four-time NFC champion (1984, 1988, 1989, and 1994).
- Four-time Super Bowl champion (XXIX, XXIII, XXIV, and XXIX).
- Two-time Pro Bowl selection (1993 and 1994).
- Two-time Second-Team All-NFC selection (1994 and 1995).

66—BRUCE TAYLOR (DB/PR; 1970–1977)

Mike Traverse

Career Numbers

18 Interceptions, 201 Interception-Return Yards, 1,323 Punt-Return Yards, 2 Touchdowns.

Notable Achievements

- Led NFL with 516 punt-return yards in 1970.
- Finished second in NFL with average of 12.0 yards per punt return in 1970.
- Finished fourth in NFL with six interceptions in 1973.
- Led 49ers in interceptions four times.
- Ranks third in franchise history in punt-return yards.
- Three-time division champion (1970, 1971, and 1972).
- 1970 NFL Defensive Rookie of the Year.
- 1971 Pro Bowl selection.
- 1970 Second-Team All-NFC selection.

67—FREDDIE SOLOMON (WR/PR; 1978–1985)

49ers Numbers

310 Receptions, 4,873 Receiving Yards, 329 Yards Rushing, 5,202 Yards from Scrimmage, 804 Punt-Return Yards, 6,065 All-Purpose Yards, 43 TD Receptions, 3 Rushing TDs, 2 Punt-Return TDs, 48 Touchdowns.

Notable Achievements

- Surpassed 50 receptions twice.
- Surpassed 800 receiving yards twice.
- Amassed more than 1,000 yards from scrimmage once.
- Amassed more than 1,000 all-purpose yards three times.
- Scored at least 10 touchdowns twice.
- Recorded longest reception in NFL in 1980 (93 yards).
- Led NFL with two punt-return touchdowns in 1980.
- Finished second in NFL with average of 21.4 yards per reception in 1983.
- Led 49ers in receptions once and receiving yards twice.
- Ranks among 49ers career leaders in receiving yards (9th), punt-return yards (9th), and touchdown receptions (tied for 8th).

- Three-time division champion (1981, 1983, and 1984).
- Two-time NFC champion (1981 and 1984).
- Two-time Super Bowl champion (XVI and XIX).
- 1980 First-Team All-NFC selection.

68—JIM CASON (DB/RB/KR/PR; 1948–1954)

49ers Numbers

25 Interceptions, 371 Interception-Return Yards, 4 Fumble Recoveries, 351 Yards Rushing, 40 Receptions, 519 Receiving Yards, 870 Yards from Scrimmage, 948 Punt-Return Yards, 703 Kickoff-Return Yards, 2,892 All-Purpose Yards, 1 TD Interception, 4 Rushing TDs, 4 TD Receptions, 9 TDs.

Notable Achievements

- Recorded at least five interceptions three times.
- Amassed more than 100 interception-return yards twice.
- Led AAFC with 9 interceptions, 152 interception-return yards, and 351 punt-return yards in 1949.
- Finished second in AAFC in kickoff and punt-return yards once and punt-return average twice.
- Finished second in NFL with 147 interception-return yards in 1951.
- Finished third in AAFC with 309 punt-return yards in 1948.
- Ranks among 49ers career leaders in interceptions (7th), interception-return yards (9th), and punt-return yards (8th).
- Two-time Pro Bowl selection (1951 and 1954).
- 1949 First-Team All-AAFC selection.

69—FRANK NUNLEY (LB; 1967–1976)

Mike Traverse

Career Numbers

14 Interceptions, 136 Interception-Return Yards, 9 Fumble Recoveries.

Notable Achievements

- Missed just three games in 10 seasons, appearing in 137 out of 140 contests.
- Recorded four interceptions in 1974.
- Led 49ers in interceptions once.
- Three-time division champion (1970, 1971, and 1972).

70—TOM RATHMAN (RB; 1986–1993)

George A. Kitrinos

49ers Numbers

1,902 Yards Rushing, 294 Receptions, 2,490 Receiving Yards, 4,392 Yards from Scrimmage, 4,507 All-Purpose Yards, 26 Rushing TDs, 8 TD Receptions, 3.7 Rushing Average.

Notable Achievements

- Surpassed 70 receptions and 600 receiving yards once.
- Amassed more than 800 yards from scrimmage twice.

- Scored nine touchdowns in 1992.
- Finished second among NFL running backs with 73 receptions in 1989.
- Tied for ninth in franchise history in rushing touchdowns.
- Seven-time division champion (1986, 1987, 1988, 1989, 1990, 1992, and 1993).
- Two-time NFC champion (1988 and 1989).
- Two-time Super Bowl champion (XXIII and XXIV).
- Inducted into 49ers Hall of Fame in 2017.

71—TED KWALICK (TE; 1969–1974)

Mike Traverse

49ers Numbers

164 Receptions, 2,555 Receiving Yards, 175 Rushing Yards, 2,730 Yards from Scrimmage, 23 Touchdown Receptions.

Notable Achievements

- Surpassed 50 receptions once.
- Surpassed 700 receiving yards twice.
- Finished third in NFL with nine touchdown receptions in 1972.
- Finished fourth in NFL with 52 receptions in 1971.
- Led 49ers in receptions twice and receiving yards once.

- Three-time division champion (1970, 1971, and 1972).
- Three-time Pro Bowl selection (1971, 1972, and 1973).
- 1972 First-Team All-Pro selection.
- Two-time First-Team All-NFC selection (1972 and 1973).
- 1971 Second-Team All-NFC selection.

72—DEREK SMITH (LB; 2001–2007)

49ers Numbers

710 Tackles, 9 Sacks, 3 Interceptions, 17 Interception-Return Yards, 3 Forced Fumbles, 8 Fumble Recoveries, 2 Touchdowns.

Notable Achievements

- Recorded more than 100 tackles five times.
- Led 49ers in tackles five times.
- Ranks third in franchise history in tackles.
- 2002 division champion.
- 2005 49ers MVP.

73—WILLIE HARPER (LB; 1973–1983)

Career Numbers

3 Interceptions, 43 Interception-Return Yards, 5 Fumble Recoveries.

Notable Achievements

- Two-time division champion (1981 and 1983).
- 1981 NFC champion.
- Super Bowl XVI champion.

74—DON GRIFFIN (DB/PR; 1986–1993)

George A. Kitrinos

49ers Numbers

22 Interceptions, 49 Interception-Return Yards, 1 TD Interception, 338 Tackles, 2 Sacks, 9 Fumble Recoveries, 667 Punt-Return Yards, 1 Punt-Return TD.

Notable Achievements

- Started 64 consecutive games from 1989 to 1992.
- Recorded five interceptions in 1992.
- Finished second in NFL with 99 fumble-return yards in 1991.
- Led 49ers in interceptions twice.
- Ranks among 49ers career leaders in interceptions (tied for 8th).
- Seven-time division champion (1986, 1987, 1988, 1989, 1990, 1992, and 1993).
- Two-time NFC champion (1988 and 1989).
- Two-time Super Bowl champion (XXIII and XXIV).
- Member of 1986 NFL All-Rookie Team.
- 1989 First-Team All-NFC selection.
- Two-time Second-Team All-NFC selection (1987 and 1990).

75—JOHN THOMAS (OT/G; 1958–1967)

Notable Achievements

- Started 84 consecutive games from 1961 to 1966.
- 1966 Pro Bowl selection.
- 1966 First-Team All-Pro selection.

GLOSSARY

ABBREVIATIONS AND STATISTICAL TERMS

C. Center.

COMP %. Completion percentage. The number of successfully completed passes divided by the number of passes attempted.

DB. Defensive back.

DE. Defensive end.

DT. Defensive tackle.

FS. Free safety.

INTS. Interceptions. Passes thrown by the quarterback that are caught by a member of the opposing team's defense.

KR. Kickoff returner.

LCB. Left cornerback.

LE. Left end.

LG. Left guard.

LOLB. Left-outside linebacker.

LT. Left tackle.

MLB. Middle linebacker.

NT. Nose tackle.

P. Punter.

PK. Placekicker.

PR. Punt returner.

QB. Quarterback.

QBR. Quarterback rating.

RB. Running back.

RCB. Right cornerback.

RE. Right end.

RECS. Receptions.

REC YDS. Receiving yards.

RG. Right guard.

ROLB. Right-outside linebacker.

RT. Right tackle.

S. Safety.

ST. Special teams.

TD PASSES. Touchdown passes.

TD RECS. Touchdown receptions.

TDS. Touchdowns.

TE. Tight end.

WR. Wide receiver.

YDS FROM SCRIMMAGE. Yards from scrimmage.

YDS PASSING. Yards passing.

YDS RUSHING. Yards rushing.

BIBLIOGRAPHY

Books

Brown, Daniel. *100 Things 49ers Fans Should Know & Do Before They Die.* Chicago: Triumph Books, 2013.

Danyluk, Tom. *The Super '70s: Memories from Pro Football's Greatest Era.* Mad Uke Publishing, 2005.

Georgatos, Dennis. *Game of My Life San Francisco 49ers: Memorable Stories of 49ers Football.* Champaign, IL: Sports Publishing L.L.C., 2007.

Jones, Danny. *More Distant Memories: Pro Football's Best Ever Players of the 50s, 60s, and 70s.* Bloomington, IN: AuthorHouse, 2006.

Maiocco, Matt. *SAN FRANCISCO 49ERS: Where Have You Gone?* Champaign, IL: Sports Publishing L.L.C., 2005.

Sterngass, Jon, *Jerry Rice.* New York: Chelsea House, 2013.

Videos

Greatest Ever: NFL Dream Team. Polygram Video, 1996.

Websites

Biographies from Answers.com
(answers.com)

Biographies from Jockbio.com
(jockbio.com)

CBSNews.com
(cbsnews.com)

ESPN.com
(sports.espn.go.com)

Hall of Famers, profootballhof.com
(profootballhof.com/hof/member)

Inductees from LASportsHall.com
(lasportshall.com)

LATimes.com
(articles.latimes.com)

Newsday.com
(newsday.com)

NYDailyNews.com
(nydailynews.com/new-york)

NYTimes.com
(nytimes.com)

Pro Football Talk from nbcsports.com
(profootballtalk.nbcsports.com)

SpTimes.com
(sptimes.com)

StarLedger.com
(starledger.com)

SunSentinel.com
(articles.sun-sentinel.com)

The Players, Profootballreference.com
(pro-football-reference.com/players)